Boeve De Haumtone
and
Gui De Warewic:

Two Anglo-Norman Romances

MEDIEVAL AND RENAISSANCE
TEXTS AND STUDIES
VOLUME 332

THE FRENCH OF ENGLAND TRANSLATION SERIES
(FRETS)
VOLUME 3

BOEVE DE HAUMTONE
AND
GUI DE WAREWIC:

TWO ANGLO-NORMAN ROMANCES

Translated by
Judith Weiss

FRETS Series Editors
Thelma Fenster and
Jocelyn Wogan-Browne

ACMRS
(Arizona Center for Medieval and Renaissance Studies)
Tempe, Arizona
2008

Published with the assistance of Fordham University.

© Copyright 2008
Arizona Board of Regents for Arizona State University

Library of Congress Cataloging-in-Publication Data

Beuve de Hanstone. English
  Boeve de Haumtone ; and, Gui de Warewic : two Anglo-Norman romances /
translated by Judith Weiss.
    p. cm. -- (The French of England translation series ; v. 3)
  Includes bibliographical references and indexes.
  ISBN 978-0-86698-378-5 (alk. paper)
  1. Beuve de Hanstone (Legendary character)--Romances. 2. Guy of Warwick
(Legendary character)--Romances. I. Weiss, Judith (Judith Elizabeth) II. Guy
of Warwick (Romance). English. III. Title.

PQ1431.B25E5 2007
841'.1--dc22

2007047715

∞
This book is made to last.
It is set in Adobe Caslon Pro,
smyth-sewn and printed on acid-free paper
to library specifications.
Printed in the United States of America

For Ivana

Contents

Series Editors' Preface	*ix*
Preface	*xi*
Abbreviations	*xiii*
Map of Boeve's and Gui's Journeys	*xiv*
Introduction	1
BOEVE DE HAUMTONE	25
GUI DE WAREWIC	97
Bibliography	245
Index of Personal and Place Names in *Boeve*	251
Index of Personal and Place Names in *Gui*	255
Appendix of Extracts	261

Series Editors' Preface

The French of England Translation Series (FRETS) aims to broaden the available range of the French works of medieval England. "French" here replaces the term "Anglo-Norman," normally used of texts composed in French in England between the twelfth and fourteenth centuries; it sometimes also replaces "Anglo-French," used of fourteenth- and fifteenth-century texts circulating between England and the Continent. Although "Anglo-Norman" has valid current uses (for example, in the continuing high-quality editions of the Anglo-Norman Text Society), it has tended to be associated with an older nationalizing history, based on post-medieval geopolitical configurations. These have assumed that the modern idea of two distinct categories of language and literature, English and French, was valid for the medieval period. In that view, the French texts composed or circulating in medieval England were neither properly "English" or "French"; as a consequence they tended to remain underexplored. It is true that a few such texts (for example, the *Chanson de Roland* and the *Lais* of Marie de France) are well known to scholars and students because of their nineteenth- and twentieth-century careers in French literary history (and in other cultures in translation); but the large and varied body of writing documented in the groundbreaking *Anglo-Norman Literature: A Guide to Texts and Manuscripts*, ed. Ruth J. Dean, with Maureen B. M. Boulton (London: Anglo-Norman Texts Society, 1999), crucial to understanding the cultures of medieval England and its neighbors, has yet to be more thoroughly investigated.

We do not claim that the term "French of England" is fully descriptive, for there are in fact many kinds of French involved, and not only in England. Wales, Scotland, Ireland and various regions of medieval Europe were also territories where the texts that we place under the rubric "French of England" circulated. But as a term, "French of England" has a usefully paradoxical quality that points to the complexities of multilingual and multicultural territories; and, given that "French" is a broader term than "Anglo-Norman" and "Anglo-French," it can denote French in, of, and from medieval England, in literary and documentary genres, especially during the main francophone period from the twelfth through the fifteenth centuries. Many of these texts have not received the attention they deserve because they have been linguistically inaccessible. FRETS has therefore been conceived with the intention of enriching the available corpus of what has been called medieval "English" literature and encouraging readers to return to the original French texts.

La Estoire de seint Aedward le rei is the thirteenth-century verse biography of Edward the Confessor, an Anglo-Saxon king who ruled England from 1042 to 1066. It is dedicated to Eleanor of Provence, queen of Henry III (1216-1272). The composition of the *Estoire* is persuasively attributed to the monk Matthew Paris (d. 1259), historian and chronicler of St Albans Abbey, Hertfordshire. Paris is best known today as the most striking and prolific Latin chronicler of his time, and as a talented artist and illustrator of his own work. But he is also an important vernacular author who composed at least four verse biographies of saints (Alban, protomartyr of England; Edward the Confessor; Thomas Becket; and Edmund of Canterbury) in the French spoken by the English aristocracy of his day. All four French lives are available in modern editions, but, except for the life of Edward, none has yet been translated into modern English. (*The Life of Saint Alban by Matthew Paris* will appear as FRETS volume two.)

The History of St Edward the King was translated into modern English for the first time in the mid-nineteenth century. The present translation seeks to correct errors made in the earlier translation (which was based on a first, unreliable edition); to render Paris's poem into a more fluid English idiom; to present it in such a way as to take advantage of a newer and more reliable edition; and to benefit from recent historical and art historical scholarship on Matthew Paris.

Like many important works in the French of England, Paris's vernacular compositions merit further study. The value of the *Estoire de seint Aedward* for our understanding of thirteenth-century visual, literary, social, and political culture is now widely accepted. The interest and importance of its manuscript illustrations have been well recognized; equally worthy of study are the rhetorical strategies and the selection and structuring of material in the text. Although the *Estoire* takes the form of a saint's life, the very term *estoire* announces that the poem is also a "history" rather than simply the more usual *vie*, "life." Matthew Paris's account of lineage and kingship across the Norman Conquest, the ethos of his courtly monastic work, the nature of his francophone audience's interests, and many other topics concerning the *Estoire* and Paris's other French writings command the attention of students and scholars of the cultures of medieval England. For all these reasons we have decided to make the translation of the *Estoire de seint Aedward le rei* the first volume of the FRETS series.

Preface

The texts used for these two translations are *Boeve de Haumtone*, edited by Albert Stimming in 1899, and *Gui de Warewic*, edited by Alfred Ewert in 1933. I have retained their numbering of the lines and, in the case of *Gui*, the bracketing of passages not in Ewert's base text.

This book has been some time in the making. Throughout, I have benefited from the wisdom and encouragement of Ivana Djordjevic, whose meticulous checking of my text has saved me from many a blunder. I am also very grateful to Marianne Ailes, Oliver Padel, Christopher Sanders, and Ian Short for their help. I am entirely responsible for any remaining errors in the translation.

Jocelyn Wogan-Browne and Thelma Fenster first suggested I undertake this task. I am indebted to them for their advice and help, and for causing me to embark on a project from which I have learned much. I am particularly grateful for their many and thoughtful suggestions about improving my translations, from which the text has benefited immensely. Martin Brett has patiently answered my numerous enquiries about historical details. I should like to thank the Sub-librarian of the Parker Library in Corpus Christi College, Cambridge; the Librarian of the College of Arms, London; the Librarian in the Lambeth Palace Library, London; and the Librarian of the Hunterian Library in the University of Glasgow for their courteous and prompt assistance.

Judith Weiss, Cambridge 2007

ABBREVIATIONS

AND	The *Anglo-Norman Dictionary* (London: The Modern Humanities Research Association, 1977-1992)
ANTS	The Anglo-Norman Text Society
Auchinleck	The Auchinleck manuscript (MS Advocates 19.2.1 in the National Library of Scotland) of the English *Guy of Warwick*
Caius	The Caius manuscript (MS 107 in the library of Gonville and Caius College, Cambridge) of the English *Guy of Warwick*
CFMA	Classiques Français du Moyen Age
Dean	*Anglo-Norman Literature: A Guide to Texts and Manuscripts*, ed. Ruth J. Dean, with the collaboration of Maureen B.M. Boulton (London: ANTS, 1999)
Ewert	*Gui de Warewic*, ed. Alfred Ewert, 2 vols., CFMA (Paris: Champion, 1933)
Flutre	Fernand Flutre, *Table des noms propres figurant dans les romans du Moyen Age* (Poitiers: Centre d'études supérieures de civilisation médiévale, 1962)
Stimming	*Der Anglonormannische Boeve de Haumtone*, ed. Albert Stimming (Halle: Bibliotheca Normannica, 1899)
Tobler-Lommatzsch	Tobler-Lommatzsch, *Altfranzösisches Wörterbuch* (Berlin: Weidmann, 1925-1936; Wiesbaden: Steiner, 1954-)

Map of Boeve's and Gui's Journeys

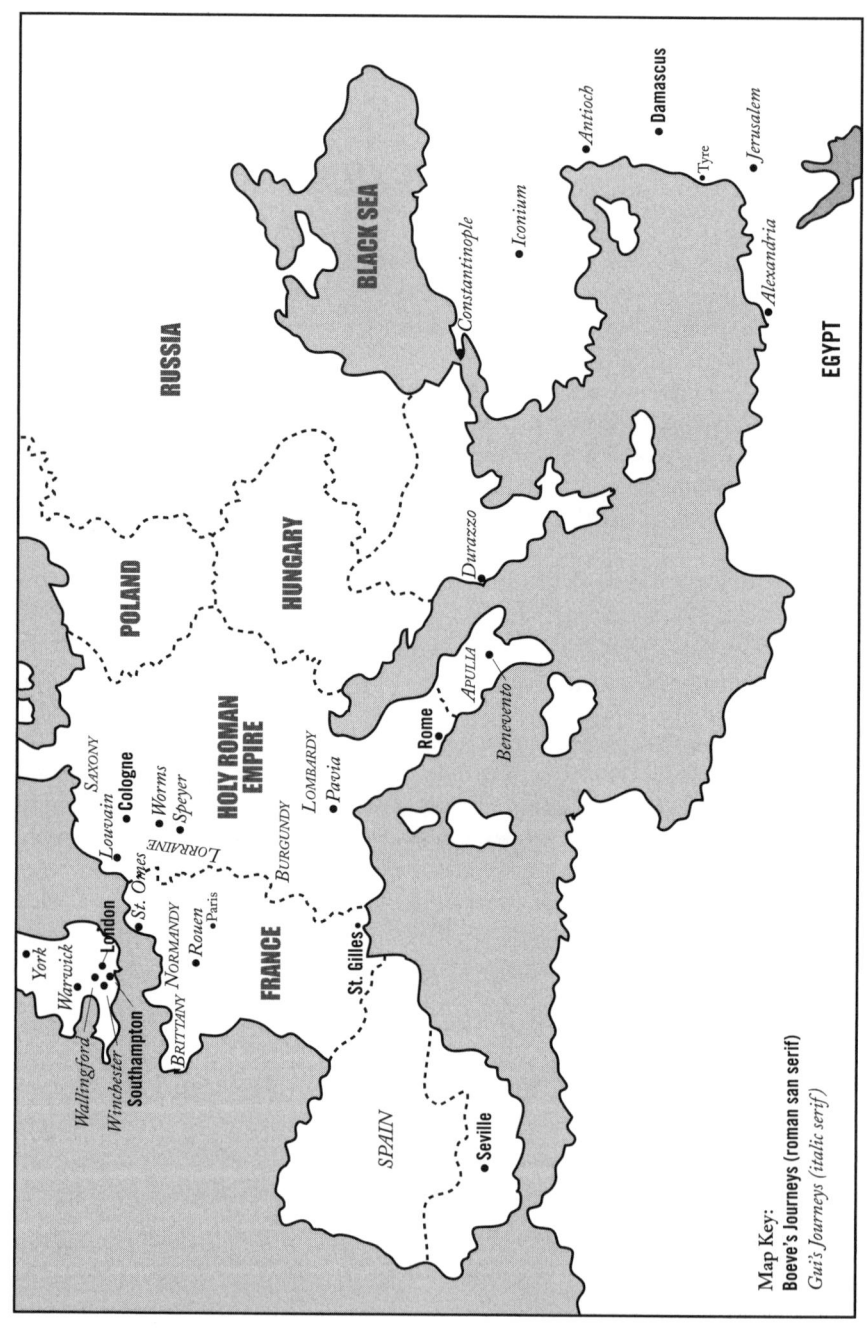

INTRODUCTION

Medieval romances, long narratives of adventures combining the real and the improbable, began to appear in the French vernacular in Britain about half-way through the twelfth century, and were designed to entertain the descendants of the Norman nobles who invaded Britain in 1066. An important context for their emergence is an interest among the new aristocracy in insular history and topography. The first, and arguably the finest, of Anglo-Norman romances, *Le Roman de Horn*, bears witness to this interest, as does Thomas's *Tristan*, both of which could have been written any time between the 1150s and 1170s. Other poems in this first wave of insular romances, on the other hand, are influenced by classical stories, which they adapt or use as a basis for their own inventions: Thomas of Kent's *Geste d'Alisandre* (c. 1175–85) and the two romances by Hue de Rotelande, *Ipomedon* and *Protheselaus* (1180–90).

Boeve de Haumtone, Waldef, and *Gui de Warewic* comprise the second wave of Anglo-Norman romances, and the stories initiated in *Boeve* and *Gui* were to prove exceptionally popular throughout Europe. They sparked imitations, adaptations, and translations in many languages, from Russian to Yiddish. Through their Middle English form they also enjoyed a long life in Britain, and were still entertaining both adults and children in the nineteenth century.[1] This popularity suggests that the literary taste of medieval people was wider and more differentiated than the canon of "great" medieval romance established in nineteenth- and early twentieth-century literary criticism leads us to believe. Such popularity would argue for the stories of both *Boeve* and *Gui* containing elements which appealed to a wider audience than their original twelfth- and early thirteenth-century ones. Both poems draw ably on a range of Anglo-Norman and Continental texts, and on favourite contemporary story motifs, to achieve strong plot-lines and vigorous characters. Initially they, like other Anglo-Norman romances before and after them, seem to have been created for patrons amongst the post-Conquest French-speaking nobility who took an interest in the past history of their adopted country and in newly-minted heroes with French names who could be inserted within it: both Boeve and Gui supposedly fight for tenth-cen-

---

[1] See Velma Bourgeois Richmond, *The Legend of Guy of Warwick* (New York and London: Garland Publishing, 1996), 313, 318, and *Der Anglonormannische Boeve de Haumtone*, ed. Albert Stimming (Halle: Bibliotheca Normannica, 1899), ii.

tury Anglo-Saxon kings.[2] But if the Anglo-Saxon past offered the initial audiences of these romances heroes with whom they could identify, they would have been equally interested in more contemporary matters: the relation of northwest Europe to its eastern neighbours. The protagonists of these narratives have prolonged careers in eastern and southern Europe, or in North Africa, fighting "Saracens".

Boeve and *Gui* embody old and new styles in insular narrative: *Boeve* is a "hybrid," combining the *laisse* or stanza form of the French chanson de geste with material characteristic of both epic and romance, and *Gui* is couched in the octosyllabic couplets which replaced *laisses* as the preferred medium for romance. Descriptions of fighting continue to occupy much of the poem, but its hero is characterised as a man of still greater religious and emotional sensibility than is encountered in epic.

1. Boeve de Haumtone

Plot Summary

Boeve is the son of count Gui, who lives at Hampton, and the daughter of the king of Scotland; she prefers Doon, the emperor of Germany, and has him kill her husband. She tries to murder her son by enlisting the help of his tutor, Sabot (or Sabaoth); when this fails, she sells Boeve to Saracen merchants who in turn sell him to Hermine, king of Egypt. Hermine's daughter Josiane falls in love with Boeve, who saves her and her father from Bradmund, king of Damascus. Boeve reciprocates her love, once she promises to convert, but enemies slander him to the king and get him sent to Damascus, where he is imprisoned for seven years. Josiane is married to Yvori, king of Monbrant, but preserves her virginity through magic. Boeve escapes, finds Josiane and travels towards England; on the way, with the help of his horse Arundel, he defeats the Saracen Escopart, sent by Yvori, and makes a servant of him. Boeve joins forces with Sabot and they defeat Doon.

The lovers are married and King Edgar restores Boeve's inheritance, but banishes him when Arundel kills the king's son. Sabot is left in charge of Boeve's lands while his son Terri, Boeve, and Josiane go into exile. After giving birth to twin sons, Josiane is abducted by Saracens led by Escopart, who has deserted

---

[2] See Judith Weiss, "Insular Beginnings," in *A Companion to Romance*, ed. Corinne Saunders (Oxford: Blackwell, 2004), 24–48, at 27–28. For further surveys of insular romance, see Susan Crane, *Insular Romance: Politics, Faith and Culture in Anglo-Norman and Middle English Literature* (Berkeley: University of California Press, 1986), and Rosalind Field, "Romance in England, 1066–1400," in *The Cambridge History of Medieval English Literature*, ed. David Wallace (Cambridge: Cambridge University Press, 1999), 152–76.

Boeve for his former master. Sabot, alerted by a dream, rescues her and returns her to Boeve, who has meanwhile had the babies fostered and has brought help to the lady of Civile, who wants to marry him. She is instead given Terri, who assists Boeve in rescuing Hermine from attacks by Yvori. Yvori is ransomed, but contrives the theft of Arundel, who is rescued by Sabaoth. Terri, Boeve, and his sons Gui and Miles, kill Yvori and capture Monbrant, then go to England to help Sabot's son, who has been disinherited by Edgar. Miles marries Edgar's daughter, while Gui inherits Hermine's kingdom. Boeve returns to Monbrant, where Arundel and Josiane die, to be followed by Boeve; Gui inherits Monbrant.

Author and Date

The genesis of *Boeve* is in the late twelfth century, but the poem depicts its hero as living at the time of the tenth-century Anglo-Saxon king, Edgar. Boeve's adventures in the Middle East, which occupy much of the poem, are influenced by the early Crusades and the literature they inspired. The poem is probably contemporary with the Continental chanson de geste *Fierabras*, which appears in shortened form in one of its manuscripts.[3] *Boeve* now exists in only one, incomplete, manuscript, but half of the poem once existed in one that disappeared during the Second World War (see below under Manuscripts); in addition, there are several fragments still extant which suggest the existence of two more manuscripts. None of these seems to preserve the earliest version of the poem, which in its existing shape is early to mid-thirteenth century.[4]

It was first proposed by Dominica Legge that many of the Anglo-Norman romances were written to commemorate particular insular noble families, and she called such texts "ancestral romances." *Boeve* was, she suggested, one such, written for the family of Aubigny, or Albini, the earls of Arundel.[5] Further research would seem to confirm that the romance probably recalls William II of Albini, the first earl, who married the dowager queen Adeliza of Louvain; she brought him the town of Arundel upon their marriage. In the poem, Boeve's famous horse, Arundel ("swallow", 542) is given him by Josiane, who becomes

---

[3] See *Fierabras: chanson de geste du XIIe siècle,* ed. Marc Le Person, CFMA (Paris: Champion, 2003), 26–27.

[4] See Stimming, lviii. Stimming invented the name "Boeve," which is in neither of the MSS (MS B uses Boefs, MS D Boves); the Continental French version of the story has "Beuve".

[5] M. Dominica Legge, *Anglo-Norman Literature and Its Background* (Oxford: Clarendon Press, 1963), 138–75, at 159. Legge labelled *Guillaume d'Angleterre, Waldef, Boeve, Fergus, Gui,* and *Fouke FitzWarin* as "ancestral romances" and linked them to specific families. Her concept, initially accepted, has more recently been challenged by Crane, *Insular Romance,* 12, 16–17 and Holden in *Le Roman de Waldef,* ed. A.J. Holden (Cologny-Geneva: Fondation Martin Bodmer, 1984), 33–34. See further, page 12 and note 31.

his wife and is virtually identified with the horse at several places in the poem.[6] William himself went to the Holy Land in the 1150s and must have there experienced at first hand "a world of shifting (and often cross-religious) political and military alliances," where "it was impossible to draw a line between friend and foe."[7] But the romance appears to be written for the Albini family as a whole rather than one member of it, since the detail about Boeve being required to pay *relief* upon inheriting his lands (2430) closely fits the experience of William's son, William III.[8]

We know nothing about the author. His knowledge of geography, both English and further afield, is, to our modern taste, imprecise: Hampton and Arundel both seem to be next door to London, Cologne has a seashore, while Spain, North Africa, and Syria all appear contiguous. But this is "cultural" geography, where exact topography matters less than imaginative closeness or distance, less than the sense that a busy European port is immediately open to close encounters with the marvellous (or monstrous) East. The poet addresses his audience, conventionally enough, as "Seigneurs" and threatens to abandon the story in the middle of a *laisse* if they do not pay him (434–36); these lords are represented as listening to him as he reads out his text (3849). He or another writer may have updated the poem by providing its first half with a continuation alluding to William III d'Albini.[9] The poet and/or his continuator employs a number of phrases throughout the romance which stress the veracity of his story—for example, *pur veritez, saunz mensounger, ne vus quer celer, pur veirs pus counter* (in truth; without lying; I don't want to hide it from you; I can relate truthfully)—but this is a fairly common device and may tell us no more than that he used the phrases as line-fillers and suppliers of rhyme. Rather more individual a trait is his taste for sardonic humour, more a feature of the first than the second half of the poem, and possibly influenced by similar humour in chansons de geste.[10]

---

[6] See Judith Weiss, "The Date of the Anglo-Norman *Boeve de Haumtone*," *Medium Aevum* 55 (1986): 237–41, and eadem, "The Power and the Weakness of Women in Anglo-Norman Romance," in *Women and Literature in Britain 1150–1500*, ed. Carol Meale (Cambridge: Cambridge University Press, 1993), 7–23, at 18.

[7] Ivana Djordjevic, "Rewriting the Crusading Experience: From *Boeve de Haumtone* to *Beves of Hampton*," unpublished paper delivered at the Leeds Medieval Conference, 2004. I am grateful to Dr Djordjevic for giving me access to this paper.

[8] See Weiss, "The Date," 239–40.

[9] Stimming was the first to postulate a poem in two parts, noticing that the first was rhymed while the second was in assonance (xlv–l.) See also Weiss, "The Date," 240.

[10] See, for example, Boeve's description of Bradmund's killing, 1204–21.

Sources and influences

The poet was clearly familiar with chansons de geste using crusading material. It is impossible to be sure if Josiane, the vigorous and enterprising *bele Sarrasine* in *Boeve*, is modeled on Floripas in the chanson de geste *Fierabras* or vice versa,[11] because the poems are probably contemporaneous. Romaine Wolf-Bonvin has noticed similarities with aspects of poems in the Guillaume cycle,[12] and it is quite possible that the character of Rainouart there was the inspiration for the giant Escopart in *Boeve*. But insular romance has also left its mark: motifs and narrative patterns from (more generally) the Tristan story and (more particularly) from *Le Roman de Horn* (c. 1170 or before) and Hue de Rotelande's *Ipomedon* (1180s) are all employed to make the first part of the story a fast-moving and dramatic tale. The exiled child, sold, like Tristan, to merchants who take him abroad, the two noble ladies who love him, one of them the only daughter of a foreign king, who makes him his cupbearer and arms him against his enemies, the seeking of the hero by an old friend in the guise of a palmer, the hero's refusal to admit his identity—all these episodes remind us of Horn. *Ipomedon* (which also shows knowledge of the figures of Horn and Tristan) probably provided the model for the comic wooing of Boeve in bed by Josiane.[13] The motif of the separated family in the second section of the romance is partly indebted to the widely-known legend of St Eustace.[14]

Themes and Issues

Boeve makes some use of the popular twelfth-century theme of exile and return, but also signals its divergence from it;[15] that is, although the hero returns at the end of the first half, with a converted Saracen wife, to claim his inheritance,

---

[11] See Judith Weiss, "The Wooing Woman in Anglo-Norman Romance," in *Romance in Medieval England*, ed. Maldwyn Mills, Jennifer Fellows, and Carol Meale (Cambridge: D.S. Brewer, 1991), 149–61, at 151–54.

[12] Romaine Wolf-Bonvin, "Escopart, le géant dépérissant de *Beuve de Hantone*," in *La Chrétienté au péril sarrasin*, Sénéfiance 46 (Université de Provence: CUERMA, 2000), 249–65.

[13] *Ipomedon* ll. 8651–8875.

[14] See G.H. Gerould, "Forerunners, Congeners and Derivatives of the Eustace Legend," *PMLA* 19 (1904): 335–448, Crane, *Insular Romance*, 105, and Jean-Pierre Martin, "*Beuve de Hantone* entre roman et chanson de geste," *Littérales* 31 (2003): 97–112, at 103–4.

[15] See Field, "Romance in England," 157, and especially her recent article, "The King over the Water: Exile-and-Return Revisited," in *Cultural Encounters in the Romance of Medieval England*, ed. Corinne Saunders (Cambridge: D.S. Brewer, 2005), 41–53, where she argues that this theme is characteristic of the "Matter of England" romances and that there isn't always "a positive conclusion" in its usage (42). See also Laura

just when it appears he can do so, he is thwarted by the unjust behaviour of the English king. Edgar at first grants Boeve's every request and showers honours upon him; his previous cowardly condoning of Doun, Boeve's wicked stepfather (2431–37), makes it impossible for the king to do otherwise, but he has to suffer Boeve's arrogance and rudeness, and he betrays his resentment as he watches Boeve win the horse race (2495); finally he learns that his son has been killed by Boeve's horse, which he was trying to steal, and in anger Edgar banishes the hero. Boeve is forced to return to the Middle East, the scene of most of his exploits and, indeed, the place where he dies: his foreign kingdom of Monbrant has become "home." In the triple concerns with land, family, and royal (mis)rule, inherited from *Horn*, the last, despite this promising material, ultimately becomes the least important: for a brief moment, Boeve stands supported by his fellow barons against Edgar, who continues to behave unjustly later on, but this conflict is hardly pursued with zeal, perhaps because there is no feeling for England and its governance as a whole. What matters is that Boeve's dispersed family should be reunited and his two sons secure kingdoms of their own, in Egypt and England; they accrue a third, Monbrant, at their father's death.[16]

His acquired family is all the more important to Boeve in that he comes from a markedly dysfunctional one, where his mother has helped engineer the brutal murder of his father and then married the murderer. Unlike Horn, therefore, Boeve does not emphasise his family background or his pride in his lineage, and he does not appear to be particularly attached to the Southampton area ("Haumtone"), despite the pointed allusion to building a castle and calling it Arundel after his horse. He can flourish in the Middle East because, unlike Horn, he does not insist on a rigorous division between Christians and pagans: he is happy to fight with Saracens against Saracens, as Gui will do after him, and to marry a Saracen (if converted) wife. Much more important than religious concerns is the loyalty of friends. His foster-father and tutor (*mestre*), Sabaoth, and Sabaoth's son, Terri, take the place of his birth-family, help him throughout his career, and are rewarded in due course by intermarriage (Boeve's daughter marries Terri's son).[17]

The long-lasting appeal of this romance must depend on its protagonists: Boeve, Josiane and (until he is killed off in the second half) the giant Escopart. A less nuanced character (and less priggish) than Horn, Boeve is arrogant, rude, rash, even stupid; it is possible the author gives him the recurrent epithet *li sené*

Ashe, "'Exile-and-return' and English Law: The Anglo-Saxon Inheritance of Insular Romance," in Blackwells, *Literature Compass* 3 (2006), www.literature-compass.com.

[16] See Crane, *Insular Romance*, 57: "the familial devotion running through the work finally comes to support the political concept of land tenure."

[17] See Judith Weiss, "*Mestre* and Son: The Role of Sabaoth and Terri in *Boeve de Haumtone*," in *Sir Bevis of Hampton in Literary Tradition: The Metamorphoses of a Romance Hero*, ed. Jennifer Fellows and Ivana Djordjevic (Woodbridge: D. S. Brewer, 2008).

(the wise) with deliberate irony since his decisions can show lack of judgement. *Curteis* also often seems a misnomer. Little description is allotted him, whether in or out of armour; his characteristics are conveyed through action and speech, whether in pretending to snore when Josiane comes to his bed[18] or in jeering with grim humour over fallen adversaries. Boeve is an imperfect hero, with an appealing if crude vigour. The same could be said of the Escopart, the converted pagan giant whose funniest hour is when he is baptized: the fact that he is too large for the font perhaps signals the impossibility of a true accommodation of his pagan faith with Christianity. He enters the poem late but then dominates many of the episodes in the first half (he is killed off in the second). The poet understood that the whole absurdity of a giant springs from his being linked to ordinary and everyday activities, too small to encompass him: hence he is described as a *lede bacheler*, a *bon garsoun* (1762, 1892: an ugly young man, in training to become a knight; a good servant/boy).[19]

Both these characters lose their appeal in the second half of the romance: Escopart implausibly deserts his new master and then disappears from the text, while the vigour and sharp edges of Boeve's character are smoothed away. The only one of the three who for a while retains some of her earlier interest is Josiane. As strong-willed and violent as Boeve himself, Josiane is in many respects typical of the *bele Sarrasine* of the chansons de geste: resourceful, enterprising, and possessed of arts, magical or otherwise.[20] In the first half, these show in her possession of a magical belt; in the second, they are seen in her musical accomplishments, somewhat awkwardly and fleetingly introduced to the narrative (2784–89, 3029–30).[21] It is noteworthy that it is through Josiane that two out of three kingdoms accrue to Boeve: one from her father, the other through her thwarted suitor Yvori.

---

[18] The scene anticipates by two centuries the scene in *Sir Gawain and the Green Knight* when the Lady of Haut Desert comes to Gawain's bedchamber and he feigns sleep. See Weiss, "Wooing Woman," 149.

[19] See Judith Weiss, "The Courteous Warrior: Epic, Romance and Comedy in *Boeve de Haumtone*," in *Boundaries in Medieval Romance*, ed. Neil Cartlidge (Woodbridge: D. S. Brewer, 2008).

[20] For the *bele Sarrasine*, see Norman Daniel, *Heroes and Saracens: An Interpretation of the Chansons de Geste* (Edinburgh: Edinburgh University Press, 1984), 73–90, and P. Bancourt, *Les Musulmans dans les chansons de geste du cycle du roi* (Aix: Université de Provence, 1982), chapters 8 and 9. Iseut's skills, in the early Tristan romances, remind us that heroines possessing magic arts of healing are, of course, not confined to chansons de geste.

[21] See Weiss, "The Power and the Weakness of Women," 12–14.

Structure, style, and aesthetic qualities

Popular texts, then and now, breed continuations: audiences want them to go on and on. Both *Boeve* and *Gui* would seem to have been given continuations.[22] Certainly the hypothesis that the second part of *Boeve de Haumtone* is a later addition (see footnote 8), possibly not by the same poet, would explain many of the romance's discrepancies and structural oddities. The first part would appear to end around *laisse* 165 or 166, with Boeve's marriage to Josiane and revenge on his stepfather, Doon; the change from rhyme to assonance (page 4, note 9 above) takes place at the start of 165. L'Escopart's baptismal name is now Gui, a fact not mentioned at his baptism in the first part, and he suddenly changes for no good reason from being Boeve's faithful follower to betraying him. The son of Sabaoth, unnamed, appears only briefly as a palmer in the first part; in the second he is Terri, Boeve's close friend. Two knights who betrayed Boeve in the first part are named only in the second; four uncles of Boeve suddenly mediate between him and Edgar in part two, but where were they in his vulnerable childhood, and are they paternal or maternal relatives? One of Boeve's twin sons is christened Miles, the name of the knight who forcibly married Josiane and whom she murdered, which suggests a strange lack of imagination on the poet's part. King Hermine's capital is Abreford later on, but all we know earlier is that the child Boeve arrives in Egypt.

To these inconsistencies (and there are more) can be added stylistic differences. Very few similes occur in the second half, whereas the first has many. Recurrent epithets attached to personal names, characteristic of chansons de geste, occur in both parts but often these epithets are very different from part to part. Above all, the handling of the unit of the *laisse* is different. The first part contains an initial section of sixty-seven short monorhymed *laisses* such as we do not find elsewhere in Anglo-Norman romance, and these show an able deployment of the form.[23] The remaining *laisses*, up to number 167, show fairly competent handling, with an average length of twenty-five lines. But the second part abandons formal control: the proportion of long and unwieldy units increases markedly, two of them running at 127 and 187 lines respectively. *Laisses* often give the impression of having been divided, or run together, with no concern for form or sense. This disregard for the form may be the work of an incompetent scribe, but

---

[22] The material from both narratives found a visual continuation in illustrations in the margins of the Taymouth Hours (c.1330), accompanying Anglo-Norman prayers. See Jessica Brantley, "Images of the Vernacular in the Taymouth Hours," *English Manuscript Studies 1100–1700* 10 (2002): 83–113.

[23] See Ivana Djordjevic, "Versification and Translation in *Sir Beves of Hampton*," *Medium Aevum* 74 (2005): 41–59, at 51.

it seems odd that he should have exercised it in the second part of the romance more than the first.[24]

The first half at least shows us some of the qualities of the original poet. Though he is insistent in his use of certain epithets and phrases, and his vocabulary does not possess the range and richness of Thomas's *Horn*, he has a gift for lively dialogue, black humour, and a gripping pace. The events of Boeve's childhood, culminating in his exile, engage our sympathies, while Josiane's forced marriage to Miles, his murder, and her rescue in the nick of time are dramatically narrated, rising to a climax; in both episodes form satisfyingly enhances content.

Manuscripts of Boeve de Haumtone

Stimming's 1899 edition uses what were then the only two extant manuscripts: B (Paris, Bibliothèque Nationale, nouv.acq.fr. 4532), and D, sold by the Parisian bookseller Firmin Didot to the Librairie Labitte and ending up with Hermann Suchier. From Suchier, D went to the University Library of Louvain and was destroyed by bombing in 1944. The two incomplete manuscripts fortunately complement each other, B containing lines 1–1268 and D, overlapping B in parts, containing 912–1081 and 1190 to the end. Stimming dated D to the second half of the thirteenth century and B to the early fourteenth century.[25] More fragments from previously unknown manuscripts have recently come to light: G, MS 466 in the Hunterian Library of the University of Glasgow, containing sixty-two lines (1003–65, with 1034–35 missing but an extra line after 1046), and L, Lambeth 1237, comprising two strips containing lines 1641–65 and 1672–96. G may date from the second half of the thirteenth century.[26]

Neither of the principal manuscripts is a good one. B, which once belonged to the antiquary Peter Le Neve (1661–1729) and then to William Constable of Burton Constable House, Yorkshire, contains in its first half accounts of various English manors; in its second half, there are two blank pages after *Boeve* breaks off, which means the scribe was possibly working from an incomplete exemplar.[27]

---

[24] On the way in which the scribe of MS B mishandled *laisse* form, see Djordjevic, "Versification," 58, n. 43.

[25] Stimming, iv. Djordjevic thinks B's letter forms could suggest a slightly earlier date: "Versification," 43, n. 15.

[26] On G, see Judith Weiss, "The Anglo-Norman *Boeve de Haumtone*: A Fragment of a New Manuscript," *Modern Language Review* 95 (2000): 305–10. The Lambeth fragments have not yet been published; the beginning of each line has been lost and they are sometimes illegible.

[27] See Djordjevic, "Versification," 58, n. 43. The romance is on parchment, the manorial accounts are on paper, in a later, probably seventeenth- or eighteenth-century hand (contrary to Stimming's "sixteenth century," iv), since the opening sentence refers to Le Neve.

Stimming thought it a careless and corrupted manuscript, and had no better opinion of D which, as earlier noted, contained *Fierabras* in its second half; he thought there were many occasions where it omitted whole lines, its scribe being perhaps ignorant of French (vi).

This gave Stimming licence to emend the text further than today we would think desirable. As he was the first to establish that three foreign translations or adaptations of the narrative of *Boeve*—the Middle English, the Middle Welsh, and the Old Norse—formed a discrete group, he changed the text in the manuscripts where it is deficient, garbled, or nonsensical to accord with readings in these foreign versions. But Christopher Sanders, in his recent edition of the Old Norse *Bevers Saga*, is of the opinion that this version derives from neither B nor D, so that reconstructing words or phrases in the Anglo-Norman from it is unwise. Ivana Djordjevic has similarly pointed out that B, at least, is probably too late to have been used by the author of the Middle English *Beves*, and Morgan Watkin showed conclusively that the Welsh version of the Boeve story, on whose nineteenth-century text and translation Stimming (who knew no Welsh) relied, is a hodge-podge full of errors.[28] Stimming also changes the order of lines, especially with D, and adds or omits words, to improve scansion or the assonance.

Some examples of emendations by Stimming which are unnecessary:

1. An innocuous word or phrase in the MS is replaced by one which Stimming, citing the Norse or Welsh versions, has invented and thinks is better:

> 258 *au tertre* is replaced by *a destre*; 892 *chaumbre* is replaced by *chaere*.

2. A repeated word is replaced by a synonym:

> 275 *truaunt* is replaced by *ribaud*. A repeated phrase is omitted: 993 *fort roi*.

3. A word or phrase is added, with Stimming citing Norse and Welsh versons:

> 1551 *e as suns*; 1841 *en sun destrer.*

4. Stimming, citing the Norse and Welsh versions, often unnecessarily reverses the order of lines which in the MS make sense:

> 1620–21, 2966–67, 3263–64. 3293–95, 3311–12.

---

[28] *Bevers Saga*, ed. Christopher Sanders (Reykjavík: Stofnun Árna Magnússonar Á Íslandi, 2001), cxliii–cxlviii and Appendix; Djordjevic, "Versification," 43; Morgan Watkin, "Albert Stimming's *Welsche Fassung* in the *Anglonormannische Boeve de Haumtone*: An Examination of a Critique," *Studies in French Language and Medieval Literature presented to Professor Mildred K. Pope* (Manchester: Manchester University Press, 1939), 371–79.

Principles in translating the text

In view of the above, I have not accepted all of Stimming's emendations. I have not commented upon all the incidences where he has changed the text, only those I thought worthy of note. Where the original order of lines was acceptable, I have reverted to it; similarly, I have retained words which there seemed no good reason to alter. The paragraphing within my translation of the *laisses* is modern.

Manuscripts B and D vary in their spelling of names: for example, Boeve's *mestre* is Sabot (and Saboc in several places in the MS) in B, but Sabaoth (and once Saber) in D; his birthplace is Haumtone or Hampton, his pagan enemy Bradmund or Brandon. For the most important names I have kept their different spellings in B and D, but retained "Hampton" throughout.

Medieval narratives move freely and somewhat unpredictably (with a few exceptions) between present and past tenses when past time is uniformly meant. I have kept to the past tense in translating narrative in both *Boeve de Haumtone* and *Gui de Warewic*. The phrasing and syntax, in particular of *Gui*, has been made more flowing, in that connectives like "and" and "for" have occasionally been added, redundant "then"s omitted, and proper names have sometimes replaced pronouns for the sake of clarity.

2. Gui de Warewic

Plot Summary

Gui, son of the steward to the count of Warwick, falls in love with Felice, the count's daughter, who demands he prove his worth before he can receive her love. Accompanied by his tutor, Heralt, he has numerous adventures on the Continent and in Constantinople, winning admiration and fame, and in the process making two good friends, Terri of Worms and Amis de la Muntaigne, and one enemy, Otun the duke of Pavia, whom he finally kills. Then Gui returns to England, slays a dragon, and marries Felice. He has been promised the count's lands, but he has a change of heart and accuses himself of having killed and destroyed for the sake of a woman, not God, in whose service he will now go in order to expiate his sins. He abandons his wife, his unborn child, and his lands and returns to foreign parts where, incognito, he fights both pagans and Christians: he helps King Triamor by defeating a huge Saracen named Amoraunt, and his friend Terri by defeating Berard, the nephew of Otun. Finally he returns to England to foil the Danes, who are intent on invading the land, by defeating their champion, Colbrond. Still unknown to everyone except King Athelstan, Gui retires to a hermitage near Warwick, and near the point of death, he sends his wife a message to bury him in Warwick. When Terri (who has married the daughter of the duke of Lorraine) hears of Gui's death, he asks for the body, which he transports to Lorraine and houses in a splendid abbey.

Gui's son Rainbrun, meanwhile, has been abducted by foreign merchants and grows up in Africa, where Heralt eventually finds himself pitted against Rainbrun in battle. Reunited, the two return to England and on the way liberate Amis de la Muntaigne from a fairy knight and inadvertently fight Aselac, Heralt's son, in Burgundy. All three join King Athelstan, who gives Rainbrun his father's county of Warwick while Heralt returns to his castle of Wallingford.

Author and Date

The Anglo-Norman romance of *Gui de Warewic* is anonymous, but its author shows his familiarity with an area around Warwick—and thus his probable origins—by mentioning that city as well as Oxford, Buckingham, and Wallingford. The poem was first edited in 1933 by Alfred Ewert who dated it to 1232–42, between the death of Henri II d'Oilly and the restoration of the war-ravaged castle of Wallingford. Ewert was convinced it had been written by a monk from Oseney Abbey (patronised by the d'Oilly family) and connected to the union of Margery d'Oilly, sister of Henri, and the fifth Earl of Warwick. He saw that the poem asserts Gui is the son of the count of Warwick's seneschal, who owns Wallingford, and he also noticed a reference in the romance to the destruction of Wallingford, "never so well restored since." (9013–20); the poet thus must have written before its restoration by Richard of Cornwall in 1242.[29] M. Dominica Legge, promoting her idea of "ancestral romance," adopted Ewert's theory and suggested the romance was written to flatter Thomas, Earl of Warwick, son of Margery and Henri, the fifth Earl.[30]

Both the dating and Legge's "ancestral romance" concept have since been challenged. Susan Crane pointed out that there was no praise of any patron in the poem or mention of the current earls.[31] In 1975 Jeanne Wathelet-Willem observed that the oldest manuscript of *Gui*, E, (BL MS Additional 38662), came from the same scriptorium as the one that produced manuscripts of the *Chanson*

---

[29] Ewert, 1: v-vii. For more details of the Oilli's patronage of Oseney Abbey, see David Postler, " 'Patronus et advocatus noster': Oseney Abbey and the Oilly Family," *Historical Research* 60 (1987): 100–2. Despite founding the Abbey in 1129, the twelfth-century d'Oillys seemed little interested in it and the first member to be buried there was Henri II in 1232.

[30] Legge, *Anglo-Norman Literature*, 162, and see above page 3.

[31] Susan Dannenbaum [Crane], "Anglo-Norman Romances of English Heroes: 'Ancestral Romance'?" *Romance Philology* 35 (1982): 601–8. Cathérine Gaullier-Bougassas agrees: "Origines d'un lignage et écriture romanesques: les romans lignagers anglo-normands," in *Seuils de l'oeuvre dans le texte medieval*, ed. Emmanuèle Baumgartner et Laurence Harf-Lancner, 2 vols. (Paris: Presses de la Sorbonne Nouvelle, 2002), 2:19–35, at 22. A.J. Holden, however, was willing to consider *Boeve* and *Gui* as "dynastic": see his review of Crane, *Insular Romance*, in *Romania* 108 (1987): 391–95.

de Guillaume and the *Pseudo-Turpin* (BL MS Additional 40142), both originally bound with *Gui*; the hand of *Turpin* and *Gui* appeared to be the same. *Turpin* could be firmly dated between 1206 and 1214, hence Ewert's dating of *Gui* to the 1230s–40s was too late. She also discovered that BN. MS f.fr. 24766, containing the *Dialogues de St Gregoire*, was in a hand very similar to *Guillaume*, *Turpin*, and *Gui*, and must again have come from the same scriptorium. Fortunately, the scribe of the *Dialogues* identified himself as brother Angier, a monk at St Frideswide's in Oxford, and dated his work as starting in 1212, finishing two years later.[32]

In 1984 Emma Mason again suggested that the romance celebrated the union of Warwicks and d'Oillys, but pointed out that Margery died in 1205 and that Wallingford Castle was renovated in 1215; the romance must thus have been written by the early part of 1205.[33] A.J. Holden's edition of *Waldef*, also in 1984, established that *Gui* was closely modelled, down to precise verbal similarities, upon this earlier Anglo-Norman romance, which he dated between 1200 and 1210, and he called Ewert's dating of *Gui*, and his hypothesis of a link to the noble families in the area, "extremely fragile."[34] Ewert had remarked upon MS E's closeness to its original, being most carefully executed and least in need of correction; Wathelet-Willem thought little time could have elapsed between it and the original. Regardless of hypotheses about patronage, we are left with a romance which seems likely to have been written before 1210.

The poem resembles *Waldef* in its general knowledge of Continental geography, mostly the lands of the Holy Roman Empire, but in addition has some familiarity with the Middle East, especially Constantinople. This knowledge is probably second-hand, and in parts vague: Persia is called a city (8384); Benevento in southern Italy seems to be close to Lombardy (1177–84); and the imperial city of Speyer appears to be envisaged as on the sea (10204) although an earlier reference to this might conceivably be interpreted as its position on the Rhine (2947). Nevertheless, there is an intriguing mention of an English colony

---

[32] Jeanne Wathelet-Willem, *Recherches sur La Chanson de Guillaume* (Paris: Belles Lettres, 1975), 27–50; Paul Meyer, "La Vie de Saint Grégoire Le Grand," *Romania* 12 (1883): 145–208; M. Dominica Legge, "La Date des écrits de Frère Angier," *Romania* 79 (1958): 512–14. Meyer prints Angier's remarks about himself and his dates, and the fact he is writing under the Interdict (1208–14). Legge thinks Angier may have started in 1213, not 1212, and finished in 1215. A caveat needs adding to Wathelet-Willem's dating of the MS of the *Turpin*: it is an Anglo-Norman redaction of the "Johannes" Turpin (commissioned in 1206), but itself somewhat later: see Ronald L. Walpole, *The Old French Johannes Translation of the Pseudo-Turpin*, 2 vols (Berkeley, Los Angeles, London: University of California Press, 1976), 1:4, 2:171–73.

[33] Emma Mason, "Legends of the Beauchamps' Ancestors: The Use of Baronial Propaganda in Medieval England," *Journal of Medieval History* 10 (1984): 25–40, at 30–31.

[34] *Waldef*, ed. Holden, 18, 29–31.

at Constantinople (4521–26) and an unusually favourable picture of the eastern empire and its ruler at a time when Byzantine Greeks were more often portrayed as treacherous and cowardly. It is possible the poet knew, whether first-hand or by report, about Manuel I Comnenus, one of the greatest of Byzantine emperors (reigned 1143–80). At any rate, the complete absence of any mention of the Fourth Crusade, with its sack and pillage of Constantinople, suggests the romance was written before 1204.[35]

Sources and Influences

Like its model, *Waldef*, *Gui de Warewic* makes use of "a host of traditional motifs and every kind of commonplace,"[36] and it has plainly drawn upon well-known twelfth-century texts like *La Chanson de Roland*, Geoffrey of Monmouth's *Historia Regum Britanniae* (probably using Wace's version of this, the *Brut*), Thomas's Tristan story, and Chrétien de Troyes's *Erec* and *Yvain*. The writer could have known the Continental romance *Robert Le Diable* (late twelfth century).[37] Above all, *Gui* is indebted to its insular romance predecessors, *Horn*, *Boeve de Haumtone*, the Havelok story in Gaimar's *Estoire des Engleis*, *Ipomedon*, *Amis e Amilun*, and of course *Waldef*; they provide him with popular story motifs such as the heroine being the sole heir to her father's kingdom, rings as signs of fidelity and tokens of recognition, faithful male friendship, and the hero as sole volunteer to fight enemy champions.[38] But the poet has also consciously varied his use of some of these: the heiress is not the feisty wooing woman of *Boeve* or *Horn*; recognition by ring is achieved only after the hero's death; and though it is important for the

---

[35] For a fuller account of this argument, see Judith Weiss, "*Gui de Warewic* at Home and Abroad," in *Guy of Warwick: Icon and Ancestor*, ed. Alison Wiggins and Rosalind Field (Cambridge: D.S. Brener, 2007), 1–11.

[36] *Waldef*, ed. Holden, 23.

[37] *Gui* 3789 ff., on the danger of sending embassies to Saracens, is reminiscent of *Roland*, 205–9; the feud between the German emperor and Duke Seguin over the death of the former's nephew (1661 ff.) reminds us of the episode with Cassibellan and Androgeus in Wace (4359 ff.), as do Gui's exploits in the Sultan's tent (3955 ff.), derived from Walwein's in Wace (11701), possibly via Lioine's adventures in *Waldef* (16529 ff.). The motif of the faithful lion whose life Gui saves must derive from Chretien's *Yvain*; possibly Felice's concern that love would diminish Gui's interest in fame and prowess has been influenced by a similar dichotomy in *Erec*. For *Robert Le Diable*'s removal of the saintly body, see Judith Weiss, "Ineffectual Monarchs: Portrayals of Regal and Imperial Power in *Ipomedon*, *Robert Le Diable* and *Octavian*," in *Cultural Encounters in the Romance of Medieval England*, ed. Corinne Saunders (Cambridge: D.S. Brewer, 2005), 55–68. The Tristan story inspires the kidnapping of Reinbrun. For further discussion, see Ian Short, "*Gui de Warewic*," in *Enzyklopädie des Märchens*, ed. Rolf Wilhelm Brednich (Berlin: Walter de Gruyter, 1989), 290–91.

[38] See Weiss, "Insular Beginnings," 26–44.

conclusion of the romance that he beget an heir, he himself shows not the slightest interest in the fate of his son and the future of his lineage. This is related to the poet's use of another cluster of stories which depict their protagonists withdrawing from most worldly concerns, leaving their wives, but continuing to fight for good causes: St Alexis, and Guillaume in the *Moniage Guillaume*.[39] Gui's discovery that, as Helen Cooper puts it, "chivalry is not enough," is what marks this romance firmly out from its Anglo-Norman predecessors and perhaps what contributed to its long-lasting success.[40]

Themes and Issues

Gui, then, is a hero unlike most of his Anglo-Norman predecessors in that he does not conquer large amounts of land in exile abroad, he does not return to defend and re-conquer his patrimony, and, from 7565 onwards, he abjures marriage, love, family, and land. The romance ends not with his, but with his son's, triumphant return to the land of his fathers. After his initial rejections by Felice, Gui develops from a participant in tournaments into a peripatetic mercenary, usually fighting for Christians but not invariably so: he is willing to go and serve the Sultan when he assumes the Byzantine emperor has maltreated him (3365–66) and, in helping count Jonas of Durazzo, he is also defending the pagan king Triamor against the Sultan of Persia. The familiar dichotomy of the chansons de geste, between good Christians and evil Saracens, present also in Anglo-Norman narratives such as *Horn* and *Boeve*, is absent here.[41]

Gui's adventures are set in two empires: the Holy Roman, with its important cities of Speyer and Worms, and the Byzantine. The first, and its ruler, is unfavourably contrasted with the second. Emperor Reiner governs weakly and with poor judgement, ceding too much power to unscrupulous bullies and mistreating loyal vassals. The peace of his domains is continually disrupted by feuding magnates. Easily misled, he is also vain and has a justifiable worry about how he is regarded by the eastern world; Gui satisfies his curiosity with trenchant criticism

---

[39] Laura A. Hibbard, *Mediaeval Romance in England*, 2nd ed. (New York: Burt Franklin, 1963; 1st ed. 1924), 137–38; Richmond, *The Legend of Guy*, 20–24. For an extended discussion of the influence of St Alexis on Gui, see Neil Cartlidge, *Medieval Marriage: Literary Approaches, 1100–1300* (Cambridge: D.S. Brewer, 1997), 99–106.

[40] Helen Cooper, *The English Romance in Time* (Oxford: Oxford University Press, 2004) 32; she suggests that the *Gui* story was popular because "it offered the familiarity of both romance and traditional devotional narrative models" (92).

[41] Lee C. Ramsey comments: "Religion is almost never a consideration in [Guy's] choice of sides." (*Chivalric Romances* [Bloomington: Indiana University Press, 1983], 64). According to Ralph Hanna, "a principled crusader [Guy] isn't." (*London Literature 1300–1380* [Cambridge: Cambridge University Press, 2005], 114). Both are writing about the Middle English *Guy*.

of his abuses of power and gives him a lesson on his duties (9966–70). By contrast, Emperor Hernis, despite his very considerable troubles with the Turks, is a better judge of men and refuses to believe calumnies against them without proof, generously rewarding those who help him. Hernis's good relations with Gui, and his use of him to fight the Sultan of Konya, may reflect Manuel Comnenus's use of both Norman and English mercenaries in his campaigns against the Seljuk Sultanate in Iconium.

Gui's behaviour to both emperors is that of the ideal vassal, supplying both *auxilium* and *consilium* (help and advice), but of course he is the vassal of neither of them but rather of King Athelstan back in England, the place of his birth to which he periodically tries to return. It is England (and Warwick), rather than Englishness which Gui evokes whenever he is asked who he is,[42] and it is possible the poet intended to create an implicit contrast between this mostly peaceable, mostly well-governed kingdom—only occasionally threatened by outside forces such as dragons or Danes, a place suitable for births, marriages, religious retreats, and deaths—and "abroad," dangerous, wracked by jealousies and feuds, and also the setting for deeply emotional partings, reconciliations, and reunions, both personal and political, which form high points of the romance.

Gui's behaviour in the second half of the romance is supposedly that of a man who repents his previous worldly career and undertakes the path of a penitent in order to serve God. Helen Cooper's summary accepts this, but may paint a slightly more generous picture than is warranted:

> He . . . sets out to replay his earlier conquests, but now against God's enemies rather than chivalric opponents. He becomes a palmer, goes on pilgrimage to the Holy Land . . . . The romance, in other words, replays the chivalric quest of its first half as penitential pilgrimage in its second half, overwriting secular adventures undertaken for honour and one's lady with spiritual seeking and with deeds of prowess performed anonymously and for the sake of God.[43]

This is persuasive, but not entirely borne out by the text, which itself has some curious inconsistencies. As Paul Price has pointed out, when Gui tells Felice of his sinful past in which he has done no service for his Creator, he describes what the text has not: he has "destroyed cities and burned down abbeys in many kingdoms" (7608–10). But far from destroying cities he has helped defend them, no abbeys have been burnt, and his actions have always been those of "an ethical and

---

[42] For example, 8781–82, 8593.
[43] Cooper, *Romance in Time*, 92; the summary is of course encapsulating both Anglo-Norman and later English accounts.

celebrated warrior." To re-launch Gui's career, augment the hero, and extend his adventures, the poet is prepared to disregard narrative coherence.[44]

But how far is Gui's seeking "spiritual," and how far is his prowess performed for God? The picture is not clear. If fighting for the "good guys" is fighting for God, then many other secular heroes must be considered as religiously motivated as Gui. Certainly it is hard to include fighting to help King Triamor in this category, even if it is a by-product of helping the Christian Jonas. Gui's "enemies" are not always God's either; rather, they are enemies of those whom, for the moment, he has decided to help, and may be Christian or pagan. We should not exaggerate his humility: though he fights anonymously, he accepts splendid armour for two of his important combats and always reveals his identity in the end, at moments of high emotion. It is unclear what his "pilgrimage" really amounts to: though he is constantly called a pilgrim, his fleeting visit to relics in Greece is more like that of a tourist (8971–74), and although he expresses the wish to go to Jerusalem "where he could seek God's saints" (7736), his trip there is equally cursory: "Then he journeyed through the land and visited the holy places. Next, he left that place" (7863–65). Here Cartlidge's summary seems apt: "the romance stresses the incompatibility of married life and adventure not in order to assert either a religious ideal or a basic hostility towards marriage, but simply to justify the hero's continued addiction to the courses of individual endeavour."[45]

Nevertheless, there are suggestions in the latter part of Gui's career that from time to time he can be seen as a type of Christ. Those who continually seek him never recognise him. When Terri, observing the armoured Gui about to do battle with Berard, reflects "this isn't the pilgrim who overtook me on the road" (10141–42; repeated 10594), he recalls for us Christ on the road to Emmaus (Luke 24: 13–31). Gui is willing to lay down his life for his friend (10237) and, having nearly done so, he meets him at a stone cross outside the city, his feet cracked and bleeding, to reproach Terri gently for his blindness: "This is Gui you see here; why will you not recognise me?" (10671–72) A similar disclosure, again outside the city and in similar words, is made to Athelstan (11321–34). Finally, though his sweet-smelling corpse is not, of course, resurrected, it is the object of great devotion and possesses curious power, suggesting possible miracles in due course (11579–608), again like St Alexis.

Gui cannot, however, be seen consistently throughout the romance as a type of Christ, and it is certainly the case that the narrative is structured around

---

[44] Paul Price, "Confessions of a Godless Killer: Guy of Warwick and Comprehensive Entertainment," in *Medieval Insular Romance: Translation and Innovation*, ed. Judith Weiss, Jennifer Fellows, and Morgan Dickson (Cambridge: D. S. Brewer, 2000), 93–110, at 107.

[45] Cartlidge, *Medieval Marriage*, 104.

searches for deeply desired people—Gui, Terri, Heralt, Rainbrun—rather than for God; these are the real "pilgrimages". Laura Hibbard was the first to observe "Guy is as much a romance of friendship as of love," and William Calin has taken her idea yet further: "The most moving sentimental episodes . . . which are truly love scenes, recount and dramatise . . . recognition and separation between Gui and his male friends."[46] Homosocial, not heterosexual, love gives rise to the high points of the romance, whether in great public scenes of reconciliation between emperor and vassal or in private scenes of reunion and parting between comrades-in-arms. "Were it not for love of my beloved I would not leave you," says Gui to Terri, "we would always stay together and never part. I must go, whether I like it or not" (7207–11) His first peacetime meeting with the man who will become his greatest friend is preceded by a description of the kind that conventionally prefaces a hero's thoughts of love: "It was a day in May when every flower blooms. Gui entered a forest . . . to hear the birds sing . . . he heard the sweet songs of the birds; he fell into profound thought" (4545–58). Though early in the poem it is Felice who causes Gui to weep and faint, these signs of acute sensibility soon come to characterise his reactions to his friends' plights, and it is notable that a final reunion with Felice is denied: that source of great potential emotion is removed, so that the wife can meet her husband again only after his death.

Structure, style, and aesthetic qualities

Though long, *Gui* tells a fast-moving story at a good pace, and every now and then rises to rhetorical heights in recounting grand scenes. The best early example of these is the reconciliation between Reiner and Seguin, engineered by Gui (2725–98), where in several manuscripts the "paragraphing" by coloured initials draws attention to a series of speeches by vassals begging the emperor to pardon the duke. Repetition here skilfully underpins a strong message: that noble men on both sides of a bloody conflict, which is tearing the empire apart, are determined to end it by putting pressure on their overlord to see reason. The poet secures a similarly impressive effect when describing the reconciliation of Terri with the emperor (10511–80). These extraordinary and moving scenes run counter to our expectations of endless fighting in romance, though *Gui* also provides plenty of that. Grand set-pieces of one-on-one combat have clearly been influenced by elements characteristic of chanson de geste, such as epithets and formulaic descriptions of fighting; such conventional writing often has little life left in it. On the other hand, the poet has enlivened the combat with Amoraunt with the depiction of Gui's armour (8387–8418), which suggests he belongs to

---

[46] Hibbard, *Mediaeval Romance*, 134 (who remarks on the influence of the Amis and Amilun story, a tale of two devoted friends, on the name of Amis de Muntaigne in *Gui*); William Calin, "*Gui de Warewic* and the Nature of Late Anglo-Norman Romance," *Fifteenth-Century Studies* 17 (1990): 23–32, at 25.

the group of the Nine Worthies (here represented by Alexander, Hector, and Charlemagne),[47] and the combat with Berard by the wicked duke's attempt to murder his opponent overnight by throwing his bed into the sea (10187–10296). The poet is also good at engineering situations of dramatic irony, most of them caused by Gui's unrecognised presence.[48] These achievements all suggest that the romance has hitherto attracted too many brickbats and not enough plaudits for its literary qualities.[49]

It is possible that the last part of the romance, the adventures of Gui's son Rainbrun, was originally not part of it and was added early on to satisfy popular demand. Legge observed: "The whole of the postscript dealing with Heralt and Rainbrun has an air of hurried compression absent from most of the earlier part of the romance" (*Anglo-Norman Literature*, 167). It certainly involves adventures of a kind quite different from earlier ones, such as the rescue of Amis from a fairy knight whose kingdom is the Otherworld, with the use of a magic sword: magic and the supernatural have been virtually absent from the rest of *Gui*. Perhaps the audience which enjoyed the father's adventures so much required those of his son be constructed around materials of proven popularity in other romances.

Though there are narrative ties between the postscript and the rest, which prepare us for Heralt and Rainbrun's exploits, there are also some inconsistencies which appear at the point of Gui's death. The hero conveys precise instructions to his wife, through an intermediary, that he should be buried in the hermitage in the wood near Warwick, and his wish that he not be moved from there is later repeated (11502–4, 11538–42). Once he dies, attempts are made to move him to Warwick, but miraculously these are unavailing, whereupon his wife recalls his wishes and insists they be respected. When she dies soon after, she is buried next to him (11594–628). The poet apparently then brings his poem to an end:

> Ensemble sunt en la compaignie
> De Nostre Dame, saint Marie;
> E issi nus doinst Deu servir
> Ke en sa glorie puissum venir. Amen (11629–32)

---

[47] See footnote 53 in Judith Weiss, "Emperors and Antichrists: Reflections of Empire in Insular Narrative, 1130–1250," in *The Matter of Identity in Medieval Romance*, ed. Phillipa Hardman (Cambridge: D. S. Brewer, 2002), 87–102, at 101.

[48] Examples are Gui hired by his enemy Otun (6199–6274) and about to help Triamor (8267–8332): in both scenes he says "I know Gui well."

[49] Legge (*Anglo-Norman Literature*, 167) repeated an early criticism of it as "one of the dullest and most tedious of our early romances" and remarked upon its repetitiveness and poverty of invention (169). *Gui*'s repetition of both formulaic phrases and particular motifs may, however, point to oral performance. Ewert deplored its irregular versification, observing that while most lines varied between seven and eight syllables, there were occasional passages in around ten (xxv–xxvi).

[They are together, in the company of our Lady, St Mary, and thus may God grant us so to serve Him that we may come to His glory. AMEN.

There then follow ten lines, 11633–42, beginning "Ore avez, seignurs, de Gui oi" (Now, my lords, you have heard about Gui), reflecting upon Gui's good end, service to God, fine adventures, and prowess, which have the air of a coda. The next event is surprising: Terri, hearing of Gui's death, comes to England and asks for his friend's body. Despite the fact that, previously, a hundred knights could not move it from the hermitage, the body is handed over to him, and he takes it to Lorraine and houses it in a splendid abbey where, we are told, it still lies.

Some of Gui's manuscripts, both from the "first redaction"[50] and from other groups, show signs of a substantial break in the narrative, either at 11632 or ten lines later, after the "coda". In Additional 38662, there is an empty space of about two or three lines after the "Amen" at 11632, then a much larger initial than usual for the coda at "Ore." Corpus MS 50 has "Amen" at 11632 but no gap until after the coda, so that 11643 ("quant li quons Terri oi aveit," when Count Terri heard) is preceded by a two-line space. Written in the margin is "Ici morut Gui de Warewik & Felice sa bele sa duz fame" (here Gui of Warwick and Felice, his beautiful, his sweet wife, die). MSS Bodmer 168 and Bodmer 67 also have an "Amen" in the margin next to 11632 and the latter has an extra large capital at "Ore." MS Royal 8.F.ix which, according to Ewert, is corrupt but mainly follows the first redaction, is complete, but actually ends at 11632, with two "Amens" and a request in Latin that the writer be blessed. MS Arundel 27 has a coda of twenty-four lines following an address to *seynurs*, with the clear statement "Ataunt finist lestorre issy" (here the story ends). MS Wolfenbüttel 87.4 has a break of ten lines after 11656 (after, that is, the account of the burial of Gui's body in Lorraine), where there is a big, capitalised AMEN. The break stretches to the bottom of that column; the story of Heralt is started at the top of the next column, in words which suggest a new beginning: "Plest vus oyr de harald le noble baron" (do you wish to hear about the noble lord Heralt?)

These manuscripts show, at the very least, scribal awareness that the narrative originally ended with the death of the hero at 11632; the coda from 11632 to 11642 may have been part of this, or added to help smooth the transition to the adventures of Gui's son. One can envisage the poet being persuaded, soon after the success of Gui's story, to write a sequel around Rainbrun; it is harder to understand why he flies in the face of the spirit and letter of his own composition in letting his hero's body be taken to be buried abroad, in a manner which is strongly reminiscent of the theft of Robert le Diable's corpse: both bodies have turned into saints' relics, and both are removed, against the intentions of the deceased,

---

[50] MSS ECHFM according to Ewert, 1: xv; for the identification of these letters, see the next section.

to places with which they have no connection.[51] On the other hand, the removal of Gui's body from England to the Continent bolsters the romance's belief in the importance of friendship at the expense of his familial ties and of his status as an English hero rooted in English lands.

Manuscripts of Gui de Warewic

Ewert knew of twelve manuscripts, all in his opinion executed in England by Anglo-Norman scribes (1:xv); Ruth Dean's *Guide*[52] lists sixteen. Three of those added are fragmentary. My list below mostly follows Dean, but separates the MSS into those of substantial length and those which are in fragments; Ewert's sigla for them are given in brackets.

MSS complete, nearly complete, or of substantial length

Cambridge: Corpus Christi College MS 50, end 13th c. [C][53]
Cologny-Geneva: Bibliotheca Bodmeriana MS 67 (once Marske Hall), second half 13th c. [M][54]
——: Bibliotheca Bodmeriana MS 168 (once Phillipps 8345), end 13th c.-beginning 14th c. [F][55]
London: British Library, MS Additional 38662 (once Edwardes), 1225–50 [E][56]
——: MS Royal 8.F.ix, c. 1300 [R][57]
——: College of Arms, MS Arundel 27, 13th-14th c. [A][58]

---

[51] *Robert Le Diable*, ed. F. Löseth (Paris: Firmin Didot, 1903), 5049-end. See Weiss, "Ineffectual Monarchs," 62–63. On the *translatio* of saints' bodies, see Patrick J. Geary, *Furta Sacra: Thefts of Relics in the Central Middle Ages* (Princeton: Princeton University Press, 1978).
[52] Dean, 90–91.
[53] See N. Wilkins, *Catalogue des Manuscrits Français de la Bibliothéque Parker* (Cambridge: Parker Library Publications, 1993).
[54] Françoise Vielliard, *Manuscrits Français du Moyen Âge* (Cologny-Geneva: Fondation Martin Bodmer, 1975), 23–31.
[55] Vielliard, *Manuscrits*, 93–94.
[56] *Catalogue of Additions to the Manuscripts in the British Museum, 1911–1915* (London: British Museum, 1925), 189–90.
[57] Sir George Warner and Julius P. Gilson, *Catalogue of Western Manuscripts in the Old Royal and King's Collections in the British Museum*, vol. 1 (London: British Museum, 1921), 267–68.
[58] See W.H. Black, *Catalogue of the Arundel MSS in the Library of the College of Arms* (London: Bentley, 1829).

New Haven: Yale University, Beinecke Rare Book and Manuscript Library MS 591, 14th c.
Paris: Bibliothèque Nationale, MS franç.1669, 13th c. [P][59]
Wolfenbüttel: Herzog-August Bibliothek, MS Aug. fol. 87.4, 13th-14th c. [G][60]

Fragments of MSS

Cambridge: University Library, MS Additional 2751, no. 16, 13th-14th c. [J]
London: British Library, MS Harley 3775, 13th-14th c. [H]
Nottingham: University Library, Oakham Parish Library, MS Bx 1756 S4, late 13th c.
Oxford: Bodleian Library, MS Rawlinson D.913, 13th-14th c. [O]
―――: Corpus Christi College MS 491, 13th c.
Ripon: Cathedral Library, MS xvii.F.33
York: Minster Library MS 16.1.7, 13th c. [Y]

Contents of the MSS

Where *Gui de Warewic* does not furnish a manuscript's sole contents, the works accompanying it suggest that scribes may have thought of it as either a historical or a hagiographical text. The works originally bound with it in E are mostly hagiographic—saints' lives, miracles of the Virgin—and from the chanson de geste tradition: the *Chanson de Guillaume* and the *Pseudo-Turpin*.[61] H contains Beneit's *Vie de Becket*, numerous short items in Latin of a historical and factual kind,[62] and a crusading song. R has fragments of the end of a poem on biblical history: Solomon, Nebuchadnezzar, and the fall of Jerusalem. C contains MS "T" of Wace's *Brut*, the chronicle *Livere de Reis de Brittanie*,[63] a list in Latin of British kings up to Henry III, *L'Estorie des quatre sorurs* (a theological debate between Mercy, Truth, Peace, and Righteousness), *Amis e Amilun*, and (the only exception to my suggestion) a fabliau. M contains the end of Wace's *Brut*,

---

[59] *Catalogue des Manuscrits Français dans la Bibliothèque Nationale*, vol.1, Ancien Fonds (Paris: Firmin Didot, 1868).

[60] Otto von Heinemann, *Die Handschriften der Herzoglichen Bibliothek zu Wolfenbüttel: Die Augusteischen Handschriften*, vol. 4 (Wolfenbüttel: Julius Zwissler, 1900), 109.

[61] For details of the contents of MS E, original and current, see Wathelet-Willem, *Recherches*. For the association of chanson de gestes with "history," see D.H. Green, *The Beginnings of Medieval Romance: Fact and Fiction, 1150–1220* (Cambridge: Cambridge University Press, 2002), 138.

[62] Items 3–18 contain chronicles, tables, lists, several entries connected to the abbey of St Albans, and a life of the hermit Robert of Knaresborough.

[63] The *Livere* has a long paragraph praising King Athelstan, in whose time *Gui* is supposedly set.

Helias's translation of the prophecies of Merlin in Geoffrey of Monmouth's *Historia Regum Britanniae*,[64] the chronicle *Livere d'Angleterre*, and *Florence de Rome* in chanson de geste form. F contains *Waldef* and *Otinel*, the latter a chanson de geste, the former an Anglo-Norman romance providing a version of English "history".[65]

The Text of Gui and Ewert's edition

Ewert established that E was the oldest and most careful of the manuscripts, with the best text of the poem, and that C was the next best (1:xxvii). He also concluded that MSS EFHMC gave the first redaction of the poem. When E misses out lines (which it does at regular intervals in the last part of the poem), he supplies them, because they are on several occasions vital to the sense and the syntax—examples are 11907–10, 12215–16, 12231–32, and 12503–8. Ewert says that such lines are supplied from C, with "quelques légères corrections" (xxvii), but in fact sometimes they are taken from M or F. He corrected the supplied lines to improve scansion (see his section VII) and to bring spelling into line with E. I have marked these extra lines by square brackets and italics and given their source whenever I can ascertain it.

My primary concern has been to translate the text of E; to this end I have very occasionally restored a line originally in E in place of what Ewert has substituted (598; 7504). In a very few cases I have preferred a reading from another manuscript. When other manuscripts from the first redaction have added two or more lines to E's text which he has not printed, but put in his end-notes, I have briefly noted this at the foot of the page.

Ewert usually borrows the "paragraph" indications supplied by means of larger, coloured initials in E, but he sometimes ignores them. These "paragraphs" are often placed at the same points in the narrative in the different MSS. Although there are sometimes very long passages between paragraphs, where we would break up the narrative (and I have done so in my translation), there are also occasions where paragraphing is clearly used for emotional and rhetorical effect. An example of this is in the grand public scene when Duke Seguin submits to Emperor Reiner (2703–98) and all Reiner's vassals urge forgiveness: each new speech is given a new paragraph in MSS E, C, A, F, M and Beinecke 591 as if to draw the reader's attention to the growing tension supplied by each intervention.

---

[64] See *Anglo-Norman Verse Prophecies of Merlin*, ed. and trans. Jean Blacker (Dallas: Scriptorium Press, 2005), 3–4.

[65] On *Waldef* and its claims as history, see Rosalind Field, "*Waldef* and the Matter of/with England," in *Medieval Insular Romance: Translation and Innovation*, ed. Judith Weiss, Jennifer Fellows, and Morgan Dickson (Cambridge: D. S. Brewer, 2000), 25–39, at 33.

Note on the Spelling of Names

The names of actual places and people have been given their usual spelling in English, e.g., Worms, Konya, York, Athelstan. Where the spelling of fictitious names varies, I have usually used the form in which they first appear e.g., Guelin, Cristor, Hesman. Exceptions to this practice are Rainbrun, Rualt, and Sequart, where I have used the more frequent spelling of the names, even if this is not the form in which we first meet them. In the case of Yun/Jun, Gui uses the false name at different times in different places and so I have kept the different spellings. In the case of Loher, it is spelt Loer only twice, once at its introduction; I have used its more frequent form.

Boeve de Haumtone

1. My lords, now pay attention to me.[1] I shall tell you tales—I know different ones—about Boeve of Hampton, the courteous knight, who defeated so many good kings by dint of his sword. If you wish to hear, I will tell you; I believe you never heard anything better. (1–6)

2. My lords, if you wish to hear about him, I will tell you, for I know much. First I will tell you of his parentage. The good count, named Gui, lived at Hampton. He was a renowned knight; in his time there was no one better than him. (7–12)

3. My lords, this Count Gui of whom I speak was a good knight, valiant and brave; but there was one thing for which men blamed him, that he had refused ever to take a wife, which I believe he later regretted. (13–17)

4. But when he was an old man and had lived a long time, he took a wife of high birth; this lady was daughter of the king of Scotland. Gui, the strong knight, took her to wife. Then came the day which, through her, brought him much agony, when his head was severed from his body. (18–23)

5. The lady was certainly beautiful and well-bred. The emperor of Germany had formerly loved her and had often asked her father for her hand, but the king of Scotland had refused and given her to Gui with the powerful demeanour. Then he lost his head—alas, what a fate!—for love of the lady he had married. (24–30)

6. My lords, this lady of whom I have told you was without question beautiful, but she was very wicked and her heart was not loyal. She had little love for her husband Gui, but rather hated him above all and held him in contempt. May Jesus, creator of all the world, destroy her! (31–36)

7. With her husband she had a handsome and capable boy called Boeve. He was more than ten, entering his eleventh year. One day the lady had wicked thoughts: that she was a beautiful woman, young and attractive, and her husband was an

---

[1] 1:1 **My lords** *Seingnurs barons*: MS B contains the first section of *Boeve* and runs from lines 1 to 1268.

old man, growing weak. No one alive, she said, would stop her having him killed in torment and pain. (37–44)

8. The lady took a very wicked decision. Without delay she called for a messenger. "Messenger, now I want you to swear not to reveal my secret; do not tell it to any man alive except the emperor who rules Germany. (45–50)

9. "Messenger," she said, "now go swiftly to Germany! Don't linger there, but say to the noble emperor on my behalf that I send him friendly greetings. And tell him no one alive should prevent him from being ready on the first day of May. (51–56)

10. "Tell him to make ready with him four hundred knights; they should be well armed and come to the forest above the sea. I will send my husband to hunt, and with few men—there is no need to fear him. And tell him never to let him escape without cutting off his head with a steel sword. (57–63)

11. "Now tell him I order him, for my love, to be quite prepared when he sees my husband and to cut off his head with a steel sword. And if he sends me the head, I will certainly do whatever he likes." "My lady," said the messenger, "just as you wish!" (64–69)

12. The messenger departed (God send him misfortune!), crossed the sea quickly without any delay and, on a good horse, arrived in Germany. There he met a knight and asked him where the emperor was. (70–74)

13. The knight told him he was at Retefor. The messenger departed quite unhindered and came to Retefor without delay; arriving before the emperor, he fell to his knees. "God save you, emperor!" said the messenger. "The lady of Hampton has sent me to you and urgently asks you to do what she wishes." (75–81)

14. The emperor replied: "My fair and gentle friend, what does that lady with her bright face command me to do?" "My lord," said the messenger, "as you will hear. The lady orders you not to delay but to equip yourself with four hundred bold and brave knights and, on the first day of May, to hide in our forest. (82–88)

15. "When you and your knights are there, the lady will send you her husband, unarmed. And if you wish to have her love, you will kill her husband and cut off his head. When you have cut off his head, send it to her, and when she has the head, you will have won her love." (89–94)

16. The emperor heard what the messenger said; no need to ask if he was delighted. "Messenger," he said, "by the body of St Richer![2] since you bring me this

---

[2] 16:97 **St Richer** *Seint Richers*: St Richard; see Flutre, 163.

news, I will give you a good swift horse, and gold and silver to load upon him." (95–100)

17. The messenger was rewarded for carrying the message. The emperor soon had the horse produced and quickly loaded with gold and silver; and the messenger thanked him and was swiftly on his way, going straight towards England. Great strife later ensued from the message he carried. (101–6)

18. Then the messenger left the emperor, taking the horse he'd given him, and, spurring him hard, arrived in Hampton. When he saw the lady, he greeted her courteously on his knees and addressed her. (107–11)

19. "My lady, I bring you greetings from the emperor. Through me he tells you to have no fear, for if his strength permits, on that precise day he will cut the head off that doughty count. And if you are glad of your husband's death, he is even gladder of your love." (112–17)

20. The lady heard him; from then until the appointed day her delight was plain. Now listen to how great a crime it is, to give a young woman to a bearded old man! The first day of May, the lady arose and came to her husband and spoke to him. "My lord," she said, "so help me Mary, mother of God, I am sick and in bad health." (118–25)

21. "My lady," said the count, "by our righteous God, if you wish for anything, let me know." "Yes," said the lady, "my fair, sweet and beloved lord, if I had fresh boar's meat, I think I could recover my health." "My lady," said the count, "by our righteous God, do you know where I might find a boar?" "Yes," said the lady, "my fair, sweet and beloved lord, there is one in your forest above the sea." "By God!" said the count, "I'll go and hunt him there." The lady heard him and went to kiss him, then embraced him most treacherously. (126–37)

22. The count mounted a swift horse, with a shield round his neck and a sword in his hand; he had neither hauberk nor jewelled helmet. Three companions mounted their horses with him. Now the count would die in pain and ignominy. (138–42)

23. When they came to the forest, they went looking for the boar. The villainous emperor rushed forward, shouting loudly: "Come on, old man! By God Almighty, you will lose your head, and your son Boeve will swing in the wind." (143–47)

24. The emperor rushed at him, but Gui's shield was very strong and he could not pierce it. Loudly he shouted at him: "I'll make you dismount, then I'll have your body quite burnt to ashes; and then I want to seize your wife for my own

enjoyment." The count replied: "So you're out to do wrong? I'll defend my wife by fighting you." (148–54)

25. 'Traitor,' said the count to him, "now what did you say? You'll cut off my head without any resistance? If there were more of us, Christ help me, I'd rate your fierce threats very low. But my trust in the Holy Spirit is complete: if I die in this way, my sins will be absolved." (155–60)

26. Count Gui spurred his horse and swiftly gave the emperor a violent blow; he knocked him out of his silver saddle and on to the ground, making him fly down from his horse.[3] Then he said to him: "My dear, gentle lord, although I'm an old man and you're a young one, I want to lay claim to my wife and my son; for by the body of St Richer, you have no right to them!" The count turned round and drew his steel sword. (161–70)

27. The count drew his sword, like a brave knight, but seven hundred knights came rushing at him. He defended himself with great courage, but they gave him ten wounds, which gushed bright blood. Alas that he was not armed to his liking! I believe he would surely have escaped. (171–76)

28. When the count of Hampton was wounded in this way, and his three companions were killed, he sank to his knees and begged for mercy. "My fair lord," he said, "take my sword, for the sake of your knights whom I've killed, and please forgive me their deaths." (177–82)

29. "My lord," said the count to him, "don't kill me! I will give you everything I have in the world, except my son Boeve and my beloved lady." "By God!" said the emperor, "I'll not do that; I'll not even spare your life; I'll cut off your head with my polished sword." (183–88)

30. The villain drew his sword, with its gilded tip, struck Count Gui, and cut off his head. He called a messenger and told him his wishes. "Brother," he said, "go quickly to the lady of Hampton, greet her from me, and take this head to her." (189–94)

31. The knight left, as he was ordered, and carried with him Count Gui's head. When he came to the lady, he greeted her in this way: "My lady," said the messenger, "the emperor sent me to you; he will come at your command and pleasure and, my lady, if you wish, he will marry you." (195–200)

---

[3] 26:165 **from his horse:** *E de sun destrer*: an emendation proposed by Stimming, citing the Norse version; the MS repeats *e encontre la tere*. On the inadvisability of using the Norse (or Welsh or English) versions to establish the original Anglo-Norman text, see *Bevers Saga*, ed. Sanders, cxliii–cxlv; his comments on "missing lines" (cxlv, n. 8) and his Appendix (384–90).

32. "Knight," said the lady, "go to the emperor and tell him that I order him, for my love, to come to me here right now. The wedding will be tomorrow, as soon as day breaks." The knight left on his good horse and related the lady's reply to his lord. (201–6)

33. Now we shall tell of Count Gui's son; those in Hampton called him Boeve. He wept loudly for his father's death. He came to his mother and addressed her. "Filthy, well-practiced whore," said the child, "why did you have my father Gui killed?" (207–12)

34. The child wept so hard he almost staggered. "Oh, mother," he said, "alas for your beauty! You're just like a whore, who should keep a brothel. But, by Him born of the Virgin, if I can live until I'm in the saddle and can carry arms and a new shield, this news, my lady, will cost you very dear." (213–19)

35. The lady heard clearly every word he said, raised her palm, and struck him sharply so he fell to the floor. The boy's tutor[4] rushed forward. He was called Sabot,[5] may God help him! He was a powerful, strong, and brave knight. (220–25)

36. Without waiting, he took the child in his arms, intending to go to his house. The lady saw him and went towards him. "Sabot," she said, "you must swear to kill the child this very day, however you choose—by hanging or flaying." (226–31)

37. "My lady," said Sabot, "at your bidding." He took the child and at once went to his lodging. Quickly he had a pig killed, collected all its blood without spilling a drop, and bloodied the child's clothes. (232–36)

38. When Sabot had bloodied the clothes, he had them tied to a large millstone and thrown into a river. Then he started to talk to the child. "Listen to me, sweet, fair and beloved son, I am bound to cherish you, out of love for your father." (237–42)

39. "Listen, fair son," said Sabot the prudent, "You, shabbily dressed and shod, will keep my lambs down in the meadow for a fortnight. Then I shall send you to another kingdom, to a friend of mine, a noble count. (243–48)

---

[4] 35:223 **The boy's tutor** *Le mestre a le enfant*: A *mestre*, also known as *nutricius, pedagogus,* and *magister,* was usually a knight who acted as a kind of mentor to a young nobleman, protecting, teaching and advising him. I have sometimes translated it as "master," as in *laisse* 40.

[5] 35:224 **Sabot** *Sabot*: In MS D, Sabot is called Sabaoth. Here and in lines 224, 229, 237, 321, 326, 331, 333, and 338 MS B has Saboc.

40. "You will stay with this man, fair son, until you have reached fifteen or sixteen. When you can bear arms, come back here and seek out the emperor like a brave and bold man and, as Christ is my help, I will faithfully aid you. As long as I live I will never fail you." The child replied: "Master, many thanks!" (249–55)

41. The child went off with his tutor's lambs. That day he led them to pasture in a meadow. He looked a little upwards and to the hill[6] and heard, from the palace which had been his father's, much merry-making, rejoicing, din, and festivity. The child wondered what this might be. (256–61)

42. "God!" said the child, "righteous Father, I am a count's son and they've made me a shepherd! But I won't refrain from speaking out and claiming my land from the emperor." He seized his club and walked until he came to the palace and spoke to the porter. (262–67)

43. "Porter," said the child, "so help you God, let me in, don't stop me. I shall speak to the emperor in front of his barons; I have a little task to do and must tell him about it." The porter replied viciously: "Get out of here, scum! May Christ curse you!" (268–73)

44. The porter replied violently to the child: "Get out of here fast, son of a whore, scum![7] You are very small and thus a great good-for-nothing." "Porter," said the child, "may Jesus protect me! I am indeed the son of a whore, because my mother's a whore, I believe. But you're clearly lying when you call me scum and good-for-nothing. (274–81)

45. "Porter," said the child, "as God is my salvation, now I'll show you I'm not scum." He raised his club, his blow did not fail, he spilled the porter's brains—shame on anyone who cares about that! "Take a rest," said the child, "you're over-heated." Then the child went up into the palace, and in front of everyone spoke boldly to the emperor. (282–88)

46. The child stood in front of the emperor with his cruel face, and boldly began to speak to him. "Listen to me, dear, gentle lord, who gave you leave to embrace this lady? She is my mother, there's no need to hide it, and if you won't ask my leave, I will make you pay very dearly for her love. I advise you to give me back my land." (289–96)

---

[6] 41:258 **to the hill** *au tertre*: Stimming emends *au tertre* (to the hill) to *a destre* (to the right), citing the Norse version.

[7] 44:275 **scum** *ribaud*: The MS has *truaunt* (good-for-nothing), used again in 276, so Stimming has replaced it with *ribaud* (scum).

47. "My fine lord emperor," said Boeve the wise, "you embrace my mother without my leave; you killed my father, whom I loved so much. Therefore, my lord, I ask you to return me my land, which you hold unlawfully and quite against my will." The emperor replied: "Silence, fool!" (297–302)

48. Boeve heard everything that the emperor said; his anger was so great that his blood boiled. He raised his club and struck him on the head, giving him three blows and three wounds, and he swore by God and the Holy Spirit he would regret it if he did not return his land. (303–8)

49. The emperor fell senseless on the table. The lady shouted: "Seize this traitor for me!" Some of the knights took great pity on the child Boeve; they got up and rushed around as if to grab him, and among them the child cleverly escaped. (309–14)

50. He ran to his tutor's house. Sabot saw him and asked him: "Fair son, where do you come from in such a rush?" "From killing my stepfather," said the child. "I gave him three wounds for calling me good-for-nothing; I think he'll never recover." (315–20)

51. "Fair son," said Sabot, "you are to blame. If you'd done what I advised, I'd praise you. Now your mother will be angry with me and because I love you she will want my head struck off." The child heard him and started to weep. Sabot took him to hide in a room. (321–26)

52. The lady appeared from her palace. She was finely dressed in a Grecian silk cloak, her shoe buckles decorated with gold; she was a most beautiful woman but her heart was loathsome. The lady called Sabot and said to him in English: "Where is Boeve, my most wicked son?" (327–32)

53. "Lady," said Sabot, "don't ask me! You ordered me to kill him, and I killed him, that's the truth. I had a great millstone tied around his neck and the body was thrown into a river." "By God," said the lady, "you're lying, Sabot. You'll be burnt or hanged if you don't bring him to me." (333–39)

54. When Boeve heard this, he was very distressed she should threaten his tutor. He would not hide but came before his mother. "Lady, what do you want?" said the child Boeve. "If you want me, here I am; don't lay a finger on my tutor." (340–45)

55. The evil-hearted lady took her son, called two knights and asked them to seize him and take him to the harbour. If they found any merchants who wanted to buy him, they were to sell him without delay, and if not, they were to drown him. (346–52)

56. Miserably they went off with the child Boeve. When they came to the sea, they found a ship full of evil Saracens. The heathen looked around them and saw the child; they would certainly, they said, pay dearly for him. (353–57)

57. The Saracen merchants bought the child, paying four times his weight in gold for him. When they had finished with their purchases, they made their boat ready and sailed over the sea for so long that they brought the ship to land in Egypt. They lowered their sails and cast anchor. (358–63)

58. The merchants sailed far over the sea. With them was Boeve, who never stopped weeping; he was utterly miserable about his father's death. In this land was a king called Hermin, a very old man with white hair; his white beard spread down his chest. (364–69)

59. The king was an old man, advanced in years. He had a daughter, beautiful, wise and very young, called Josiane; no rose in the shade had a more lovely colouring. (370–73)

60. What more can I say to describe the girl? No one as beautiful lived in the world at that time. Then all the merchants came to court and brought Boeve the brave with them. They most courteously presented him to the king, and he was very grateful to them for this child. (374–79)

61. "Child," said the king, "tell me where you come from. By my god Mahomet, I never saw a child as beautiful as you before, whether near or far. If you believe in Mahomet, be sure that no wicked tales will ever separate you from me." The child replied: "Don't say that!" (380–85)

62. Then the child said: "I was born in England, son of Count Gui of the city of Hampton. My mother had him killed in pain and ignominy; an emperor took her, against my wishes. But, so help me, mother of God, if I can live to bear arms, he will pay for it dearly." The king heard him and felt great pity. (386–92)

63. "Child," said the king, "what is your name?" "My lord," said the child, "I'm called Boeve." "Child,' said Hermin, "by my god Mahomet, if you turn heathen, you'll be a valiant man. My only heir in this world is a daughter, and I will give her to you along with my kingdom." (393–98)

64. "King," said the child, "you talk foolishly. Not for all the land in heathen parts nor for your daughter with it, rosy-cheeked as she is, would I renounce Jesus son of Mary. Mahomet can't even do as much as an ant, for an ant can move and he can't. Shame on him who trusts in Mahomet!" (399–405)

65. "Child," said the king, "your heart is most constant, and since you will not honour Mahomet, you shall serve me by day with my cup at meal-times. When

you come of age, I shall knight you and you shall carry my standard in battle." (406–10)

66. The king felt much love for Boeve the wise. This deeply angered some of the knights, and because he was so close to the king and because merchants had bought him, they all called him wicked slave. (411–15)

67. When the child had reached fifteen or sixteen, he was very handsome, strong and well-formed. There was no knight in the court so bold as to joust with him, so strong was he. Then a boar arrived in the country, which spared no one, neither great nor small, so that if twenty bold knights came along, all well equipped with weapons, the animal would fear them no more than it would a partridge. (416–24)

68. Boeve often heard talk of this boar. One day he mounted a good, fast horse; he would not don a hauberk, but hung a steel sword by his side and took in his fist a lance of apple-wood. And the king's daughter started to look at him; she felt such love for the young man that it later made her weep many a tear, and caused Boeve much trouble—as you will now hear me tell truly, if you will give me some of your silver, or if not, I will now leave it be. Boeve came to the forest to seek the boar but had no need to worry for he found him right away. The boar saw him and began to paw the ground and open his great throat as if he wanted to devour Boeve whole. Boeve soon saw him, spurred his horse, and firmly held his lance with its unbroken head. He struck the boar in its open mouth, the point reached its heart, and the boar died[8] quickly without lingering. And Boeve drew his sword to cut off its head, and took the stump of his shattered lance and stuck the boar's head on it. The beautiful Josiane sat on the battlements and began to watch the young man closely; whatever she saw him do pleased her. (425–52)

69. "By Mahomet," said the girl, "how dashing Boeve looks! Lucky the woman who could be his beloved! If I don't have his love, I shall die." So said the girl, with many tears and sighs. Boeve knew nothing of her thoughts: she would commit great folly if God did not help her. Now the god of love held her in his grip.[9] (453–59)

70. Boeve knew nothing of her thoughts. He came at full gallop out of the forest. Ten foresters appeared—may they never be forgiven! They had all treacherously sworn to kill him. (460–63)

---

[8] 68:446 **and the boar died quickly without lingering** e *lui sengler tost murt saunz nul demurer*: the MS has *e lui sengler tost vint saunz nul demurer* (and the boar came on quickly without delay). Stimming emends *vint* (came) to *murt* (died), drawing on the Norse version.

[9] 69:459 **in his grip** *en sa laterie:* literally, in his enclosure.

71. His enemies came spurring towards him, shouting: "You'll go no further! By Mahomet the mighty, you'll lose your head!" Boeve heard them, and made to draw his sword, but unluckily he had left it behind when he killed the mighty boar. Now God protect him! (464–69)

72. Boeve made to draw his steel sword, but he had left it behind when he killed the boar. The foresters approached, each one on horseback, and four struck him. May God give them grief! (470–73)

73. Boeve grasped the stump of his lance and knocked two down dead straightaway. Then he felled two more, no matter whom it upset, then the fifth and then the sixth, with no more remorse. Boldly Boeve rushed at the rest. (474–78)

74. The four saw that six were slain and that Boeve was neither wounded nor harmed; they turned their horses and fled. The girl with the bright face watched him. "Ah, Mahomet!" she said, "how dashing Boeve is! If he doesn't become my lover, I now must die." (479–84)

75. With that, Boeve could be seen spurring towards his lord, the king; he presented him with the boar's head. "Boeve," said Hermin, "you are very brave. Mahomet save and protect you!" Having said this, the king left him and went up his strong tower and looked out of a window; he saw approaching a heathen king and his whole army. There were certainly a hundred thousand of them, strong and brave. (485–94)

76. King Hermin was up in his tower. He looked down and saw Bradmund, king of Damascus—may God confound him!—and a hundred thousand heathen with him, who uttered violent threats against Hermin and swore by Mahomet that they would have his daughter, and Bradmund, that fierce king, would marry her. Hermin heard them and nearly fainted with anger. (495–502)

77. "Hermin," said Bradmund, "give me your daughter. By Mahomet, if you refuse, I'll leave you neither castle nor city nor even half a foot of your land. Josiane shall lie by my side, and then she'll be given in grief and shame to the poorest man in my land!" "By Mahomet!" said Hermin, "you're lying, scoundrel; nothing will happen as you say." Then he descended from the tower, called all his knights to him, told them all about Bradmund, the strong king, and asked for their counsel: "My lords, what do you advise?" Josiane began to speak and said: "My lord, hear me! By Mahomet, if you knight Boeve, be sure he will give you valuable help. For with my own eyes I saw him when he was weaponless and ten foresters challenged him; he had no sword because he had left it behind when he killed the mighty, raging boar; he had only the stump of a thick lance and with it he killed six of them and maimed the rest. But they fled, so frightened were they." "By Mahomet!" said the king, "he shall be knighted."

Then Boeve was called forward. "Boeve," said the king, "listen to me: I shall knight you and then you will carry my banner into battle in front of my barons." "My lord," said Boeve, "let it be as you wish." He laced up his leggings very tightly, then put a hauberk on his back, weighing less than ten coins in money but nevertheless very close-knit; it could not have been damaged by a sharp weapon. King Hermin attached his gilded spurs and girded his sword on to his left side. No better blade was ever forged from steel; it was as long as an arm and as wide as a foot. It was called Murgleie and had conquered many kingdoms. The girl gave him a valuable horse. No better horse could be found: God never made an animal, you can be sure, that came within a mile[10] of overtaking it. Boeve leapt on the horse without needing stirrups, with a shield round his neck and a sword in his hand; he galloped a short distance and then turned back. The beautiful Josiane spoke to him. "My lord," she said, "God help you! Be sure to use the horse to good purpose." "Lady," said Boeve, "never fear! But please, go up into this tower; watch me in the fray, and if I don't use the horse to good purpose, take it from me when I return and have the spurs cut from my feet." "By Mahomet!" she replied, "enough said." Boeve blew a strong blast on the horn, whereupon everyone in the city donned arms. (503–60)

78. Then Hermin with the white moustache arrived. He gave the command of his knights entirely to Boeve, and Boeve went forward with the standard. A lion was painted on his shield, which showed the knight's ferocity, and he had forty thousand followers. Against him came King Bradmund, a hundred thousand wicked Saracens with him; God, how many more men he had than Boeve! Rudefoun, a heathen, carried Bradmund's banner; he had no love for God, only Mahomet, and was hairier than any pig-skin or fleece. He carried the lance straight, with a long standard, and the pennant was fastened with four silver nails.

Brave-hearted Boeve saw him, jabbed sharp spurs into Arundel, and went to joust with the wicked Rudefoun. He struck him hard above the device on the shield round his neck so that it was not worth a feather, nor was the double hauberk worth a button. He pushed the lance with the whole standard through his body, knocking him dead to the sand. Then he said to him: "Son of a whore, wretch, better you had stayed at home."

Then Boeve said to his men: "Strike, friends! Ours is the first blow, we'll easily defeat them." His fellows heard him and came on ferociously and cut down four hundred of Bradmund's men, who never again would see wife or home. Boeve drew Murgleie, hanging by his side, and cut off heads and fists, legs and chins. His enemies saw him and shuddered: as the lark flees before the falcon, so his evil enemies gave way around him, and because their standard-bearer was dead, the boldest of them all wished he were at home. (561–96)

---

[10] 77:545 **a mile** *un arpent*: a measure of both area (where it corresponds to about an acre) and length.

79. When Boeve had killed Rudefoun, the standard-bearer of angry-faced Bradmund, Bradmund's knights were so aghast that, upon seeing Boeve with his shining blade, they fled from him like the thrush when she sees the falcon in flight. Boeve's companions were so encouraged that they feared the enemy no more than sheep. Bradmund saw Boeve[11] and shouted loudly: "What are you doing? Strike, my friends! If Hermin's people aren't hanged or slain, you'll never get a penny[12] from me."

Boeve heard him and gave a great laugh. "Tell me, wretched Bradmund," he said, "what were you looking for in this land? Did you think you could have fair-faced Josiane? You'll have the gallows, I tell you truly, for your men are mostly killed and those still alive will soon be humiliated." Then bold Boeve struck around him, sending heads, fists, feet, and legs flying onto the field. What more can I tell you? Before noon all King Bradmund's men were killed, and Bradmund took flight through a valley. (597–620)

80. When Bradmund saw he could hold out no longer, he began to retreat through a valley. He had had two of Hermin's men bound, intending to take them with him to his own land, and he swore by Mahomet he would have them flayed. But Boeve of Hampton would make him leave them alone and sing a different song. Boeve saw that Bradmund was about to leave; he struck steel spurs into Arundel and made the horse go faster than a sparrow-hawk. Swiftly and without delay he reached Bradmund and, with Murgleie in his hand, gave him such a blow that he flew to the ground. Then he dismounted, intending to cut off his head. (621–34)

81. When Bradmund saw Boeve the noble, he got up from the ground and sank to his knees. "Mercy, my fair, sweet lord Boeve!" he said. "After the blow you struck me, I'll hand over four hundred cities to you, by Mahomet my god! And more than three thousand castles and keeps, for I shall hold all my lands from you." (635–41)

82. "Bradmund," said Boeve, "I won't agree to that, but you will become the vassal of Hermin the fierce, you will hold your land from him without disloyalty, and you will do whatever I order you to and never be so bold as to resist." "By Mahomet!" said Bradmund, "I'll do that gladly." Then Boeve let him return to his own land. Ah, God, what harm ensued from not killing him! For later Bradmund made him fast many a long day; he was in his prison for seven whole years, as you will now hear me tell. Boeve untied the two knights, whom Bradmund had wanted to take away with him, then came to King Hermin, who had such

---

[11] 79:605 **Bradmund saw Boeve** *Bradmound les voit*: I use the original wording (*Boefs*) of the MS here; Stimming, following the Norse version, substitutes *les* (them).

[12] 79:608 **penny** *Parsis*: a Parisian penny.

cause to love him. "Now, my lord, by God who made heaven and earth," he said, "fierce-looking Bradmund has paid you homage and will hold his land from you without disloyalty." "Boeve," said Hermin, "I have every reason to hold you dear. My fair daughter," said the king, "go and disarm him and serve him food in his room." "Right away, my dear, gentle lord," she said.

Swiftly Josiane removed the knight's armour. When he was disarmed she led him into a fine chamber above an upper room. She brought him meat, which he needed, and she herself began to carve it. When he had eaten, she began to talk; now she revealed all her thoughts to him. "My fair lord Boeve, I won't hide it from you: love of you has made me weep many tears and many a night made me lie awake far too long. So, fair lord, I want to beg you not to refuse my love. If you refuse, I can't survive, I must die and perish for grief." "My fair lady," said fierce-faced Boeve, "for God's sake give up this foolish love, for the king will have me shamed and disgraced. (642–79)

83. "My fair lady," said Boeve, "for God's sake give up this great folly. Already King Bradmund has asked for your hand; there's no king, I believe, in the whole world, no prince, emir, count, or baron, who would not desire you if they saw your face. I'm a poor knight from another land; I've not yet seen my house or my land." Josiane said to him: "Fair lord Boeve, by my god Mahomet, I love you better in your tunic than a king with ten kingdoms. Son of a noble lord, give me your love." "No, I won't," said Boeve, "by the body of St Simon!" The girl heard him and blushed red as embers; she felt such grief that she fainted. (680–94)

84. When she rose, she wept bitterly. "By God, my lord Boeve, you tell the truth: there's no king, prince, nor emir in the world who would not willingly take me, if it suited me. You've refused me like a depraved peasant. You'd be better off mending ditches and rubbing down saddled horses with straw and running basely on foot like an errand-boy than being a knight in an honoured court. Go back to your own land, base good-for-nothing that you clearly are; Mahomet who made us all, destroy you!" "Fair lady," said Boeve, "you lie, by God! You know I was never a peasant or good-for-nothing, and now you've slandered and insulted me. You gave me a horse: go and take it; I don't want you refusing it me. I'm telling you truly, I'll go back to my country and you'll never see me again for the rest of your life. You won't have the sword, I can tell you, because I bought it most dearly in battle, when I won a kingdom for your father."

The girl heard him, her heart almost burst and she fell down in a faint—it was a pitiable sight. And Boeve swiftly left the room and went to a burgess's house in the midst of the city and there quickly went to bed, very angry at Josiane's words. In her heart, Josiane reflected that she had slandered and insulted him. She called a messenger, one of her intimates. "My fair brother," she said, "you shall do my bidding." (695–725)

85. "Messenger," she said, "you must go and tell lord Boeve to come and talk to me. If I've slandered him, I will make amends." "I'll willingly go," said the messenger. He swiftly arrived at brave Boeve's lodging, and started to kneel to him. "My fair lord Boeve, I won't hide it from you: Josiane earnestly begs and entreats you to come and talk to her for a little while." "Brother," said Boeve, "you can tell her you were quite unsuccessful. But because you carried the message, I will give you my tunic of expensive silk."[13] The messenger thanked him and made to return. (726–39)

86. The messenger came back and told Josiane everything Boeve, the renowned fighter, had said. Josiane gave the messenger a quick glance. "May God help you," she said, "tell me who gave you that tunic ornamented with gems." "By Mahomet, my lady, the worthy Boeve." "Mahomet!" said the girl, "he's as well-bred, generous and courteous as any emir. He's no peasant, I see that now. (740–49)

87. "Since he won't come and talk to me, I shall go to him, no matter whom it offends." With no cloak on, she went on her way. Boeve saw her coming and began to snore, pretending to sleep; he had no wish to speak to her. Josiane came and stood before his bed. "Wake up, my fair sweet and dear friend," she said, "I want a few words with you." "Lady," said Boeve, "let me rest. I've fought fiercely today with my steel sword, and you've poorly rewarded me by calling me a base hireling." The girl heard him and began to weep, her face wet with bright tears. Boeve watched her, and pity touched his heart. (750–64)

88. "My fair lord Boeve, have pity on me! I'll soon make amends for the wrong I've done, for I tell you, I'll leave Mahomet and put my belief in God who suffered on the cross; I'll be a Christian for love of you." "Lady," said Boeve, "willingly and with pleasure." Now peace is made, God be praised! They kissed each other most lovingly. But the kiss that wise Boeve gave her brought him misfortune; he regretted it before the year was out.

But the same two knights whom he had rescued, shackled, from Bradmund, came to King Hermin and accused him. "My lord king," they said, "you've a right to be angry when that wicked, manifest slave, Boeve of Hampton, has slept with your daughter—that's an outrage." But the crazed wretches were lying, for he had merely kissed her once. May Jesus, born of His mother, destroy them! The king heard them and bowed his head. "Do you think this could be true?" he said. "Yes," said one of them, "by Mahomet my god!" "My lords," said the king, "now what do you advise? Ever since he came to me, I've loved him so; if I have him killed, you can be sure I'll feel such sorrow that I'll soon die of it." "My lord,"

---

[13] 85:738 **my tunic of expensive silk** *mon bliaunt de saie de utre mer*: *Outremer*, "beyond the sea," was the name given to the Middle East.

said one of them, "here's good advice. Have a letter drawn up and sealed well and make Boeve himself take it to the famous King Bradmund. (765–94)

89. "My dear, gentle lord, the letter will tell Bradmund to put him in such a prison that you will never hear another word from him again. And you must make him swear by his faith that he will show the letter to no one except King Bradmund the warrior." "By Mahomet!" said the king, "that I'll willingly do." Then he had Boeve summoned to him. "Boeve," said the king, "you must go to the king of Damascus, to carry this letter to Bradmund, your vassal, whom you defeated the other day, and you must swear to me by your faith that you'll show the letter to no one except King Bradmund the warrior." (795–808)

90. "My lord," said Boeve, "I'm at your command! Give me the letter and my speedy horse and my fine, sharp sword Murgleie." "Sir," said Hermin, "you talk foolishly: the horse's pace is too violent for you. You shall have a quiet, ambling palfrey. And Murgleie, your sword, is too heavy: you shall have another, less troublesome." "My lord," said Boeve, "I'm at your command." He took the letter and left right away, travelling fast. Now God guide and protect him!

He crossed the mountains and the valleys too; he rode for three days and saw no living soul. On the morning of the fourth day, as he rode along, he found a palmer sitting under a tree. At that very moment he was at his dinner: he had four large wheat loaves before him, and two full barrels of spiced wine. The palmer saw the knight coming from close by. "Get down, fair sir, by almighty God! As God is your help, come and dine with me!" "Palmer," said Boeve, "God protect you! I know for sure you've never acted churlishly." He dismounted soon and fast; he was starving and ate hugely of the food that the palmer gladly gave him.

Boeve looked at him and said laughing: "My friend, where do you come from? Don't deceive me." "Sir," said the palmer, "I won't deceive you. Indeed I was born in England the great, in the strong and noble city of Hampton,. My father is called Sabot[14] the brave; he strongly urged me, as I was leaving, to search in this land for a child, who was sold to the heathen—a great shame. He's called Boeve; may God help him! I can't find him, which much distresses me." "Palmer," said Boeve, "you're talking nonsense, for the child I hear you mention has been hanged." (809–47)

91. The palmer heard him and began to weep; he swooned from the grief he felt. When he recovered, he cried out loudly: "Ah, God of majesty, what shall I do now that my sweet friend has been wrongly killed? Knight," said the palmer, "what are you carrying? If it's a letter, now show it me." "Don't even think about it!" said Boeve, "don't speak of such a thing, for I'll not show it to anyone alive except Bradmund, the powerful crowned king." "Indeed!" said the palmer, "you're

---

[14] 90:840 **Sabot** *Sabot*: MS Saboc.

not sensible; it could be your death, only you don't know it." "Don't even think about it!" said Boeve, "don't believe it: my lord wouldn't do that for three hundred cities." Then they kissed and separated. (848–62)

92. Boeve then mounted his swift horse, left the palmer, whom he had every reason to cherish, and rode off singing. He would not stop till he came to Damascus, the most splendid city under the sun, for there was neither tower nor battlement in the town which was not covered with silver or pure gold. On top of the main tower King Bradmund had set—this is no lie—a golden eagle, holding between its claws a shining carbuncle which gave out such a radiant light that—I won't hide it from you—however dark it was, one could walk along as if God was making the sun shine brightly.

Boeve entered the city with a bold heart, and heard singing inside a temple, for that day the pagans were glorifying Mahomet and there were more than a thousand priests of their faith there. Boeve entered the magnificent temple, took the statue of Mahomet by its forelock, and hurled it at a priest of their faith, whom he saw standing there; he broke the statue's neck and made it collapse. The others saw it and dared not remain, and all went to tell their King Bradmund how a powerful knight had arrived who had quite shattered their Mahomet. "By Mahomet, leave him be!" said Bradmund. "That's my lord, Boeve. I don't dare talk to him; let him do[15] just what he likes."

That day Bradmund had assembled his great court and sat in an ivory chamber[16] amongst his knights. Then fierce Boeve appeared. King Bradmund saw him, rose, and quickly said to him: "Fair, sweet, and dear lord, welcome, come and rest. What brings you on a journey to me?" "By my head!" said Boeve, "you will soon know. Read me this letter without delay, or I will cut off your head with my steel sword." When Bradmund heard him, he began to tremble; he was frightened of Boeve and started to stand up. (863–902)

93. Bradmund was frightened of Boeve the powerful and snatched the letter away. When he saw it, he was delighted. He then took Boeve by his right wrist, because he feared he would draw his sword, and said to his knights: "Get up, and bind Boeve tightly. Hermin orders me to string him up because he has bedded beautiful Josiane." The knights seized him right away and swiftly[17] loaded

---

[15] 92:890 **let him do** *Lessez li fere*: Stimming substitutes *fere* (do) for *dire* (say) in the MS, citing the Norse version.

[16] 92:892 **chamber** *chaumbre*: I have restored the MS reading *chaumbre* here; as Sanders remarks (*Bevers Saga*, 386), it is unobjectionable. Stimming substitutes *chaere* (throne).

[17] 93:912 **The knights seized him right away and swiftly** *Ceo chevalers le pernent toust e ignelement*: From this line, MS D starts and runs parallel with MS B till 1081 and from 1190 till 1268, after which MS B stops. D 93:912: they seized him tightly.

his feet with heavy chains,[18] locking[19] round his neck a heavy neck-iron, weighing at least fifteen quarters of wheat.[20] "Boeve," said Bradmund,[21] "by my god Tervagant,[22] if you hadn't defeated me with your sharp sword, you would be hanged right now, but I will still give you sufficient punishment:[23] from now on, you can be sure, you will be in my prison, thirty fathoms deep. There will be nothing to your taste there except snakes and adders, sharp steel spikes,[24] and each day[25] only a quarter-loaf of bran and barley, vilely baked." "My lord, at your command!"[26] said Boeve. "I must do everything you want."[27] (903–27)

94. "Boeve," said Bradmund, "now be seated: you shall have a meal just one last time."[28] When he had washed, they brought him food; Bradmund himself cut up the pieces. When he had eaten, Bradmund cried: "Knights,[29] what are you about? Why don't you seize him?' And they quickly[30] seized him and took him to the prison and threw him inside. Indeed, if the Lord God[31] had not helped him there, his neck would have broken before he reached the ground, but God helped him out of mercy. His neck and feet were tightly bound. The prison was full of vermin: snakes and adders and large reptiles with tails;[32] they rapidly advanced on Boeve and stung him.[33] Boeve groped about, found a stick, and killed all the

---

[18] 93:913 **loaded his feet with heavy chains** *e les pez li lient de chaines mult fortment*: D omits this line; see Stimming's Introduction, vi.

[19] 93:914 **locking** *ferment*: D: hung.

[20] 93:915 **fifteen quarters** *quinze quarters*: A quarter is a measure of volume, and equals eight bushels.

[21] 93:916 **Bradmund** D's version of this name is Brandon throughout.

[22] 93:916 **by my god Tervagant** *par mun dieu Tervagaunt*: D: by Mahomet Tervagant.

[23] 93:919 **still** *nekedent*: D omits "still" and adds: and torture.

[24] 93:923 **spikes** *pikes*: D: stakes.

[25] 93:924 **each day** *chescun jour*: D: in the day

[26] 93:926 **at your command** *ore seit a tun comaund*: D: now do what you command.

[27] 93:927 **I must do everything you want** *Tut ceo me estoit fere cum vus vent a talent*: D: I must suffer everything you want.

[28] 94:930–34 B omits these lines; see Stimming's Introduction, vi. D 930–4: "And then you'll be thrown into my prison, thirty fathoms deep, you can be sure; you'll find there nothing to your taste." "My lord," said Boeve, "as you wish! I must do everything that pleases you."

[29] 94:938 **Knights** *chevalers*: D: lords.

[30] 94:939 **quickly** *toust*: D omits this word.

[31] 94:941 **Lord God** *dampnedé*: D: the Lord of heaven; Stimming supplies "lord."

[32] 94:946 **snakes and adders and large reptiles with tails** *serpens e coluvers e granz verms cuez*: D: snakes and adders and many other vermin.

[33] 94:947 **stung him** *le unt envenimé*: D wished to sting him.

snakes and adders;[34] and[35] he was most unhappy in the prison. Not a single day[36] did he get his fill of bread; if he wanted water, he had to find it at his feet.[37] Two knights there were wicked[38] guards over him. (928–53)

95. "Now help me, God!" said Boeve of Hampton. "Every misfortune comes to a poor man. But, by St Peter of Rome, if I can escape, I'll take the crown from proud King Hermin. May I be shamed the day[39] that I don't give him such a blow that he never afterwards speaks to any man. (954–59)

96. "I am most wickedly betrayed here.[40] I believe I have not deserved his betraying me so badly:[41] I conquered a kingdom for him with my sharp sword." Boeve said this, and wept bitterly;[42] but later he had an excellent revenge. One night it happened that, while he was asleep, an adder darted at[43] him and bit him badly on the forehead. Boeve woke up at once, seized the adder and with his stick beat it bloodily to death.

Now we shall leave Boeve and tell of Hermin and of beautiful Josiane. Josiane[44] knew nothing of this treachery; she came to her father and asked him: "Where is Boeve now whom you loved so very much?"[45] (960–75)

97. "My fair daughter,"[46] said the king, "I won't hide it from you: Boeve has already crossed the sea. He has gone to England to kill his stepfather and harshly avenge his father's death.[47] He told me the other day he will never return. "Ah God!" said the girl, "how can I survive? Ah sir Boeve, I loved you so much! Surely love of you will kill me;[48] now I've lost you, I don't care to live. Ah sir Boeve, how

---

[34] 94:949 **the snakes and adders** *les serpens e colures*: D omits "adders."
[35] 94:950 **and** *e*: D: and then.
[36] 94:951 **Not a single day [did he get]** *un jour ne [out]*: D: on no day.
[37] 94:952 **if he wanted water, he had to find it at his feet** *si il veut de le ewe, si prenge a son pe*: D omits this line; see Stimming's Introduction, vi.
[38] 94:953 **wicked** *mal*: D omits this word.
[39] 95:958 **the day** *icel jour*: D omits "the day".
[40] 96:960 **I am most wickedly betrayed here** *Jeo sui ci trai mult felunement*: D: he has most vilely betrayed me.
[41] 96:962 **his betraying me so badly** *que il me dust trair si tres ledement*: D omits this line; see Stimming's Introduction, vi.
[42] 96:964 **and wept bitterly** *e plurist mult fortment*: D: while weeping bitterly
[43] 96:967 **darted** *vint. . . fort launzaunt*: D: came threateningly towards
[44] 96:973 **Josiane** D: For Josiane.
[45] 96:975 **Where is Boeve now whom you loved so very much?** *Ou est ore Boefs, ke par amastes taunt?*: D: Father, where is Boeve, where does he dwell now?
[46] 97:976 **My fair daughter** *Bele file*: D: My fair [one].
[47] 97:979 **and harshly avenge his father's death** *e la mort son pere cruelment venger*: D: because he wants to avenge his father's death.
[48] 97:983 **will kill me** *me fra afiner*: D: will make me die of grief.

false-hearted you are since you didn't want to talk to me when you left. But if you are a courteous and noble knight, you should not forget your love." (976–88)

98. So the girl said, and grieved bitterly at heart. For Boeve's love she kept herself chaste, and she likewise looked after the horse and the sword. Then a powerful and warlike king arrived, called Yvori de Munbraunt,[49] with fifteen kings, all crowned, as his vassals. He came to King Hermin asking for his daughter, and Hermin most graciously consented. Josiane the beautiful heard him; in all her life she had never been so wretched. She had learnt a little magic: she made a tight belt of silk.[50] The belt was made in such a fashion[51] that if a woman put it on underneath her clothes, there was not a man in the world[52] who would have any desire to sleep with her, or approach the bed where she lay. The girl girdled herself very tightly, so that Yvori de Munbraunt would not be able to touch her. One day Yvori and his men mounted their horses, with Josiane amongst them, weeping bitterly, and took the road straight to[53] Munbraunt.[54] (989–1010)

99. Now I shall tell you a little about the horse: Josiane had brought it with her. Once it had lost the brave[55] knight, there was no person in the world[56] who dared touch it nor attend to it[57] except the girl. Josiane had it tied up in a stable, fastened tightly with two iron chains.[58] If anyone wanted to give it food, he had to descend from an upper room. King Yvori began to think he would show his great daring one day[59] by forcibly mounting the horse. He entered the stable and wanted to mount it. The horse saw him and began to lash out behind. With its back

---

[49] 98:993 **Munbraunt** In D, the name is Monbrant here and throughout. Monbrant occurs in *Maugis d'Aigremont* as the name of a Saracen kingdom; this chanson de geste of the first half of the 13th century seems to be indebted to *Boeve* in many details. See *Maugis d'Aigremont: Chanson de Geste,* ed. Philippe Vernay (Lausanne: Francke Berne, 1980), 1.195, and Stimming, 140; he omits *fort roi* (powerful king) which B993 repeats after Yvori.
[50] 98:1000 **she made a tight belt of silk** *une ceinture fist de seie bien tenaunt*: D: she made a belt of silk immediately.
[51] 98:1001 **in such a fashion** *par tele devisement*: D: through such magic.
[52] 98:1003 **there was not a man** *il n'i avereit homme*: MS G begins here.
[53] 98:1010 **the road straight to Munbraunt** *le chemin [. . .] tut dreit a Munbraunc*: G: the road towards Monbrant..
[54] 98:1008–10 **One day . . . Munbraunt** *Un jour . . . Munbraunc*: These lines are missing in D; see Stimming, vi.
[55] 99:1013 **brave** *vaillaunt*: D: good.
[56] 99:1014 **in the world** *en secle*: D: under heaven.
[57] 99:1015 **attend to it** *li [. . .] endrescer*: D: prepare it.
[58] 99:1017 **iron chains** *cheines de fer*: D omits "iron".
[59] 99:1021 **one day** *un jour*: G omits "one day."

foot, without hesitating, it struck and landed a blow to the middle of his chest,[60] so that he fell to the ground, and as he fell he hit his head on a wall behind, so it was cracked, and if his knights had not come[61] to help him, the horse would have killed him, beyond recovery.[62] His knights took him, carried him off, and put him to bed in his chamber; they summoned doctors who healed him.[63]

Now we will leave them there; we want to return to Boeve of Hampton, in the prison of fierce-looking Bradmund.[64] Boeve had already been there seven[65] long years. One day he began to talk like this:[66] "Fair Lord God, who deigned to create me and redeem me on the blessed[67] cross with your blood, I beg you, fair sweet Lord, sincerely and whole-heartedly,[68] that you do not let me remain[69] here long; let me rather be hanged or flayed alive,[70] or help me soon[71] to escape from here." The two jailers[72] heard him and began to speak.[73] (1011–46)

100. [74]"By our god Mahomet, you will indeed be hanged!"[75] One of the jailers,[76] you should know, came down to him on a rope. And Boeve saw him and got up to meet him. The jailer-knight raised his fist with force[77] and gave him such a

---

[60] 99:1026 **landed a blow to the middle of his chest** *en mi le piz fest le coup asener*: D: struck in the middle of his chest a resounding blow.

[61] 99:1030 **if his knights had not come** *si ses chevalers ne l'usent venu eider*: D adds "speedily."

[62] 99:1031 **killed him, beyond recovery** *le ust tué saunz nul recoverer*: D and G add "without delay" and omit "beyond recovery."

[63] 99:1034–35 **they summoned . . . leave them there** *maunderent . . . issi ester*: These lines are missing in G.

[64] 99:1037 **fierce-looking Bradmund** *Bradmund a vis feer*: D: Brandon the fierce.

[65] 99:1038 **seven** *set*: D and G: six.

[66] 99:1039 **began to talk like this** *comence issi a parler*: D: began to talk and said.

[67] 99:1041 **blessed** *beneite*: omitted in D and G.

[68] 99:1042 **whole-heartedly** *enter*: D omits.

[69] 99:1043 **remain** *demurer*: D and G: endure.

[70] 99:1044 **alive** *vif*: D and G omit.

[71] 99:1045 **soon** *toust*: D omits.

[72] 99:1046 **two jailers** *deus chartrers*: D: two knights; G omits "two."

[73] 99:1046 **speak** *parler*: D and G: shout.

[74] 100:1047 **By our god** *Par nostre deu*: Before this line G adds an extra line, 1046a: "The jailers spoke loudly." This makes for a much better start to *laisse* 100, and one that is more characteristic of *laisse*-linking in chansons de geste than in the other MSS. But it is also possible that, in the original poem, *laisse* 100 began with line 1046.

[75] 100:1047 **By our god Mahomet, you will indeed be hanged**: *Par nostre deu Mahun! ensi pendu serrez*: D: By Tervagant and you will be hanged; G: by god, traitor, today you will be hanged.

[76] 100:1048 **One of the jailers** *Le un de chartrers*: D and G: one of them.

[77] 100:1051 **with force** *fortment*: D and G omit.

blow below the eye[78] that he knocked Boeve flat[79] at his feet. Boeve speedily[80] got up again. Now[81] he realized he was very hungry. "Oh God!" he said, "how feeble I am,[82] for when I was first thrown into this prison, had I had my[83] steel sword in my hand and been challenged by a hundred Saracens,[84] I wouldn't have given a damn,[85] and[86] this one's felled me with a tiny blow! But, so help me God, if I don't at once avenge myself on him, I'm not worth a single penny."[87] He gave him such a blow with the hewn stick[88] that he knocked him stone dead at his feet;[89] he looked, and from his side took a steel sword.[90] (1047–68)

101. The other[91] knight began to call out: "Friend, hurry up,[92] don't stay so long; bring Boeve here and we'll[93] kill him." Boeve heard him and set out to fool him; Boeve[94] said to him: "My dear, gentle lord, I'm so heavy,[95] he can't carry me; but, my lord,[96] please come and help him." The other replied: "Most willingly." He

---

[78] 100:1052 **eye** *oi*: D and G: ear.
[79] 100:1053 **flat** *plat*: D: down.
[80] 100:1054 **speedily** *hastivement*: D: wretchedly.
[81] 100:1055 **Now** *ore*: D: then.
[82] 100:1056 **"God [...] how feeble I am"** *"dieus! [...] mult sui enfeblé"*: G omits "God" and adds "now" before "am."
[83] 100:1058 **my** *mon*: D and G: a.
[84] 100:1059 **Saracens** *Sarazins*: D and G: pagans.
[85] 100:1060 **a damn** *un oef pilé*: B and G: *Un oef pilé*, literally, a peeled egg; D: *un dener demoné*: I wouldn't have cared a brass farthing.
[86] 100:1061–62 **and this one's felled me with a tiny blow!** *e pur un petit coup ke cesti me ad doné me ad il abatu*: D has: "while" rather than "and" and adds "now" after "this one's."
[87] 100:1063 **on him** *de li*: D and G omit these words. At the suggestion of Dr Ivana Djordjevic, I have changed Stimming's punctuation of 1062, so that the new sentence begins mid-line: *me ad il abatu. Mes si me eide dé, / Si jeo ne seie de li ore endreit vengé, / Jeo ne me preise mie un dener moné.*
[88] 100:1065 **hewn stick** *bastun quarré*: MS G ends after this line.
[89] 100:1066 **at his feet** *a sun pé*: D omits.
[90] 100:1067 **he looked, and from his side took a steel sword** *e regarde a sun le si prist un braunc asceré*: At the suggestion of Dr Thelma Fenster, I have emended the MS reading of this line to include an *e* (and) after *e regarde* (he looked). The next line, 1068, is missing in B; see Stimming, vi. D gives: "which this same knight had carried."
[91] 101:1069 **The other** *Li autre*: D: And the other.
[92] 101:1070 **hurry up** *hastez vus*: D omits.
[93] 101:1071 **we'll** *frum*: D: I'll.
[94] 101:1073 **Boeve** *Boefs*: D: And he.
[95] 101:1074 **I'm so heavy** *jeo sui si pesaunt*: D adds: with iron.
[96] 101:1075 **my lord** *sire*: D omits.

began to descend the same rope. Boeve soon⁹⁷ saw him, cut the rope, and he fell down on to a steel spike⁹⁸ so that his heart was pierced through. Now the two⁹⁹ knights¹⁰⁰ were dead.¹⁰¹ But it was unfortunate that the fierce-looking Boeve killed them, because now there was no one to give him food. He fasted three whole days, I can truthfully say; then proud-hearted Boeve knelt and began to pray hard to God to favour him with escape. (1069–87)

102. When Boeve had prayed to God for a while, his bonds were quite shattered, through the power of God, king of compassion. And Boeve saw this and never before had he been so happy: he jumped fifteen feet high for joy, I reckon, up into a cellar, and feared nothing. It provided a very tall and wide underground passage—this is all true. Boeve followed the path to the end and emerged from the ground in the midst of the city. And Boeve looked all round; it was then dark night and people were in bed. (1088–99)

103. Now Boeve had escaped from prison. He had grown very thin—we know this for certain—and in prison his hair had grown so long that it hung down to his heels. His arms were thin, nothing but bone. (1100–4)

104. Boeve began to look all around. In a room he saw candles burning. He went there without delay, entered the room, and saw many weapons, steel swords, silken garments and robes, which he needed, but he could not find anything to eat there. He began to arm himself all on his own, for he had no page or squire. When he was armed quite to his liking, he found a palfrey and, like a knight, mounted it and wanted next to leave the city. The town's watchmen stopped him and asked: "Where do you come from, young man?" Boeve heard them and decided to fool them. "My lords," said Boeve, "let me pass; I am the knight of Bradmund, the fierce-faced. (1105–21)

105. "I'm going after Boeve, who has escaped; you can be sure I'll catch him." The watchmen said: "Then go quickly; may Mahomet, to whom you are devoted, guide you!" And Boeve quickly went out of the city. (1122–26)

106. When day came, it brought him great trouble. He came to a crossroads, which made him go astray; he had been so long in prison, I shall not hide from

---

⁹⁷ 101:1078 **Boeve soon saw him, cut the rope** *Boefs tost le vist, la corde va couper*: D omits soon, and has *teste* (head) instead of rope; Stimming substitutes rope.

⁹⁸ 101:1079 **down on to a steel spike** *jus desur un pik de ascer*: D: down on the middle of the ground.

⁹⁹ 101:1081 **the two** *les deus*: D: both.

¹⁰⁰ 101:1081 **knights** *chevalers*: D: jailers.

¹⁰¹ 1082–1189 **But it was unfortunate . . . supper time** *mes mar . . . hure de soper*: These are missing in MS D; see Stimming, iv-v.

you his confusion at not knowing which way to go. He thought he was going in the right direction, but—you should know the truth—he had to go back to where he had come from. Around high noon he looked about him and caught sight of Damascus, which is so famous. At once he began to ponder in his heart. "Oh God!" said Boeve, "where can I go? Even if I were now to be burnt in a fire, here I must sleep and rest." Then he got down from the swift palfrey and laid his head down on his undamaged shield. When he awoke, he mounted the palfrey, but, as you should know, he was very weak from fasting; for three days, I can truthfully say, he had not eaten. Singing merrily, he began to ride until he saw the crossroads, and there took the right way. Now we shall return to Bradmund the warlike. (1127–46)

107. Bradmund rose that same day and called his nephew Graunder to him. "Graunder," he said, "go quickly to the prison and tell my jailers to come here to me." As commanded, Graunder quickly went there and, coming to the prison, called the jailers, but you can be sure that he found none. Seeing this, Graunder lit a lamp and climbed down into the deep dungeon, where he saw that the jailers were dead, for Boeve had killed them. He came straight to Bradmund and told him everything: "My lord, I went there, by Mahomet! (1147–58)

108. "In the prison the jailers are dead and done for, and Boeve has escaped, he has broken his bonds." Bradmund heard him and was very angry and went blacker, certainly, than coal. He took a knobbly stick and thrashed his god Mahomet so hard that he almost totally smashed him. "Mahomet," said Bradmund, "wicked and faint-hearted god, if Boeve isn't defeated this very day and hanged high on a gallows, you won't get even a straw's worth from me again." (1159–69)

109. When Bradmund had thrashed his god, he shouted: "Arm yourselves quickly, my knights, and come here; we're going after Boeve and we'll catch him soon. It vexes me greatly he wasn't hanged long ago." The knights, about three thousand of them, each threatening Boeve, grabbed weapons; and King Bradmund armed himself thoroughly, mounted a good horse, and went off ahead of the others. And his nephew Graunder mounted another horse: a better one never carried any knight, and he had given four times his weight in gold for it. Graunder spurred after his uncle Bradmund. (1170–81)

110. Bradmund went in front, his nephew behind; three thousand knights followed them at great speed. Bradmund went in front on a good horse and soon reached Boeve climbing a hill. When Bradmund saw him, he began to shout: "Come back, false scoundrel; you killed my two jailers in prison the day before yesterday and you'll be strung up high before supper time." "My lord," [102] said

---

[102] 110:1190 **My lord** *Sire*: Here MS D resumes.

Boeve, "I daren't return;[103] I'm quite weak from watching and fasting. And you're well-fed, you can easily overcome me. But all the same[104] I would like to see if I can give you a little blow.' (1182–94)

111. Bradmund, a very cruel[105] man, heard him, spurred his horse violently towards him,[106] came swiftly[107] at Boeve, and gave him such a blow that the shield clanged and split.[108] Boeve of Hampton was furious: he[109] drew his sword and gave him such a blow that he cut off the whole top of his head. (1195–1201)

112. When Bradmund had struck Boeve the wise,[110] and split his shield striped with gold,[111] Boeve of Hampton was furious. With his good sword he gave him such a blow[112] that he spilled his brains: Bradmund fell down dead. And Boeve of Hampton jeered at him. "By God!" he said to Bradmund, "it's turned out well for you[113] that you've been ordained by such a good bishop: you certainly look like a learned chaplain."[114] Then Graunder arrived at quite a gallop,[115] a sharp bolt in his fist,[116] on his prized horse. He shouted loudly: "Boeve, listen to me: before I eat,[117] you shall be hanged." "Fellow," said Boeve, "I advise you to turn back and gather up your uncle;[118] carry him home, for he's newly ordained priest. And if you come any closer, so help me God's mother,[119] I'll make you his deacon with my steel sword."

[103] 110:1190 **return** *returner*: D: stay.
[104] 110:1193 **But all the same** *mes nequident*: D: But now.
[105] 111:1195 **very cruel** *mult cruel*: D: very fierce.
[106] 111:1196 **towards him** *envers ly*: D omits.
[107] 111:1197 **swiftly** *tost*: D omits.
[108] 111:1198 **clanged and split** *fendi e resoune*: D split all over.
[109] 111:1200 **he** *il*: D: then he.
[110] 112:1202 **had struck Boeve the wise** *out feru Boefs, le sené*: D: had hit Boeve.
[111] 112:1203 **his shield striped with gold** *son escu, ke fust d'or bendé*: The *AND* thinks this is heraldic, in which case Boeve's shield would have a diagonal gold stripe from the top right to the bottom left.
[112] 112:1206–7 These lines, between "such a blow" and "that he spilled", are missing in B; see Stimming, vi. D 1206–7: that he razed a quarter off his jewelled helmet, cut off all the nape behind.
[113] 112:1210 **"By God!" he said to Bradmund, "it's turned out well for you"** *"Par deu!" dyt a Bradmund, "bien vus est encountré"*: D: By God, he said, Brandon, it's turned out well for you.
[114] 112:1212 **chaplain** *chapeleyn*: D: priest. Boeve jokes that the missing hair on the top of Bradmund's head resembles a tonsure.
[115] 112:1213 **at quite a gallop** *tretut enleessé*: D: quite rested.
[116] 112:1214 **a sharp bolt in his fist** *trenchaunt quarel en poyn*: D: swiftly riding.
[117] 112:1216 **before I eat** *einz ke jeo mangue*: D: before you pass.
[118] 112:1218 **your uncle** *vostre uncle*: D adds: with you.
[119] 112:1220 **God's mother** *la mere de*: D: God.

Boeve thought in his heart that, if he could win the good, prized horse, he would not be afraid of any man born. He took the lance from Bradmund, whom he had killed, and split and smashed Graunder's strong shield;[120] his hauberk was worth no more to him than a penny, for the crimson pennon was plunged into his body.[121] Boeve[122] pulled it out and knocked him dead in the meadow.[123] Then he took the horse by the golden bridle, quickly mounted without needing the stirrups,[124] and went off at a gallop in front of the others,[125] riding[126] quite confidently and fearing nothing, pursued vigorously[127] by the others. In[128] a little while Boeve looked about him; he had come to a river, half a league wide, which distressed him. Boeve took his lance[129] and sounded the water; it was deep and very fierce[130] and, truthfully, the current was so swift it swept his sword out[131] of his hand. (1202–41)

113. When[132] Boeve saw this, he was aghast. "Oh God!" he said, "fair king of Paradise, who was born of the Virgin in Bethlehem, and suffered death on the blessed cross for us,[133] and was buried in the tomb, and harrowed hell, and rescued your friends,[134] and pardoned the Magdalen her wanton pleasures, and now sits at the right hand of your powerful Father, and will come on the last day to judge the quick and the dead and, according to his deserts, will give each one

---

[120] 112:D1226 **Graunder's strong shield** *le fort escu Graunder*: D: the shield.
[121] 112:D1228 **the crimson pennon was plunged into his body** *le vermail gonfanoun ly est en cors bayné*: D: the crimson standard was struck into his body.
[122] 112:D1229 **Boeve** *Boefs*: D: and he.
[123] 112:1229 **and knocked him dead in the meadow** *si le abat mort en le pre*: D: and he fell down.
[124] 112:1231 **mounted without needing the stirrups** *mounte sus, le estru ne sout gre*: D: mounted entirely to his liking.
[125] 112:1232 **went off at a gallop in front of the others** *devaunt les autres s'en va tretut enlessé*: D: deliberately went off in front of the others.
[126] 112:1233 **riding** *chevacha*: D omits.
[127] 112:1234 **pursued vigorously** *fortment chacé*: D: harassed fiercely.
[128] 112:1235 **In** *En*: D: And in.
[129] 112:1238 **lance** *launce*: D: sword.
[130] 112:1239 **it was deep and very fierce** *si ele fut parfounde e de graunt ferté*: D omits this line; see Stimming, vi.
[131] 112:1241 **out** *hors*: D: almost out.
[132] 113:1242 **When** *Quant*: D omits.
[133] 113:1243–45 **"fair king . . . suffered death on the blessed cross for us"** *"beau rey . . . la beneyte croiz mort pur nus suffris"*: D omits fair, blessed and for us.
[134] 113:1247 **harrowed hell, and rescued your friends** *enfern brisas e'n outas tes amys*: D: descended into hell for your friends.

his due,[135] I beg you, Jesus Christ,[136] for mercy: I would rather be in peril and drowned in the river than here seized by the heathen."[137] (1242–54)

114. When Boeve had prayed to the Lord God,[138] he spurred the good horse on both flanks and launched into the river, thirty feet out.[139] And the good horse put up a big struggle;[140] the current was swift and carried him downstream and the good horse swam upstream,[141] frothing mightily from his proud mouth.[142] And Boeve loosed[143] his bridle and by main force they crossed over. When they were over, Boeve was very glad, and the good, prized horse shook himself so violently that he sent Boeve flying, four feet away. Boeve[144] jumped up and remounted. Now he saw truly how hungry he was.[145] The Saracens saw he had crossed over and, all dejected, turned back.

To himself, the excellent Boeve said he would willingly and gladly give all his weapons and the horse he rode, too, for half a loaf of sifted wheat. He rode so far along a rough track that he came to a castle of hewn marble. Boeve looked around and saw its square tower; on the battlement he glimpsed a beautiful lady leaning out, lovely and fair-complexioned, as he could see. Boeve approached her and called out loudly. "Honoured lady,"[146] he said, "for the love of that god to whom you are devoted, give me some food, just this once." (1255–85)

---

[135] 113:1251 **and according to his deserts, will give each one his due** *e solum sa decerte rendras chescun ses meryz*: D: and at your right hand will give to your friends.

[136] 113:1252 **Jesus Christ** *Jesu Crist* D: Lord Jesus Christ.

[137] 113:1254 **here** *isci*: D omits. Boeve's prayer, as in *laisse* 167, fits the pattern of the epic prayer, common in chansons de geste, of which there are many examples in *Fierabras*, an item in MS D. On epic prayers, see G. Raynaud de Lage, "L'Inspiration de la prière' 'Du plus Grand Péril'," *Romania* 93 (1972): 568–70.

[138] 114:1255 **to the Lord God** *dampnedeu*: D: to God in this way.

[139] 114:1256–57 **good horse; launched . . . thirty feet out** *bon destrer; fert sey . . . trente pez mesurez*: D omits good and all of line1257; see Stimming, vi.

[140] 114:1258 **the good horse put up a big struggle** *ly bon destrer se est fortment pené*: D: The horse struggled here.

[141] 114:1260 **and the good horse swam upstream** *e ly bon dester est contre mount noé*: D omits this; see Stimming, vi.

[142] 114:1261 **frothing mightily from his proud mouth** *de la fere goule est fortment escomé*: D: and the horse snorted mightily from his mouth.

[143] 114:1262 **loosed** *abaundoné*: D: relinquished.

[144] 114:1267 **Boeve** *Boefs*: D: then Boeve.

[145] 114:1268 **Now he saw truly how hungry he was** *ore veyt il bien ke mult fu afamé*: D: now Boeve rode off, who was very hungry. After this line, B breaks off. Text henceforth from D.

[146] 114:1283 **Honoured lady** *Dame [. . .] tu cher honuré*: Stimming supplies *tu cher honuré* for the corrupted second half of the line.

115. "Knight," said the lady, "you're talking nonsense. You're a Christian and you're asking for food? By my god Mahomet, you can talk as much as you like. My husband is a strong and fierce giant; I'll go and ask him right now to give you a meal with his big club." "Lady," said Boeve, "by our righteous God, I'll either eat or die." The lady went off to tell her lord that outside a knight had arrived who wanted to get a meal by force. "My lady," said he, "I'll go and punish him." He took a javelin he wanted to throw and a hunting-spear he wanted to cast, and with his club in his hand he made a mighty bound. Then coming to Boeve he said to him: "Knight, where have you stolen this good horse? It's my opinion and complete belief that my brother Brandon used to have such a one." "You're right," said Boeve, "as God is my help! I made Brandon a priest with my steel sword. Yesterday, on this side of Damascus, I killed him; I believe he'll never be able to sing mass." The giant heard him and advanced to hit him, thinking to strike him with his club, but he missed him and hit the horse, so that he felled it to the ground. (1286–1312)

116. Boeve jumped to his feet and drew his steel blade, returning the giant's blow unsparingly, and because the giant had refused him food, like an angry man Boeve struck him on the head, cutting the skin right off. Boeve might have split him down to the belt. The giant threw a javelin at him which passed through his thigh, wounding Boeve very badly. Again the giant raised his spear, thinking to strike wise Boeve, but he missed and fell down. And Boeve jumped on him and quickly put his foot on him, cut off his right arm, then his left, and his two feet, and finally his head; the soul went to the devil.

Then Boeve entered the castle.[147] "My lady," said Boeve, "give me some food." "My lord," said she, "you will have plenty." "My lady," said Boeve, "you'll get poor thanks for it." The lady brought him—who was starving—plenty to eat: twice-baked bread, crane, wild goose and good light-red wine.[148] And Boeve ate like a madman. Now he was full, God be praised!

When Boeve returned to health and felt stronger, he recovered his might and his courage, but not all, to tell the truth. When he had eaten, he was very angry about his good horse, which had been killed. "My lady," said Boeve, "give me a horse." "My lord," she said, "willingly and with pleasure." She gave him a skewbald horse, and he mounted it and made his way towards Jerusalem. He confessed to the Patriarch, telling him all his sins, and how his father was killed, and how he served Hermin, the mighty crowned king, and how he captured Brandon, a king of great experience, and how he was sent to Damascus, and

---

[147] 116:1329 **Then Boeve entered the castle** *A tant est Boves en le chastel entrez*: This is Stimming's reconstruction; the line makes no sense in the MS.

[148] 116:1335 **good light-red wine:** *bon vin clarré*: Clarry was a spiced wine very similar to hippocras, a wine also flavoured with spices, and made from a blend of red and white wine.

how he was thrown into prison, and how he escaped from there, and how he defeated the powerful giant. And the Patriarch took pity on him and gave him a tame mule and thirty-four pure gold besants,[149] and in a kindly way commended him to God. Then Boeve decided that he would not go to the city of Hampton. (1313–61)

117. Boeve then decided he would not yet return overseas but would talk to Josiane. He went back to Egypt, but he could not find her there, so he had to go to Monbrant. One day Boeve met a knight; he had known him before and kissed him. "My friend," said Boeve, "tell me how bright-faced Josiane is." "Indeed, I'll tell you," said the other. "The much-feared Yvori has married her. His name is Yvori de Monbrant, and if you want to speak to Josiane, you must go straight to Monbrant and to Carthage too and the city of Famer; then you'll come to Monbrant without delay." Boeve thanked him and turned about and made for Monbrant,[150] along the wide road.

When he arrived in Monbrant, he heard that King Yvori had gone hunting and all his knights with him; only Josiane and a squire were left. Boeve heard this, felt great joy at heart, and came to the palace, wanting to enter. But he waited a bit, not wishing to hurry, and heard Josiane weeping bitterly and greatly lamenting Boeve of Hampton. "Ah, lord Boeve!" she said, "I loved you so much. Indeed love of you will drive me mad: since I have lost you, I no longer care to live." Boeve heard her and felt pity in his heart. He entered the palace dressed like a palmer and then asked Josiane for a meal, in the name of God. "Palmer," said Josiane, "welcome; you'll certainly have a meal." And she herself served him food. When he had eaten, she began to speak, and said to him, weeping, "Dear lord, in the name of the righteous God, where were you born?" (1362–1401)

118. "My lady," said Boeve, "I was born in England." When Josiane heard this, she was glad at heart. "As God is your help, palmer," she said, "do you know a knight called Boeve at all?" "Yes," said Boeve, "certainly: I was told his father was kin to me. It's not yet a year since I saw with my own eyes that he'd killed a mighty giant with his shining sword, and also Brandon, the powerful crowned king. My lady," said Boeve, "it's certainly true that Boeve has returned to his own land, the fine city of Hampton. He has killed his stepfather with his steel sword and properly avenged the death of his father; he's taken a beautiful wife with a rosy complexion—no more beautiful can be found." "Wife!" said Josiane, and fell swooning to the ground. Barely restored to life, she cried: "Alas that I was born! alas, what a fate, to have lost Boeve!" (1402–22)

---

[149] 116:1358 **besants** *besans*: A besant was a Byzantine gold coin.

[150] 117:1380 **for Monbrant** *avers Monbrant*: D omits Monbrant, supplied by Stimming.

119. Josiane's heart was desolate. Then she looked at Boeve and said: "As God is my help, palmer, if you weren't in that pilgrim's cloak, I would say you were Boeve the proud." "Indeed I'm not he," he said, "you're talking nonsense. But I've often heard talk of a horse; do you have him within? I'd like to see him; it would give me pleasure to see if he is as fierce as people say." Then Bonefey the squire came forward. "Bonefey," said Josiane, "do you see this palmer? Who do you think he is? Come and see." "My lady," said Bonefey, "as God is my help, I believe it's Boeve of Hampton!" When the horse, which was bound by two chains, heard the name of Boeve of Hampton, his heart was filled with joy from what he understood: he ran through the court neighing loudly and knocked down everything he touched. The girl said: "Now, sir palmer, you can hear how excited the horse becomes as soon as he once hears Boeve named." "By my head, now I want to try if I can mount him just once." Josiane was distressed, but could not refuse him. Arundel saw his lord approaching; the horse was so proud he did not deign to move; he stayed quite still and would not leave the spot. (1423–53)

120. Straight away Boeve mounted, and the horse became very excited. He neighed and pawed the ground—you can be sure he recognized his lord; he behaved more proudly than anyone alive and began to gallop. Then Josiane (she who was famous for her beauty) said: "By God, palmer, now I know truly you're the man I longed for! Boeve, by God, get down! You have your horse, you will have your sword." "My lady," said Boeve, "give me my sword! You should know I'm going to England." "No you won't, by God!" said the girl. "You'll take me with you when you go." (1454–68)

121. "My lady," said Boeve, "put all that aside. You are a noble queen and I'm a young man, and, by Jesus Christ whom I should revere, by rights I should hate, not love, you. Your father had me imprisoned for many a day. And there is something else I must tell you: I recently made my confession to the Patriarch and he ordered me not to take a wife unless she were, without deceit, a virgin. If you were a virgin, it would be amazing: you have been seven whole years with Yvori." "Boeve," said Josiane, "put all that aside, because, by that God I should revere, I can show and convince you that Yvori has never succeeded in touching my body. Let's go to England; when I have been baptized, if I'm not a virgin when it comes to the test I beg you to send me back here naked save for my tunic, without a penny or even a farthing." "Agreed," said Boeve, and embraced her; you can imagine how joyful they were.

Back came King Yvori from hunting, and fifteen lords with him who owed him loyalty,[151] with leopards and lions and other fierce beasts, and more bears than a cart could carry. (1469–94)

---

[151] 121:1492 **who owed him loyalty** *ke li devent honorer*: The MS has *ke il deuent coroner*, who are to crown him.

122. When Josiane saw him, she was sick at heart. She called her squire, the valiant Bonefey. "King Yvori is already on his way back; I believe we can't escape." "My lady," said Bonefey, "don't shed so many tears! I'll give you what I think is good advice. At the castle of Abilent, Yvori has a brother, the strong [king][152] Baligant. When Yvori arrives, Boeve should approach him and tell him that, without any doubt, his brother is under siege, together with his men, inside a castle in the city of Abilent. When he hears this, he'll be very distressed; he and his knights will quickly arm themselves and advance fast towards Abilent, and we will stay behind with few people. Thus we can escape, I believe." "By my head!" said Boeve, "that is excellent advice. God who made the firmament preserve you!" (1495–1513)

123. When Yvori arrived with his followers—to tell the truth, he had fifteen lords under him—he showed his beloved the prey he had caught. Then he looked at Boeve and called out loudly: "Tell me where you come from; I want you to do so." "My lord," said Boeve, "I have been in Nubia and in Carthage and in Esclavia and at the Dry Tree,[153] in Barbary and in Macedonia, throughout heathen lands, but I never went to the castle of Abilent. I could not enter it for all the gold of Pavia, for the king is besieged by Ydrac of Valarie. I tell you truly, if he gets no help, without protection he will be seized and hanged." Yvori heard him, his blood boiled, and he believed Boeve told the truth and did not lie. "By Mahomet!" he said, "how difficult life is! If my brother is hanged, I shall lose my own life." Then he armed his knights and made his way to Abilent. He left a king at home to watch over his beloved: he was called Garcie, old and white-haired, and with him were sixty knights who would not fail him. (1514–36)

124. When this was done, then he left him. Josiane, the maiden famous for her beauty, saw she was to be closely watched, and it made her very miserable and sad. Her squire Bonefey comforted her. (1537–41)

---

[152] 122:1502 **the strong [king] Baligant** *le fort roi Baligant*: Stimming adds *roi* (king), citing the Norse version.

[153] 123:1519–21 **Nubia; Carthage; Esclavia; the Dry Tree** *Nubie; Cartage; Esclavie; l'Arbre Sek*: in the MS the first three words appear as *"Ambie, "Cartagie,"* and *"Clavie."* According to Stimming (146), the Dry Tree is a legendary tree in Hebron which dried up at the death of Christ. See *Kyng Alisaunder,* ed. G.V. Smithers, EETS, o.s. 229, 237 (London: Oxford University Press, 1957, repr. 1969), 2:146, which cites the use of the Dry Tree in several texts, including *Boeve,* to signify "a remote or extreme point on the earth's surface," and adds: "the tree is withered in consequence of the Fall." Stimming identifies *Esclavie* as "the country of the Slavs, then heathen;" it is probably the same as *Esclavonie* (see n. 268). Mandeville includes these place-names in his *Travels* (see the Middle English version, ed. P. Hamelius, EETS, o.s. 153, 154 [London: Oxford University Press, 1917–19, repr. 1960]).

125. "My lady," said Bonefey, "stop crying; I will still help you to make a successful escape. I will go down to the meadows here: I know of a powerful herb which I shall load on to my horse. I'll pound the herb and extract its juice, then carry it down to the cellar and mix it into the wine-casks. When it's night-time and they are at supper, I'll give copious amounts of it to the king [and his men][154] and the juice will make them so drunk they won't know which way to go; you'll see them sleep and snore like pigs. Boeve and I will both arm and you will [also][155] get ready and we'll make for England without delay. Before Garcie can wake up, I think we'll be far away.' (1542–59)

126. Bonefey did as he had said: he came back from gathering those same herbs, pounded them in a mortar, extracted their juice, and put it all into the wine casks. He gave plenty to the king and his men. When Garcie had drunk, he quite lost his senses, and so did all the knights on whom he depended. (1560–66)

127. Then Boeve and Bonefey armed themselves, and the beautiful Josiane made ready. She called Boeve to come and speak with her. "My lord," she said, "we will load ten good horses with fine, pure gold; we want to take them with us." "Don't think of it!" said Boeve, "St Peter forbid! For once I'm in England, by the sea, and I can kill my stepfather, I'll have as much wealth as I want." "My lord, I believe you," said Bonefey the squire. "My fair, sweet, and beloved lord, you will have plenty, but that's not yet, you must know; first you must strike great blows. If you take some gold, you will need it, for with it you can hire knights who will certainly help to kill your stepfather. I've heard it said many times in my life: 'a bird in the hand is worth two in the bush.'"[156] "I agree," said Boeve, "as God is my help!" And then they loaded ten pack-horses with gold and at once set off on their wide road.

The next morning Garcie the proud, who was supposed to watch over Josiane, woke up. When he woke, he began to wonder why he had been so very drunk. In his ring there was a bright carbuncle from which a man who could conjure with it properly could learn about everything he asked. Garcie, who well knew that art, conjured with it, and saw openly and clearly with the stone that Josiane had gone off with the palmer. When he saw this he was astonished. He ordered all his knights to arm. "My lords," he said, "go and get ready! The palm-

---

[154] 125:1551 **[and his men]** *e as suns*: these words are added by Stimming, citing the Norse and Welsh versions.

[155] 125:1556 **also** *aussi*: added by Stimming, citing the Welsh version and syllable-count.

[156] 127:1585 **a bird in the hand is worth two in the bush:** *ke meuz valt un ke ay ke deus ke dey aver*: Proverbial: see Elisabeth Schulze-Busacker, *Proverbes et expressions proverbiales dans la littérature narrative du moyen âge français* (Paris: Champion, 1985), 251, no. 1300. See also Hue de Rotelande, *Ipomedon*, ed. A. J. Holden (Paris: Klincksieck, 1979), line 1092.

er to whom we gave supper has taken bright-faced Josiane away. If Yvori finds out, he'll have us burnt." The knights heard him and began to arm; they boldly spurred after Boeve, all threatening to cut off his head. Boeve and Bonefey the squire saw them coming. "By my head!" said Boeve, "I want to turn back and give King Garcie a blow. And, by that God I should revere, whoever threatens to behead me will never again want to come near me, for I'll defeat and overthrow his men. Because, if I can attack them with Morgeley,[157] you'll see me cut off so many heads that all the dogs in the land will have enough to eat."

"My lord," said Bonefey, "get rid of that thought. Do you think you alone can harm all these? Don't take it to heart,[158] my dear, gentle lord! Two such as you could not withstand them. But I want to give you better advice: in front of us I know there is a great cave underneath the ground, where we can go. When you are inside, you need fear nothing; not a single man of them will be able to find you." (1567–1626)

128. "Bonefey," said Boeve, "that's excellent advice. By almighty God, let's go into the cave!" Bonefey quickly led them to the cave and they entered—may God protect them! King Garcie looked for them everywhere, but his men did not find them, nor any living man who could tell them anything at all, and they returned gloomy and wretched. And Boeve, Bonefey, and the beautiful Josiane were quite safe in the cave, but they had no food, which distressed them. In tears, Josiane spoke to Boeve: "My lord," she said, "God help me, I am so hungry that I think I can't last[159] much longer." "Lady," said Boeve, "God help me, I am very sorry for it—be sure of that. But now I will go and see if I can find a swift stag;[160] Bonefey will protect you until I return. " "My lord," she said, "thank you; if you love me, don't be long." "I won't, by almighty God," said Boeve. Boeve went spurring off, and Bonefey stayed to protect the maiden.[161] (1627–51)

129. At this moment two fierce[162] lions appeared, with their large and terrifying bodies. They rushed at Bonefey the squire and at the girl—whom God protect from harm! Bonefey saw them, hurried to arm himself, and, like a brave squire,[163] mounted his horse; he struck one with his lance of apple-wood, but the

---

[157] 127:1615 **Morgeley** *Morgelei*: D's version of MS B's Murgleie.

[158] 127:1621 **Don't take it to heart** *ne pernez pas en cors*: This translation is the *AND*'s and Stimming's suggestion. Another possibility is: "don't risk it." Stimming reverses the order of 1620 and 1621, which I have restored.

[159] 128:1641 **I can't last** *ja ne purai durer*: The Lambeth fragment begins here. See Introduction, 9.

[160] 128:1645 **swift stag** *cerf corant*: L: stag or buck.

[161] 128:1651–129:1652 **to protect the maiden. At this moment** *la pucele gardant. A tan*: There is no sign of a break in *laisse* between these lines in L.

[162] 129:1652 **fierce** *fers*: L: very fierce.

[163] 129:1657 **like a brave squire** *com vailant esquier*: L: like a brave young man.

lion's skin was so tough he could not pierce it. The two lions stood on their hind legs; one seized Bonefey and the other the[164] horse and they tore him to pieces till there was nothing left.[165] The girl saw it and began to tremble; she started to cry out for fear of the beasts. The lions heard her, leaped nimbly over,[166] and seized her, with no intention of sparing her. They would have devoured her without delay, but they could not eat the child of a king. Nonetheless they would not leave her alone: they gave her many wounds and made her flesh stream with blood. Then the two of them dragged her[167] until they came to the top of a rock. The girl's thoughts were wretched;[168] she started to cry out for Boeve: "Ah, sir Boeve, you stay too long![169] Now these beasts want to kill me! You'll never see me sound and whole again."

Then Boeve returned from hunting, having speared a buck with his lance of medlar wood.[170] He looked around and saw his squire Bonefey's arm,[171] lying there; on one side he saw Bonefey's whole foot and on another the horse's thigh. He called out:[172] "Josiane, where are you? Come and speak to me." When he had no reply, he could bear it no longer but fell fainting from his horse to the ground.[173] And then Arundel the horse saw him; he neighed and pawed the ground as best he knew, and felt great sorrow. Boeve got up and his heart grew bolder; he mounted Arundel and spurred forward. And Boeve looked on top of a rock and saw two lions guarding the girl so that no one in the world would dare touch her. Josiane saw Boeve and cried:[174] "Come and avenge the death of Bonefey the squire." "I will," said Boeve, "you can be sure I'll deal with them with my two hands." The two lions heard him and rose; Josiane held on to one by

---

[164] 129:1661 **the** *le*: L: his.
[165] 129:1662 **and they tore him to pieces till there was nothing left** *tretut li desachent, nent lessent ester*: L replaces this line with another, which is hard to decipher but may end with *targer*. A half-line similar to D 1662 — *nent lessent ester* — in L replaces half of 1663: *ne lessent ren entier* (they left nothing intact). It looks as if D 1663 — *La pucele le vist si comence a trembler* (the girl saw it and began to tremble) — appears in L at 1665, but there is only part of the last word in the line left, *enble*r.
[166] 129:1665 After *enbler* the first fragment of L stops.
[167] 129:1671 **dragged her** *le . . . treyner*: After this line, the second fragment of L begins at 1672.
[168] 129:1673 **wretched** *dolent*: L: very wretched.
[169] 129:1675 **too long** *trop*: L: a very long time.
[170] 129:1679 **medlar wood** *mecler*: L: apple-wood.
[171] 129:1681 **his squire Bonefey's arm** *la brace Bonefey, son esquier*: L: his noble squire.
[172] 129:1684 **called out** *comensa . . . a crier*: L: shouted.
[173] 129:1687 **fell fainting from his horse to the ground** *de le destrer chet palmé en graver*: L: fell into the middle of the path.
[174] 129:1696 **cried** *comensa a crier*: After this line, the second Lambeth fragment ends.

the skin of its neck, as firmly as she could, so that it could not move. Boeve told
her to let it go. (1652–1704)

130. Boeve dismounted and went on foot, because he did not want his horse to
be harmed. He gripped his strong shield and seized his steel sword. "Let the second raging lion come." "No, I won't," she said, "so help me God! Not until you've killed the first." "By God!" said Boeve, "that would be a mistake, for if I were in England, my kingdom, and I boasted before my barons that I had killed two lions, you would come forward and swear by God that the truth was that you held one of them until I had killed the other. But I don't want that for all Christendom. Now let him go, or, if you don't want to, I will leave and you will stay." "My lord," she said, "no, take him! May Jesus Christ, born of a mother, protect you." The lions approached Boeve very angrily; one of them lifted its front feet and shattered Boeve's strong shield. Boeve drew Morgeley and struck him; he gave this lion a severe blow, but it was so old and tough he did not harm it. And it opened its mouth as if mad, fully intending to kill Boeve the wise. Boeve thrust his sword into its mouth so that it sank to its heart; when he pulled out the sword, the lion fell dead. Then the other came up, infuriated, tearing Boeve's hauberk as if it were a worn-out fur. It raised its front feet too, and Boeve cut them off with his sword. It fell to the ground and could not move, though it snarled fiercely. (1705–40)

131. When Boeve had killed the rampant lions, he mounted Arundel, the swift [horse].[175] He glanced ahead a little way and saw, reposing on top of a hill, a churl who was certainly nine feet tall. In his hand he held a heavy club, which ten men could hardly carry, and by his side a good sharp sword. The space between his eyes was a foot wide, his forehead was as large as an elephant's buttocks, his skin was blacker than ink, his nose was misshapen and knobbly in front, his legs too were long and thick, and his feet long[176] and flat. He was a hideous fellow, a faster runner than a bird on the wing. When he spoke, he barked as horribly as if he were a vile baying hound. (1741–57)

132. The churl was extremely large and very fierce; his hair was as long as a horse's mane, his eyes as big as two saucers, his teeth as long as a boar's, his mouth huge — he was a most ugly young man. (1758–62)

133. And the churl was large and misshapen; his arms were long and strong, his nails so long[177] that I tell you, there's no wall in Christendom which, truthfully, if he were nearby one day, he would not quickly demolish, for he would tear out

---

[175] 131:1742 **[horse]** *destrer*: added by Stimming.

[176] 131:1754 **feet long** *pez longes*: I have restored the MS reading of *longes*; Stimming substitutes *larges* (wide).

[177] 133:1765 **long** *longes*: I have restored the MS reading of *longes*. Stimming substitutes *dures* (tough).

a stone quicker than someone could count twelve pence. When he saw Boeve, he called out loudly: "Traitor, turn back! Return my lady whom you're taking with you." And Boeve, amazed, saw how large and misshapen he was, and laughed. (1763–75)

134. "Tell me,"[178] said the brave Boeve, "by the god you believe in, where were you born and of what race? And what is your name? Hide nothing from me." "I'm a fierce pagan," he said, "and my name is Escopart, the strong and brave,"[179] "Pagan," said Boeve, "you look very ugly: is everyone in your land so large and terrifying?" "Yes, by Tervagant!" said the Escopart. "When I was in my land, everyone, great and small, mocked me and called me a dwarf and said I'd never grow. I was so ashamed of their mockery that there was no way I could bear it; I came speedily to this land, and I've served Yvori de Monbrant ever since. And you're taking his beautiful wife away, but by the powerful god Mahomet . . ."[180] "Pagan," said Boeve, "you boast too much, but before we part all will be clear: if I don't force you to admit defeat, and kill you, I won't think I'm worth a glove." Then he spurred the swift Arundel and struck the Escopart on his chest in front. His lance broke, and Boeve rode past him. The Escopart stayed upright and on his feet, and never staggered. (1776–1802)

135. When Boeve had broken his lance, the fierce Escopart struck him in the chest and for fun began to snarl; he would make the boldest of men shudder for fear. He grabbed his club and charged, and Boeve dodged; he knew very well how to protect himself. The club overshot, it could not stop, and hit a tree, which it felled. Then the Escopart seized his sword, wanting to hurt Boeve. When Arundel, the good horse, saw that he would hurt his master, he raised his forefeet and struck the Escopart around the heart so that he could not stand fast. He fell to the ground and tried to rise, but the horse would not allow it; he would not go away

---

[178] 134:1776 **Tell me** *Di moi, velein*: *Velein* is supplied by Stimming but missing in MS.

[179] 134:1781 **Escopart** *Ascoparz* also appear in the Egerton MS of *Fierabras* 1028 as the name of a race fighting the French; see Louis Brandin, *"La Destruction de Rome et Fierabras," Romania* 64 (1938): 18–100. The definite article in *Boeve* 1784 shows the Escopart to be a member of a race. Albert of Aix, in his History of the First Crusade, describes the Azopart, an Ethiopian tribe who frequently attacked the Crusaders with maces and flails, very similar to the black-hued Escopart with his mace. (*Recueil des Historiens des Croisades: Historiens Occidentaux* [Paris, 1879], Book 4: 490, 494, 592.) See also Paul Meyer in *Romania* 7 (1878): 437–40. When Escopart is directly addressed (as in 1822 by Josiane), his race has become his name.

[180] 134:1793 **god Mahomet . . ."** *deu pussant, . . .!"* Stimming points out (148), citing the English, Welsh, and Norse versions, that a line or two is missing after this one, since the sentence is incomplete, but Sanders, *Bevers Saga*, cxlv, n. 8, observes that the lines could have been added independently by the foreign redactors and thus were never a part of the Anglo-Norman version.

but sat on the Escopart's belly, striking again and again and nearly killing him. Boeve dismounted, intending to cut off the Escopart's head. Josiane saw him and spoke: "Escopart, I advise you to become the vassal of Boeve the fierce, and he and I will have you christened." "Don't even think about it," said Boeve, "give up that thought: I believe he'll do none of that. But, by that God I should revere, whom this man allowed to die on the cross,[181] I'll cut off his head with my steel sword unless he agrees to what you say." The Escopart began to roar so that the whole wood rang: "Boeve, don't kill me, I want to be a Christian." (1803–33)

136. "Escopart," said Boeve, "can I trust you?" "Yes, by St Peter!" said Josiane. "He would rather let himself be torn apart by horses than do you wrong. I will stand surety for him, fair and beloved lord." "By God!"[182] said Boeve, I can't but be pleased by that." The Escopart got up and did him homage. (1834–40)

137. Then the noble Boeve mounted up,[183] and Josiane his beloved mounted too. The Escopart found his club, which he had earlier thrown at Boeve. They travelled very far until to their joy they came to the sea.[184] When they reached it, they found a ship full of faithless pagans, ready to attack Christendom. When the pagans saw the Escopart, they said to each other: "We're in luck: I see the Escopart arriving in a hurry. He will certainly help us with all his might, for there's no better seaman than him." The Escopart asked them: "Where do you come from? Where were you born?" "Sir," they said, "as you know, we are Saracens; you know us very well. We are looking for Boeve who took Josiane away." The Escopart said: "Now leave the ship fast or, by Jesus Christ, you will pay for it." Then he crushed them with his club, braining all of them, except those who drowned from fear. And the Escopart jumped in the ship, both feet together; he carried his lord and lady inside and then took Arundel, the good and highly-prized horse. (1841–67)

138. The Escopart took Arundel, worth so much, and carried him in his arms into the ship, and he did not forget his lady's little mule and all the gold and silver there was.

Now I shall tell you about Yvori: I do not know who told him that Boeve of Hampton had taken Josiane away and that he had defeated the Escopart. Yvori

---

[181] 135:1828 **this man allowed to die on the cross** *ceo lessa en croiz murer*: The Escopart seems to be considered as representative of the "heathens" who put Christ to death.

[182] 136:1839 **By God** *Par deu*: *deu* is missing in the MS.

[183] 137:1841 **mounted up** *monte en sun destrer*: Stimming adds *en sun destrer* (his horse), citing the Welsh and Norse versions.

[184] 137:1845–46 **They traveled . . . to the sea**: *Tant ont erré par lur jurné / ke il sont venu a la mer de grez*: I have translated *de grez* as "to their joy," but it is possible that it means "Greek": "they travelled so far that they came to the Greek sea."

told his uncle Amustrai about it.[185] King Amustrai had nine galleys, and he threatened Boeve fiercely and swore by Mahomet he would have his head. He encountered him in mid-ocean. (1868–79)

139. King Amustrai cried out in a loud voice: "Are you the Escopart? Reply quickly!" "Yes," said the Escopart, "by the body of St Simon!" Amustrai said to him: "By my god Mahomet, you will pay dearly for this treachery." The Escopart heard him with bowed head. He grabbed the stump of a mast and said to him: "Get back, wretch! I don't rate you worth a button." When King Amustrai heard him, he quaked so much that he would not have awaited his coming even for a kingdom. And they sailed on with a great din; Boeve had gained a most useful page.[186] (1880–92)

140. After sailing over the sea, Boeve of Hampton arrived in Christendom, at the city of Cologne. The bishop of the town had gone that day to the seashore and there met Boeve of Hampton, the strong knight. To tell the truth, the bishop was his uncle, but did not know they were related. Boeve saw him and greeted him; the bishop saw him and asked him: "Where are you from, my lord? You have good manners." "My lord," said Boeve, "I was born in England, son of Count Gui, who was wrongfully killed." The bishop heard him and kissed him. "Fair nephew," said the bishop, "welcome. Who is this girl with you?" "My lord," said Boeve, "she loved me, and I her, to tell the truth. I was seven years in prison for love of her, and so she now wants to be baptized, since she has renounced Mahomet." "Nephew," said the bishop, "God be praised! If my strength permits, I will have her baptized at once."

Thereupon the Escopart arrived in a rush, driving before him the horses loaded with silver and gold. The bishop saw him and marvelled, crossing himself three times out of fear. "Oh nephew!" he said, "who is this demon?" "My lord," said Boeve, "I won't conceal it from you: he is my page, and very valuable." "Page?" said the bishop, "God forbid he enter my house as long as I'm alive." "Yes he will, if you please," said Boeve, "he must be baptized today." "What?" said the bishop, "will he be christened? All the men of this city won't be able to hoist him into the font." When the Escopart looked at the bishop, he truly took him for a shepherd, because he was shaven and tonsured.

Then the bishop said to Boeve the strong: "Fair nephew, you are most welcome; I know for certain you are a strong knight when you have won such a page.

---

[185] 138:1875 **Yvori told his uncle Amustrai about it** *Amustrai, son uncle, de ceo li mustra*: Stimming suggests there are either some missing lines here (citing Norse and Welsh versions) or that the line should read *Amustrai, son uncle, detrès li enveia* (sent Amustrai his uncle after him).

[186] 139:1892 **page** *garson*: compare the earlier irony of *bacheler* (young man), 1762.

Now you should harass your stepfather. Sabaoth,[187] your tutor, is very angry because his son told him you were wretchedly and shamefully hanged. He is lodged in a strong castle, which he set up, on a rock in the sea; it can never be won by force. He was expelled in grief and shame from his own land for love of you. I advise you to go to him and then make all-out war on your stepfather, and I will give you a hundred[188] strong knights: you can be sure they'll give you plenty of help." "My lord," said Boeve, "thank you." Then they went to the bishop's palace. The bishop was very happy: they went to the church of the Holy Trinity and then the beautiful Josiane was baptized. The Escopart was so long and broad[189] (1893–1956)

141. that he could not get into the font. They prepared a great tub full of water in order to baptize him; twenty men were there to lift him, but between them they could not move him. (1957–61)

142. "My lords," said the Escopart, "your efforts are useless. Let me get in; you can pull me out." "True," said the others. The Escopart jumped in, feet together, so that he fell to the bottom, and in the font he was named Gui. The water was cold so that it chilled him. (1962–68)

143. The Escopart began to yell and to upbraid the bishop vigorously. "What is this?" he said. "Base, wicked shepherd, do you want to drown me in this water? Let me go; I've had enough of being a Christian." Then he jumped out, not eager to stay. Whoever could see him jumping about, naked, would think—I won't deny it—he was a hungry devil.[190] The Escopart went off to dress and clothe himself, and they went to the bishop's palace for a meal. After the meal, Boeve got ready, for he wanted to go to England. The bishop gave him five hundred knights. Josiane saw this and began to weep. She came to Boeve: "You are much to blame for wanting to leave me here behind you; now princes and their knights will come and take me by force and I won't be able to stop them." (1969–87)

144. "My lady," said Boeve, "don't be frightened. I will leave the Escopart with you, who will help you when you need it." "My lord," she said, "as you command! I pray to God, who created us all, that I can look after myself until you return." Then she kissed him and he mounted his horse, and the knights that the bishop had given him went on their way towards England. Boeve called them and spoke

---

[187] 140:1939 **Sabaoth** *Sabaoth*: D's version of MS B's Sabot or Saber.

[188] 140:1949 **a hundred** I have restored the MS reading of *c*. (a hundred). Stimming substitutes *cinc cens* (five hundred), citing 1982 and the Welsh and Norse versions.

[189] 140:1956 **so long and broad** *si longe e si lee*: The *laisse* ends without completing the sentence. Stimming suggested there were two lines missing (150). See *laisses* 166–67.

[190] 143:1977 **a hungry devil** *un deble ke vousist manger*: literally, "a devil who wanted to eat."

to them. "My lords," he said, "if you agree, we will not yet go to Sabaoth the wise, not until I've talked to my stepfather; you can be sure I'll trick him very well." "My lord," they said, "as you wish. We're ready to do your will." (1988–2003)

145. Then Boeve spurred off, and his knights with him, with God's blessing. They crossed the sea without stopping and came to Hampton without delay. The emperor, whose name was Doun,[191] saw Boeve, and advanced to meet them—may he never be forgiven! He looked at Boeve and questioned him: "Where are you from, knight?" Boeve replied: "My lord, from France, from Dygon[192] castle." The emperor asked him: "What is your name?" "My lord, I'm called Gerraud,"[193] Boeve replied. (2004–14)

146. "Gerraud," said the emperor, "are you a soldier?"[194] "Yes," said Boeve, "I won't deny it; I need to earn many possessions." "Gerraud," said the emperor, "by the faith I owe St Richer, I would very much like to hire you. I have to make war on a villain called Sabaoth; he's in a strong castle in the sea here so that I can't harm him." "By our righteous God, my lord," said Boeve, "does he annoy or harm you?" "Yes, Gerraud, my dear friend," said the emperor, "he wants to destroy my castle by night; he despoils my land of food and drink, sparing neither man nor woman, taking sheep and oxen with him." "My lord," said Boeve, "you should not overlook this. If you wish to pay me, I will go and seize and bind Sabaoth for you, and bring him safely to this castle." "Indeed," said the emperor, "I agree to what you request." Boeve said: "What I ask is small: load this ship for me with food and drink and then give arms to all my knights." "Willingly," said the emperor, "so help me God!" Instantly he had arms handed over to him, and they departed, crossing the sea without delay till they reached Sabaoth's castle. (2015–41)

147. Sabaoth saw Boeve arriving rapidly. He came to meet him, asking: "Are you a knight? Tell the truth!"[195] "I am," said Boeve, "I will not conceal it." "Tell me," said Sabaoth, "where were you born?" "Master,"[196] said Boeve, "In the city of

---

[191] 145:2008 **Doun** Despite his role earlier, this is the first time the emperor is named.

[192] 145:2012 **Dygon** According to Flutre, 230, this is Dijon.

[193] 145:2014 **Gerraud** Boeve's assumed name appears in various forms in the MS: here, Gyrant, at 2015, 2018, and 2025, Gerrand, at 2213, Gyrald. I follow Stimming's usage.

[194] 146:2015 **soldier** *souder*: *souder* means a soldier for hire, a mercenary.

[195] 147:2044 **Are you a knight? Tell the truth!** *Estes vus chevaler? Dites verité!*: The MS has: *Dunt este vus chevaler e ou fust vus ne* : "from where" (*dont*) or, alternatively, "so (*dunc*) are you a knight and where were you born?" changed by Stimming because of the repetition in 2046 and also to make sense of 2045.

[196] 147:2047 **Master** *Mestre*: *Mestre* can also mean "tutor": see note to line 223.

Hampton." Sabaoth heard him; never had he been so joyful. With both feet together, he leaped towards him, kissed him thirty times, and welcomed him with great delight. They went off to eat.

Now I shall tell you about the much-admired Josiane, left with the Escopart at Cologne. One of the land's counts saw her one day: because she was so beautiful, with her rosy complexion, in his heart he felt great love for her. He often came asking for her, and she refused because she was very wise. When the count heard, he swore by his head he would take her by force, however well guarded she was. (2042–59)

148. "Miles," said Josiane, "leave me be. I advise you to do nothing to me, because the Escopart will certainly avenge me." When Miles, the wicked devil, heard that she relied on the fierce Escopart, he began to think about treachery. Then he came to the Escopart and spoke to him: "By God who is your help, Escopart, my brother, Boeve summons you to speak with him; he is in that tower you can see in the sea." The Escopart believed him and said to him: "Dear lord, I beg you to take me there." "Willingly," he said, "without delay."

They entered a boat and put out to sea. When they came to the tower, the Escopart proceeded to enter, and Miles barred the entrance from outside. The Escopart looked through the whole tower, but he could not find his master. He saw Miles turning back, came nearer and shouted: " By the righteous God, Miles, where are you going?" "Escopart," he said, "you are welcome to know: I want to marry the beautiful Josiane." The Escopart heard this and became angry: with his hard nails he scratched at the wall and knocked all of it into the sea. And he jumped into the water and began to swim. He saw merchants passing by in a ship. "My lords," said the Escopart, "let me get in with you." When they heard[197] the monster calling out so loudly, they thought it must surely be Lucifer; out of terror they all jumped into the sea, and the Escopart got in and began to sail. That same day a messenger came to Boeve of Hampton to tell him what had happened: "My fair lord Boeve, I won't hide it from you: whether people like it or not,[198] Josiane is married." Boeve armed and mounted his horse and took the wide road to Cologne.

Now I shall tell you about the fiendish Miles, who had married Josiane against her will. Against her will he led her to church, against her will he took her to bed at night, sat down before the bed, and began to take off his shoes; he was in a great hurry to dishonour her. Josiane saw him and sighed. She took

---

[197] 148:2089 **heard** *oirent*: MS: *virent* (saw).

[198] 148:2096 **whether people like it or not** *ky ke deut peyser*: literally, "regardless of whom it harms."

her expensive silk girdle,[199] made it into a noose, as she knew how, and threw it round Miles's neck. (2060–2108)

149. My lords, now listen to what I've told you! Before Miles could enter his bed, Josiane the beautiful took her girdle and threw it around Miles's neck, no doubt about it. The bed in which he slept was high and he sat on one side of it; the girl jumped on the other side, pulled him to her, and broke his neck. (2109–16)

150. And in the morning when day broke and the light of the clear dawn arrived, all the knights nearby arose and came to the chamber where their lord was. Knights and noblemen loudly called to him, but all in vain, for he was dead and beyond recall. (2117–22)

151. The knights cried out: "My lord, get up." All in vain, for he had been strangled. The girl said: "Your efforts are in vain: this night I strangled Miles." The knights heard her and broke down the door, seized the girl, bound her arms, lit a fire outside the town, and without any pity took the girl there. The girl cried out: "Ah, God in majesty, save my soul, for my body is lost." (2123–32)

152. The noble girl kept weeping and crying: "Ah, sir Boeve, you have lost your beloved. Fair Lord God, son of St Mary, what folly you made this girl commit, to love a knight she didn't know! I gave my love to you, sir Boeve; now you've forgotten me and I shall die." (2133–39)

153. When the girl had mourned thus, there was no man alive who would not have pitied her. She asked for a priest and they gave her one; she kept him a long time, to tell the truth. At that moment Boeve arrived on the renowned Arundel, met a shepherd, and asked him: "Brother, what is that fire which I see lighted?" "My lord," he said, "it's a great shame: a girl who strangled a count, who married her by force, will now be burnt, unless God has pity on her." "It won't happen," said Boeve, "as long as I'm alive." He spurred strongly towards the fire. (2140–52)

154. Thereupon the Escopart came rushing in from the other direction, and met the shepherd in the middle of the field. The Escopart shouted to him: "Brother, what is that fire they've lit over there?" When the shepherd saw him, he turned to flee; "Bless us!"[200] he shouted. And the Escopart seized him by his hood. "Be quiet," he said, "now listen to me and tell me who lit that fire." "Mercy, by the Creator!" he said. "In that fire[201] they're burning a girl whom a count yesterday

---

[199] 148:2106 **her expensive silk girdle** *sa seynture de sey de oltre mer*: literally, her girdle of silk from the Middle East; see note to line 738.

[200] 154:2158 **Bless us** *Benedicité*: Bless [the Lord].

[201] 154:2163 **In that fire** *en ceo fu*: these words are missing in MS and supplied by Stimming.

evening married by force." "By my head, you're lying, it won't happen, for she will get good help, if my club holds out." The Escopart went after Boeve and in a short while overtook him. (2153–68)

155. When they reached the fire, they did not delay: Boeve drew Morgeley and made heads fly, and the Escopart struck out with his club, felling dozens. Boeve told him: "Now set about hitting." "I will," said the Escopart, "as God is my help; only a magician will escape." When they had killed their enemies, Boeve went to unbind Josiane and they embraced. The Escopart said he was thinking of the journey and of asking the bishop for a palfrey. The bishop gave them one at once, and they got ready. When the Escopart came back, they made Josiane mount and did not stop from there to the castle. Seeing the girl, Sabaoth went to kiss her; they stayed there as long as they desired. But the white-haired Sabaoth wished to lose no time: he meanwhile had his castle fortified, his walls raised, and his moats repaired, so that no one could come inside the castle without the order of Sabaoth the warrior. Once he had done that, he was satisfied. (2169–92)

156. One day in the morning Boeve got up and called a messenger, and he came; he was no page but a strong knight. The story says he was called Karfu. "Brother," said Boeve, "God save you! Go to Hampton without stopping. Tell the emperor, when you see him, that the knight who was there the other day is called Boeve, and tricked him. Tell him I'm sending him word he will be hanged, for I have reinforcements: hauberks, shields, and good knights, powerful and strong, and I have a mighty[202] giant. But, as Jesus is your help, speak boldly!" "Willingly," he said, "no one will stop me." When he was armed, he mounted his horse and came to where the emperor was, at Hampton.

When he saw the emperor, he did not hold his tongue. "Traitor," said Karfu, "you'll be crushed! The knight who was here the other day was not called Gerraud, as you were told, but Boeve—God give him strength! The noble Count Gui was his father; you wrongfully killed him, which will cause you grief. Through me Boeve sends word that you'll be hanged. Traitor, wicked thief, where is your valour now?" The emperor heard him and seized a sharp knife, meaning to strike the messenger through the body, but he missed and struck his beloved brother, felling him dead at his feet. And Karfu mounted his long-maned horse. (2193–2223)

157. He said to the emperor: "You're a stupid fool, to kill your best friend instead of me. Yet if you had had a better aim, I'd say there was some good in you. But

---

[202] 156:2205 **mighty** *mun grant vertu*: This line has a misprint: it should read, following Stimming's footnote, *mult grant vertu* (very great might), not *mun g.v.*

I believe something ruined your game: you've been humping[203] your wife over there. (2224–29)

158. "Fool," said Karfu, "listen to me! Shame on your hand which attacked me![204] It's Boeve of Hampton who sent me to you: he gave you three blows when he was little and nearly killed you." "God!" said the emperor, "I shall surely go crazy." "By my head," said Karfu, "you'll have your blood let:[205] I've never known better medicine." (2230–37)

159. Then the brave knight departed, leaving the emperor quite mortified. The messenger came to Boeve the brave and told him everything he had just found. Then both large and small laughed, and old Sabaoth and Boeve too, so that they could barely keep on their feet. Now we shall tell you about the emperor. He was very unhappy at the news: he summoned his men in Germany the great to come to him, for now his need was great. And he summoned the king of Scotland too, father of his beautiful wife, to help him and his men, for the need had never before been so great. And knights came, and men at arms too, and many archers and other lowly people. (2238–54)

160. Princes and knights came to Hampton, summoned by the enemy. Then he gathered the princes together. "My lords," he said, "be quiet! You know very well, I surely don't need to tell you, that Sabaoth has done me great wrong. Now a knight has come to help him, Boeve of Hampton, very strong and proud. I sold him to pagans who came from overseas. Now he has returned, eager to make war on me; with him he brings a very fierce giant—more like a devil of Hell than a man: I heard him called the wicked Escopart. My lords, will you help me to fight him?" "Yes, most willingly," they replied. "Fear nothing: we will go and besiege him. However strong and fierce the Escopart is, while we surround him he cannot hurt you. We will bring him alive to this castle; you shall behead him and Boeve, and set fire to Sabaoth the white-haired." Doun heard them with a joyful heart.

Then the knights went off to arm; they prepared tents and shelters, and divided their army into two companies. The king of Scotland, proud-faced Boeve's grandfather, led the first, and Doun, of whom you shall hear, led the second. There were many men, the army was a mighty one: for every man from the castle,

---

[203] 157:2229 **humping** *caubé*: Stimming does not know this word (152), but it would seem to come from *cobrer/covrir*, to cover, and is cited by Tobler-Lommatszch in an animal context. Karfu is being as insulting as possible.

[204] 158:2231 **which attacked me** *ke sy enseyna*: Stimming suggests (152) substituting *ke m'assena* (which attacked me) or *ke me seigna* (which blessed me) for the original wording, which makes no sense.

[205] 158:2236 **you'll have your blood let** *l'em vus legera*: literally: you will be relieved. See Stimming, 153.

there were a thousand men. Sabaoth and Boeve acted in a praiseworthy way: they divided their army into three groups. Sabaoth the warrior led the first, Boeve, the brave knight, led the second, and the Escopart, who was so strong and fierce, the third. (2255–89)

161. Sabaoth led and directed his large army. He had the gate opened and went out with his followers; ten thousand knights accompanied him. Doun saw him and called out loudly: "Go to meet him! See he doesn't escape from you." The king of Scotland mounted his horse from Orfanie and approached Sabaoth with his army.[206] Upon seeing him, the white-haired Sabaoth pierced his shield, leaving the body unprotected, and felled him dead, shouting: "Ah, wicked scoundrel, Jesus curse you for letting such a company down at the first opportunity!" Then he drew his shining sword: no weapon was safe from his blow. They wiped out the first group; seeing that, the emperor did not feel like laughing. (2290–2305)

162. Doun mounted and his followers did too; with him, they spurred against Sabaoth. Boeve saw this and came out of the castle on Arundel, his good, prized horse; armed knights came out with him and did not hesitate to set about fighting. Spurring Arundel, Boeve swung his shield in front of him and killed Yvori the Grey at the first blow; he also knocked Oube de Mondoie[207] down dead. (2306–14)

163. When Boeve had killed Oube de Mondoie, his companions struck their blows—God give them joy! Each killed his opponent; each was intent on it.[208] Boeve saw the emperor and reddened with anger. "By God!" he said, "traitor, should I catch you, God grant I never go on pilgrimage until I've got your big head!" (2315–21)

164. The emperor said to him: "Wicked, cowardly wretch, why these violent threats? If you want to fight, come out into the field!" Boeve heard him; never was he so pleased. They withdrew a good two miles[209] from the fray. Boeve took his lance, swung his shield forward, and knocked the emperor flat on the ground. And as he fell, his shield split and his good sword likewise broke. The emperor jumped up, very frightened. He found a stone lying at his feet; as he was quite strong, he raised it high and angrily hurled it at Boeve, so that Boeve's shield was

---

[206] 161:2296 **with his army** *o sa hoste banie*: with his army summoned by bann, i.e., proclamation.

[207] 162:2314 **de Mondoie** MS: *de Mundie*; 2315: *de Modeye*.

[208] 163:2317 **each was intent on it** *nul ne se amoye*: literally, "not one wasn't intent on it."

[209] 164:2326 **miles** *arpens*: See note to line 545.

badly broken. Boeve drew Morgeley and at once struck him, but the Germans[210] then spurred forward and soon quickly re-horsed their lord. (2322–38)

165. They entered the fray intent on striking. At that moment the Escopart arrived, club in hand, with the third company of fifty knights, and felled the enemy by the dozen. Boeve said to him: "Escopart, dear friend, do you see the emperor on the white horse? If you bound him, you would do well." "My lord," said the Escopart, "just as you wish! Now let me clear a path with my club." The Escopart struck, sparing no one, and, coming to the emperor, seized him bodily and carried him to the castle, where he had him bound. He returned to the army to help his lord. The Germans saw they could not hold out, and their lord was captured and in great trouble: they paid homage to Boeve in order to save their lives. Then all entered the castle.

Doun saw Boeve turn towards him. "Sir Boeve," he said, "I won't dissemble: asking mercy[211] will be useless. I will willingly forgive you my death provided you kill me with a single blow." "As God is my help," said Boeve, "I won't!" Boeve had lead brought and prepared a pit nearby, which he filled with boiling lead. Then he had Doun thrown in. "Now," said Boeve, "my lord Doun can bathe; if he is cold, he can get warm." A messenger came running to the empress, telling her news of Doun the proud. She heard it and took a steel knife and pierced the messenger straight through the heart. She went to the top of her tall tower and threw herself off it and broke her neck. Boeve heard tell of it, but had no wish to weep. He rode to his court without delay and, like a bold and proud man, took possession of his inheritance, governing Doun's land. My lords, he repaid all those who had come to help him, like a true and noble knight.

Boeve entered the city; all the citizens asked him for mercy and showed him masses of treasure. His vengeance on all his enemies was complete. Boeve sought his beloved, who was on the castle rock, and sent for Josiane so he could marry her; the bishop of Cologne was summoned there and came willingly and with pleasure. Then they brought the lady to the church and the noble and proud Boeve married her. When that was done, they went off to eat. Once they had sufficiently eaten and drunk, they asked for wine and went to bed. The moment was propitious: children were conceived. Boeve begot two sons, as he was destined to do: one was Miles—that was his name—and the other Gui,[212] the brave and wise. But later they endured great suffering. You shall hear further on how it happened. (2339–98)

---

[210] 164:2337 **Germans** *Alemans*: missing in MS and supplied by Stimming.

[211] 165:2358 **mercy** *merci*: Stimming adds *merci*, citing the Welsh and Norse versions.

[212] 165:2395–96 **one was Miles [. . .] the other Gui** *li un fu Guiun [. . .] li altre Miles*: I have restored the order of the names in the MS. Stimming (see 154) provides the reversed order from the Norse and Welsh versions of the romance.

166. Boeve stayed half a year at Hampton. Boeve called his brave knights: "My lords, make ready as I order you: we shall now go to speak to the king." And the count mounted and went spurring off (2399–2403)

167 to London, where they were well lodged.[213] He and the bearded Sabaoth turned around[214] and did not stop till they reached the palace. They found the king on the marble steps and greeted him, as you can hear: "My lord king, God save you and your barons. May God—who for sinners was born of the Virgin, endured thirty years in the Holy Land, fasted for forty days to save his people, then was betrayed by Judas for only thirty pieces, was given to the Jews to torture his body, deigned to die for us on the cross and have his body entombed, was resurrected within three days, and will come to judge us all on Judgement Day—save the king and all the barons."[215] "My friend," said the king, "where were you born?" "Upon my word, sire, now I shall tell you: my name is Boeve, of the city of Hampton, son of Count Gui whom you used to love so much." "Friend," said the king, "God be praised! I have every reason to cherish you: come and kiss me."

The king restored all his inheritance, and Boeve thanked him five hundred times. Sabaoth, his tutor, rose, called Boeve, and said: "My lord, come here, and quickly give him the levy."[216] "Sir," said Boeve, "a curse be on my head if I ever in my life give him the levy! My lord, it was extraordinarily shameful: when Doun killed my father with his sword, the king then gave him my mother with my inheritance and allowed me to be exiled.[217] This wrong he has done me must be redressed."

The king said: "Your mother had him killed—may Christ bring her trouble! She had your father made away with and murdered. I don't want a penny from you. Keep your revenues, your fiefs, and your cities." "My lord," said Boeve, "now I thank you." "Boeve," said the king, "I hold you very dear and I've restored to you your rich inheritance—towns and castles, keeps and strongholds. I greatly loved Gui, who brought me up with kindness; I have poorly rewarded his son." "My lord," said Boeve, "since you repent, I forgive you here and before God." And the king said: "Now that is well spoken."

---

[213] 166:2403–167:2404 **spurring off to London** *esporonant Jeskes a Lundres*: Compare the absence of break between *laisses* 140 and 141. Stimming (154) posits a substantial omission here.

[214] 167:2405 **He [...] turned around** *il se returne*: Stimming points to the lack of satisfactory meaning here, and suggests substituting *remonte* (remount).

[215] 167:2409–19 **My lord king, God save you ... all the barons** *Deu vus salve, sire roi ... tuz le baronez*: Another "epic prayer"; see 1243–52.

[216] 167:2430 **levy** *releve*: The *relief* was a levy paid by an heir to the crown, in order to get his fief. See Weiss, "The date," 237–41.

[217] 167:2433–34 **My lord ... sword** *Sire ... espé*: At the suggestion of Dr Djordjevic, I have altered Stimming's punctuation of these lines.

The king called his chamberlain inside. "Brother," said the king, "give me the staff which belonged to Gui of Hampton by the sea, and give it to Boeve, his son; the rod[218] is of pure, damascened gold." Then the king said: "Boeve, come here: I give you the keys to England."[219] "My lord," said Boeve, "now you give me my possessions: thank you, you have given me my fief."

The next day was Pentecost, in summer. The king rose and sent for Boeve, and they went to church; Archbishop Giré celebrated mass for them. Before mass, the king was crowned and Boeve secured his crown.[220] The king went to the altar, knelt down, and made the offering with good will. His renowned princes made their offering with him. They heard mass and returned.

The knights spoke among themselves: "My lords, today is Pentecost in summer: we should test[221] our well-rested horses." The race-course was arranged, the money was brought: forty marks were placed at the end of the race. Two knights—may God soon destroy them!—had two swift and speedy horses, one piebald, the other dappled. Now the horses were brought into the area. Boeve had Arundel, the swift horse, mounted to the saddle by his gold stirrup, and talked to the king. The other knights moved on ahead; the two of them stole into the race-course. The knights all assembled.[222]

---

[218] 167:2456 **rod** *verge*: a staff of authority, but it is unclear of what sort—perhaps an entitlement to carry a royal staff in front of the king in procession.

[219] 167:2458 **I give you the keys to England** *jeo vus renke de Engletere le clef*: The MS has *jeo vus renke de Engletere le chef* (I make you leader over England). See Stimming, 154.

[220] 167:2466 **secured** *ad [. . .] fermé*: It is not clear what is happening here. From Eadmer's account of Henry I wearing his crown at his second marriage, it would appear that it was secured by a strap under the chin (*Historia Novorum*, ed. Martin Rule, Rolls Series [London: Longman, 1884], 293). Alternatively, Boeve might be supporting Edgar's crown: fourteenth-century illustrations commissioned by Charles V show French peers doing this at his coronation. See Anne D. Hedeman, "Copies in Context: The Coronation of Charles V in his *Grandes Chroniques de France*," in *Coronations: Medieval and Early Modern Monarchic Ritual*, ed. János M. Bak (Oxford, 1990), 72–87.

[221] 167:2473 **test** *prendre*: Stimming suggests substituting *prover* (test) for *prendre* (take) here, citing English and Welsh versions.

[222] 167:2474–84 **The race-course . . . assembled** *Deus chevalers . . . sont ensemblez*: This seems to be a corrupted passage. I have adopted Stimming's suggested re-ordering, placing 2474–76, *Deus chevalers. . .l'altre pomelez* (Two knights . . . dappled) after 2478, *a le chef de curs un quarante mars getez* (forty marks were placed at the end of the race), and placing 2479, *En la place sunt les chevalers amenez* (the knights were brought into the area) after 2484; he suggested substituting *chevals* for *chevalers*. He changed the MS's *parout* (appeared) in 2482 to *parlout* ("spoke," emendation supported by Skarup), and considered 2484 (*Li chevalers sont ensemblez*) repetitive and dubious. I have changed Stimming's comma in 2482 (*o le rei parlout, avant sun passé*) to a full stop, and I have taken "they moved on ahead" to refer to the knightly contestants. I am grateful to Drs Ailes, Djordjevic, Padel, Sanders and Skarup for their help with this passage.

"My friend," said the king, "no more of this. On pain of losing limbs, don't let them get ahead of you."[223] "My lord," said Boeve, "you're talking nonsense; the horse has saved me from many a difficulty." The young man talked so long to his lord that the two others were four miles[224] ahead. Boeve let the prized Arundel run and angrily spurred his sides; he rushed along the route. Dust rose, mixed with wind. "Look," said the king, "he's a devil." In a short while he had overtaken them. Two knights, born at Wastrande, had two grey and dappled horses; they followed at his side for a good three leagues so that neither passed the other. "Horse," said Boeve, "how badly you're doing! Now you're not doing well, when these emaciated hacks follow you so closely. Once I saw you overtaking three such, when I killed the emir Tenebres[225] and Josiane first knighted me." When the prized Arundel heard his lord, he took more pains than a tried and tested servant; he set out and rushed forward: there was no bird, had it competed with him, which could have kept up with him for a mile. He descended a valley and climbed up again. Boeve went ahead, the knights were left behind; he did not halt at all from there to the goal. He took the money he found there, went to the sick, and gave it to them.

Boeve looked at the land where he had won the race. "Oh God, righteous Father!" said Boeve, "my father used to govern this land. I will establish a castle here, and because of my horse, that good steed, I will call it Arundel." He returned without stopping, not eager to pause till he reached London, and dismounted on the marble steps.[226] "Sir," he said to Sabaoth, "leave me be! I've won more today on my swift horse than all my family in Hampton by the sea."

The king's son coveted the steed. "My lord, please give me your horse." "My friend," said Boeve, "you're talking foolishly, for if England were yours, and you were its crowned king, and renounced the whole land in my favour, I would not give you my prized horse." The young man heard him and was very angry. He had a counsellor—may God send him to the Devil!—who said to the king's son: "My lord, we are forty dubbed knights here. While Boeve serves your father at his meal,[227] we will go to his lodgings and take the horse." Boeve then went to his lodging, secured his horse with three large chains, took his staff, and went

---

[223] 167:2485–86 **My friend . . . get ahead of you** *Amis . . . attendez*: more problematic lines. Another possible reading of *Ne les attendez* (2486) is "you cannot catch them up."

[224] 167:2490 **miles** *arpens*: "mile" also translates *arpent* in 2511. See note to line 545.

[225] 167:2505 **Tenebres** As Stimming points out (155–56), Tenebres has not appeared in the poem before.

[226] 167:2525–26 **marble steps**. "Sir" *marbrin degré*. "*Sire*": Stimming thinks a line has been omitted between 2525 and 2526.

[227] 167:2538 **serves your father at his meal** *servera vostre seynur a manger*: This was a mark of royal favour—see later, 2567, 2588–89 and compare *Le Roman de Horn*, ed. M.K. Pope, 2 vols. (Oxford: ANTS, 1964), 1: ll.461–63, 935–38.

to court. The king saw him and called to him: "My fair lord Boeve, how did you fare?" "My fair lord, well, thank God! I have won the race and got the prize. Directly on a hill at the end of my land, there I shall build a good fortified castle and, indeed, will call it Arundel." And the king said: "I will gladly allow that."

Along came the king's son and forty well-armed men; they went to Boeve's lodging and cut through all the chains and destroyed them. The king's son went closer; the horse raised his forefeet and struck the young man, knocking the eyes out of his head. They found him stone dead, and took him up and made a bier on which they placed him. Shouting, they entered the noble palace. "My fair lord king, misfortune has struck you: Boeve's horse has killed your son." The king heard them and almost went mad. "My lords," he said, "seize the duke for me. I will have him hanged, for he has greatly angered me." "My lord," said Boeve, "please do not do so. I willingly served you at your meal! My good master," said the prudent Boeve, "go and find out what Arundel really did."

Sabaoth did not stop till he reached the lodging; he found the young man[228] dead and returned to Boeve. "On my honour," said the bearded Sabaoth, "your horse has killed the king's son." "My lord," said Boeve, "it is great misfortune to hear of this event; I would rather be disinherited." "Boeve," said the king, "leave me in peace; before me I see my son borne on a bier." And he said to his men: "Seize him at once; by God, he will hang, there will be no bail." And they leapt to Boeve's side and seized him by his richly-trimmed ermine coat. When they had seized the brave Boeve, Brise de Bretoue rose to speak, and Glos de Gloucester felt strongly, and Claris of Leicester would not slip away. They said to the king: "You wish to insult us: we saw him serving before you and coming and going with your cup. It is not right you should have him killed." (2404–2590)

168. "If he gives up the good and prized horse, we consider he ought to be spared." And Boeve said: "What are you saying? The horse has served me in many lands, and whoever has a good servant should not abandon him." (2591–95)

169. The counts[229] said: "Indeed, he speaks the truth." And the counts begged the king so hard that Boeve renounced his land and gave it to Sabaoth, and the king readily agreed to it. The swift Arundel was brought to Boeve. He mounted him by his golden stirrups. "Horse," said Boeve, "I have loved you greatly, since for you I'm losing my splendid inheritance. Curse him who cares! I've won plenty, and I'll win plenty more if I'm well enough to do so." He grasped his shield and his gleaming sword and took his leave before the assembly of barons. Everyone, old and young, watched him. Boeve turned back and approached the king. "My lord," he said, "now I must go, since I can't remain here any longer. For God's sake, I beg you not to forget my lord Sabaoth, who is so dear to me. But, by our

---

[228] 167:2571 **the young man** *l'enfant*: MS has *lur homes* (their men).
[229] 169:2596 **The counts** *Les contes*: missing in MS.

righteous Lord, should you want to expel him from the land which was my father's, even if I'm four seas away, I will come to help and aid him. I will never defy you except on the day you have deserved it." (2596–2621)

170. With that, he spurred his horse and departed. "By St Mary," said Edgar the noble,[230] "now I've lost my child this way, I shall never again be joyful." Boeve, the brave knight, departed and travelled back to Hampton. (2622–27)

171. When Boeve came to the city of Hampton and saw Josiane, famous for her beauty, he called all his knights to him: "Swear fealty to Sabaoth, my tutor." And they replied: "Never speak of such a thing!" And Boeve replied: "Indeed you must do so, for the king has given him all my fiefs, and I am totally exiled from the land."[231] "My lord," said Josiane, "how did you fare?" And Boeve replied: "Thank God,[232] but my horse has killed the king's son." How the knights wept! Each said to the other: "Alas that we were born, since we are losing our best friend in all Christendom." Josiane called to Boeve: "My lord, whom shall we take with us?" "My lord," said Sabaoth, "Terri, my son."

At that moment the fierce Escopart appeared, whom Boeve had baptized and christened and in Cologne had given the name of Gui. "My lord," said Gui, "what is your plan? Will you take me with you or leave me here?" "My friend," said Boeve, "stay with Sabaoth. I will give you Large[233] with two hundred knights." "Thank you," said he, then turned away, miserable and angry. The day passed; the night grew dark and the scoundrel took to the road, came to the sea, crossed it quickly, and made great haste as far as Monbrant. The king saw him and called to him: "My friend," said the king, "where have you been for so long?" "My lord," he said, "I won't deny it: I've been looking for your wife. A year has passed since she went off with the bold palmer whom you lodged in this sumptuous palace." (2628–64)

172. "By Mahomet!" said the king, lord of Monbrant, "where did you find him, brave heathen?" "In England, my lord, where he has large domains; to tell the truth, he's been expelled from them for a misdeed. His grey horse killed the king's son. I know the way and the main roads well; now give me a hundred Saracens." And he did so at once. Then they went on their way: may God destroy them! (2665–73)

---

[230] 170:2623 **Edgar the noble** *Edegar, le franc*: The English king's name appears for the first time. In the MS he is called *le franc corone* (the noble crowned [one]); Stimming omits *corone*.

[231] 171:2635 **land** *terre:* missing in MS.

[232] 171:2637 **thank God** *La merci damedé*: Stimming suspects a missing *ben* (well) before this phrase.

[233] 171:2652 **Large** *Large*: This appears to be the name of a city. Compare "Larthe" in the Norse version (Sanders, *Bevers Saga*, 239).

173. The scoundrels set out on their road. Lord Boeve got up next morning and asked leave of Sabaoth, the count palatine, and he granted it, in the name of St Martin.[234] He and Terri packed up silver and fine gold and, as a sad fate would have it, put to sea. (2674–79)

174. On land, grief was great and intense. Sabaoth fainted, and so did all the brave knights; they watched them as long as they could, then went back up into the great palace. (2680–83)

175. Boeve and Terri[235] sailed vigorously. Then they crossed the sea, mounted excellent horses, and did not stop till they reached a forest. Boeve rode with Terri alongside and, between them, the beautiful Josiane. Then the lady was seized with pains in the belly. Boeve heard her; it was no laughing matter. "What shall we do?" said Boeve to Terri. They helped the lady down from the mule, made a shelter with their steel swords, and put the excellent lady inside. Pain seized her and she let out a great cry. "Lady," said Boeve, "honourable and noble woman, shall I stay with you to serve your body's needs, to help you, when you want me to? I will, indeed, be able to see your child;[236] never in my life will I despise you for it." "My lord," she said, "certainly not! It's neither a right nor a custom, nor have we ever heard of a man seeing a woman giving birth.[237] Go away, withdraw from here, and leave the decision to God; St Mary will be at the delivery." They left, miserable and unsmiling. Josiane stayed in the shelter; the moment was propitious, and she gave birth to two sons.

At that moment the Saracens appeared and found the lady delivered of two sons. They took her quickly and left the sons behind; she was so feeble she could not cry out. They crossed the bridge and the wide moorland. Boeve and Terri came back to the shelter and heard the children crying. "By God!" said Boeve,

---

[234] 173:2677 **St Martin** *Seyn Martin*: The Albini family, possible patrons of *Boeve*, came from St Martin d'Aubigny; on the other hand, none of the religious houses they patronised were dedicated to this saint. But their predecessor in holding Arundel, Roger de Montgomery, was a major benefactor of Séez, dedicated to St Martin (from a personal communication by Dr Djordjevic).

[235] 174:2684 **Boeve and Terri sailed** *nagent Boves e Terriz*: MS has *negent Boves le paleyn* (Boeve the count palatine sailed). Stimming substitutes *e Terriz* (and Terri), citing the plural verb and the Norse version.

[236] 175:2699–2700 **to help you . . . see your child** *pur vos aider . . . vostre enfant . . . bien ver*: In the MS the order of 2699 and 2700 is reversed, so that *vostre enfant purray mult bien ver* (I will indeed be able to see your child) appears before *pur vos aider . . .* (to help you . . .).

[237] 175:2704 **a man seeing a woman giving birth** *enfant de femme dust home ver*: Cf Eugen Kölbing, ed., *The Romance of Sir Beues of Hamtoun*, EETS e.s. 46, 47, 65 (London: Kegan Paul, Trench, and Trubner, 1885, 1886, 1894), 335, who cited other examples of later narratives where it was thought improper for a man to be present at childbirth.

"I've delayed too long." He rushed quickly into the shelter and found two sons lying on the leaves. "Ah, Josiane, what has become of you? I've loved you more than any of God's creatures." They cut pieces from their coats edged with ermine and in them wrapped the two little sons; Boeve carried one and Terri the other. They looked for the lady through far-off realms, then mounted their swift horses;[238] when they could not find her, they turned back in anger.

Now we shall leave Boeve the marquis and tell you about the white-haired Sabaoth. He was asleep in a vaulted chamber and had a dream which greatly distressed him: that a hundred lions had attacked Boeve and taken his prized horse from him. And then Sabaoth the white-haired dreamt he went to St Gilles[239] to seek forgiveness. He woke up and told his dream to lady Eneborc. "No doubt I just dreamt it all." "My lord," she said, "pay heed to me for a while! Go, don't put it off: he has lost the lovely Josiane. I'm telling you the truth—he is left with two sons."

Sabaoth went off in pilgrim's garb and managed to reach a vessel;[240] he commended its excellent seaman to God, covered the ground in distant lands, and never stopped till he reached St Gilles. The noble knight entered the church, begged St Gilles to have mercy on him, made his offering, and then came out. Twenty men from his country came out with him. Immediately they met the lovely Josiane. Sabaoth saw her and was overjoyed. "My lady, where are Boeve and my son Terri?" "My lord," she said, "listen to my words: in a wood I had two sons. When I gave birth to them, by God's mercy, my lord and Terri were far off. Then all these Saracens arrived, who are now taking me to Yvori, the strong king."

"Tell me, my lady," said Sabaoth, "are these Saracens?" "Yes, my fair lord, there's the scoundrel, Gui, whom Boeve had baptized and christened." Sabaoth seized his pilgrim's staff, struck the traitor near the eye, and knocked him down dead. In a loud voice he shouted: "Strike, my pilgrims!" Each man struck another. Hearing the uproar, the town's citizens arrived and butchered them all to death, and Sabaoth speedily took charge of the lady. "My lord," she said, "by God, who never lies, how can you take me through the land?" "My lady," said Sabaoth, "don't be frightened; I will dress you like a man." And the lady said: "We

---

[238] 175:2725–26 **Boeve carried one... swift horses** *li un a porté Boves... corant destrés*: My translation follows Stimming's reversal of the order of 2725 and 2726 in the MS.

[239] 175:2736 **St Gilles** *Sen Gile*: Probably St Gilles-du-Gard, near Nimes: many pilgrims flocked to the saint's shrine in the reliquary abbey there. The town had an active port, an important fair, and a market for overseas merchants. St Gilles specialised in curing mental illness, paranoia, and fears of the unknown.

[240] 175:2744 **reach a vessel** *a un dromun vint*: Stimming suggests a line was missing after *a un dromun vint*, citing the English and Norse versions, but the sense is complete without it.

are in great need." Sabaoth stayed behind, the pilgrims departed, and he dressed the lady and they went straight off to the market. She bought a herb—you never saw a better—and with it she dyed all her body and her face. Then they went looking for Boeve and Terri. (2684–2781)

176. They did not stop till they reached Abreford. Then Sabaoth fell very ill. One day Josiane became pensive, and began to sing about Boeve. And lords came from distant lands, giving her horses and clothing, with which to buy what might be needed. She took good care of Sabaoth the warrior for a full seven years and three months.

Now we must return to Boeve, the valiant and wise, the courteous warrior. He and Terri rode on until they emerged from the wood. There they met a courteous forester. Boeve saw him and spoke to him: "What kind of man are you, my fair and dear lord?" "Indeed, sir, I am a forester. And you, who are you, my young lord? You look very weary and in pain." "Truly we are," said Boeve. "I had a wife, you never saw a fairer. She gave birth to these two sons. Now I have lost her and I'm very distressed." "Give them to me," said the forester, "and I will have them baptized and raised. I won't take a penny from you till the day you return." And Boeve thanked him five hundred times and then gave him one of the children. "What will his name be?" said the forester. "Gui," said Boeve of Hampton-by-the-sea. He quickly carried the child to the holy church, commended him to God, and they went on their way. The other child was given to a fisherman, with five marks towards raising him. And thus the children were baptized and raised.

Then they mounted, commending them to God, and did not stop till they reached Civile.[241] They took lodging with Gerner, who treated them well in return for pledges. When they had eaten and drunk enough, and seen to their horses, their beds were made and they lay down. The very next day, at first light, a battle began,[242] with a good forty thousand armed men, famous knights and lords.

The young Boeve, mounted on Arundel who was not sluggish, was the first to emerge, and struck their standard-bearer; using the full length of his lance, he toppled him over dead, while Terri, a brave fighter,[243] served another the same way. They seized the man's fine horse by the reins and gave it to their host, as payment towards their lodging. The city would certainly have been burnt down

---

[241] 176:2818 **Civile** *Civile*: Stimming (276) thinks this is Seville.

[242] 176:2824–27 **The very next day ... famous knights and lords** *Dreit a demain ... de chevalers e de barons mult preysez*: Stimming's note to this "garbled" passage postulates a missing line (159).

[243] 176:2832 **fighter** *guerrer*: omitted from MS; the word could equally be *chevaler* (knight). See Stimming 160.

and plundered [had Boeve not arrived in time].[244] When he saw everything thus surrendered,[245] he shouted to them in a loud, clear voice: "Defend yourselves, base and dejected people! The city's possessions are yours: I won't take a penny's worth of them." Then Boeve fought Armiger, who in the sight of them all landed in the sand. And Boeve took three prisoners; he did not know where they were from. He presented them to the young maiden.[246] Boeve turned sideways, struck a count, and cut his head off. The maiden had gone up the tower and seen the great blows struck by the wise Boeve; she gave all her love to him. At that moment the fighting stopped and Boeve and Terri went to their lodgings; their host prepared a meal and they ate and drank copiously. At that moment, the others entered the palace and the maiden thanked them profusely, but most of all she wanted the best man, who had presented her with the three prisoners. The lady called Reiner, her steward. "Go quickly," she said, "and bring the knight to me." He went off, but was unsuccessful. When the lady heard, she was rather cross, set out and went towards them. When Boeve saw her, he rose to meet her. She greeted him as you shall hear. (2782–2865)

177. "I sent a man for you; you didn't deign to come, morning or evening." "Lady," said Boeve, "I didn't think of it for, if I can, I shall leave tomorrow. I'm looking for my true-hearted wife; I lost her in a forest, one morning recently. Thank God, I was left with two sons." The maiden said: "That's an extraordinary story. My lord, marry me," said the girl. (2866–74)

178. "My fair sister," said Boeve, "give up this idea. Even for everything you have, I would not do it." What more shall I tell you, to deflect slander?[247] But they talked and quarrelled so much that each was very angry with the other, and the lady threatened to have his head cut off. "My lady," said Boeve, "let me speak! I will take you to wife on this condition: if bright-faced Josiane doesn't return within seven years, I will delay no longer but, with your leave, take you for my wife." Then the lady said: "You have spoken very well, and I will willingly give you four [months][248] in addition, but please give me Terri if you find your wife." And Boeve replied: "That is agreeable to me." At that point, the dispute was

---

[244] 176:2835 [**had Boeve not arrived in time**] A missing line after 2835, *ja fust la vile ars e robé*, has been suggested by Stimming from the Welsh and Norse versions, but see Sanders, *Bevers Saga*, cxlv, n. 8.

[245] 176:2836 **saw** *veu ad*: Stimming's emendation (*veu* for MS *vus*) to a nonsensical line in the MS (160).

[246] 176:2845 **the young maiden** *la pucele*: As Stimming remarks (160), here the lady of Civile is mentioned as if we have heard of her before.

[247] 178:2877 **What more shall I tell you, to deflect slander?** *Key vus dirai plus pur defere losoenge?*: Stimming unnecessarily alters the line to *pur estre losengé*. I am grateful to Dr Djordjevic for her reading of the line.

[248] 178:2887 [**months**]: missing from MS and suggested by Stimming (160).

over.[249] That night they were served with food and drink in abundance. Next morning, the counts rose and crossed the bridge to church. Then Boeve married the lady,[250] and Bishop Sené celebrated mass for them. When mass was over, they entered the palace, asked for water, and washed their hands; they were well served by able knights. Boeve asked for those counts whose oath of fealty[251] he had earlier taken during the battle: "In the name of God, I release you." And they did him homage and swore fealty. This is how the duke and Terri acted.[252] The day passed; it grew dark, and they went to sleep in the splendid palace until the morning and the dawning of the day.

Duke Vastal summoned his men and Duke Doctrix rode to meet him; they intended to make war on the lady of Civile with forty thousand armed men. Like madmen, together they spurred their horses[253] and did not stop till they reached Civile, pitilessly devastating the land. Boeve of Hampton rose in the morning, heard the noise, and went to get his men,[254] summoning them to arm. They donned hauberks and jewelled helmets, girded swords on their left sides, and mounted their swift horses. First Boeve mounted Arundel, followed by Terri, the famous knight, on his own horse; with him came fifteen thousand armed men. Boeve let swift Arundel charge forward and, in front of the others, struck Ysoré; he pierced his shield, damaged his hauberk, and with outstretched lance felled him dead. Terri violently struck Lancelin[255] and knocked him, injured, a full lance-length away. Boeve shouted: "Strike, my excellent knights!" And they did so with their polished swords, each cutting down his man as they rode past. (2875–2932)

---

[249] 178:2891 **At that point, the dispute was over** *A cele parole la tenson est finé*: In the MS this line comes before 2888: *mes, ci vus plet, Terri me donez* (but please give me Terri).

[250] 178:2895 **Boeve married the lady** *ad Boves la dame esposé*: Such a marriage could be annulled, under certain conditions, if the partners initially promised marriage "in the future tense"; see David Herlihy, *Medieval Households* (Cambridge, MA: Harvard University Press, 1985), 80–81.

[251] 178:2901 **fealty** *feuté*: Stimming (161) argues that it is unlikely Boeve could have taken fealty from his prisoners in battle and suggests the word may be an attribute belonging to battle for which another — such as *champel* (pitched battle) — could be substituted. But his objection to Boeve's action seems unnecessary.

[252] 178:2904 **This is how the duke and Terri acted** *Estevus ke le duc e Terri ad ovré*: In the MS, the line reads: *Estevus le duc Terri ad ovré* (this is how Duke Terri acted). See Stimming 161.

[253] 178:2912 **their horses** *lur chevals*: missing in MS.

[254] 178:2916 **to . . . his men** *as sons* Stimming proposes the addition of *as sons*, citing the Welsh and Norse versions.

[255] 178:2928 **Lancelin** *Lancelin*: Laucelin in MS.

179. The battle was great and the fray was violent. The people of Civile won the field, and the others fled through a low valley. Boeve rode ahead of the others, and Terri was not slow either: those he reached had no protection from death. Boeve pursued the duke of Vastal; after Boeve turned the head of his war-horse, each man struck great blows at the other's shield. Then the duke's lance broke, and the brave Boeve struck him down in the field. Then he drew sharp Morgeley, and the other cried to Boeve: "Lord, I surrender." He offered his sword and Boeve took it. Boeve pursued the strong Duke Doctrix; he gave him a great blow on the overlapping scales of his mail-coat and knocked him dead, a full lance-length away, in the field. (2933–49)

180. The booty Boeve acquired was very fine. The battle was well and truly over; next they went to the splendid palace to eat. The noble maiden loved Boeve very much. (2950–53)

181. They dwelt together for seven years without there ever being carnal love between them. One day the lady called Boeve to her: " Now I shall soon have my will of you." "That may well be so." said Boeve the wise.
Now we shall leave the wise Boeve and must turn to Sabaoth the renowned. Thank God, he was cured of his illness. And Sabaoth said to Josiane: "We shall go and look for my liege lord." She replied: "Sir, you are right." They mounted their horses and went on their way. One day, just at nightfall, when they were looking for their lord through distant lands,[256] they came to the city of Civile and lodged with a worthy man. Sabaoth went to the palace; in front of the gate of the splendid palace, on a bench, sat Boeve the wise, and next to him his close friend. Sabaoth saw them, approached, and greeted them as you shall hear: "God save you and all that you have!" "And you too! Where are you from?" "My lord, I'm a pilgrim from another land. I have a few followers in the city, and for charity's sake ask you for supplies." "My friend," said Boeve, "you shall have plenty." He called Terri and said to him: "Look how like the bearded Sabaoth he is." And then famous Terri said: "Because you are so like my father, I shall give you plenty of food." "My lord," said Sabaoth, "God reward you! People used to say you were my son." And Terri went pale and begged his forgiveness. He quickly returned to Boeve. "See, here is Sabaoth, my own father." All of them now felt redoubled joy and quickly embraced; they asked for news of Josiane and he told them, because he knew all about it: "She is lodged with a worthy man." Meanwhile she went to rub off that herb which he had bought.

---

[256] 181:2966–67 **One day, just . . . distant lands** *querant . . . avesprés*: I have restored the original order of 2966—*querant lur seynur par ample regnez* (looking for . . . lands)—and 2967—*un jur quant dreit fu avesprés* (one day . . . nightfall), reversed by Stimming citing the Norse version. Stimming has emended 2967, a corrupt line.

Then Boeve and the wise Terri took the lady and brought her up into the palace. The duchess saw how lovely and rosy-cheeked she was, and said to Boeve: "Is this your cherished wife?" "Yes, my lady, I won't hide it from you." "Take your wife, and give me Terri." "That pleases me, by God!" said Boeve. The ladies rejoiced. Then Boeve asked for his sons: the forester, who was in charge of Gui, came, and the fisherman did not want to dawdle, because the messengers had told them the children's father was duke of the city of Civile. They made such progress on the way and the road that they arrived in Civile one bright morning. The courteous forester entered the palace, holding the young Gui by the hand, and the fisherman held the other, Miles the swift. Boeve saw them and welcomed them courteously.

Boeve's sons entered the palace; when he saw them, he was overjoyed and embraced them a hundred times over, giving their guardians many thanks. The splendid feast was soon under way, and the duchess married Terri. Young and old went to eat; Boeve and his sons willingly served them, and Josiane went in front with them. When they had finished eating,[257] the minstrels, well prepared, sang. Josiane tuned her fiddle[258] and played three songs for the love of Terri. That day many well-prepared knights[259] were ready to serve. Boeve's sons, who were well educated, went to play after the meal.[260] You can be sure that there was a great crowd. (2954–3034)

182. When Duke Boeve had separated his sons from the others, they next seized the chessboard and played against each other, for they were very skilled. Boeve asked for weapons of great worth and dubbed their guardians noble knights; he gave each of them four excellent war-horses and plenty of pure gold. They asked leave to depart and left. Great and small paid homage to Terri, and so did all the barons in the palace,[261] the dukes and the counts, as the book says.

Now you will hear a fine song about King Yvori and King Hermin. Yvori made war on him night and day, according to a palmer coming from the east. Boeve heard him and sent for Terri: "We shall send messengers through distant lands." They gathered fifteen thousand bold knights. (3035–52)

183. "Lord Boeve," said Terri, "I want to go with you." "By God, my lord," said Boeve, "don't do so. Should I summon you, come and help me. I shall take with

---

[257] 181:3027 **When they had finished eating:** *kant vent ke urent mangez:* literally, "when it came to [the fact that] they had finished eating." Stimming's emendaton of *vent* to *veit* is not necessary. I am grateful to Dr Djordjevic for this reading.

[258] 181:3029 **fiddle** *viele*: MS *vile*; a fiddle or a viol.

[259] 181:3031 **knights** *chevalers*: supplied by Stimming, but the missing word could also be *sergent* (men at arms) (Stimming, 163).

[260] 181:3033 **play** *juer*: almost certainly here means "fight" or "tussle."

[261] 182:3044 **and [. . .] all the barons in the palace** MS: *e tuz le barons que sont en paleis*. Stimming, citing the Norse version, alters the MS reading to *en pais* (in the land).

me Sabaoth the bearded, who would rather be cut to pieces than let me down." And Boeve had stayed so long at Civile that Terri had a son, I tell you truly, and Boeve a beautiful rosy-cheeked daughter; Terri's son was called Boeve and Boeve's daughter, Beatrice. Boeve saw to mounts for his family, Josiane and her daughter, whom he cherished. With them they had fifteen thousand armed men; they did not stop till they reached Abreford and sent a messenger to the king.

King Hermin was up in his tower and saw Boeve coming with fifteen thousand armed men. He called his princes and his vassals: "My lords, here outside I can see a deadly army." Then the messenger entered the palace. When Hermin saw him, he summoned him. "My lord," said the messenger, "don't be afraid! Boeve has arrived, the glorious and brave. Don't be fearful or scared, for he brings fifteen thousand armed men." And the king said: "God be thanked!" When he saw Boeve dismount, the king at once knelt, and Boeve ran to him and raised him up.[262] "Mercy!" said the king, "for the love of God! If I have done you wrong, it will certainly be put right." "My lord," said Boeve, "thanks, but we shall never be reconciled until I am avenged on those who judged me unfairly and wrongfully." "By God!" said the king, "you shall have them." He sent for Gocelyn and Furez;[263] Boeve seized them and had them cut to pieces. Reconciled, the king and Boeve entered the palace. Josiane saw them and came to them, and the king embraced her tenderly. "Now," said Josiane, "are you and Boeve reconciled?" "Yes, fair daughter, God be thanked." Josiane said: "You have indeed done very well: there is no better man in Christendom."

Then they entered the noble palace. Josiane entered her own chamber, took a *rote*[264]—a finer was never seen—and composed three lays before ceasing. Then the lords sat down to eat, and the children returned from their lodging. The king saw them and called them to him, and they came willingly and with pleasure. He kissed them, then asked them: "Which of you is the elder?" "Upon my word," said Miles, "you should know it is Gui: he is taller, strong and burly." They took off their cloaks and had a drink of wine. The king saw them and called them to him: "I will make Miles a duke and you a crowned king: my kingdom will be given to you." "My lord," said Gui, "please don't do so; please give it to my father, who will keep and protect it well. I have not yet been dubbed knight." That day the court was very joyful. They asked for wine and went off to bed.

---

[262] 183:3080; 3083 **the king at once knelt, and Boeve ran to him and raised him up** *le roi c'est tost agenulez*; *E Boves curt si li ad redressez*: I have restored the order of 3080 and 3083, changed by Stimming, citing the Norse version. See Sanders, *Bevers Saga*, 389.

[263] 183:3089 **Gocelyn and Furez** This is the first time the two knights who slandered Boeve (775–800) are named.

[264] 183:3100 **rote** *rote*: The rote was a triangular zither, with strings on both sides of the sound box. See Christopher Page, *Voices and Instruments of the Middle Ages* (London: J.M. Dent, 1987), 123.

Now we shall leave Hermin and tell of Yvori, the enemy. At Hermin's court there was a spy, who heard all about Boeve the wise, Sabaoth, Miles and Gui, the tried and tested, and about Josiane, whom Boeve had married. He went to Monbrant, found Yvori, and told him. And Yvori summoned his men from the whole country and came to Abreford with forty thousand soldiers and occupied a meadow outside the city; the noise they made was huge. And Boeve armed himself in the noble palace: he donned his hauberk and jewelled helmet, girded Morgeley on his left side, and mounted Arundel from the golden stirrups. With him were thirty thousand armed men. And Boeve gave swift Arundel free rein and in front of the rest struck an emir; he knocked him a full lance-length away, dead. And Sabaoth felled another dead. Boeve shouted: "Strike, my knights!" And they struck willingly and with pleasure. You could see a fierce battle start there — so many lances broken and shields pierced, Saracens struck down one on top of another. It turned out badly for Yvori de Monbrant: that day he lost fifteen thousand armed men. Then his troops retreated to the city of Monbrant. And Boeve and the bearded Sabaoth returned; the booty Boeve conquered was huge. King Hermin met them and said to Boeve: "Your renown is great." They disarmed and went to the palace.

Yvori de Monbrant — may God destroy him soon — returned and asked for his steward: "Fellow," he said, "what do you advise me? I've lost my men, which fills me with anger. The king has sent for a Frenchman;[265] I know for sure he is Josiane's lover." "My lord," said the steward, "you shall have good advice: send messengers from here to Babylon and summon the emir without delay." "And Yvori replied: "Now that's well said." Letters and covenants were quickly sealed; the messengers went on their way, not stopping till they reached Babylon. They soon told the emir about it, and he brought fifteen crowned kings with him, and each king brought fifteen thousand armed men. They arrived in Monbrant in summer. When Yvori saw them he was delighted. He went up and greeted them, brought them to the palace, and told them how King Hermin had treated him. And he told them he had taken his treasure and his wife Josiane, acclaimed for her beauty. Then the emir said: "My lord, can you prove it?" "Yes," said Yvori, "by pitting my body against his." "By God, that is well said," said the emir. (3053–3179)

184. Boeve had a spy at Monbrant, and when he saw such an assembly of lords, he at once made his way to Abreford to tell Hermin and the brave Boeve. When Boeve heard, he was angry and mortified. He quickly sent a messenger to Civile, to Duke Terri, to come and help him. And Terri brought a large number of men, a good fifteen thousand with bright and shining helmets, and with him he

---

[265] 183:3158 **Frenchman** *François*: it is surprising that Boeve is here referred to as French; see also 3614, 3622, and 3628 (all referring to his troops). But see Ian Short, "*Tam Angli Quam Franci*: Self-definition in Anglo-Norman England," *Anglo-Norman Studies* 18 (1995): 153–75.

brought his son Boeve. They rode so speedily by day and night that they reached Abreford as dawn broke. When Boeve saw them, he was very glad, mounted Arundel, and came towards them. He called to Terri and said, laughing: "How is your noble wife?" "Well, by God! She is strong and spirited and has given me three sons, great God be thanked! Look, here is the eldest, Boeve, skilled at riding." "By my head!" said Boeve, "that delights me even more." He kissed his godson; then they dismounted and Boeve told them about Yvori de Monbrant. (3180–3201)

185. Boeve and the duke entered the palace. The beautiful Josiane was delighted, and the king came to do honour to the duke. Miles and Gui came running; Terri was very pleased to see them. "My lord," said Terri, "to horse with all your knights! Let's go to Monbrant without delay! For a man who makes war should not hesitate." Then their equipment arrived; princes and dukes armed themselves, mounted their long-maned horses, went out of the gate, and rode hard, day and night. They lay in ambush outside Monbrant, in a leafy thicket, and when dawn came their army contained ten thousand about to seize their prey outside the city wall. In Monbrant the din and clamour grew; inside were more than forty thousand armed men. (3202–20)

186. Through the gate came the evil Saracens. In front of all the rest came Favon; he owned towers and castles in Arabia. He cried in a loud voice: "Wretches, you won't escape unharmed." And Terri heard him, as did noble Saber;[266] he struck sharp spurs into his horse, landed a great blow of a full lance-length on Favon, and felled him dead on the sand. The might of the evil Saracens was now growing; then Boeve arrived with thirty thousand companions. The fray was so deadly to see: so many shattered lances, so many split shields, so many knights collapsing on the sand! Boeve gave Arundel, the horse from Aragon, free rein, struck a Saracen, Fauseron, in the head, and knocked him quite dead from the saddle-bow. The others struck like good knights. (3221–37)

187. The battle was very harsh and violent. Boeve and Terri delivered very good blows, and Sabaoth the white-haired did not hold back; whoever his blow reached was doomed to die. At that moment Yvori appeared with ten thousand vicious men from Arabia. Boeve met him on the excellent Arundel and, in front of all the rest, went to strike Yvori; he gave him a great blow on his shield paint-

---

[266] 186:3225 **Saber** this is the only time this spelling of Sabaoth's name is used. Stimming changes the order of lines; in the MS 3225—*E Terri les condust e Saber li barons* (and Terri led them as did noble Saber)—stands before 3222, *Devant toz les altres est venu Favons* (in front of all the rest came Favon). Stimming changes *les condust* in 3225 to *l'entendit* (heard him).

ed with flowers, broke the valuable breast-harness [and saddle-girths],[267] and knocked him a full lance-length on to the field. He drew Morgeley and jumped on him, giving him a great blow on his shield painted with flowers; he would have dispatched and killed him, but Yvori cried: "Take me alive! I will give you as much ransom as you want." "By God!" said Boeve, "now I agree." He had him taken to King Hermin and his daughter, bright-faced Josiane; no man alive could rescue him. Sabaoth and Terri fought in the fray; Sabaoth killed the emir of Esclavonia,[268] then shouted: "Montjoie![269] Strike, brother knights!" His men heard him and were greatly cheered; the Christians pursued the enemy like brave and bold men. (3238–62)

188. The pursuit covered a good four miles; the pagans fled as far as Monbrant.[270] And Boeve returned to the great city of Abreford. Brave knights went to their lodgings; the children ran to disarm Boeve. "My lord," said Gui, "we are grown-up now: knight us and equip us." "My fair son," he said, "not this year; you are too young to suffer hardship." When they were disarmed, Boeve and Terri and the brave Sabaoth went in and saw Yvori sitting on a bench. "Will you accept a ransom?" said the king of Monbrant. (3263–75)

189. "Will you accept a ransom, my fair friend Boeve, or do you wish to hang and humiliate me?" "No, by my head!" said Boeve, "You will swear me oaths by your gods, Apollo, Mahomet, Tervagant and Baratron[271] too." And the king replied: "In such a fashion, willingly." The king swore to all that was asked; he named a ransom of silver and pure gold. (3276–83)

190. "Thirty horses laden with gold and silver; three hundred beds decorated with gold and silver, with all the quilts and pillows; three hundred cups, all with lids, and three thousand goblets of pure damascened gold; a hundred lions and a

---

[267] 187:3247 **[and saddle-girths]** *les cengles*: These words are added by Stimming, citing the Norse version.

[268] 187:3259 of **Esclavonia** *d'Eclavonie*: MS *de clanouie*: Stimming interprets this "garbled" name here as Eclavonie, and as Esclavonie in his Index of names. According to the editor of *Maugis d'Aigremont* (493; see n. 49) Esclavonie is the country of the Slavs.

[269] 187:3260 **Montjoie** *Monjoie*: this is a Frankish battle-cry; see *La Chanson de Roland*, ed. Frederick Whitehead, rev. T.D. Hemming (London and Bristol: Bristol Classical Press, 1993), 1181 etc.

[270] 188:3263–64 **The pursuit . . . Monbrant** *Li enchace dure . . . Monbrant*: I have restored the original order of these lines, which Stimming inverts, citing the Welsh and Norse versions.

[271] 189:3280 **Baratron** *Baratron:* On the names and possible derivations of the pagan gods Baratron and Tervagant, see Henri Grégoire, "L'Etymologie de Tervagant," *Mélanges offerts à Gustave Cohen* (Paris: Librarie Nizet, 1950), 67–74, at 69, 71.

hundred [bears],[272] chained, and a hundred pack-horses laden with lustrous silk mantles and with three thousand bowls with smaller dishes, all well worked in silver. I will give you all this in exchange for my life—fifteen thousand white hauberks adorned with gold lacquer and as many green jewelled helmets.[273] May I now be released?" "By my head!" said Boeve, "you shall give no more. Once the treasure has been shown to me, you can go, you will not be stopped."

Yvori called a messenger: "Go to the city of Monbrant and tell Fabur, my privy steward, to send me the ransom as I have described it." The messenger departed and found Fabur and told him how the king was held to ransom: "See here the letter I've brought you." Fabur took the letter, looked at it, and said to the emirs: "Now listen to this! Yvori isn't dead but in prison; he is held to ransom, and in this letter he asks for it." All the treasure was quickly assembled.[274] And they gave thanks to Mahomet that Yvori had survived; seven thousand pagans accompanied the treasure and arrived at Abreford in one day, and Boeve took it and Yvori departed. To tell the truth, that caused great harm, which then led to great injustice for Boeve, as you shall hear if you listen.

Now we shall stop speaking of Yvori and must return to Hermin. He was very sick and lay in an upper room. "My God," said Hermin, "through your goodness I have kept my kingdom for a long time. By God, bring me Gui, he shall be king tomorrow. I shall have him crowned, and Miles made a duke; I shall not change my mind. Thus I will bequeath my land." When Boeve heard this, he wept. The king had himself carried to church; he summoned the bishop and confessed, and was absolved of all his sins; he had made his peace with God. He sent for Gui and the wise Miles and dubbed them knights, as well as Boeve, Terri's son, and another two thousand. Then he had the crown brought before him and Gui crowned with it. Twelve bishops and abbots were there; the offering placed on the altar was large. Then the king died and angels carried his soul to God.[275] Gui was now a crowned king[276] and Miles an honoured duke. That day Hermin was placed in his coffin. When he was buried, they mounted their

---

[272] 190:3289 **bears** *urs*: added by Stimming, citing the Welsh version.

[273] 190:3293–95 **I will give ... helmets** *tant vus dorrai ... heumes gemmés*: I have restored the original order of these lines. Stimming puts *tant vus dorrai pur la vie aver* (I will give you all this in exchange for my life) after 3294, *e autretant de vert heumes gemmés* (and as many green jewelled helmets), citing the Welsh version.

[274] 190:3311–12 **All the treasure ... survived** *Tut le tresor ... il est eschapé*: I have restored the original order of these lines; Stimming placed *E mercient Mahom ke il est eschapé* (and they gave thanks to Mahomet that he had survived) after 3310—*a rançon est venu e ci l'ad demandé* (he is held to ransom and here he asks for it), citing the order in the Welsh version.

[275] 190:3341 **angels carried his soul to God** *l'alme aportent li angle a deus*: Hermin dies a Christian, but there is no mention of his conversion.

[276] 190:3342 **king** *roi*: The words "the king" after this refer to Gui (as in 3489, 3505, etc), until Boeve is made king of Monbrant, 3698.

horses.²⁷⁷ The one said to the other: "Cross the field and let's think about a joust! Fight me, for we don't know when we'll be put to the test. When my famous father sees us bearing arms, he'll be very glad." Then knightly blows were exchanged.²⁷⁸ "By my head!" said Boeve, "these were only youths; after this, if they live long enough, they will be as good as their father." They broke their lances on their shields, but their hauberks were strong and not damaged; the young men were good and neither fell. "Saint Mary, our Lady!" said Boeve the famous, "mercy, Lady, spare the children." In a loud voice he cried: "Stop your fighting!"

When the boys heard their father,²⁷⁹ they quickly went into the palace; when their father saw this, he went to meet them. When they had eaten, Sabaoth rose, came to Boeve, and asked leave to go. "My lord," said Sabaoth, "I have been with you seven years without seeing my wife or my lands." "My lord," said Boeve, "go, with God's leave. Take your wife a cloak edged entirely in pure beaten gold, and give her from me a golden cup—no better exists—and present her with twelve rings as a gift from me—no better were ever forged." He took leave of Boeve and all the others, and left in the guise of a pilgrim. Then the bearded Sabaoth made his way towards Civile, to Terri the famous, but he did not speak to him. (3284–3378)

191. The grizzled Sabaoth crossed the sea, and in Rome was given a severe penance by the Pope because he had been so long away from his wife. Then he came to St Gilles and to the great tree,²⁸⁰ took ship and sailed until he arrived in Hampton just as noon struck. He came to the gate of his large palace and met his wife and his son Robant; he asked for lodging for God's sake and in His name, and for the love of Sabaoth, the noble and white-haired. And the lady said: "Henceforth you will lack for nothing." They came walking up to the hall. "My lady," said Sabaoth, the courageous knight, "Boeve, the brave and bold, sends you greetings and regards on the part of the noble Sabaoth, and on the part of Boeve's most powerful sons, and on the part of the beautiful Josiane, and on the part of Duke Terri, your dear child." When the lady heard this, she was overjoyed. "Did you ever see Sabaoth the old?" "Yes, lady, and Boeve, not long ago; and Boeve sends you a large and fair mantle, all worked in pure shining gold—there's none like it as far as Abilent—and twelve rings and a big cup." Well then, are you then, my lord, Sabaoth the old?" "Yes, fair lady, by St Laurence!" (3379–3405)

---

²⁷⁷ 190:3345 their horses *es chevaus*: missing in the MS and supplied by Stimming, citing the Welsh version.
²⁷⁸ 190:3351 **Then knightly blows were exchanged** *Ore purrez vere cops de chevalers*: literally, then you could see knightly blows.
²⁷⁹ 190:3360 **father** *ancez*: an untraceable word, but one which may be a mistake for *ancesur*, forbear.
²⁸⁰ 191:3382 **St Gilles** *Sent Gile*: see note to line 2736. Nothing is known about the great tree there; see Stimming 166.

192. When she heard him, she began to look at him; by the lines of his mouth she knew the warrior. Then the lady ran to embrace her lord. Now Sabaoth is in Hampton by the sea, and we must return to Boeve.

Yvori had a thief in the city of Monbrant; no walls would keep him out, however smooth. He had nails as long as a moulted hawk's, and was called Gebitus in his land. Yvori summoned him: "Friend, come here; I've seen many of your magic arts. If you can steal Boeve's horse for me, I shall give you plenty of castles and riches." And the thief said: "By Mahomet, you shall have him." Then the scoundrel set off and came to Abreford when it was night; like a bird he climbed the wall and came to the stable without stopping. He saw Arundel, the famous horse; he opened the door without asking for a key and placed such a spell on the horse that he could seize him by the legs. Then he mounted him and rode towards Monbrant and came to the city at daybreak. And the king showed great arrogance, swearing by Mahomet and Apollo, his gods, that Boeve would run into great trouble. Boeve's squires got up in the morning; when they did not see the horse, they were furious. A groom went to Boeve and told him; when Boeve heard, he was nearly frantic.

Now we shall stop talking about Boeve and must return to Sabaoth, lying in his chamber beside his wife. He dreamt that Boeve was wounded and the main bone in his thigh was broken. He told his wife of the dream when he woke. "My lord," she said, "you delay too long; he has lost either his wife or his valuable horse." "Alas!" said Sabaoth, "now I'm in trouble." He took his pilgrim's palmbranch and iron staff, took his leave, and set off, not stopping till he reached Abreford. Sabaoth entered the splendid palace. Boeve was very glad of his coming.[281] "Master," said Boeve, "my horse has been taken; Yvori's thief has stolen my horse." "Alas!" said Sabaoth, "I stayed away too long." He took his staff, left the palace, and took the road with great anger, not stopping till the evening. A groom was giving Yvori's horses a drink, and Sabaoth came up to the ford; there the old, bearded man sat down. (3406–58)

193. When Arundel saw him, he recognised him very well. Sabaoth said to the groom: "As you hope Mahomet will save you, where does this horse come from? There's nothing to be seen like him. Show me his rear, I've seen the front." And the young man said: "You'll soon see." He turned the rear of Arundel the longmaned towards him, and Sabaoth nimbly leapt behind the man, raised his staff and struck him next to his eye, so that he knocked him dead. Once Sabaoth had mounted the long-maned horse, he came spurring straight towards the city.[282] (3459–69)

---

[281] 192:3448–49 **Sabaoth ... coming** *Sabaoth ... lee*: These two sentences are in inverted order in the MS.

[282] 193:3468–69 **Once ... horse; he ... city** *Kant ... quernu; dreit ... venu*: The two halves of this sentence are in inverted order in the MS.

194. In a loud voice he shouted: "Yvori de Monbrant, Arundel is taken; bad luck is coming your way." When Yvori heard this, he was mortified and angry and shouted in a loud voice: "To horse, my kinsmen!" A whole thousand quickly armed, all chasing Sabaoth the old; Fabur impetuously rushed ahead of the rest, mounted on the son of the mettlesome Arundel. And Sabaoth quickly fled, pursued fiercely by hundreds and thousands. Josiane was high up in the palace;[283] she looked through a window towards Monbrant, and she saw Sabaoth come galloping on Arundel. She came to Boeve and her son Gui: "My lord, arm all your men; hundreds of Arabs are pursuing Sabaoth. He is bringing Arundel, for whom you were so distressed." "Arm, my lords!" said the young Gui. With that, a good fifteen thousand took arms. The king went out first, on a grey horse, followed by Miles on a piebald and Boeve, son of Terri, on a black horse. Fabur now reached Sabaoth and had given him a first blow when the king spurred up, broke Fabur's lance with his sharp blade, and struck him on the front of his helmet, splitting it down to the mouth. At once he shattered the hauberk and knocked him down, a full lance-length, bleeding and dead. Sabaoth climbed into the saddle of the good grey horse to give swift Arundel a rest, for he did not know that Boeve had come into the field. And Miles gave his horse its head and struck an emir; Boeve, Terri's son, killed a giant; and each killed and defeated his man. The king ordered: "Strike on!" [and][284] now they all struck. They were very weary from the long pursuit. The fight lasted till the bell for vespers; only four hundred of Yvori's men returned. And Gui [and Miles][285] returned with fine and rich booty, not resting till [they] reached Abreford. Their father and mother were glad and joyful at their children's return from battle; they gave glory to God who created Moses. Five hundred men ran to disarm them.

Then a consultation about Monbrant started. "My fair son," said Boeve, "harm will befall us if the barons let us down. Let's send for Terri to come and help us; I shall give your sister to his son Boeve." "My lord," said the king, "at your command." (3470–3521)

195. The king sent for a messenger: "You will go to the city of Civile and tell the noble Duke Terri to come and help us, out of his goodness." The messenger went on his way without stopping and found Duke Terri at Civile; he greeted him and spoke: "The king of Hermin's people sends me to ask you to help and succour him." "By my faith!" said Terri, "gladly and willingly." He summoned his men from throughout the kingdom; four dukes and four counts gathered

---

[283] 194:3480 *en paleis en haut*: Stimming adds *mandement* (dwelling) after *en haut* to emend the assonance and the short line. See Sanders, *Bevers Saga*, 389.

[284] 194:3506 **[and]** *e*: added by Stimming, citing the Welsh version, as also in 3508 (*E l'estur dure . . .*).

[285] 194:3510 **and Miles** *e Miles*: added by Stimming, citing the Welsh version, though the verb in 3511 is singular (*n'out recetement*).

there, each accompanied by ten thousand armed men. Terri called to them and addressed them in this way: "My lords, we will go into a foreign land, for I dare not fail famous Boeve." The duke called for his good horse, and they crossed the land and distant kingdoms and came to Abreford at dawn. The king had climbed into a tower and saw the lords from the city of Civile. He came to his father and told him that Terri had arrived with his barons, and his father replied: "God be thanked!" Then the knights, who acted wisely, dismounted; Boeve and Josiane went to meet them, and Boeve told them how Yvori had attacked them. Terri replied: "They'll be the worse for it: I've brought a fierce band of men with me."

Now we shall speak of Yvori, the proven deceiver. The next day Yvori rose and summoned fifteen emirs and fifteen kings, and they came willingly and gladly. They rode together, furiously, not stopping till they reached Abreford. Those inside the city heard the noise; the king shouted: "To arms, by God!" They mounted their horses quickly and soon, and came out of the gates in serried rows and ranks. Then Yvori called Judas and Masebré. "My lords," he said, "I need advice as to whether I should take arms against the famous Boeve. Never was a better fighter knighted, while I am the best out of all my kin." The king of Damascus[286] said: "Then fight him." Yvori quickly mounted his horse and shouted to the famous Boeve in a loud voice: "My lord, Duke Boeve, wait a little. Inside the city you have a great band of lords, and here outside I have kings and emirs. If they come to blows, losses will be great. If you'll agree to a one-on-one fight, and if I'm killed or vanquished and captured, I'll make you a confirmed king and emir; all my land will be renounced in your favour as well as the fine keep in the city of Monbrant." And Boeve replied: "I say the same to you, and I willingly grant you battle." Then they extended their hands and promised it. Quickly they armed themselves. (3522–81)

196. Now, armed and on excellent horses, they crossed the ford[287] and reached the other side. Boeve invoked God, who does not lie; Yvori invoked Mahomet and Apollo. Then they mounted their glossy horses and struck each other great blows on their Persian shields. Their hauberks were strong and did not break. Their swords shattered from the blows they gave; they rode past each other with neither falling. Boeve drew Morgeley and went to strike Yvori, giving him a great blow on his gleaming helmet; he cut the precious stones and ornaments down the middle, hit the horse in front of the saddle-bow, and slit it in two. When this happened to the horse, Yvori fell. He rose and Boeve dismounted; he did not want Arundel to be harmed. When Yvori saw Boeve had dismounted, he drew his sword and gave him a great blow. (3582–3600)

---

[286] 195:3566 **Damascus** *Damacle*: *macle* in MS.

[287] 196:3583 **crossed the ford** *le gué passent*: There is a possible reference to a combat on an island (a *holmgang*) here; Stimming (168) cites the English and Norse versions in support. See Gui's combat with Amoraunt, 8449–51.

197. On top of the helmet, where the gold was, he knocked out precious stones and ornaments. And Boeve was ashamed of receiving this blow: turning suddenly at full gallop,[288] he struck him with great force, breaking his neck and cutting off his head. The body fell to the ground, the soul went to Beelzebub. When the pagans[289] saw this, they charged into the ford, and King Gui turned his long-maned horse round, and Boeve stopped and went to his horse, and Miles arrived like a valiant and brave man. The battle at that crossing was terrifying. Gui the king spurred his horse and struck Bralu, the king of Damascus and Brandon's son. The French did well and showed great courage; Miles gave his horse free rein and felled a king. (3601–15)

198. Another was killed by Boeve, Terri's son, and a third knocked down by the white-haired Sabaoth; Terri of Civile killed an emir. And Boeve of Hampton struck such a blow that the battle rapidly became very fierce. He crushed the Saracens next to a stream. The French acted like bold and brave men, seizing three emirs and fifteen kings. Then they went to Monbrant the famous. The emir, the Saracen lord, said: (3616–25)

199. "If you want to have the land of Monbrant, you need to arm yourselves with pagan weapons." The French armed themselves, the brave knights. The emir of Cordes[290] said: "I shall lead the way. If you wish I'll become a Christian and believe in God and abandon Tervagant." And the fifteen kings said the same to them. Upon that, they spurred forwards; the emir was the first to enter Monbrant. King Gui followed him quickly, with the fifteen thousand following him. Outside was Boeve, committing great slaughter. When the pagans saw this, they were most unhappy and at once dropped the portcullis.[291] And yet King Gui entered with twenty thousand brave knights. Now he came to Yvori's palace, and the pagans saw him and turned to flee; neither great nor small were spared. If they did not invoke God and ask to be baptised, never again would they see wives or children.

At that moment, Duke Boeve arrived and entered the city with all his men, and King Gui went to meet him. "My lord," said he, "I present you with the land

---

[288] 197:3604 **a tor François** *at full gallop*: Although the text does not say so, Boeve has clearly remounted.

[289] 197:3607 **when the pagans saw this** *Kant ceo veient paien*: Stimming adds *paien*, which is missing in the MS.

[290] 199:3629 **Cordes** Cordoba; see Flutre 226.

[291] 199:3638 **When the pagans saw this** *Kant ceo virent paiens*: The train of events is unclear. Yvori has been defeated, so Monbrant should fall to Boeve (3576–77), but Boeve and his troops still have to fight for it. He takes prisoner three emirs; one or two of these (one from Cordoba, one unspecified), offer him advice, and they, and fifteen kings also captured, accept Christianity, become Boeve's allies, and enter Monbrant. It is the pagans within the city who try to keep the Christians out by dropping the portcullis.

of Monbrant." "My fair lord," said Boeve, "thank you." They sent for Josiane in the great city of Abreford, and all the clerks and learned bishops, and they came without delay. They also sent for the king of Damascus. Whoever wanted to embrace Christianity suffered no loss but was meekly baptized. The king of Damascus said: "Listen to what I think: I want to be christened and will abandon Tervagant." The others said: "We wish the same." Gui[292] said: "Bring Tervagant forward." And they placed him in an upright position. "Mahomet," said Boeve, "you were never powerful; now, today, perform a great miracle!" He took a club and struck Tervagant, and Bishop Morant threw holy water over him; a red dog came rushing out. "Now see," said Boeve, "what you believe in." The king of Damascus said: "Our belief is erroneous and so was our ancestors'. May God overthrow anyone who henceforth believes in him!" The kings and the four emirs said: "We will never believe in him as long as we live." They quickly sent for their wives and their children, for their friends and their relatives, and everyone came willingly and humbly. God never made a cleric so expert at reading aloud[293] who could describe to you how big the gathering was: the great baptism was extraordinary, lasting a good four months before it ended. Bishop Morant exhorted them powerfully;[294] his sermon was such that they were all in tears and beat their breasts in repentance. God was glad and the devil was wretched. (3626–84)

200. Now hear how wise Boeve was: he sent for the Pope, who willingly came, took to the water and set sail, two bishops and other clergy with him. They did not stop till they reached Monbrant, and there the Pope of Rome arrived. (3685–90)

201. Great and small came to meet him. It was Pentecost, a splendid feast-day. They carried the crown forward, and the noble Pope blessed it and put it on the head of brave Boeve; next he crowned beautiful Josiane. Then there was much joy. At that moment, four messengers came before the king, crying in a loud voice: "Where is the noble Sabaoth?" When Sabaoth heard this, he rose to his feet. "I am he, " he said, "whom you seek." "The king is disinheriting your son

---

[292] 199:3661 **Gui said** *Dist Gui*: Stimming has substituted *Boves* for *Gui*, citing the Welsh and Norse versions.

[293] 199:3677 **cleric so expert at reading aloud** *clerc si bien lisant*: Stimming (169) suggests "at studying." Wace describes himself as a *clerc lisant*, a cleric with probably specific duties such as writing, teaching, reading aloud, interpreting texts etc., i.e. a lector or reader (in minor orders). See Wace, *The Roman de Rou*, trans. Glyn S. Burgess (St Helier, Jersey: Société Jersiaise, 2002), xvii.

[294] 199:3680–81 **lasting a good ... powerfully** *bien dure ... Morant*: Stimming, citing the Norse and Welsh versions, has inverted the order of these lines in the MS, where *bien dure quatre moys ke ne fist fenant* (lasting a good four months before it ended) occurs after 3681, *Bien les sermonne l'eveske Morant* (Bishop Morant exhorted them powerfully); see, however, Sanders, *Bevers Saga*, 390.

Robant." When Sabaoth heard this, he was angry and unhappy. Sabaoth said: "This is bad: the king disinherits me and leaves me nothing." "My friend," said Boeve, "wait out this year." "My lord," said Sabaoth, "at your command." Sabaoth said to the messenger: "Now return, and tell my wife and my son Robant to wait for me at the great rock." The messengers returned without delay. The assembly of barons was large and there was great joy; the court lasted for a full two months. The Pope departed, and Boeve remained at the court in Monbrant. Then Duke Terri came before him: "My lord, I will take my leave if it pleases you." "You shall not go now," said the king of Monbrant, "we shall go and help Robant in England." Duke Terri said: "At your command." The king got ready and summoned his men; he left ten thousand foot-soldiers to protect his land, and with him took forty thousand brave knights. Then the noble Boeve went to England, and Terri and his two sons went readily with him, along with old Sabaoth and many brave knights. They arrived at Cologne with Bishop Morant. (3691–3727)

202. Then the king[295] set sail vigorously and arrived on the sands at Hampton. The lady and fair-haired Robant came to meet him. When the king saw him, he addressed him: "My lord, noble sir, how do things stand?" "By God, my lord, the king holds everything we possess." "By my head!" said Boeve, "we shall conquer it for you." People from the town spurred to the city of London and described Boeve and his great army, such as men had never seen. When the king heard, his forehead broke out in sweat; he summoned his lords from throughout England. (3728–39)

203. They heard the news and came willingly, not stopping till they reached London. The king saw them and addressed them thus: "Boeve has arrived; he bears a crown and his son rules over all Hermin's subjects. I think he has come to make war on me, and I fear the approach of death. I have a daughter, who is my heir: I will give her to his son, if you advise me so." The counts said: "We certainly consent." The king summoned the bishop of London and four counts, wise Boeve's uncles; they[296] went speedily to Hampton and courteously told Boeve about the marriage and greeted the king, as you shall hear, on behalf of King Edgar, their liege lord. When Boeve saw his uncles, he kissed them. They told him the news about the marriage. "My lords," said Boeve, "give him many thanks, but I dare not; I think he is angry because he has oppressed Robant so much." "Not at all," said his uncles, "he has no such thought." That night the counts brought him there, but he did not come to London so poorly equipped that his people did not number twenty thousand armed men. They came before the king with all speed,

---

[295] 202:3728 **the king** *li rois*: Here and at 3754, "the king" is Boeve, king of Monbrant.

[296] 203:3752 **they** *cil*: I have followed the reading of the MS and omitted the *e* (and) which Stimming inserts before "they," citing the Welsh and Norse versions.

and the king saw Boeve and raised his head. "Come here, my lord king, and kiss me; I will give my honoured daughter to your son." When Boeve heard him, he gave him many thanks. And King Edgar said: "Illness afflicts me. Have your son Miles brought before me so that my daughter may have him for husband." He had them married in the chapel: the bishop of London performed the ceremony. Then they were brought back to the splendid palace. King Edgar said: "Miles, come here! I have given you my daughter and my kingdom." "Many thanks, my fair lord," said Miles the wise. In front of the barons, Miles was crowned. That day the king died and his soul went to God. They kept watch over him until dawn,[297] and in the morning his body was buried. Then they had Miles crowned; barons and counts gathered and did him homage once they had eaten.

Now Boeve was a crowned king, as were his two sons, as God had destined it. They were well revenged on all their enemies. They stayed there for a fortnight and then returned. Boeve entrusted his son to Sabaoth, and he vowed and swore that all his life he would not fail him. The king made for the city of Hampton, came to its port, and took ship; he rowed and sailed so swiftly that they arrived this side of Cologne. Terri took leave to return to his land; in their lifetime they would not see each other again. That night Boeve came to the city of Cologne, [and][298] in the morning took his leave and once again crossed lands and countries and arrived in the good city of Rome. There he made Morant archbishop of his kingdom. (3740–3804)

204. And Boeve and his son travelled quickly: they took to the sea and sailed, not stopping till they reached Monbrant, where they went up to the palace of gleaming marble. They found Josiane, the queen, lying sick. She saw her husband and called him forward: "My lord, I am very sick; I shall not last long." When King Boeve heard this, he was beside himself. "Lady, if you die, I will die too." "My lord, who will rule your great estates?" "Lady, I don't care, I commend them to God. I've still got three children, thank God, who can rule our great estates." At once he called for the archbishop:[299] "Do whatever my lady commands." And the archbishop replied: "My lord, gladly." He confessed her and said what she desired. Boeve went looking for his war-horse; in the stable he found it lying dead and cold. He came away abruptly in tears, met his son Gui, and told him lovingly: "Now my horse is dead, and your mother is dying in there." When Gui the king heard him, he was almost frantic, and came to his mother to bring her comfort. "My lady, you will be the death of my brave father: I've never seen anything

---

[297] 203:3781–82 **and his soul . . . dawn** *e l'alme . . . ajornez*: In the MS 3781, *e l'alme s'en va a dampnedeus* (and his soul went to God) and 3782, *La nuit ly veilerent deskes ajornez* (they kept watch over him till dawn) are inverted.

[298] 203:3801 **[and]** *e*: added by Stimming, using the Welsh version.

[299] 204:3818 **the archbishop** *l'erseveske*: the MS has *son eveske* (his bishop), repeated in 3819.

as great as his grief." "My fair son," she said, "call Boeve to me." The young man called Boeve, and he came running. When he saw the lady, he took her in his arms and commended Gui, their child, to God. Then the lady died and Boeve too; the angels carried their souls to the blest. That night they kept watch until the next day. It was not at all the king's desire that they should lie in the ground, like other people. He had a tomb of gleaming marble made for them; they were carried to church by bishops and great kings, to the church built in honour of St Laurence. Gui was crowned king over the land of Monbrant. May God who made the firmament save us! Our song is ended, it lasts no longer; I will tell you no more in words or in song. (3805–46)

205. Thus finishes the tale, properly told, of Boeve of Hampton with the fearless face. I have read it to you and you have heard it. It would be courteous to give me my reward. (3847–50)

Gui de Warewic

Since the time God was born, and since the establishment of Christianity, many marvellous things have happened which are not known to all men. For this reason, one should make many inquiries, and try hard to do well, and follow the examples of good men, of the deeds and words of those in the past, who lived before us. Splendid adventures happened to them, because they always loved truth, faith, and loyalty. We should indeed remember them by hearing and telling about their good deeds. Whoever hears much, and remembers it, often becomes very wise. He who acts wisely and eschews folly is held as commendable. We wish to tell the tale of a well-regarded count, of a seneschal of his, brave and loyal, and of the seneschal's son, a young man both noble and handsome, and how he loved a most beautiful maiden, the count's daughter.[1] (1–26)

In England there was a count who lived in the city of Warwick. He was wealthy and powerful, clever and wise—a good knight. His wealth lay in gold and silver, silken garments, tableware, strong castles, and prosperous cities. Throughout the kingdom he was much feared: there was no one in the whole land who dared to make war on him whom he would not at once seize and put in his dungeon. He greatly loved good knights and often gave them rich gifts. Thus he was respected, feared, and esteemed throughout the kingdom. He was a count of great renown, lord of the whole region; in those days the whole honour[2] of Oxford was his, and he was called lord of the whole county of Buckingham. (27–48)

The count was named Rualt; he was a most noble baron. He had a daughter by his wife. I cannot describe the daughter's great beauty, but she was regarded as the most beautiful alive. Now I ought to tell you a little about her great beauty: her face was pink and white, long and shapely and pleasing; she had a lovely mouth and a becoming nose, sparkling eyes and blonde hair; time would seem to stand still to anyone contemplating her. Her body was well made, of a good height, and her glance was gentle. She was courteous and learned, instructed in all the arts: her tutors, all hoary and white-haired, had come from Toledo and

---

[1] 1 **Since the time** *Puis cel tens*: C has eight lines which act as a coda to its previous item and an introduction to *Gui*.

[2] 45 **honor** *l'onur*: An honor is a lordship of several manors, held by one paramount baron.

taught her astronomy, arithmetic, and geometry. She had a very proud heart. Because she was so wise, she was sought by dukes and counts who came from many lands for her sake. But she would love none of them because she was so noble. Felice was the name of the beautiful girl, who was greatly loved for her beauty. She was the flower of all beauties; no one was so beautiful at that time, nor would a search of many lands find one so beautiful. It would take too long to describe her beauty completely. (49–82)

We will leave the girl and talk about the seneschal, who was most courteous and wise. He was a man of noble birth, wealthy and courageous; no one was better at that time, nor was there any so esteemed for feats of arms, for he had been in many lands to pursue his renown. Thus he was most worthy of praise. He was born in Wallingford and all the region there belonged to him, so he was noble and proud; on this side of the sea there was none so good nor who always served his lord with such great honour. There was no count in the whole land who dared to wrong his lord without the seneschal being aroused, for love of his master, to attack and forcibly capture him at once, to the point of going as far as Scotland. He kept all his lord's land so honourably, and in such peace, that if a man were to carry about a quantity of silver, he would not encounter a single robber or thief wanting to steal a pennyworth from him. I've heard the seneschal was called Sequart; such a man should be much esteemed. He was loyal, brave, and good as long as he lived. I never heard of a better seneschal or of a more praiseworthy. (83–116)

This Sequart had a most courteous and wise son. He was beloved by all, and wanted to give what he had to everyone. He served Count Rualt, his rightful lord, who loved and cherished him above all others; he made him sleep in his chamber and be his cupbearer. As long as he was with him, Rualt honoured him greatly because of his good father, whom he loved so much. The son's name was Gui of Warwick, and he was held in high regard in the court by knights and men at arms, both high and low. There was no one so humble in the household who did not receive a rich gift from him. No young man in the kingdom was so loved and praised. Because he was both handsome and brave, and surpassed everyone in goodness, they all constantly looked at him. He was very handsome and well-proportioned; Dame Nature had gone to great trouble to make such a fine creature. He possessed every virtue, and every one spoke very well of his jousting and fencing, and his skill in both spurring and restraining horses. (117–46)

This Gui had a tutor, called Herald of Arderne. He was courteous and learned, and instructed Gui very well in dealing with dogs, birds, goshawks, falcons, and girfalcons. If anyone asked Gui for anything,[3] he gave it him readily—he often

---

[3] 153 **If anyone asked Gui for anything** *Ki que unques rien li demanda*: the French does not make it clear whether it is Heralt or Gui who is generous, but one of the English MSS of *Guy of Warwick* (Caius 107) specifies Gui (the passage is omitted from the Auchinleck manuscript).

made rich gifts to poor knights and prisoners, bestowing on them palfreys, hunters, and chargers most willingly. Each, according to who he was, received a fine gift from him. (147–60)

It happened that the count held a feast on the day of Pentecost. People were gathered as usual in his fine city of Warwick: counts and barons were there, from many lands, as well as ladies and young women, the loveliest in the land. Many maidens entertained their lovers there, from amongst the knights who had arrived, and the knights did likewise with the maidens who had come. When they had returned from church and entered the hall, the count sat down to eat. He saw Gui before him, the son of Sequart the seneschal (whom God keep from harm). So he summoned him, and ordered him to go to the chamber and greet his daughter Felice, and to serve her that day, to her great pleasure. "My lord," he said, "I will most readily do your command." He entered the chamber dressed in a tunic of rich cloth that suited him very well—nothing could have improved on it. He was fair, handsome, and well proportioned; the maidens were very attentive to him. He knelt before Felice and gave her her father's greeting: how he had been sent to her that day to serve her according to her wishes. And then she replied: "Fair sir, I thank him!" Then Felice asked him who he was and what was his birth. "I am son of Sequart, the seneschal, whom your father loves and considers trustworthy; he has brought me up in his court and I thank him for the great kindness he has shown me." (161–204)

"So you are Sequart's son?" said she. "They say you are well-bred." Then water was called for and the maiden washed her hands. Gui took pains to serve her well and as much as she wished; he applied himself to good service. There were more than thirty maidens there, who that day all fell in love with Gui, but that was of no concern to him, for another love afflicted him. He had been taken so unawares by love for the beautiful Felice with her radiant face that he had no idea what to do at any moment, so overwhelmed with love was he. From then on, he kept sighing and was pensive. When he saw her radiant face and fair body, he was struck with wonder about such a lovely creature. He did not dare show her any love; he hardly dared look at her in case anyone were to notice. Then he considered what to do, but for now he wanted to stay quiet and reveal himself to nobody. [4] He went to the maidens and charged them with serving the lady; then he begged leave of them and with that left the chamber. He returned to his lodging quite sorrowful and distressed. His retinue asked him what was the matter and why he was sad. And he told them that such an illness had come upon him that he thought he would die; he thought he would never recover. They lamented greatly over him in court; nobody's grief for him was feigned, because he was frequently of service to them and often provided fine lodgings. (205–46)

---

[4] 230 **reveal himself to nobody** *A nul ne se voldra descovrir*: After this line, F adds 8 lines.

Now Gui was in great uncertainty; he sighed and thought what to do about this feeling of love that pulled him about so badly. He often called himself unfortunate. "What shall I do, alas, wretch that I am? Alas the day I ever saw bright-faced Felice! I daren't show her the pain I feel because of her, both night and day, nor will I ever show her—I won't dare do it. And then isn't she the daughter of my lord, whom I should greatly respect? If I loved her and he knew of it, he could then punish me and he would have me burnt or beheaded, strung up high or drowned in the sea. So what shall I do, alas? I love someone I'll never have." (247–64)

Now Gui was in such anguish that he did not know what he could do, so he got up when he should have been lying down, and stayed awake when he should have slept. He could neither eat nor drink, nor could anyone ever comfort him. In his heart he decided nobody alive should know about it. "Better to pine," he said, "until I must die here, than that the count should have me killed or puts me in his dungeon." Gui led his life in this way until the festival was over. Then he reflected: "What shall I do? How wretched I am! There is no respite from suffering; I don't dare tell her about my pain. It's a frequent saying: they say that necessity knows no law. Love forces me to go; whether I like it or not, I must show the misery and severe pain which continually afflict me. My misery is nothing to her; at the moment she cares little for my life. Whether good or bad comes of it, indeed I won't any longer, on any account, hesitate to go to her. I'll put myself entirely at her mercy; she can kill me, do what she likes with me. It's certainly better if she kills me than that I continue to live in this way." (265–98)

Then Gui came to court, weak, wretched, and distressed. He knelt before Felice and said most piteously: "Noble Felice, I beg you for God's sake to take pity on me, wretched creature that I am, so that I don't find you so cruel to me that you don't hear my prayer. From now on, I can no longer conceal—it is love that makes me speak—the great pain and misery which I suffer both night and day for you. You are what I most desire; my heart can't leave you. I love you above all else; the threat of death will not prevent me loving you always, as long as I live. There's nothing under heaven, whether good or evil, which I wouldn't do for your love; I wouldn't refuse it on pain of death. You are my life and my death; I have no solace without you. I love you much more than myself; I would die in great distress for you. If you don't show me pity, I shall be in great danger. If you knew the great sadness I have for love of you, and the severe pain and grief which I suffer for you both night and day, I would know for sure that you would have mercy on me." (299–332)

The lovely Felice replied: "Aren't you that Gui who is the son of Seneschal Sequart? Now I think you're really a fool for asking me for love; you're certainly too bold. At heart you value me little and think me a fool when you ask me to love you. It's a poor school that has brought you up. Am I not your lord's daughter? You do me great dishonour when you are so foolish as to ask me to become your beloved. I have never found a man who has said as much to me, or made such requests for love—neither duke, count, nor baron. Were I now to love a boy who is my vassal, and rightly so, my beauty would be very ill-used. Were I now to love you, and refuse so many noble men, dukes, counts, and barons (all the way to the mountains there are none so mighty) who want me above all else, while never having seen me, I would be marrying well below my rank and never enjoy life again. You imagined a foolish thing, Gui, when you spoke to me of love, for, by the faith I owe my mother, if I go and tell my father, he'll cut off your limbs and have you pulled apart by horses, which would serve as a good warning against folly to those who would dishonour the daughter of their lord. Get up quickly, go; see you never come back!" (333–72)

Then Gui left in sorrow, despondent, wretched, and distressed. He returned to his lodging. His heart was so full of pain it nearly burst. He sat down, then got up. Since he dared not seek out Felice once more, he no longer knew what to do. He went off into a chamber and shut himself in; there he was, displaying such grief, rending his clothes and tearing his hair, that anyone under heaven seeing his misery would have pitied him. He complained bitterly about love, which caused him such torment: "Love, relieve this pain you have sent, so deadly for me! Love, in this unexpected situation you treat me with such cruelty! Love, you brought this madness to my heart: relieve me a little so I can rest! Then I would be better able to endure the hurt. I 'm suffering so much and lamenting: Love, make me crazy, so I can punish myself; I've taken on too much trouble!" (373–400)

Love made him fall to the ground; love made him suddenly shudder; love made him remove his clothes. He kept calling himself miserable and weak. "What shall I do, and what can I do? I certainly don't want to live! Most of all, I want to die, for that would please me. Oh death, what keeps you? I am so defeated by love! Why don't you come and take me? I've quite gone out of my mind. I'll never again have joy in my life, and I certainly don't care who hears it. I've well deserved to die, when the woman who hates me more than anything else is the very one I love more than my life. This will make me go quite mad. He is considered a madman who hangs such a burden around his neck that he can carry it no further and must thus collapse. That's just what I have done; alas, what shall I do? I desire the one woman I shall never have." (401–24)

He went to the window and looked at the castle tower. "Tower, how beautiful you are!" he said. "My lady, at the moment enjoying herself, lives in you. For love she rewarded me ill. Would you were demolished and strewn over the ground! Then I would see my beloved who's made my life so hard!" Again he wept, sighed, and was melancholy; then his grief began once more and he fell, he swooned, he rolled around the floor in pain. Love had injured him so much that he cursed the hour he was born. "Curse you, Love! You possess too great a power; I can't defend myself against you and must place myself at your mercy. Better at once to die for you than languish for a long time in pain. Ah, Felice, would I had never seen you and served you in your chamber. I took great pains to serve you.

You know how to reward my good acts very badly. I love you, but you don't love; love isn't evenly divided. I get the bad and you the good; you feel nothing of what I feel. You are very cruel when, for a look that you once gave me (and then spoke no more to me), I must die. From the moment you looked at me, you poisoned me with your gaze; my heart has perished from the poison, from which my body will never be cured." (425–62)

Gui led his life like this every day of the week. It distressed his father deeply, as well as lady Sabine, his good mother, and the count's heart too was heavy on his account. And the knights in the paved hall grieved greatly for Gui. The count sent him his doctors, to discover what illness he had. The doctors quickly went to Gui and found him despondent and wretched. Then they asked him where his illness hurt him most. Gui replied: "I feel great heat, much hotter than burning fire, which burns and destroys all my body—that is my life day and night. Cold follows the burning heat and is worse for me, for I'm colder than ice and so don't know what to do. Each limb fails, making me swoon three or four times. Such, sirs, is my entire life; I don't know what else I can tell you about it." A doctor said: "It's fever." "True," said Gui, " it's extremely difficult to treat."[5] (463–90)

The doctors went away and he stayed behind, lamenting most bitterly: "Oh God, dear Lord, what shall I do? How long will this torment last? Why can't I die now, since I can't see her as I wish? Why does Felice deny me this? What wrong have I done her? Nothing, indeed, except that I've loved her so much: that I can never regret. If I entreat her, her father will find out—what does it matter?—and will have me torn limb from limb. But he doesn't know, and if he did, he can't do worse than kill me; if he killed me it would be wrong. Should death deter me from going to talk to her and showing her my huge suffering? If one dares to love, there's nothing under heaven bolder than love. If she reproaches me in any way at all, I will call love to witness that love made me come there; I could not find the strength to hold back." (491–514)

Then Gui got up and went to the door. "God!" he said, "I'm behaving so much like a fool. My folly will rebound on my own head,[6] as I now go seeking my death!" He leant on the door and fell in a faint; and then, when he got up again, he said: "Oh God, what shall I do? It's no wonder I'm dismayed. I shall go to court, whether good or ill comes of it." (515–26)

Gui then came to court, pale, blanched, and crushed. He went into an orchard and found the beautiful Felice there; he sank to the ground at her feet and said to her, weeping: "I have come to beg you for mercy. You can certainly kill me and it would be a good thing: I have broken your orders by coming when you forbade me to. I want to show you what I feel: what severe pain you have given

---

[5] 490 **difficult to treat** *enrevre*: literally, "obstinate, stubborn."

[6] 518 **al col** *on my own head*: literally, on my shoulders. Against E's reading of *me vendra al col*, I prefer the reading of M, *me revertira* (C: *vertira*).

me, and the sufferings, the anguish, the miseries which you make me endure every day, from which I shall never be free unless you give me joy. Love for you has so afflicted me I am going from bad to worse. Now I shall admit it to you: I just have to die. My heart will stay with you—whether you like it or not, so it will be. They can send the body away, but the heart remains unaffected. As long as I'm alive, I shall love you, and seeing that I must leave, I shall die. If it were up to me, parting wouldn't happen, as long as there's life in my body. You can't forbid me to love you; you make me experience suffering and pain. When your father gets to know I love you so much, he will have me killed in great agony, in severe torment and anguish. It will be of great solace to me to suffer death for you; I'll suffer it very gladly because it will please me. From now on, I care nothing for my life and what happens to it." Then he fell down in a faint. (527–67)

The beautiful Felice looked at him and was seized by great pity. Then she told a maiden to take him in her arms and move him away from there. This girl then came running, full of compassion for Gui. "By the God upon whom we call," she said, "if I were the most beautiful in the world and daughter of the mightiest emperor who was ever crowned, and Gui was as overwhelmed for love of me as he is for you, I don't think I'd refuse to love him, if he wanted to love me in this way." (568–82)

Gui recovered from his swoon; the maiden was holding him in her arms. "Gui," said Felice, "you're behaving very foolishly. Do you want to lose your life on my account? I want to send for my father now and show him all this: what great dishonour you do him when you entreat my love. He will have you condemned in his court and dismembered before everyone." Then Gui replied: "God! would that it were now so, that you were the cause of my death! Whether rightly or wrongly, I am quite ready to accept it, for whoever prefers death to life is now happy to have that drink.[7] I no longer care what anyone says about it." (583–600)

Gui again fainted. Great pity seized Felice. "Gui," she said, "your love is great; it has driven you quite mad. Now I would like to do something for you so that you'll not be able to ask for more: there is no lady or maiden so beautiful in the whole of this land whom you cannot have as you please, if you desire this so much." "Felice," he said, "no more of that! Why do you want to mock me? Am I not sufficiently unfortunate that you don't care for me? Now I have lived too long and I shall go mad; from now on I'm beginning to go out of my mind." "Gui," she said, "now listen to me! I've changed my mind. Don't think it insulting if I tell you what I think. I don't want to love any young man unless he's

---

[7] 598 for [. . .] is now happy to have that drink *Car ben art ore icel beivre*: I have reverted to E's reading at 598: *Car ben ait ore icel beivre*. The Caius MS of *Guy* has: *For such a drinke me is yiue*, 643; see Ewert's conjecture on *Car beu ai ore tel beivre* as the source of EFHM.

a knight—handsome, courteous and renowned, brave and bold, prized for his feats of arms. When I have seen you receive weapons, I will grant you my love if you become as I have asked you." (601–28)

When Gui heard this news, nothing so good had ever happened to him, so he swooned for joy. Felice had indeed comforted him. He took his leave of her and went at once to his lodging. He had to go to court as fast as he could. One day seemed like ten, to his mind, until he could get the weapons. When he was hale and hearty, he went off to the court; everyone was delighted to see him healthy. Gui came before the count and greeted him courteously: "My lord, I ask you for weapons: give them to me at once! If you wish, I shall receive them and serve you as my lord." Count Rualt replied: "You shall have them most readily, Gui!" Then the count made ready; he wanted to knight Gui splendidly, and twenty of his companions with him, sons of noble barons who were with Count Rualt and had served him in order to get their weapons. (629–56)

It was on Trinity Sunday that the count knighted Gui, and for love of him twenty knights that day were equipped with silk clothes, rich taffetas, grey furs, fine cloaks, handsome weapons, good horses—the most expensive in the whole land. The least of them all could not have been better dressed in any respect, even if he were an emperor's son, or better equipped with good hauberks, fast war-horses, palfreys, hacks, and pack-horses. Not a spur was wanting for either squire or page. (657–72)

Gui was now well armed; he was handsome, fair, and well-proportioned. Then he went to Felice and spoke most lovingly to her. "My fair love, you know very well what a hard life I have had because of you and how my body has been afflicted. But now you've greatly comforted me. Because of you I've received weapons, and now I've come to you to hear your wishes. You are what I most desire." "Gui," she said, "not so fast! You are not yet esteemed for feats of arms. You are worth no more than you were the other day, except for being dubbed and called knight. When you have been in battles, and are renowned for tourneying, and have captured knights and attacked towers and castles, and when your fame and the report of your great valour runs throughout the land and the country, then you should ask me for love." (673–98)

When Gui heard Felice speak, whom he loved so sincerely, he rejoiced at the maiden's words. He took leave of her and went off to his father, Sequart. "Father," he said, "listen to me: I'm a knight, newly dubbed; now I want to cross the sea to advance my renown. "My fair son," said his father, "God send you joyfully back! I will most readily give you some of my gold and silver; take what you like and use it as you wish." Then he called Heralt, who had been Gui's tutor. "Heralt, my friend, listen: cross the sea with my son. He is very young, a mere child, so henceforth I commend him to you, and also to you, Thorout, and you, Urri. I put great trust in you: you shall go off together with Heralt and carefully look after my son." They were brave and bold knights, the most courageous in their land, and they replied: "We shall do so; we shall gladly go with him." (699–728)

Gui took as much gold and silver as he wanted; he went off to the sea and crossed it as soon as he could. He arrived in Normandy to start looking for knightly adventures. He took lodgings at Rouen, with the richest man in the city, and had himself most splendidly equipped, for he had enough gold and silver. Gui called his host and then asked him for news of the tournament, and where it would be; he had seen so many shields brought there. "What," said the host, "so don't you know? Haven't you heard? A very important maiden, daughter of the emperor of Germany, has had a tournament proclaimed: you have never heard the like of it. There isn't a knight in all Spain or as far as the Breton coast,[8] in any way famous at arms, who won't test his mettle there; there won't be a knight with a sweetheart who fails to perform deeds of valour there; there, a knight can show his worth and much advance his renown. Knights from all countries are going and will cover themselves there with glory. I'll tell you some other things that I've heard people say: a man who's valiant will be able to win great honour there. The maiden of whom you heard me speak, daughter of the Emperor Reiner, will bring to the tournament an entirely white, moulted gerfalcon (you'd never hear tell of a better; whoever wins it will be valiant) and a most valuable horse, not to be exchanged for a country. It is whiter than fine linen; you won't find its equal among a thousand. There are two good white greyhounds; better ones never ran on a leash. Whoever wins the tournament and comes off best on both sides will be given the gerfalcon and the white horse, so greatly prized, and the good greyhounds will be given him, and the love of the maiden, unless he has a fairer sweetheart." (729–82)

When Gui heard the news, he was overjoyed and said to his companions: "My lords, now let's be glad! God willing, in the morning we shall set out." He gave the host a palfrey in exchange for the news he had told him. Gui got up in the morning and took the road, as did his companions, who were brave and good lords. They would not stop travelling until they came to the tournament. Gui arrived at the tournament; he saw knights from many places, and large bands arriving in the middle of the wide, open country. When they were all gathered, they got ready to joust. Out of the lists came a knight who was noble, handsome, and proud. Gui asked a man from Lorraine who it was who had come out of the lists, and he replied: "I'll tell you what I think, my lord: it's Guaer, the emperor's son, recently knighted, very courageous, who's now making ready to joust, if he can find a knight." (783–812)

When Gui of Warwick saw Guaer preparing to joust, he came out of the lists; he certainly looked like a bold knight. Then the knights proceeded to strike each other with great violence. Guaer first struck Gui of Warwick in the middle of the shield so that his whole lance shattered; the hauberk was good and did

---

[8] 750 **the Breton coast** *la mer de Bretaine*: this phrase could mean the British sea or the sea of Brittany.

not break. Gui quickly returned the blow, knocking him down to the ground. Gui seized his horse and took it away, dismounted from his own, and mounted Guaer's. Then he began to tourney; he no longed deigned to consider the horse but made an effort to do well and take knights, as if in war. He took so many good knights that day, and was victorious in the fray through strength, and smashed so many lances, that everyone close by marvelled: there was no knight however good whom, if he struck him, he did not knock to the ground. (813–36)

The wicked Duke Otun of Pavia was very jealous of him. Arrogantly he proceeded to joust with him—no good came to him from it. Gui struck him through the middle of the shoulder, knocking him down to the ground. Then Duke Reiner of Saxony, who thought himself very fierce, came up, spurring violently; he made a great show of hitting him. "Young man, it was a bad idea to hurt the duke of Pavia. It's your misfortune to have laid hands on him; he's my first cousin and it's I, Duke Reiner, who now want to avenge him. Turn round and joust with me!" "By my faith, I agree!" said Gui. Gui turned round and proceeded to strike, with no wish to hold back: he struck him on the top of his shield and knocked him far from his horse. He took the horse by the reins, came to the duke, and said to him: "My lord, take your horse; now you owe me recompense." Later the duke, like a noble man, rewarded him when he most needed it. (837–64)

Then the duke jumped to his feet, at heart distressed with Gui: "Sir knight, don't hide it from me: what is your name, where were you born?" Gui at once replied: "I shall tell you most willingly, my lord: I am called Gui of Warwick and I was born in England." Then the duke of Louvain came up, a sharp spear in his hand; he attacked Gui fiercely. When Gui saw him coming, he fought him; they proceeded to strike each other great blows, making their spears fly into pieces. Then they drew their steel swords and proceeded to give each other great blows; they made pieces fly out of the weapons and out of the shields, for they were very valiant.[9] (864–82)

And Heralt went forward and jousted with the duke of Moriane;[10] he knocked him far from his horse, quite prone on the ground. Then he struck Duke Galdemer,[11] knocking him far from his horse. He acted well, like a bold knight, as did Thorout and Urri with him. Then the battle started—you never heard of anything more fierce! So many lances could be seen shattering, so many knights falling to earth, and so many knights coming together, each strongly jousting with the other! I couldn't name them for you: it would be too much of a delay. There's no clerk, able to read, who could decide on the best of them. The

---

[9] 882 **they were very valiant** *mult sunt preuz*: After 882, C adds 2 lines.

[10] 884 **Moriane** E has *Normendie*; Ewert substitutes Moriane from C. Perhaps the same as 7186, *Moraine*. Flutre (274) suggests this is Moravia, or perhaps Maurienne, as in *Protheselaus*.

[11] 887 **Galdemer** Perhaps the same as Waldemer, 1932, 2094 etc.

local people said that Gui came off best that day, and on the next day too he won the prize in the tournament. Gui was praised on all sides; the renown was all his. When it reached the last day, as everyone was leaving the fray, Duke Reiner came spurring up, who was very brave and valiant. "My lords, now listen to me; if I say amiss, put me right. This gerfalcon and this horse, and these greyhounds I see there, should belong to him who won them. It seems to me that's Gui of Warwick. Whoever wants to deny that won't lack for a fight." They all said with one voice: "Indeed we agree with your decision." It was proclaimed throughout the tournament that the gifts would go to Gui. (883–922)

When the tournament had come to an end, Gui went back to his lodging. There he had himself disarmed; he had exerted himself in tourneying. Then at once a courteous, wise, and well-spoken youth arrived, who dismounted at Gui's lodging, came towards him quickly and greeted him courteously, saying, as you shall hear: "God save you, Sir Gui, as the most valiant man in the world! You have won the prize in the tournament, and so I make you this present on behalf of the lovely Blancheflur, daughter of our emperor: this entirely white, moulted gerfalcon, these greyhounds, and this horse, and together with all that, her love, if you haven't a beloved more beautiful." Gui replied like a courteous man: "Friend, I thank her! If it pleases her, I will most readily receive this present, and willingly receive her friendship;[12] I want always to be her knight. My friend," said Gui, "now listen to me! What I am about to tell you, you shall do: I want to give you weapons and make you a knight in splendid fashion. You and your friends will receive gifts from me; I want to do you great honour, for love of the beautiful Blancheflur." "My lord," he said, "thank you! But I did not come here for weapons. I shall go back to the maiden and will be able to tell her what I've seen; I shall give a good report of you to my lady Blancheflur." (923–62)

The young man departed and Gui, who had achieved a great deal, remained. He called two young men and ordered them to accept the present he was giving them, go at once to England, and present it to Count Rualt, his worthy liege lord. When they heard the order, they set off at once, went to England, and found the count at Warwick.[13] They told him how Gui had won the white gerfalcon, the horse, and the prized greyhounds, and how he was renowned throughout the land, and how the emperor's daughter had sent him to the fray, where everyone famous for feats of arms was gathered. He who had bested them all had earned this present and the love of the maiden who was so noble and beautiful. When the count heard this, he was delighted that Gui was so esteemed. His father was

---

[12] 941; 947 **love; friendship** *driuerie, druerie*: Blancheflur's "love" and Gui's "friendship" both translate *druerie*. A *dru* could range from "beloved" to "knight attached to and serving one especial lady"; context would suggest the latter.

[13] 974 **found the count at Warwick** *Le cunte a Warewic troverent*: After 974, F adds 2 lines.

very glad and happy about it, as were all those in the land who were Gui's good friends. (963–92)

From now on, Gui went tourneying to advance his reputation. In Germany and in Lombardy, in France and in Normandy, there was no tournament or battle where Gui did not win all the distinction. He stayed for more than a year and was famous throughout these countries. He won praise and glory and made many good friends in these regions. He returned to Rouen and resumed his lodgings. "My lord," Heralt said to him, his valiant companion, "let's go to England! Now we certainly can do so: you're the best at tourneying, you can return to your own land. You ought to get to know the king and you can easily do so, and you should make yourself known to the lords of the land." "My lord," said Gui, "I agree. The journey is in your hands, not mine. Tomorrow, early in the morning, we will set off; we will go to the sea and quickly cross it." (993–1020)

In the morning Gui rose and went straight to the sea; as soon as he could he set sail, and straightaway arrived in England. Then he went off to the king and got to know him well, and also the counts and the barons, who offered him splendid gifts. After that he went off to Warwick, where he found Count Rualt, who gave him an excellent reception, for Gui was most welcome. The count gave him his gold and silver, silk garments and tableware. His father was delighted with Gui, who had such renown and his mother was much more so; equally delighted were all the people of the land. Gui went to Felice and very gently greeted her: "My fair love, I have come; I certainly owe my life to you. Were it not for you, I would be dead and destroyed, my body in a wretched plight. You made me take up arms and then told me what you wished: since I have taken up arms and crossed the sea and, far off in a foreign land, become quite famous for using them, I should be given your love for which I have been so eager. Now I have come, my fair love, to hear your wishes." (1021–54)

Felice at once replied: "Not so fast, sir Gui! You are not yet so famous that there is no one as good in the kingdom. You are very brave and valiant, bold and courageous in battle. If I were to love you above all else and give you my love, you would become so infatuated that it would make you quite lazy; you would no longer want to bear arms or enhance your reputation. It would be wrong of me, I think, if through me you lost your renown. I won't conceal my thoughts from you, but want to make them quite clear: you will not have my love unless you are so good that no one is your equal in any land or as famous for bearing arms, or until you are the flower of chivalry and quite the best in the world. When you are like that in every way, when there's no one better than you under heaven, I will give you my love, to do with it as you please. No one but you will have my love, as long as I live." (1055–82)

When Gui heard Felice speak, he gave heartfelt sighs: "Now I know that you mock me, when you command me to be the best in the world; that will never happen. I shall go off to foreign lands, and because of you I shall certainly do my best and won't fear death. If I die, it will be for you." Then he asked her for leave and, all in tears, kissed her. He went to his lodging; he barely stayed there because he wanted to go to Rualt, to ask him for leave to go. Gui came to the court and dismounted at the door of the hall; he went up to Count Rualt and told him what he wanted: "My lord count, now listen to me: I ask for leave—give it me! I want now to cross the sea to enhance my renown more. Should I be praised for feats of arms, you should be so much the happier: if you have men of great valour, it will bring you much honour. In every way you will be more feared by the powerful men of the kingdom." (1083–1112)

"Sir Gui," said Count Rualt, "tell me if you want for anything—gold or silver or good horses, silk garments or splendid tunics? Why will you cross the sea? Give up that idea, Sir Gui! Don't I have dogs and birds, rapid chargers and fine horses? Whenever you like we shall go hunting plump stags and boar; with our gerfalcons and with our falcons, we will go after the cranes and herons. Thus we can amuse ourselves. I want to give you this counsel, Sir Gui: in time you can very well cross the sea and you'll be much more comfortable." "My lord," he said, "thank you, but I shall stay here no longer." He took his leave and went away; it grieved the count very much. Then he came to Sequart, his father, who was very upset with him. "Father," he said, "I want to leave; I'm asking your leave and I will go away. I now want to seek renown overseas, in a foreign land; I don't want to stay here, to dwell in this land any longer. A young man of any bravery should exert himself, while he's young, so as to be much praised, and honoured in his old age. So, as long as I'm a young man, I want to seek renown."[14] "Fair son," he said, "give up that idea! Don't cross the sea again. You stay here with us: we shall be so much happier." "Fair son," said his mother, "do take your father's advice. Stay this year with us and you can cross in the time to come. Were we to lose you and remain without a son,[15] we would never be happy but would die in great anguish. Who, when we are gone, would rule our castles and fiefs?" (1113–60)

Then Gui replied: "I commend you to God, dear father, and my mother too. I want to leave at once." Gui went away and they stayed, sadly lamenting. He went off to the sea, found the wind was favourable, crossed and arrived in Normandy. There he did many knightly deeds, and from there he went to Brittany. There was no tournament as far as Spain where he did not go to tourney; everywhere he was much praised. He stayed so long in Spain that he became famous for feats of arms. From there he went to Lombardy, where chivalry was then to be found; there he was much esteemed. The Lombards loved him and held him dear because he was generous and open-handed, courteous, brave, and valiant. As he was coming from a tournament in the area of Benevento, he was wounded in the body by a sword, which caused him a great deal of pain. Then Duke

---

[14] 1146 **I want to seek renown** *Mun pris voildrai purchacer*: After 1146, F adds 2 lines.
[15] 1155–56 **Were we to lose you and remain without a son** *Si nus nul fiz n'avioms, E nus vus ore perdisuns*: I have followed Ewert's emendation here.

Otun, who was very wicked and cruel, thought about Gui of Warwick, whom he had never liked after Gui had wounded him in Brittany:[16] since he knew for sure that Gui was wounded, he sent for Count Lambert and one of his prized knights, and with them fifteen valiant knights, bold, brave, and courageous. He made them go to a crossing which he knew, through which Gui of Warwick was to pass. (1161–98)

"My lords," said Duke Otun, "now listen to what I say. You are my men and my trusty retainers; you should be loyal to me and do everything I command, as I shall at once tell you: go quickly and avenge me on a villain, a scoundrel who has entered my lands and wants to make all-out war on me. He's Gui, who has a sword-wound to the body. Now all swear to me by the saints that you will go to the forest of Plains and lie in ambush there, where Gui of Warwick must pass, and bring him to me and kill all his men, for I shall put him in my prison, from where he will never be ransomed. He will die in pain and disgrace, for he will never escape from there." "My lord," they said, "we'll go and carry out your orders." Then they went off, all very well armed, straight to the crossing where Gui of Warwick was to pass, who did not know of the great danger he would soon be in, if God did not protect him. (1199–1228)

Gui travelled gently, ambling along on a little mule, and suffering greatly from the wound at the place in his body where he had been struck. He expected to cross the ford right away, but Otun's men contested it strongly. When he heard the horses neigh and saw the helmets gleam, "God!" he thought, "now we're betrayed; we are all dead and done for." He quickly got off the mule, mounted his horse, seized his weapons, and said to his companions: "Now defend yourselves like brave men! Each of you should defend himself, and I will protect myself if I can; I will sell myself as dearly as I can to the wicked Lombards." "My lord," said Heralt, "as God is your salvation, run away! And we shall defend this crossing; by God, we will die for you! Better to die without you than that you should perish with us." Gui replied at once, like a knight full of courage: "If you die, I shall die; I shall stay here together with you." (1229–56)

Then a Lombard came up, who was extremely ill-bred. "Gui," he said, "surrender now! By my head, you shall not escape! I've sworn to Duke Otun that I will hand your body over to him before it crosses the ford." Gui of Warwick encountered him, vigorously struck him a mighty blow, and made his soul leave his body. He went to hit another Lombard, in no way sparing him; with an energetic stroke through the body he cut him down into the sand. Then Heralt, his valiant companion, came spurring up; he went to meet a Lombard and did him great harm: he pierced his body with his sword and threw him down to the ground. Then Thorout came spurring up, who knew plenty about fighting. He

---

[16] 1190 **had wounded him in Brittany** *en Bretaigne le nafra*: Gui wounded Otun in Normandy; see 733.

encountered a Lombard before he had crossed the ford, making his head fly from his body with his sharp steel blade. Then Urri came spurring up; no one there was so bold. He made to strike a knight, as he wished to keep the fight going; he pierced him through the body and knocked him flat on the ground. You could have seen battle anew—so many terrible blows exchanged on conical helmets and tough shields! Then Count Lambert came up, a wicked and savage knight; he killed our brave Urri. When Herald saw this, he was very distressed; he went to fight Count Lambert, wanting to avenge Urri's death. With great violence he hit him; neither shield nor hauberk could save Lambert. He split his heart in two and knocked him down far from his horse. (1257–1302)

Then Huencun came up, a brave and valiant knight, nephew of Duke Otun; there was none more courageous in Pavia. He killed our Thorout next, in front of Herald the marquis.[17] When Herald saw him fall, and saw him die in front of him, he was deeply unhappy and distressed, and very eager to avenge him; never had he been so unhappy. He pressed forward, straight towards Huencun, like a fasting lion eager for its prey, and with his sword struck him violently through the body. He knocked him off his horse in front of the Lombards, who saw him. When lord Gunter, a proud and fierce knight, saw this, he struck Herald crosswise, damaging his hauberk; he thrust his sword through his body and flung him far from his horse. (1303–26)

When Gui saw Herald overthrown and flung from his horse, he nearly went mad with grief; if he could, he would certainly avenge him. He went to strike Gunter of Pavia. Shield and hauberk were no help to him: he cut through his heart and lungs and knocked him dead onto the sand. Now Gui was in difficulties: he had lost all his companions and remained there alone. He had seen all his companions killed and was wretched, not knowing what to do; he knew no one to whom he could tell his grief. Only three Lombards were left, who attacked him on all sides. Two of them were unharmed, the third wounded through the body by a large sword. Gui hacked at one of them and cut his head from his body. Then Guischard came spurring up, a most arrogant Lombard. "Gui," he said, "surrender now! You can't defend yourself any longer: I can see your shield lying on the ground, entirely cut into little pieces, your helmet quite smashed, your strong hauberk broken. You are wounded in the side, your blood is streaming over the links of mail; I can see from your appearance you're not able to defend yourself. Today I'll hand you over to Duke Otun and he'll put you in his prison." (1327–60)

Gui replied: "No you won't, Guischard! You won't hand me to Duke Otun as long as I have my sharp sword and this much strength. I won't surrender to you

---

[17] 1308 **marquis** *marchis*: A *marchis* is the prefect of a March, i.e., a border. Heralt would seem to have been promoted. Maybe the word is only there for the rhyme, see 3715, 5698. Similar promotions occur later, e.g., 3715.

as long as I can defend myself." Then Guischard struck him on his bright, shining helmet, cutting off one of its quarters; the blow fell on his shoulder, hacking off more than seven links of mail, but it did not injure his flesh. When Gui felt the blow, he was angry to the core; he struck Guischard with great fury, like a most valiant knight, separating his shoulder almost half a foot from his body. Guischard fled, Gui pursued him, but the horse carrying Guischard was good and Gui turned back. Guischard, very distressed, went off towards Pavia, in a wretched plight. (1361–84)

On his way back from hunting, the duke wanted to return to Pavia. He saw a knight come galloping, causing his horse much distress. Then the duke stopped until he recognized Guischard, who looked very like a frightened man bringing bad news. Then Guischard approached; the duke called him to him and said: "Who has upset you? Have you been fighting, then? Where's Gui? Isn't he captured? What is he, alive or dead?" Guischard replied: "I'll tell you about Gui of Warwick and where I left him. We found him at the crossing by the ford and we opposed him with force, killing all his companions. We didn't capture him: he killed and slaughtered all of us; I alone survive." "Where is Huencun then?" "My lord, he lies dead in the sand." "And the brave Count Lambert?" "I left him lying dead and bleeding." When the duke heard this, he was very distressed and angry. He was most miserable and dismayed because of the men he had lost. (1385–1414)

Gui returned; he nearly went completely mad when he saw his companions dead and their bodies lying on the ground. Then he gave way to great grief, lamenting his companions: "Ah, valiant knights! How brave and courageous you were! You are all dead for love of me; alas that you ever saw me![18] How should I forsake you? Why can't I die with you? Curse the Lombards—they were so wicked and cowardly! Why am I left alone in this way, because they didn't kill me with you? Ah, Heralt, noble friend! What a brave fighter you were! Who will help me in battle from now on? You paid me much honour; I have given you a poor reward, for I have done you nothing but harm. You have lost your life because of me; I shall never again have help from you! Ah, Count Rualt, my lord! Your advice was really valuable: had I stayed with you and crossed the sea at the right time, I would not have suffered such harm as I have now received in this wood."[19] What with his grief for the companions he had lost, and his bleeding wound, he fell to the ground in a swoon. (1415–48)

When he came round from his swoon, he bitterly lamented his companions. Then he mounted his horse and went off to a hermitage. "Hermit," he

---

[18] 1424 **alas that you ever saw me** *Tant mar veistes unc mun cors*: After 1424, C adds 8 lines, blaming Felice for his knights' death.

[19] 1444 **as I have now received in this wood** *Que ore ai receu en cest boscage*: After 1444, C adds 4 lines.

said, "come with me: take this valuable horse and bury these two bodies for me, which are lying dead beneath the forest." "My lord," said the hermit, "I will do so. Go ahead, I will follow you." Gui gave him the bodies of Thorout and Urri the renowned. Then he mounted his horse; he wanted to carry Heralt with him. Now Gui left the battle behind, with much grief. He carried with him the body of Heralt, his companion whom he loved so much. He went at once to an abbey which he saw by the road. There he found a good abbot and spoke piteously to him. "Lord abbot," said Gui, "God, who makes the heat and the cold, save you! I beg you, as a most saintly man, out of holy charity to receive this body and to have it buried. He was a most courageous knight who today was killed in a battle. I will reward you when I can, if I live." The abbot said: "I consent. Who are you? Tell me!" (1449–82)

"I am a knight from a foreign land; we were attacked at a crossing by thieves and scoundrels. They killed my companions, and I myself was wounded there, by a great sword through the body." Gui went off, grieving mightily; his wound gave him great pain. He went to a hermit he had earlier come to know and straightaway had his wounds dressed in secret. He was in great fear of Duke Otun, who was so wicked and cruel. (1483–96)

The abbot I spoke of felt great pity for the knight, whom Gui had left with him, so he had his body carried to a house to be disarmed. When he was disarmed, a monk, knowledgeable about herbs, looked at the great wound which lacerated his body. He noticed from the wound that he had not been dealt a mortal blow and could still be healed if someone wanted to help him in some way. (1497–1508)

Now Gui was healed of his wound. He took his leave of the good hermit and then went off to Apulia, to its king who held him in much honour, and who offered him plenty of gold and silver and whatever else pleased him. He went tourneying throughout the land and was much loved and cherished. He was so long in the country that he bore the prize for tourneying. Then he took leave of the king. Next he went to Saxony, [*to Duke Reiner, a most noble man, who did not hesitate to pay him honour. He stayed so long in the land that he was highly praised for feats of arms. Then he thought hard and decided that he had been there long enough. He wanted to go to his own country and did not want to stay there any more.*][20] He left Saxony and came to Burgundy, to Milun who was duke then. The duke showed him great respect, freely gave him land, and paid him honour as much as he could. Then they went off tourneying together and were much acclaimed for feats of arms. (1509–36)

Gui was now much prized and loved throughout the land. There was no poverty-stricken knight or forsaken prisoner who might ask him for something

---

[20] 1521-8 to **duke Reiner** ... **stay there any more** *Al duc Reiner ... mes demorer*: these supplied lines are not in E; they seem to be a composite of FHMC.

of his to whom he did not very quickly give it, and to young men who wanted to be of service he gave as many weapons as they wished. Queens and ladies of the kingdom now greatly desired Gui, but he would not love any of them; he had given his love to Felice. Whether for gifts, whether for generosity, whether for goodness, whether for prowess, no knight as far as Antioch was so famous. (1537–52)

As Gui was returning from hunting, he saw a poor man going in front of him. Then he called him over and gently asked: "Worthy sir, where do you come from? Tell me, don't hide it from me!" "My lord," he said, "from Lombardy, where I led a very hard life: there I lost my lord, a knight of very great valour. Duke Otun had us betrayed—may he never be forgiven for it! I want to journey in this manner, always to pray for my lord's soul." Gui said: "Who was your lord, whom you loved with such great love?" "He was called Gui of Warwick; there was no one more famous in the world." When Gui heard him give his name, he began to sigh. "Worthy man," he said, "tell me: upon your word, what is your name?" "In the kingdom where I was born I am called Heralt of Arderne." (1553–76)

When Gui heard Heralt named, he dismounted from his horse and took him in his arms. Never had he rejoiced at anything so much. He kissed him more than a hundred times and wept for joy. "Ah, Heralt, my good companion! Don't you know Gui, whom you once used to love so much? Why won't you speak to me?" When Heralt heard Gui named, he could not remain on his feet; he fell swooning to the ground. Gui raised him up again in his arms. Anyone could have seen their joy, each weeping for joy over the other! Then they sat down there and each told the other what had happened. Gui told Heralt how he had carried him from the battle to be buried in an abbey; he would not leave him behind. Heralt told him how his wound was healed and how he sorrowfully went through many lands, looking for him. Then they mounted Gui"s horse and went back to the city. Gui then had him bathed and splendidly equipped with good, fine silken garments, grey furs, and noble cloaks. (1577–1608)

When Heralt was thus equipped, they went to Duke Milun and told him what had happened to them and how hard things had been for them. Then they took their leave of the duke, wishing to return to their own land. The duke wanted to retain them, but they were not pleased to stay there any longer. Gui took his leave and left. They proceeded straight to Flanders and lodged at St Omer; they would go straight to the sea, not wanting to stay there any longer. Gui went over to a window and looked into the street; he saw a very poor pilgrim coming along the road. Quickly Gui called him over and kindly asked him: "Pilgrim, do you want lodging? It's night, you can't go any further." The pilgrim quickly replied: "My lord, thank you!" Gui then asked him if, in the kingdoms where he had been, he had heard talk of any war in any land. "My lord," he said, "I will tell you of one war I know of; neither you nor any man this side of the sea ever heard tell of a fiercer." Gui replied: "Tell me about it!" (1609–41)

"My lord," he said, "I certainly will. The powerful emperor, Reiner, who rules Germany, has besieged the duke of Louvain and slain and killed his men, because of his nephew, whom the duke killed. But he did it in self-defence in a tournament this year, which was held in response to a challenge. The mighty Duke Seguin was there, to whom Louvain is subject, and Duke Reiner from Saxony, and Duke Loher from Lorraine, and knights from the whole land, who came there to seek renown. When the tournament was ended, Duke Seguin proceeded to leave; he had felled a knight who was brave and of great strength. Then Saduc came spurring up to fight the duke of Louvain; he was very envious of his fine knightly exploits. Saduc was the emperor's nephew, his sister's son. He had exerted himself in the tournament, but he had now removed his hauberk and was without armour.[21] He was a knight of great renown. 'My lord, Duke Seguin, turn around! Joust with me for once! You are much admired as a knight: now this will indeed be put to the test.' (1642–74)

'Saduc, let me be!' said the noble Seguin. 'I don't care to joust with you because I hold you too dear to my heart; you're my lord's nephew. I will never harm you, because I see you're now without body-armour; it would be too insolent. If I now jousted with you, it would look as if I didn't like you.' Saduc said: 'You're too much of a weakling, since you don't dare joust just once. Now I consider you a coward. If you don't joust with me, so help me God, I'll strike you from behind. Protect yourself; I challenge you! From now on I am your enemy.' Saduc struck the duke in great haste, unwilling in any way to spare him, and the duke quickly wheeled around and they struck each other boldly. First Saduc hit the duke in his quartered shield; he wounded him in the arm so that his whole lance shattered. Duke Seguin hit him back, in no way sparing him. He struck him through the body and knocked him dead to the ground. (1675–1704)

The fight broke up and there was great grief. The body was carried to an abbey, to be buried. The duke returned to his city, Arascune;[22] he had walls rebuilt and put to rights his tall towers, his castles, his cities, and the strongholds of his land. He had them stocked with good men, for he wanted to defend himself bravely. He had heard tell from others that his lord would make war on him. When the emperor had heard that his nephew had been killed, from throughout his empire he summoned his army to join him very quickly; he summoned kings and dukes, counts and barons of the realm. They came from all the lands which were subject to the empire. When he had gathered his army, he besieged the duke of Louvain. He will never leave the land until he has either killed or captured the

---

[21] 1669 **without armour** *en pleines armes*: In Middle English *en pleines armes* means "without armour" (cf *Middle English Dictionary* under *plain*, 3 c, which cites the English *Guy of Warwick*, Auchinleck 6477: *"In pleyn armes wil we fight"*). See also 4700 and 6571. In all three places, "without armour" is the only phrase to make sense in the context.

[22] 1710 **Arascune** *Rascune*: This is perhaps Tarascon; see Flutre, 197.

duke, destroyed his castles and cities, killed and cut down his people. Only one city was left to him, built on the Rhone: that is the city of Arascune—as far as Barzune[23] there is none stronger." (1705–36)

When the pilgrim had told the story and Gui had listened to all of it, he then began to think whether he should stay or go. "Lord Heralt, what do you think best? Give me some good advice, as to whether we should go and help the duke or return to our home. I will do whatever you advise; I will trust your counsel." "Sir," said Heralt, "I will give you valuable counsel, because I am loyal to you. It is my duty to give you good counsel: prepare yourself splendidly and go and help Duke Seguin, along with fifty companions, and offer them plenty of noble gifts. One ought to help him who needs it most. You will gain fame and glory so that you'll always be respected for it." "Lord Heralt, thank you! This is most noble counsel. Now I am certain you love me, when you give me such advice." (1737–62)

Gui very quickly made preparations and proceeded straight to Louvain, together with fifty knights, who were most valiant and fierce, the most prized in all France; Gui took them with him. They arrived in Arascune and were nobly received and lodged in the city, and were very happy and pleased. In the morning Gui rose and went to church; he heard matins and mass and then returned to his lodging. He saw people running through the streets as if to defend themselves. Gui called his host and at once asked him: "Sir host, tell me, what is this great confusion about?" "My lord," he said, "I will tell you, I won't hide it from you: the emperor's seneschal, a most valiant knight—all the way to Spain there's none braver—is bringing a noble band with him and three famous knights, very bold and renowned. They have arrived in front of the city. Any knight they encounter will not leave but be captured, held or killed." (1763–94)

Gui asked for his weapons and armed himself very well, and he and his companions then mounted Gascon horses and left the city. The seneschal saw them and, like a praiseworthy knight, he went towards them. When he saw them coming, he had a great desire to fight with them, and he said to his companions: "Wait now, my lords! I see a knight approaching who seems truly proud and fierce, on an excellent horse, which he would not exchange for a country. If I don't get the horse, I'll never be happy." Then he came down from the vantage-post and at once went towards Gui. The lords struck spurs into their horses and hit one another; they struck hard at each other's shield, exchanging great blows. Gui at first struck him and knocked him off his horse; then he made a sudden turn at full gallop,[24] like a brave and courteous knight. Next he drew his steel

---

[23] 1736 **Barzune** *Barzune*: Ewert suggests this could be Bayonne. A has *Rome*, HC has *Baiune/Baione*.

[24] 1821 **a sudden turn at full gallop** *le tur franceis*: a *tur franceis* is a kind of wheeling turn, usually performed on horseback.

sword and cut a quarter off his helmet. Then he defeated him in battle, and at once he released him on parole. (1795–1826)

When the Germans, who were brave and warlike, saw their lord captured in the fight, they made haste to come to his help. Before he was led off the field, many mighty blows had been given. Gui turned around suddenly, and his companions too; they struck the Germans; they would not spare them in any way. When the knights in the city had taken good note of this, they went off to their lodgings to arm, in order to aid Gui. Then they all went out together and bravely helped him. You could see so many blows given there—so many knights fighting together, and lances and swords exchanging so many strokes, so many horses wandering around aimlessly and so many knights shouting and howling, so many knights pierced through the body and knocked dead to the ground! Sir Gui made great efforts that day, and so did lord Heralt, to defeat the Germans, making them suffer and feel pain; with the help of the important city, Gui accomplished a great deal. They defeated the Germans—they slew, killed, and captured them. (1827–58)

Gui turned back, with the booty he had won, and he and his companions took many noble prisoners. They returned to the city, each one going to his lodging, and they became proud and exuberant about the defeated Germans. Gui returned to his lodging and there disarmed. When the duke heard the news—better news had never reached him before—that Gui of Warwick had come and captured the emperor's seneschal, he mounted a horse, quickly went to Gui's lodging, and politely spoke to him, happy and pleased at his arrival. "Gui," he said, "the bravest in the world—welcome! I've wanted you more than anything else: thank God you have come to me. From now on I shall be feared by my mortal enemies, who have destroyed my land. I make you lord and owner of my city and of the tower, and of castles in my land. From now on I will ask you to assume authority over them; you do what you want with them. I want to travel about, according to your counsel, and discomfiting my mortal enemies." (1859–92)

Like a courteous man, Gui replied: "My lord duke, many thanks! I will help you as much as I can and as best as I can advise." Gui handed the seneschal over to him, which made him happy and pleased; through him he believed he could come to good terms with the proud Emperor Reiner. Then they learned about each other, and talked of their plight. Immediately Gui sent his messengers—who were very brave, courteous, and wise—to the countries where he had been, and summoned a large collection of knights. And in hundreds and thousands they willingly came to him. Thereupon, through Gui, who was from now on most loyal to him, and by his advice, the duke would conquer the castles which he had lost. (1893–1912)

When the emperor heard that Gui was with the duke, and had killed his men and imprisoned his seneschal, he was mortified and angry about the men he had lost. He said to his barons: "My lords, what shall we do now? I shall never be happy again if I'm not quickly avenged on Duke Seguin and Gui, who have injured my men." "My lord," said the duke of Pavia, "don't be distressed! Before a third day passes, you will be amply avenged on them. Take those of your barons most praised for feats of arms, Duke Reiner of Saxony and Waldemer the constable, and I shall go along with them; I shall lead a fine body of knights. Send us to Arascune: should Gui and the duke be found, if we don't hand over those traitors to you and put them in your prison, I don't want to hold castle or tower or any part of the fief of Pavia." The emperor replied: "That is good counsel. My lord, Duke Reiner, go! And my lord constable, you go too, and with you the duke of Pavia with his good body of knights, to the fine city of Arascune. Should Gui or the duke be found there, whoever can seize the traitors will have my friendship for ever." (1913–50)

"My lord," they said, "we're going; we will carry out your command." They took their leave of the emperor and went to their lodgings. They rose early in the morning and armed themselves splendidly. The dukes with their impressive troops overran large fields; they came straight to Arascune, 20,000 shields in number. When the city-dwellers saw them, they made to defend themselves: they hastily armed and gathered large groups of people together. When they were gathered, and ready to fight, the duke called Heralt and addressed him kindly: "My lord Heralt, you will take three hundred armed knights; you will first go and assail them boldly and speedily attack them. And you, Sir Gui, take a thousand knights, the nimblest in the city. If Heralt should need you, be sure to help him quickly, and I will come with my followers, with the men I've gathered. If we fight with them, please God we shall entirely defeat them." (1951–80)

Heralt readily attacked them; he wanted to keep the battle going. He saw Duke Otun at the outset, noticing him in the first body of troops. "My lord duke, Otun of Pavia, do you remember the wicked deed you did in Lombardy, when you betrayed my lord and me? Please God, we shall be avenged before sunset." They struck each other so that they fell from their horses; then they drew their steel swords and exchanged great blows. The duke defended himself fiercely and Heralt attacked him very keenly. Through the field, most angrily, here came the duke's followers pounding on, who rescued their lord. They were very eager to capture Heralt, but he defended himself with his sword. Now here came his men spurring up with great force, putting Heralt back on his horse. Then they exchanged blows, neither wanting to spare the other. Heralt exerted himself greatly that day, making a big attack on the duke and killing more than a hundred of his men, who were left dead there. The duke was unhappy at heart when he saw his men killed, and he said to his companions: "And now what will you do, my lords? Don't you see a vassal who has done me harm and shame, who's killed all my men, your kin and your friends? If you don't avenge me on him, you won't have my friendship!" Then they at once gathered and joined battle fiercely with Heralt. It turned out badly for him, since he lost his companions, but he would soon recover them, for much help was coming. They pursued Heralt forcefully, but he opposed them bravely. (1981–2028)

When Gui saw Heralt coming, leaving the bitter fray with his helmet partly crushed and his shield cut to pieces, his horse wounded from having been in the fierce fighting, he loudly shouted his war-cry. He attacked the duke, rescuing Heralt's companions and those of his own men who had been seized and captured. Wherever he saw Duke Otun, he fiercely called out to him: "Duke, why did you treat me treacherously, and make my men die a painful death, at the crossing in the forest of the Plains? So help me God and his saints, from now on I defy you as my mortal enemy; I shall never be happy unless I am revenged on you!"

The knights turned round the heads of their horses and struck each other great blows with sharp spears; their shields were no more use than a glove. The duke struck Gui first, splitting his golden shield; the hauberk was good and did not break, so that the whole spear shattered. Gui struck the duke back with a sharp spear through his body. Then they drew their swords and gave each other hard blows. Gui would certainly have taken off his head when help appeared, in the shape of some thousand knights, all brave and agile, who all proceeded to strike Gui; they were very eager to kill him. But Gui defended himself like a lion; whomever he struck, he knocked him down dead and bloody. (2029–68)

Then they took their lord away and carried him, wounded, out of the fray. Gui constantly shouted his war-cry and exhorted his men to do well. Then they struck; many good lords would die there before the day quite ended, because Gui made great efforts to capture and slaughter the Lombards. He wanted to revenge himself on the duke for the grief he had caused him when he carried out the wicked act through which many men lost their lives. Then Gui could be seen hitting very well and thus killing his enemies, and so could his companions, who struck most courageously. With swords and lances and with sharp spears, they killed many of the Lombards, who were defeated, killed, captured, and slain by their valiant deeds. They fled, Gui pursued them; the spot was filled with the dead. Gui pursued them and, like those who are defeated, they fled. (2069–92)

Then Duke Reiner came up, and Waldemer the constable, their mighty bands with them, who rode down the fields. They met Gui in a valley and firmly challenged him. Gui withdrew to a plain, his noble band with him. "My lords," he said, "now listen to me! You see these large bands coming, Duke Reiner of Saxony and Count Waldemer of Cologne and many knights with them? We shall not shake them off: they have surrounded us on all sides and will certainly attack us fiercely. Whether we defend ourselves or not, we shan't shake them off. Better to die with honour than flee in dishonour. So let's defend ourselves well: if we are killed or captured, may it redound greatly to our glory that we have been here!" They all said to him, as one man: "May Almighty God never help him who ever fails you, so long as he can defend himself!" (2093–2120)

Then they went to strike the Germans; there would be no sparing them. They started a great battle, hitting them from both sides. Before the battle ended, many a good warrior would be maimed. Gui went to strike Duke Reiner and knocked him far from his horse. Then he struck a German, and neither his shield nor his hauberk was worth an acorn. He struck him through the body and felled him dead to the ground. Heralt went at Waldemer and made him quit his stirrups. He did not want to stop there, but went to strike a knight through the body with his sword, throwing him down from his horse. Thereupon Guelin came spurring up, cousin to Duke Seguin. He struck Count Bertulf and threw him far from his horse. Gui strove to strike well and his companions did likewise; they killed many of the Germans, for they attacked them fiercely. When Duke Reiner and the constable, Waldemer, saw this, their men killed in front of them in pain and great torment, they shouted their war-cry in a loud voice, then gathered together in a throng. Boldly they went to strike Gui; he disdained to flee but offered them a most severe resistance, so that many good fighters died. They attacked him most violently and killed many of his men. (2121–58)

Then Duke Reiner came up and went to meet Guelin; he struck him through the body with his keen, sharp sword. Guelin fled, vigorously spurring his horse, and came to Duke Seguin. The duke saw and recognized him, but was very distressed to see him bleeding as he approached. "My lord duke, what are you waiting for? Why don't you go and help your men? Already they have been defeated—why don't you go and help them?" When the duke heard what the brave Guelin was saying, he struck spurs into his horse and said to his companions: "My lords, now do your best! Don't hesitate to help Gui! If he's either killed or captured, we are all defeated." (2159–80)

They went off at high speed to help Gui and his companions. Duke Seguin came spurring up, vigorously striking the Germans. He struck a knight and parted his soul from his body. He gave Gui much help and severed the heads of many men. Then they joined the main battle and made every effort to deal good blows. The Germans next struck, attacking with swords and lances. They threw spears and sharp javelins and on both sides landed good blows, and they cut into shields and hauberks and made men fall over dead; they cut off fists and arms and feet. Bodies lay on the ground, butchered. Good, brave knights, sons of noble lords, who had come from afar to seek renown, lay butchered upon the fields: when their fathers found out, they would be overcome by grief. (2181–2204)

Then Duke Reiner came up. He killed our good Garner, lord Gui's companion and good friend, born in France. Gui saw this and was distressed; he at once struck Duke Reiner and knocked him far from his horse, then he drew his sharp sword and went to strike him a great blow. He was very eager to avenge Garner. Next, like a most valiant warrior, he captured Duke Reiner in the fray. Duke Seguin then came up, spurring his good horse. He struck Lord Waldemer and soon made him fly out of his stirrups, capturing him with great effort. Both were wounded in the body. Now the leaders had been taken; the Germans, defeated, fled towards their own army, with Duke Seguin and Gui pursuing them. (2205–26)

Now here came Terri of Worms, son of Alberi. Thirty knights, very proud and fierce, were with him. They came fully armed from the army to give the Germans rapid help. Wherever Terri met the Germans, he cried to them loudly: "My lords, where are you going? Turn back with me and attack our enemies, who have discomfited you, or I will tell the emperor you have done him great dishonour by deliberately fleeing from only a few men!" He made them turn around there and begin a great battle. Terri struck a knight, with no appearance of wanting to cherish him. In his turn Gui fiercely struck, so that Terri's shield was no more use than a button. Then they drew their swords, forged in Lorraine. They struck each other great blows on helmets and strong shields; they struck so violently that they made the gold and precious stones fall out of them. The lords fought as fiercely as lions. (2227–56)

Then Duke Seguin came up, whose appearance was not poor. He killed one of their Germans, cutting his heart in two. When Count Terri saw this, he was deeply angry; he went to strike Duke Seguin, he could not restrain himself. They gave each other great blows from their swords, which were of sharp steel. Then Heralt, who never failed in the hour of need, came spurring up. He struck a knight and made him fall dead to the ground. When the strong, brave, and good Count Terri saw this, he strove mightily to strike Heralt. He cast him far from his horse, and loudly shouted his war-cry; the Germans soon rallied to him. They attacked Duke Seguin, slaying and killing his men, vigorously driving them back, wounding, slaughtering, and killing them. When Duke Seguin saw this, he was angry; that was the limit! Furious, he said to Gui: "How shameful: a single knight giving us such trouble!" Gui replied: "Turn round! Attack them boldly! Better to die with honour than flee the field with shame." Then they struck the Germans and by dint of great effort defeated them. Terri kept coming to meet them, inflicting much harm with his steel sword. (2257–94)

The Germans fled, their sharp steel swords in their hands. Duke Seguin returned and made his way to the city, together with Gui of Warwick and his companions. With them, they brought their prisoners, the dukes and counts and barons. Then, happy and rejoicing, they entered the city and went off to their lodgings with great gladness. The duke went to his tower; he looked after his prisoners with great honour, for he had Duke Reiner of Saxony, Count Waldemer of Cologne, and Gunred, the seneschal, a man of great valour, to eat with him and paid more respect than himself. The duke called his sister, a maiden of high reputation: "Sister, take charge of these prisoners for me and lead them into your chambers, especially Duke Reiner, whom at heart I have so much reason to love!" "My lord," she said, "I will do so; I will serve them to the best of my ability." (2295–2322)

But Emperor Reiner did not know what great disaster had occurred. He was playing chess with the king of Hungary, of whom he was very fond. Then Terri arrived, spurring his horse, a sharp sword in his hand. Its scabbard was cut to bits in the battle in which he had been. With so many violent sword-strokes visible on it, his gleaming helmet was crushed, its golden band[25] cut to pieces, right down to just above the nosepiece. Blood streamed down his body, but Terri took no notice of it. His strong shield was so full of holes, not half a foot of it was intact. "Emperor," he said, "now listen to me! You will hear bitter news about your barons, who are captured. They will never return to you: some are taken and captured, some are killed and destroyed. Duke Reiner and Duke Waldemer of Cologne are captured, and the count of Pavia has been wounded through the body by a strong sword; he is in great fear for his life and doesn't think he'll ever recover." (2323–50)

When the emperor heard what Count Terri said, he was angered and much distressed; he almost went out of his mind. He swore a mighty oath that, if omnipotent God would help him, he would never be happy until the city of Arascune was taken and the traitor captured and hanged, burnt at the stake or drowned in the sea. He had his horns sounded and all his troops armed; next he arranged bands of troops so they were ready to fight. They occupied the fields beside a mountain and in front of the city. Guaer went ahead with five hundred bold knights who would be reluctant to flee from battle. As those in the city were looking at the Germans, and at the countryside quite covered with shields and polished hauberks, Duke Seguin appeared, well armed and on a charger. "Gui," he said, "what shall we do? Should we go out and attack them, or go and defend our walls? We can await them more securely." "My lord," said Gui, "I shall tell you; you will do well, as I know. We shall take a thousand knights and attack them boldly. I see Guaer, son of Reiner, positioned in front of the city, and with him five hundred knights, all armed, on their horses. They have already advanced in front of their army, eager to seize us. If we need help, we can easily go back." (2351–92)

Then they took a thousand knights, the boldest and bravest, and went out of the city, jointly making a great display of ferocity. They approached the Germans to fight them; from now on there would be no need for reconciliation. Each side struck ferociously and often knocked the others off their horses. Gui went off to strike Guaer and on a hill felled him and his horse; then he captured him in the fray. The others left, defeated and fleeing back towards the large army. They were energetically pursued; many of them were wounded and captured and were left lying in the plains. (2393–2408)

When those in the army learnt that their knights had been defeated and that Guaer, the emperor's son, had been captured in the battle, they made haste and speedily went to attack Duke Seguin. They started a bitter battle in which

---

[25] 2333 **golden band** *cercle d'or*: This could either be the brow-band round the edge of a conical helmet or (less likely) a vertical band of the "spangenhelm" type. See Ian Peirce, "The Knight, His Arms and Armour c. 1150–1250," *Anglo-Norman Studies* 15 (1992): 25–74.

many knights suffered death. Many were killed on both sides, but the duke had the worst of it, because he had lost men through having come out initially with few followers; his pride led him far away from his soldiers and the city. Nevertheless, he and the valiant Gui were doing well, and Heralt of Arderne too, who was landing mighty blows. Then Terri came spurring up, the brave and bold knight; he struck Duke Seguin, landing him far from his horse. But the duke quickly jumped to his feet, entirely consumed by anger; he drew his steel sword and like a noble lord defended himself well. Whomever he reached, he struck down dead, for he was a brave and strong knight. Terri attacked him most keenly, and so did the Germans; they surrounded him on all sides, throwing spears and sharp javelins. They wounded the duke in various parts of his body and they considered him dead. (2409–42)

When Gui saw the duke on the ground, he felt such grief he did not know what to do. He struck a knight and made him die on the spot. Then he drew his steel sword and struck a knight who had seized the duke, removing his head from his body. Then he made the duke mount his horse and they went off to meet their enemies. But these foes would not leave the place and took the lives of many men. "My lord duke," said Gui, "now listen to what I say: we shall return to your city; we can't defend ourselves any longer. A hundred thousand knights have armed and soon will all be gathered. If we wait here any longer, we'll all be considered madmen." Then they quickly gathered together and returned to their city. They went to defend the parapets, where they wished to await battle. (2443–66)

When the emperor heard his son was captured, he said loudly to his men that they should at once attack the city, and they speedily did so. They attacked the city; archers threw spears and shot, crossbowmen let fly round about, scaled ladders and hoisted crocs;[26] they never rested from the assault. They threw stones, and cast stones from catapults; they broke down the walls, which were so fine. Those inside defended themselves well and gave those outside a fierce fight. That day the Germans died with much suffering. They attacked the city fiercely; that day they accomplished nothing. In the evening they withdrew. The emperor was most mortified he could not avenge himself on them nor overcome the city. Each day he had it attacked most fiercely, but the duke and Gui and Heralt made many strong assaults on his followers. They often killed his men, which made him wretched at heart. (2467–94)

It was on a summer's day that the emperor had his meal, summoned his huntsmen, and said he would go hunting with a small retinue, in the forest, early (lest Duke Seguin should find out), seeking fat stags and boars, in which the countryside abounded. A spy from the army heard all this and came straight to Arascune. He went to Duke Seguin and addressed him: "My lord duke," he said, "listen to this! Now you'll hear good news: Emperor Reiner will go hunting early,

---

[26] 2475 **crocs** *crocs*: A croc was an instrument for winding up crossbows.

in the forest, with few followers; he will take with him hardly anyone except his small retinue. I'm not lying to you: he doesn't want you to know about it. You'll be able to catch them all." (2495–2518)

When the duke heard him speak, he was quick to kiss him. "My friend," he said, "it will profit you if it's true what you've told me. I'll give you a hundred besants[27] for it and, what's more, I'll make you a rich man." Then he called his barons—Gui and Heralt the wise and lord Belin and lord Gunter, lord Heldemer from Teutonic lands, and Joceranz who was from Spain (there was none wiser as far as Germany)—to give important advice; for that act he was worthy of much love. "My lords," he said, "what do you advise me, now you are gathered here? We could be avenged on our emperor, Reiner, who is going hunting early with his private retinue, much prized for knightly deeds, and on his other lords." "My lord duke," said Gui, "I will advise you the best, I believe: take a thousand knights, the bravest and best, and I will go with them. If I can find the emperor, I will beg him courteously to come and stay with you in your city of Arascune. He and all his companions shall be nobly lodged and we shall serve them splendidly. [*And you will stay here and not go towards your lord.*][28] Make the palace ready and prepare sumptuous dishes. And if he won't come willingly, we'll attack them so hard that we'll bring them to you by force. Whether they like it or not, we'll capture them all." (2519–60)

The duke replied: "Well said! Sir Gui, quickly, without delay, take a thousand knights from those you most trust. Make them lie in wait in the forest. If you can find the emperor there, on no account fail to bring him to me!" Gui went off to arm himself thoroughly, then mounted his good horse, a thousand good knights with him, all armed on horseback, all prized knights, brave, valiant, and bold. (2561–74)

The emperor rose in the morning and equipped himself well. He and his companions went to the forest of Leons, entered it, and uncoupled their dogs. They discovered a large boar, very proud and fierce. Huntsmen were pursuing it vigorously and so was the emperor, when he looked to his right and saw the gleam of polished helmets, hauberks and shields, and heard the noise of longhaired horses. "God!" he said, "now we're betrayed! Terri, good friend, come here! Can't you see, at the top of that hill, many armed knights? They have surrounded us on all sides and they'll capture us all, dead or alive. They are Duke Seguin's companions—God give him a bad end!" He saw Gui advancing first, well armed, on his horse. (2575–98)

---

[27] 2523 **a hundred besants** *Cent besansz*: A besant was a gold coin from Byzantium. See p. 52, note 149.

[28] 2553–54 **And you will stay here and not go towards your lord** *E vus ici remaindrez, Sur vostre seignur nen irez*: These lines are missing in E and are supplied from C.

"My lord emperor," said Terri, "by the true God, I beg you to leave here quickly. For God's sake, sire, don't delay! And I will stay here; if I can encounter Gui, I will do great harm to him and to those I meet. Before I'm killed or captured, you will have passed beyond this land." The emperor said: "I won't do that; I'll stay here with you." Then he quickly armed himself and mounted his good horse. Gui came spurring up, carrying a branch in his hand, which between them all meant peace. He greeted the emperor in a loud voice: "May that Lord who creates the day bless you, my lord emperor, and your barons here, who will give wise advice. Duke Seguin sends word to you, through me, that he wishes to love you loyally, and that you should come and stay with him. He wants to provide splendidly for you and your companions, with cranes, swans, and herons. He will hand his good city over to you and the castles which he has fortified. And if he has done you wrong in any way, he will make amends to your liking." (2599–2630)

When the emperor heard him speak and show such great affection, he called to the king of Hungary, and Otun and the wise Terri and Count Herkenbalt of Helene and Waldenot and Cherenbalt. "My lords," he said, "what shall we do? We cannot leave this place." Waldenot said: "My lord emperor, the duke does you very great honour, when he hands over to you his castles and his city, which has so enriched him, entirely at your pleasure. You should reward him for this, unharmed. He will be judged in your court; go and stay with him! And if he does what he has said, he cannot do more for you." The emperor said: "I agree, on condition that I do not see him until I have conferred with my barons. I want to act on their advice, whether for peace or war." They went together towards the city and talked about reconciliation between themselves; then they arrived at the city and were most nobly received. The emperor was lodged in the city of Arascune, where he was most nobly served, as were his companions, with wines, spiced wine and clarry, mead, hippocras,[29] mulberry wine, and with swans, cranes, peacocks, and all kinds of game. Gui made great efforts that day to serve them with great honour: in the house there was neither squire nor page nor anyone, however humble, who was not served most nobly, entirely at their orders. (2631–72)

The emperor rose in the morning and went to the church of St Laurence, and with him his counts and his barons, who came from many regions. Duke Seguin was not there, because the emperor did not wish it; he had himself attended to along with his prisoners, who were very noble lords. In the morning he rose and spoke to his prisoners. "My lords," he said, "now I ask you to come with me to beg our lord the emperor to give up his anger with me, this very day, if it is his pleasure." And they replied very readily: "We shall go with you and ask

---

[29] 2663–64 **clarry; hippocras** *claré, boschez*: *claré* was a blend of red and white wine with added spices; hippocras was also wine flavoured with spices. See above p. 51, note 148.

him most willingly." Then he took off his tunic—many men pitied him—and remained in his shirt. Now listen to the way he wanted to go to the emperor: he carried an olive branch in his hand and went barefoot through the streets. Many dukes and counts went with him, so that they could ask the emperor as soon as they saw him. (2673–2700)

When they entered the church, they fell at the emperor's feet. "My lord emperor," said Seguin, "this very day my end will come. I do not want to endure your anger any longer. Rather, have me killed quickly. Take this sword, sire, and cut my head off my body! I don't want to suffer war from you; I would rather bequeath you all my land and leave the kingdom, never to return. Do what you please with me and I, my good lord, will agree entirely. As for the folly I committed when I killed your nephew, I did it in self-defence, in the presence of the duke of Saxony and many other knights, whom I saw there. If there is anyone who contradicts this, saying I killed him out of wickedness, and if I can't defend myself against that, have me hanged, sire!"[30] (2701–24)

"Sire, good father," said Guaer, "the duke is a most noble lord; he will be able to serve you in time of need and give good protection to your borders. If you don't pardon him, you will get no more joy from me." (2725–30)

"Sire," said Duke Reiner, "you should cherish the duke greatly. Since he placed himself at your mercy, do what you please with him. As for your nephew whom he killed, he did it in self-defence. If there is anyone who contradicts this, I will fight for the duke in your presence, right away; I will certainly defend him against the accusation of wicked deeds. If you don't have mercy on the duke, you will certainly get war from me." (2731–42)

"My lord emperor," said Waldemer, "I won't hide my thoughts; I love the duke above all others, for he has done me honour and great good. We are sworn companions. If you wrong him in any way, I shall return to Cologne and gather my country's army. Be advised that I'll destroy your castles and your cities!" (2743–52)

"Sire," said the seneschal, "the duke is extremely brave. He has done you very great honour; no greater will ever befall you. Since he has taken you inside his city and surrendered himself to you, whether to live or to die, and to do what you want with him, what he does, you should do and seek mercy in the same fashion. My noble lord, be quick to abandon the anger and wrath you have against him!" (2753–64)

---

[30] 2681–2724 **In the morning . . . "have me hanged, sire!"** *Par matin . . . "sire, me facez pendre!"*: Seguin's dress and behaviour is reminiscent of the penitential actions of Henry II after Becket's murder. See *La Vie de S. Thomas Becket*, ed. Emmanuel Wahlberg (Paris: CFMA, 1936), 5946–55, and William of Newburgh, *Historia Rerum Anglicarum*, Book 2, chap. 35.

"Sire," said Gui, "good, gentle lord, so long as I become your man and serve you henceforth as lord whenever you need me, I beg you to hear my prayer and have mercy on the duke, to cherish him." (2765–72)

"My lord emperor," said Terri, "have mercy on Duke Seguin! If through him you have lost your nephew, Count Saduc, he will take the place of your nephew and serve you in case of need." (2773–78)

When they had all entreated the emperor, he kept his head bent. "My lords," he said, "now listen to me! You all ask me to renounce my anger against the duke for the death of one of my kin, my sister's son, a most valiant knight, the man I loved most in the world; I shall never be joyful again. I see the duke amenable and without pride. I will give up my anger against him. From now on he shall be one of my intimates; let everything be readily forgiven him." Dukes and counts thanked him and said repeatedly: "Thank you!" Each fell at his feet and kissed him, weeping for joy. There they were reconciled and became friends and the armies dispersed. (2779–98)

But now here came Duke Otun; no one in the realm was more wicked: "My lord emperor, what have you done? Because you have kissed the traitors and pardoned the death of Saduc, you will always be humiliated. Henceforth, who will fear you? Everyone will wrong you, for their own advantage, since you pardon them their wrongs; they will visit great shame and disgrace on you. Had you hanged them, you would be much more feared. Duke Seguin and Gui never did you anything but harm, and now they will be your intimates and you will love them more than the rest." (2799–2814)

When Gui heard the duke speak, he jumped to his feet like a noble knight. "Duke," he said, "you lie when you speak of wrongdoing, whether the duke's or mine! I shall defend us, as I ought to do. But you are a traitor and a scoundrel. May God curse you, since you had me betrayed and my men die in pain, and if you maintain this by force of arms, that what you have heard is not true, I shall prove it physically; I shall cut your head from your body." He would certainly have punched him, which would have thrown him to the ground, but the barons separated them. The emperor swore by St Denis that if anyone were so bold as to defame another in front of him, he would have him burnt or beheaded or dismembered. Peace was made throughout the palace; neither Greeks nor Germans spoke a word. Then Duke Reiner came up to ask Duke Seguin for the hand of his sister, Erneburc, and he gave him her with much honour: she was a well-educated maiden, none more excellent in the kingdom. He took her and married her and then brought her to Brunswick. (2815–46)

The emperor called the wise Duke Seguin: "My lord duke, I have much reason to love you: now I want to give you a wife. I have an unmarried niece and, out of my great affection, I will give her to you." "Sire," he said, "thank you!" He kissed his feet and rejoiced. Then they held the wedding festivities. None more splendid had ever been seen. (2847–56)

Gui then went to the duke and asked him for leave to go. "My lord duke, now I want to depart; I have no wish to stay any longer in this land. I have been of service to you in your war. If you need me, be sure to send for me, and I shall come to you, be certain of that!" "My lord," he said, "if you please, I don't deserve that yet. Stay with me! This very day I will give you half my castles and my cities, and half the fief of Louvain." But Gui took his leave and departed, and the duke wept for sorrow. (2857–72)

The emperor left, taking Gui with him. He offered him castles and cities, large domains and splendid fiefs, but Gui did not want to accept them, no matter what happened. He went to Germany, to the noble city of Speyer. The emperor paid him much honour and he stayed a while with him. Then, to amuse himself, he went to the riverbanks, which were full of game birds; and, whenever he liked, he went hunting the fat boars in the forest. One day he came back from hunting and saw a ship arriving. He went to it and greeted the sailors. "Sirs," he said, "where are you from, who have come to this shore? I can easily see from your appearance that you carry great riches with you." "My lord," said a well-spoken sailor, "we come straight from Constantinople; we are going in search of a peaceful country. We are merchants in that land, expelled because of great warfare. The mighty sultan of Konya,[31] so puffed up with pride, has, with fifteen Saracen kings and thirty emirs from an evil race, besieged the noble Emperor Hernis in Constantinople. No tower or city or castle in the kingdom is left to him which has not been burnt and totally destroyed. He has fled to Constantinople and is defending himself there against Saracens, Turks, Persians, and Moravins.[32] You can travel for a hundred leagues without seeing one man talk to another. We have barely escaped all being slaughtered. We have come to this land; we carry plenty of miniver and grey fur, gold, silver, and precious stones, possessing many kinds of power. You can see good silk cloth from Alexandria, oriental marten skins, and many other goods of all kinds." (2873–2924)

When the sailor had told all his story, Gui commended him to God. He went back to his lodging and called Heralt of Arderne. "My friend Heralt, let's go and ask leave of the emperor! I want to go off to Constantinople, to help and aid the emperor, whom the mighty sultan has besieged. People from the land have told me the kingdom has been destroyed and laid waste and Christianity has been brought low." Heralt replied: "I agree. You will get much glory from it, I believe." Gui took leave of the emperor, who granted it only very reluctantly; he offered him many castles and towers, noble cities and great domains. Gui took a hundred knights, the bravest and boldest he could find in Germany, and the most acclaimed. He quickly embarked and sailed as far as Constantinople,

---

[31] Capital of the Seljuk sultanate, 11th through 13th centuries.

[32] 2912 **Moravins** According to Flutre, 195, this Saracen people might be the "Amoraives," i.e., the Almoravids, a Berber dynasty, powerful in North Africa and southern Spain in the 11th and 12th centuries.

where he took lodgings in the city. When the emperor was informed that Gui of Warwick had come, he rejoiced at his arrival; he sent for him by means of two counts and spoke to him most affectionately: "Sir Gui of Warwick, you are welcome as the most highly esteemed man in the world! I have heard you greatly praised! I am in much need of your help. Wicked Saracens have besieged me, leaving me no castle or tower which they have not entirely burnt and laid waste, but only this city. I lost forty thousand men in one day, all slaughtered with great suffering. They have killed my men and my son. Now I entreat you, good friend: if you can avenge me on them, and deliver my land from the villains, I will give you my beautiful daughter and half of all my land with her." (2925–70)

"My lord," he said, "thank you! And I tell you truly that I will serve you faithfully as long as I am with you." Then he took leave of him; from now on they would be good friends. He returned to his lodging. He heard a din and shouting in the city, and asked what such outcry in the city meant, as well as knights he had seen arming throughout the town and men at arms climbing to the battlements. "My lord," said a citizen, an Englishman, born in England, "it's emir Cosdroein, nephew of the powerful sultan; he's very brave and aggressive, and I think there's no one in the world more valiant. His weapons are all poisoned with deadly venom. There's nobody in the world whom he would not speedily knock down dead if he strikes him. He hurt us very much the other day when he killed the emperor's son, who was a brave knight who had given him many a hard fight. There wasn't a knight in this city who dared encounter him when he was angry. He has arrived with a large band of knights, and with him the mighty king of Turkey and many thousands of brave Turks; there are none braver in any land." (2971–3002)

Gui said to his companions: "My lords, let's now quickly arm ourselves and go and attack the Saracens. Let everyone strive to strike well." They armed speedily, then mounted their horses[33] and struck them at once; no one was spared. Gui struck the emir, whose shield and hauberk were not worth a straw.[34] He put his steel blade through the emir's body and felled him to the ground. Then he drew his sharp sword and cut his head from his body. He sent it to the emperor, who was joyful and happy to have it. Heralt struck the king of Turkey, the most wicked man in all Syria. He hit him through the body and he fell flat on the ground. Then Tebalt came spurring up, born in France and very valiant; he struck Helmidan—none more wicked as far as Milan—with great violence, put his lance through his body, and instantly felled him dead. Then Gunter came spurring up, a knight from Germany. He struck Rodoan—you haven't heard of anyone more wicked this year—cut his heart in two, and knocked him dead on the spot. Then Morgadur appeared, the emperor's seneschal; he was a brave

---

[33] 3008 **then mounted their horses** *En lur destrers sunt puis muntez*: After 3008, F adds 4 lines.

[34] 3012 **were not worth a straw** *ne li valt un ail*: After 3012, H stops.

and bold knight, though always evil and treacherous. He struck a Saracen and knocked him flat on the field. Then they all struck boldly together in the fray. Gui could be seen fighting very well—he made so many Saracens die that day, as did Heralt along with him. Both strove hard to harm, defeat, and slaughter wicked Saracens. The Saracens put up a great fight because they were very courageous warriors. (3003–50)

Then Esclandart came spurring up, a cruel Saracen and the son of the king of Burie, brave and full of knightly qualities. He knocked down our lord Tebalt, whom he struck in the body with his sword. Then he killed one of our Frenchmen, born in the region of Blois. Then Remirant appeared, a brave and valiant Saracen: he killed our Guineman, a German from Germany. Then Amilert appeared, a wicked and savage Saracen; he killed our lord Guimer, a knight from Lorraine. When the noble Heralt saw this, he felt nothing but anger; he struck Amilert and fiercely knocked him dead. When Esclandart saw this, he was impatient to avenge Amilert; he at once went to strike Heralt. Heralt met him boldly and they hit each other with great violence and were knocked off their horses. Then they drew their steel swords and gave each other great and mighty blows, cleaving hauberks and shields. They were bold and brave warriors. They struck such blows with their steel swords that they made sparks fly from their helmets. (3051–81)

Heralt was pursuing him hard, threatening to cut off his head, when plenty of help arrived. A hundred Turks, aiding him, all attacked Heralt and would have certainly hurt and killed him, except that Gui saw him and was distressed. He went to help him with great ferocity. Then he drew his steel sword, made a Saracen's head fly, and another just the same; the third he at once knocked dead. Like a noble knight, he helped Heralt and got him mounted on his horse. Then they encountered the Saracens and made many die that day. That day many killed one another, but the Saracens had the worst of it, for Gui and his companions, and his Greeks with him, defeated and drove them away, and they lay slaughtered in the fields. They fled straight to the army, and Gui followed them vigorously. Before they had passed the hills, they were all dead and slaughtered. Esclandart kept fighting them and doing the Christians much harm; he galloped off on an Arab steed and, without any resistance, occupied the hills. His shield was full of holes and his jewelled helmet was shattered. (3083–3114)

When Gui saw him, he was grieved that he had to leave in such a state. "Esclandart, " he said, "turn around! Truly, you are quite safe; you needn't fear anyone but me. In the name of your faith, I ask you for a joust." Esclandart asked: "Are you Gui? Now I defy you! Indeed, I swear by my religion and by Mahomet, in whom I believe, that I'll never be happy until I've cut off your head. I've promised it to a maiden, the sultan's daughter, who is very beautiful." They turned their horses' heads and struck each other hard like good warriors. First Esclandart struck Gui fiercely on the shield, cutting off the links of mail with his sharp sword. If almighty God had not protected Gui, Esclandart would certainly have soon maimed him and given him a deadly wound through his body. Gui struck him back with great violence; neither shield nor hauberk could save him from being run through the body by Gui's lance with great force. Esclandart quickly fled, and Gui did not catch up with him. He was much vexed and returned to his companions. Then they went back to the city; they had defeated the Saracens and there was great joy throughout. The emperor sent for Gui; he paid him great honour, as he should have done. "Gui," he said, "I have great reason to love you: I want to give you my daughter. You are a man of much courage and you will be emperor after me: those who attend on me will do the same to you." When the seneschal heard this—there was no more wicked knight in Greece—he was very jealous of Gui; if he could manage it, Gui would lose his life because of him. (3115–58)

Esclandart fled, spurring strongly towards the army. There was the stump of a lance through his body; he gripped the saddle-bow with his hands, and in front and behind the blood streamed down his body. His helmet hung to one side, his face was all bloody, he could not hold his shield, and he was very fearful of dying. He arrived in the Sultan's tent. The Sultan saw him and recognized him. "Esclandart," he said, "where have you come from? You've been in a bitter battle. Were you alone in the city? Tell me, who wounded you so badly?" "My lord," he said, "I will tell you the bad news I know of: you have lost emir Cosdroein, your nephew whom you loved so much; you have lost the king of Turkey—he'll never help you again!—and some thousand excellent Turks are dead in front of the city." Then the Sultan, who was listening to him carefully, replied: "Did help then arrive for the city, by which I have lost my Turks?" (3159–86)

"Indeed, my lord," said Esclandart, "a fierce, cruel fellow—that's the fine help which arrived. There's no such armed man in the whole world. His name is Gui of Warwick: he's fiercer than a lion. No one could endure his blows without immediately having to die. With him were a hundred valiant knights, the most successful in Germany. He hit me so hard through the body that I feel sure I'm mortally wounded." The Sultan swore a great oath by Mahomet, whom he worshipped, that he would never be happy until he had taken the mighty city; he would attack it before the third day had passed. When a spy, who would not hide anything from Gui, heard all this, he came to the city and told Gui of Warwick everything about how the Sultan was to come and attack the city by force. But the emperor did not know that the news was so bad; when he found out, his heart would indeed be sad and dark. (3187–3214)

The emperor was very happy that he was avenged on his enemies; he asked for his birds—goshawks, falcons and gerfalcons—and wanted to go to the riverbank to amuse and entertain himself. Then he called for some of his brave and courteous Greeks; they went to the bank, which was full of game birds. Then the seneschal came up, who was very wicked and faithless. "Gui," he said, "I have much reason to cherish you, and in my heart I hold you very dear. I have splendid, strong, and fine domains and castles; I want them to be at your disposal.

I'm eager to have your friendship. Let's go and have some fun, my lord, and enjoy ourselves in chambers playing backgammon and chess in the presence of the maiden, Laurette,[35] your beautiful mistress." "My lord," said Gui, "let's go; since it pleases you, we can do so." (3215–40)

They went straight to the chambers and entered hand in hand.[36] They came to the maiden, who called to them courteously: "My lord Gui, welcome! Come and sit down and amuse yourself." Gui took her in his arms and kissed her and talked most affectionately to her. Then they asked for the chess-pieces and played in front of the maiden. They set out the first game, but the seneschal soon lost it. Then they began another, and Gui quickly won it, and the third likewise, which upset the seneschal. He stood up angrily, because he was cross and furious. "My lord Gui," he said, "stay here and amuse yourself with the maiden, and I will go into the city; I'll be back soon." Morgadur left the chamber, mounted a valuable horse, and went straight off to the emperor. When the emperor saw him come, he went to meet him and asked him for news. "Now, my lord seneschal, is it good or bad news? Why do you come spurring up like this? Tell me, I order you. If you have heard about the Saracens, tell me, don't hide it from me." (3241–74)

"My lord," he said, "I shall tell you, without concealing your shame. You have retained a mercenary. He wants to humiliate and deceive you; he has prostituted my lady your daughter. He entered your chambers by force and has raped your Laurette. And if you don't want to believe me, make haste to return: you can find him embracing and kissing your daughter in your chamber. Therefore I came to tell you about it, not wanting to hide your shame. If you have him seized and put in your dungeon, then sentenced in your court to be hanged or drowned in the sea, you will be much the more feared by everyone in your realm. So don't desist, either because of him or his help. After you have sentenced him and are rid of the traitor, I want to go to Germany, to the mighty Emperor Reiner; I will bring you his help, and I will certainly save your land from your mortal enemies, who have killed and slaughtered your men." (3275–3304)

"You shouldn't talk of such things," he said. "From now on, seneschal, let this be! Gui would not harm me, nor would he do what you have said, even were he to be dismembered, so loyal a knight I know him to be. Because I have promised him my daughter, I do not want to break the agreement." When the seneschal heard that the emperor would not listen to him, he was very grieved. He returned quickly to the city, and entered the fine chambers where Gui was amusing himself with the maidens. As soon as he entered the chambers, he called Gui to one side. "Gui," he said, "I have much reason to cherish you, so now I want

---

[35] 3237 **Laurette** In GAP, as also both English versions, the emperor's daughter is called Clarice.

[36] 3242 **entered hand in hand** *Main en main i sunt entrez*: Cf *The Romance of Horn*, ed. M.K. Pope, 2 vols. (Oxford: ANTS, 1964), 795–96 and 1050: both Haderof and Horn enter Princess Rigmel's chamber hand in hand with the seneschal, Haderof.

to tell you: the emperor has been informed that you have shamed and disgraced him, you have raped his daughter and entered her chambers by force. If he can catch you or seize you, he will have you burnt or strung up high. I command you, go away; don't delay for anything. If you are found in this city, you will be handed over to a painful death." (3305–32)

"My God!" said Gui, "this is indeed wrong, that I should here receive death for something of which I am not guilty or of which I've never thought. When he went off this morning, he loved me very much, from what he said. Who can ever trust fine promises and fine speech? For the emperor told me, and truly promised me, that he would do me great honour and good. Now he wants to give me a painful death because of the word of a scoundrel, an envious slanderer." He went out of the room, miserable and angry at heart, went to his lodging, and called all his companions. "My lords," he said, "now let's arm ourselves; we'll stay here no longer. Someone has denounced us to the emperor; we shall all be cut down and killed. But, by the faith I owe my Creator, who makes night and day, before we are captured or killed we shall slay so many of theirs that it will be clear to the proudest of them we are wrongly accused." They speedily armed and at once took horse. Then they went in order out of the city, in serried ranks; they wanted to go to the Sultan, to get to know and serve him. (3333–66)

Then the emperor appeared, who was returning from hawking. The weather was fine, the day bright; he saw the gleam of helmets and asked a passer-by: "Who are these armed knights?" "My lord," he said, "indeed it's Gui; in anger he's leaving here to go straight to the Sultan's army, shield round his neck, sword in hand. He certainly looks as if he's angry: he sits his horse fully armed." When the emperor heard this, he lowered his head and struck spurs into his horse, which moved faster than a falcon. He very quickly overtook Gui. "Gui," he said, "go no further! My friend, don't do this! Why do you want to leave me? If I have done you any wrong, whether in word or deed, I beg you, tell me. If anyone has criticized you, I want to be reconciled with you; above anything in the world, I want to cherish you. I can well believe that the Sultan, who holds all Persia in his hands, has summoned you, and I know very well he will get you and I shall lose you. He can give you gold and silver; he can endow you splendidly with magnificent fiefs. For this you want to forsake me and side with him against me?" (3367–3400)

"My lord." said Gui to the emperor, "I shall never be a traitor. I was told and informed this very morning, in the city, that you didn't care for my service, that I served you with deceit and that I had been denounced to you. For this reason I didn't want to stay but wanted to go and serve someone who could reward my pains. I shouldn't be against you for all Damascus." The emperor took him in his arms, kissed him lovingly, and said: "My friend Gui, turn back! Barons, my lords, entreat him! Land, and whatever else belongs to me, is now at your command. I won't believe a living soul who slanders you in any way." Then they kissed each other there and returned to the city. Gui knew now for sure that the seneschal had betrayed him, but he did not let it show, nor did he say a word to him. (3401–26)

"My lord emperor," said Gui, "listen to what I tell you: tomorrow, early in the morning, we shall be attacked, for that's how things stand, by impious Saracens and their large bands. They will attack the city tomorrow and destroy it as far as they can. The Sultan himself will come, who has sworn by his gods to attack the city; he won't leave, even were he to die, until the city is destroyed and taken, and the land laid waste." The emperor replied: "Whatever you want shall be, Sir Gui: I've transferred all responsibility to you, subject to God's providence. If they attack us, we shall defend ourselves. The city is strong, we have no fear." Gui called to the constable, a noble and wise knight with a white beard, called Cristor, lord and duke of Armarie. "Sir Cristor," he said, "listen to this: you can be sure we shall be attacked. We must decide whether we want to defend the city, or go to fight them in the narrow defiles between the mountains, for there we can encounter them and do them great harm." (3427–58)

"My lord," said the constable, "these words should be binding. Have it proclaimed throughout the city that in the morning everyone who can bear arms should be armed and that anyone who stays behind is a coward!" In the morning they armed, twenty thousand hauberks in number. Then twenty thousand shields—no lie here—went out of the city. "My lords," said Gui, "now listen, you who are gathered here. The Saracens are coming to attack us, I want you to know, and we shall go to fight them in the narrow defiles between the mountains. Now think of doing well and of defending your country well; now think of your friends and your kin, whom they have killed; think of your lands, of your cities, destroyed and laid waste; now think of avenging yourselves and fighting them with vigour. If you don't defend yourselves well, and you're chased off the field, we shall all be killed or captured and stay in servitude for ever. So let's go and fight them; everyone should strive to do well, and I, who will never let you down, shall go with you." They all said: "Thank you! Sir Gui, you speak very well." Then they came to the pass in the mountains, when they saw the Saracens and saw the country round about covered with armed men. (3459–96)

The sultan summoned Hesman of Tyre, who disdained to flee out of fear, a brave and valiant king, greatly feared in many lands. "King," he said, "I order you to come forward with twenty thousand Turks. Go and attack the Christians; take care to capture all who are there on top of that mountain: they have done us great harm." The king went off with his men and occupied the mountains by force; in his pride he believed he would pass through the gorge, but on the contrary he would meet great obstacles. At the entrance to the gorge, Gui called to his men: "My lords, barons, now we need your help! Now put your minds to defending yourselves! If they can take the pass from us, we shall fare badly, unless God, who created everything, looks after matters. We are on the mountain and they are in the valley; they have taken their stand in the middle of the gorge." They threw stones and shot with bows; they hurled spears and sharp javelins;

they struck with swords and sharpened blades; they threw sharp and piercing bolts; they killed Saracens furiously. Gui did a very clever thing: he let them come up into the gorge, then had them attacked behind and in front, and by hundreds and thousands they killed the wicked Saracens. (3497–3528)

When the king of Tyre saw his men dying with such suffering, he grasped a sharp javelin in his hand and greatly threatened the Christians. He proceeded to hit a knight, knocking him dead to the ground. When Gui of Warwick saw this, he went over there, without resistance; he carried a javelin in his hand, bent his arm back, and threw it. It struck King Hesman[37] so that it knocked him bleeding to the ground. They cut down and killed the Saracens, who howled and cried amongst the mountains. (3529–42)

When the sultan saw his men dying a violent and painful death, he called for the king of Nubia, who was full of wickedness. "King," he said, "don't you see how my men are being killed? I see them defeated and, indeed, all dead; I see the bodies lying amongst the mountains. So help me Mahomet, Tervagant, and Apollo, the omnipotent, if I'm not avenged on them, I'll never feel joy again. Now we shall go and attack them, and seize the mountains by force; we are a hundred to one of theirs—we shall surely seize them all at once." They overran the mountains round about as the scoundrels attacked our Christians. In the wide and in the narrow passes, the Greeks defended themselves well; they struck with axes and swords and gave hard blows with broadswords. The battle was very bitter; many lost their heads and their ventails.[38] God! how well Gui did that day, like a warrior of great valour! He stopped in a gorge, like a knight of great power, holding in his hand a sharp broadsword, and, in front and behind, the Saracens attacked him. Everyone he reached came to grief. He had lost his shield, which lay at his feet, cut to bits. He killed so many Saracens that they lay dead on top of each other; he killed so many in a short time that he made a pile of them up to his waist. (3543–80)

Brave Heralt was like a boar in ferocity. He held a Danish axe in his hands and killed and crushed Saracens; foam flew out of his mouth. In his courage he looked the picture of a worthy man; his strong hauberk was damaged and through it his bleeding flesh was visible. The Saracens attacked him fiercely and he defended himself like a good warrior. Each of Gui's companions defended himself like a brave fighter, and, alongside them, the Greeks defended themselves well on this occasion. Then they got hold of cartwheels, as many as seventy, I believe, and they joined them together with great posts and made an amazing device. There were so many very sharp iron stakes all around it that no

---

[37] 3539 **Hesman** *Helmant*: Spelt Helmant here and Helman, 8286.
[38] 3566 **ventails** *la ventaille*: The mail coif underneath the helmet was fitted with a ventail, a shaped flap of mail which could be drawn across the mouth for added protection. See Peirce, "Knight," 255.

man alive whom they touched was not cut into a thousand pieces. The engines of war to defeat the Saracens were so horrible—sharpened stakes on all sides. They threw them down from high mountains, and with them large, quarried stones, such as a hundred men could push, in order to maim the Saracens. Some thousand of them were knocked down by the stones, so that they were all killed or injured. It turned out very badly for the Saracens that day; they suffered greatly and were killed. (3581–3614)

Night came, the day ended. The Saracen army were in a bad way, for so many of them had been killed that day! The people of that land said there were so many killed that a man could not go for fifteen miles,[39] without, however much he tried, having to walk on the dead, whether on a hand or a foot or a severed arm. Then Mirabel appeared, a newly-dubbed Saracen who had been struck through the body. He came straight to the sultan. "My lord sultan, go! Don't you see your men being killed? Our gods hate us heartily; they will not help us in any way. From now on, withdraw and go to your camps; have the wounded carried with you, you could still need them. Summon your whole body of vassals and give your mind to revenge." Then they withdrew and carried the wounded with them; they arrived in their camps wretched, beaten, and dismayed. (3615–42)

The sultan called for his gods and had them brought before him. "Ah, gods, how odious you are, always wicked towards our people! I have done you much service and honour; today you have poorly rewarded me. I will reward you: I will do you service with a large stake." He took a stake made of apple-wood and began to abuse his gods, raining great blows on their sides, tearing the tops of their heads off, and smashing their legs and their arms, often calling them weak and feeble. "You never did me any good, nor can you do any more than a dog." Then he took them by the feet and threw them outside into the mud. Next he summoned his whole body of vassals; there was no Saracen as far as the Red Sea, however wealthy or powerful, whom he did not summon, from great necessity. (3643–64)

Gui called his companions. "My lords," he said, "God be thanked: today has turned out very well for us, thanks be to God, all-powerful Jesus! We have defeated our enemies; let us return to our city." They carried the wounded with them and returned with much joy. Now Gui was very much lauded; the people of the land loved him greatly and the emperor held him very dear, believing he could get his kingdom back through him. Whatever pleased Gui was done, and no one ever criticized him. When wicked, treacherous Morgadur, the scoundrel, saw this, he started to think how he could trick Gui. He decided on a wicked act, such as you never heard of: he resolved in his mind that he would make Gui go as messenger to the fierce sultan. If he went, he would never return. (3665–88)

---

[39] 3620 **fifteen miles** *quinze arpenz*: an arpent is a measure of length.

Morgadur came to the emperor and addressed him most affectionately: "My lord emperor, listen to this: you will surely hear good advice. If you want to trust me, I am sure you will not do amiss. I am your man and your faithful subject, so you ought to trust my advice. I would not give you any that wasn't good, for I don't want to be considered wicked. The sultan has summoned his men from throughout all the pagan lands, it's true; there's not an old man or child in the land who might bear arms whom he has not summoned through his missives, in order to besiege you, fair lord. His army will grow every day, whereas the number of your men will continually be diminished. Then he will capture the city; none will be there to defend it. Therefore, my lord, prepare yourself; think about acting for the best. You already have a knight, the best who ever mounted a horse, the brave Gui of Warwick: there's no one in the world so valiant. He and the marquis[40] Heralt of Arderne are both very good friends to you. You can certainly trust them; even if their limbs were to be cut off, they would not fail you. So send word to the mighty sultan that you want to decide on a day with him: since he wants to conquer your kingdom and possess the land by force, he should pick the knight by whom he can settle its fate in battle. And you should pick another, whom you trust completely, and who can defend your land. Suggest this to the sultan, and if your man should defeat his, if that is accomplished in the fight, you should have your land without opposition. Tell the sultan this: if by chance his knight should kill or maim yours, you will give him tribute for your land. Swear to this agreement between you." (3689–3736)

The Emperor Hernis replied: "Now I will follow your advice, seneschal. I will summon all my barons; if any of them dares to go and carry the message to the mighty sultan, I will consider him very brave and wise. I am sure none will dare to go, for he would be most uncertain of returning." Then the emperor had his barons summoned, his mercenaries and his Greeks. "My lords, barons, now listen: you are gathered together out of great necessity. I want to send word to the sultan that he wrongly wants to dispossess me, and that I no longer will endure his war. He should let me rule my land in peace. If he contests the ownership of my land, then he should choose one of his Saracens by whom he can settle the matter, and I in turn will find a knight to fight his Saracen and defend my land well. And if his man defeats mine, I will indeed hand over power to the sultan, give him tribute for my land, and hold it all from him. If mine defeats his, he should leave my kingdom and my land in a friendly fashion and never return to do evil. Whoever can carry out this mission and then return safely to me will always have my love, and I will greatly honour him." (3737–70)

When the emperor had made his speech, there was no knight in the room who replied in any way, but everyone in the palace was silent until Cristor,[41]

---

[40] 3715 **marquis** *marchis*: See note to line 1308; *marchis* is again a rhyming word.
[41] 3776 **Cristor** *Clistor*: Here spelt *Clistor*, but in 3449 and 3451 *Cristor*.

the old and bearded constable, rose. His beard reached to his waist, his face was broad, his look was proud. He was dressed in a fine tunic and arrayed with marten fur. "Listen to me, my lord emperor, and don't consider my words harsh. However well-born he may be who gave you this advice, that you should send your valiant man there and knowingly have him killed, may he be cursed five hundred times, because he hardly loves you. Don't you remember the seven lords from Greece, from amongst the noblest Greeks, whom you sent to the sultan on a mission there? Alas that you thought of it! He sent only their heads back to you, and after that no one ever dared to go. I don't believe you will find a knight who dares to go on the mission. I don't say so from cowardice: if I had as much strength in my arms, and were the age I was forty years ago, I would certainly carry the message and wouldn't refuse it, regardless of death. But I'm old and my hair is quite white and I've quite lost my great strength. More than a hundred years have now passed since I was dubbed knight. While I was a knight, I would often go on great missions. Now I'm old, I'm no longer competent. From now on I must be a counsellor." (3771–3810)

Heralt looked at Gui; with little provocation he would have asked to be allowed to carry out the mission, if he had not thought Gui would consider it insulting. When Gui of Warwick had heard that no one offered to go, he did not want to come forward. He had wanted to hear from others, and to know their feelings for certain, and whether anyone dared to carry the message. Then he rose to his feet. "Emperor," he said, "now listen to me: for you I will go on the mission to the fierce-faced sultan. I won't fail, out of fear for my life, to give him the message; in the room no one, however lowly, will fail to hear my words clearly." The emperor said: "Gui, don't go; don't even think of going! I would not, for this city, have you go on the mission. I did this only to test whom I could really trust. Now I know your mind well: you would certainly carry out the mission." (3811–36)

In great anger, Gui replied: "My good lord, I certainly won't fail to carry the message, even were I to die on the spot; fear of death won't stop me executing the mission." Then he left the palace. The Greeks said amongst themselves: "What a brave knight Gui is! May God, who suffered, defend him from danger and let him come back safely!" Then Gui came to his lodging and found his companions much dismayed, for they wanted to accompany him but he did not want to take anyone with him. "My lord," said Heralt, "I will go with you; if you die, I shall die there." "Sir Heralt," he said, "you will not; by my head, you shan't go!" At once he asked for his armour; it was brought to him courteously. He put on greaves: no finer were ever forged. Then he dressed in a strong hauberk: whoever had it on would never fear death. He laced a helmet on his head: a better knight never handled it. Its golden hoop could not be exchanged for half a city, for so many good stones were in it, which were precious and dear. Then he girded on a sword made in an enchanted island, hung a shield round his neck, and jumped on to his horse without using stirrups. In his hand he took a sharp spear. Then he went out of the city. All those in the city wept for pity for him: they thought he would never return but would have to die among the Saracens. (3837–78)

Then Gui took the way leading to the Saracen army. He never stopped travelling, crossing the mountains and valleys. He came to the Saracen army and saw many tents and pavilions, and valleys and large mountains all spread with tents.[42] He saw the royal pavilion and the golden eagle right at the top, and the gleaming carbuncle set in the front, which gave out as much light at night as if on a summer's day. He soon came straight to the pavilion, travelling at top apeed. He entered the tent on horseback and spoke to the sultan, whom he found at a meal, along with his large band and with seven kings also eating there, who were making many threats against the emperor. (3879–3900)

Gui then appeared in the tent and spoke proudly: "May that Lord who lives on high, who makes heat and cold, and who let himself suffer on the cross to free us sinners from Hell, and who makes the sturgeon in the sea—may He curse you and all those I see in this place, who believe in your false religion! Our emperor, who has good and fierce followers, who have defeated, killed, destroyed, and harmed your Saracens, tells you this: that you should leave his land. If you dispute ownership of it, you should then find a knight through whom you can claim it, and the emperor will find another who, God willing, will take on the battle. If by chance your man should defeat his in battle, he will pay you tribute for his land and serve you as his lord. Should it happen that our man defeats yours in battle, you will speedily hand over the emperor's land to him and make good his great losses. I tell you, on behalf of our emperor, to decide on a day for this. If you don't agree to this, and claim a right to the land, I am here to defend our right, if anyone dares to take on the battle. I will defend my lord's land in your court now, without further ado." (3901–36)

The sultan said: "Who are you, who have come to my court? I have never yet come across a knight who stood up to me in this way." Gui replied: "I will tell you, and I will not hide my name from you. I am called Gui of Warwick in the land where I was born." "So are you that same Gui? How dare you come here! You killed my nephew, Cosdroein, and cut off his head with your own hand, and you have killed my men. I won't eat so long as you are alive! Your emperor had little love for you when he sent you on a mission here. I shall be thoroughly avenged on you; you will be handed over to pain and injury." He ordered Gui to be seized and speedily put in his prison until the end of the meal, and then he would be sentenced to a painful death. Saracens jumped up, wanting to seize him. "By my faith, " he said, "I'm waiting too long!" He drew his steel sword and struck spurs into his horse. "Sultan, " he said, "you shall pay for this: you will be the first to lose your head." He made the sultan's head fly from the golden chair he sat in onto the table, seized the head with his left hand, and at once left the pavilion.

---

[42] 3886 **spread with tents** *tenduz de pavilluns*: After 3886, F adds 2 lines.

On the way he cut the heads off many who wanted to hamper him. By force he carried off the head, wrapping it in the skirt of his coat. He quickly rode through the army on his horse, which carried him at great speed. (3937–74)

Now you could see the Saracens mount their horses! They could scarcely arm, so anxious were they to catch Gui; for the most part they were in full armour. Gui went off along a slope, and the Saracens pursued him; by hundreds and thousands nimble Saracens chased him. On all sides they attacked him and he had many encounters with them. You never heard of a lone knight who dared to fight them more fiercely. If God, son of Mary, did not look after him, he would be in great fear of his life. (3975–88)

Now I want to talk about Heralt, who never stopped lamenting. No one could describe the misery and anger he felt. He could be seen lamenting so bitterly, wringing his hands and tearing his hair, for his good lord Gui! He thought he would never see him again. "Ah, fair lord, sweet friend Gui, now I know for certain I will never see you again, and I, wretched and unfortunate man, what shall I do then?" From his great grief, he fell onto his bed, and there he went to sleep, like someone very distressed. It came to him in a dream that he saw his lord Gui approaching, spurring a good horse, a sharp sword in his hand. Boars and lions had attacked him, giving him much trouble: they had entirely smashed his shield and torn off a flap from his hauberk. So violently were they attacking him that it was with great suffering that he was defending himself. Then Heralt woke up and was very alarmed by the dream. He sent for his companions. "My lords," he said, "to arms: we shall go and help our lord Gui — he is in great need of help." (3989–4020)

They armed hastily and mounted their horses; quickly they went out of the city on to the metalled road[43] and vigorously spurred along it. They were very afraid for Gui lest he had been killed or captured, mortally wounded or harmed. When they looked in the direction of the army, they saw many wicked pagans, in armour. They saw the fields round about covered with Saracens on their good, swift steeds, all pursuing Gui with ardour: they were there to kill him. In the midst of them they saw Gui, defending himself like a lion. The Saracens had attacked him on all sides, but he defended himself like a brave fighter. They seized him by the bridle, but he defended himself with his sharp sword, cutting arms and hands off many, for his plight was dire. (4021–42)

Then they rode off at great speed, fiercely intent on helping Gui. Heralt proceeded to strike a Saracen; Apollo was no use to him. Heralt gave him a great blow on his shield with the painted border, which knocked him far from his horse. Each man in his turn struck his opponent, cutting many times into his

---

[43] 4024 **metalled road** *chemin ferré*: (see also line 11375). The roads laid by the Romans provided the standard for hundreds of years. "Metalled" refers to their topmost layer which, according to region, could be waste iron from flint or nearby workings.

liver and lungs. They gave the Saracens a hard fight and killed many of them. Heralt had the good fortune to have succeeded in helping his lord. There was great delight amongst them and they quite wept for joy. All of them kissed Gui, since God had saved him from danger. The Saracens, sad and very angry, returned; they took the body of their lord and with great distress carried it away with them. They went straight back to Konya, considering themselves totally defeated.[44] (4043–64)

Gui returned most joyfully, making his way straight to the city. He put the head on a lance so that everyone could see he had defeated it. He had it carried in front of him, and many men pointed to it. He entered the city; the people rang the bells for joy. When they saw the head being carried, they wept for joy and said that from now on they would have complete peace from the Sultan. "May almighty God bless the man who has delivered us from torment!" Gui came to the court and handed the head over to the emperor. "My lord emperor," he said, "hear this: the head you see carried here is the head of the mighty Sultan; I cut it off with my own hand and now present it to you. You have the right to receive it." (4065–86)

When the emperor saw Gui coming, he could not refrain from weeping. He kissed him more than a hundred times. Many men wept for compassion; throughout the city people celebrated the end of their great war. In the centre of the marketplace Gui had a very sturdy marble pillar erected; he had a brass head placed on top, inside which he put the Sultan's head. He had it splendidly adorned, topped with a precious crown, to warn others against entering the land with evil intent. (4087–4100)

"Come here, fair and sweet friend!" said Emperor Hernis. "Gui, thirty days from now I want to do you very great honour. I wish to give you my daughter; I've set my heart on it." "My lord, thank you!" he said. "If I have served you well, that pleases me." The emperor said to his people that during the day they should speedily prepare his baggage-train because there was no need to stay any longer; he wanted to go through his cities and make good his great losses. The emperor rose in the morning, heard mass at St Martin's church, and mounted an ambling mule. He took Gui with him, and dukes and counts from his land who had served him in his war. They journeyed till noon in the weather that was hot, as in summer. They looked into a plain, below a spring, and saw a lion approaching; it could only go at a walking pace. With its mouth agape, it was very weak, walking slowly and with difficulty. After this, they saw a serpent vigorously pursuing the lion. Its head was large, its eyes big; from afar they looked as if they were burning. It had sharp teeth and a wide mouth—a man could have not survived inside it—and its body was hideous to look at, nor was there anyone who could have encircled it. It was ugly and extremely long, a most repulsive creature. They

---

[44] 4064 **defeated** *confunduz*: After 4064, F adds 2 lines.

were looking at it with amazement, no one daring to set foot where it was, when Gui asked for his horse, mounted it without waiting, took his shield by its leather thongs, and said to his companions: "My lords, stay here; see that you don't come with me." Then he took a sharp sword and left his companions and went off right away and at great speed; now he would help the lion if he could. (4101–50)

When the dragon saw him coming, it left the lion and went to attack Gui. With gaping mouth it came flying, and Gui raised his sword in its direction. He stuck it into its mouth with great violence, pushed it into the body as far as his wrist, and quickly stuck his lance into the other side. He spun the serpent onto the ground. Rapidly he drew his steel sword, rounded his horse on the dragon, and severed its head from its body. His companions looked at the beast with amazement. Gui came back at a walk, and the lion followed him at a great rate, walking playfully in front of him and showing him much joy. It began to lick his feet and jumped up at the neck of his horse. Gui got down at once, and the lion stretched out at his feet. Gui stroked it, affectionately rubbing its ears and patting its flank. The lion at once jumped up and then began to entertain him, jumping up at him like a greyhound. Gui remounted his horse, and the lion went playfully in front of him or following at his stirrup; it followed him everywhere, into every place. Then Gui went to the emperor and told him everything he had done. They looked with amazement at the lion, which bore such love towards Gui. Then they came to the city where the emperor's quarters were. Gui went to his lodging and felt great love for the lion; it lay down in front of his bed, never to leave him. (4151–90)

When the emperor had travelled throughout his land and his kingdom, he returned to Constantinople and sent for Gui.: "My friend Gui, now get ready; tomorrow you shall marry my daughter. Now the set time has come; I don't want it to be extended any longer." "My lord emperor, thank you!" replied Gui most readily. Gui dressed himself richly and in the morning went to the church, along with his companions; they followed behind, two by two. Each was dressed in silken clothes stitched with gold thread. All the people in the city looked at them in astonishment, so splendidly were they adorned on their good, fresh horses. Gui came to the church and saw there many dukes and counts; archbishops and bishops were there to carry out the nuptials. "Gui," said the emperor, "come here! I give you my daughter; take her. Half my land along with her I grant you, Sir Gui; you shall be emperor after my death. Receive this promise in front of my barons." The Germans were very pleased, and Gui replied like a courteous man: "My lord emperor, thank you; now this is a most noble gift!" (4191–4224)

The archbishops came forward, all robed for the wedding. The gold rings were brought, and then for the first time Gui thought of his sweetheart, whom he loved so much. In only a short while he had forgotten her. "Ah Felice, my fair love! To what an end is love now come! Now I know very well I've done wrong, when I've loved another because of her wealth. Now I repent of it, and I regret it; I don't want to love any other but you. I would rather love you by yourself, without gold and silver, than another with all the world and all the riches that are in it." Then he sat down on the ground and said that such sickness had seized him that he could no longer stand up; his heart, he said, was going to burst. "My lord emperor," said Gui, "my fair, sweet lord, I beg you without hesitation to postpone this wedding until the illness which has afflicted me is alleviated." The emperor said: "It grieves me to have to postpone the wedding." (4225–52)

The emperor was very sad, and all the others too. They all left, sad, angry, and distressed, and the maiden lamented bitterly. She often sighed for Gui, her beloved, and thought she would never get him back. No one could comfort her as she wept and swooned frequently that day; no woman ever lamented so much. Then Gui mounted a mule (not a living soul knew of his deceit) and went straight to his lodging. He kept to his rooms for a fortnight, without ever going out, and disclosed his whereabouts to no one. You could see the lion grieving so much for his lord, whom he saw suffering pain, that he would hardly eat; never was an animal so distressed. Gui called Heralt and revealed all of his secret. "My lord Heralt, I ask for advice now: should I take the emperor's daughter or wait longer? I won't avoid telling you that in England I have a sweetheart, the daughter of noble Count Rualt, the lovely and excellent Felice. I can't love anyone else but her, my lord Heralt; I won't hide it from you." (4253–84)

Heralt replied: "I'll give you the best advice I know. If you take the emperor's daughter, you will continue to be rich and powerful, and you will be emperor after him. God grants you very great honour: no one in the world will be so noble or so rich or so powerful. You will have some thousand barons, who have more castles and cities than the valiant Count Rualt. You should not refuse the honour." "Be quiet!" said Gui, "don't talk like that! Now, Heralt, I know you don't love me when you advise me to leave my beloved. Were I to lose my life, I would not do it." "My lord," said Heralt, "I'll be quiet; I won't talk about it if it doesn't please you. When you asked me for advice, I didn't know you loved her. I wanted to give you the best advice I was sure of, my lord. If you love Felice so much, you must be wrong to leave her." (4285–4308)

At the end of the fortnight Gui got up; everyone in the city rejoiced. He came to the court and was received with very great joy. With him went his lion, about which a great quarrel was about to erupt. The emperor rejoiced to see Gui, and all the court did too. The emperor retained him at his meal, to gladden and solace him. The lion roamed through the palace. It occasioned much talk amongst the Greeks, about the brave deed Gui did when he killed the dragon and acquired the lion. The seneschal was very envious, and decided to kill the lion. After the emperor's meal, Gui stayed for a while that day. The lion, quite peaceful and in no way fierce, went out of the palace, and went to lie and sleep in the hot sun in an orchard. Then Gui took his leave and went to his lodging. The seneschal entered a room and looked through a window; he saw the lion lying asleep and thought of a most wicked act—that he would kill it while it slept, so much did he want to be avenged on Gui. Then he took a sharp sword and struck it through the body. The lion, quite terrified, shuddered as if mortally wounded. A maiden saw everything and cried loudly to the seneschal: "My lord seneschal, you have done wrong and in the future you will be reproached for it. When Gui learns about it, truly it will grieve him bitterly." (4309–48)

Moaning, the lion went through the court, dragging his bowels behind him. He went to his master's lodging and found Gui in a room. He came directly in front of him, fell into his lap, and began to lick his hands to show him he loved him. When Gui saw the lion was wounded, he wept for pity. "Almighty God!" he said, "who has treated me so badly? My God, whoever has struck my lion to death has now dealt me such a crushing blow! By that God who endured suffering, I would not have it happen for all this city or for all that belongs to the kingdom, so wretched am I at heart." He watched the lion die, and he looked at it in his lap. "My God!" he said, "how unhappy I am! In front of me I see one of the things I most loved die. I have a great desire to avenge him; if I knew for sure who had wounded him, he would at once be thoroughly avenged. However powerful a duke or count he may be, however much a noble of the realm it be, except for the person of our emperor, I will kill him painfully." Then he girded on a steel sword, mounted a swift horse, and spurred off to court. The knights saw from his face that he was unhappy and angry; they all went to meet him. (4349–84)

"My lords," he said, "now I entreat you: if any of you can tell me who killed my lion, I will give him a very great reward. I will become his liege man and give him a thousand gold besants, fifteen hauberks, and fifteen horses, the dearest in the whole kingdom." They replied: "My fair lord Gui, you can be sure that we don't know." Then he entered the hall and asked many men. He angrily entered one room after the other and met a lady. "Sir Gui," she said, "fair and sweet friend, is your lion dead or alive? I saw him struck through the body; I wouldn't hide it from you, sir Gui." Gui replied: "My beautiful friend, tell me, don't hide it! I will become your man and serve you like my lady." She answered, "I saw Morgadur—God curse the scoundrel!—strike the lion through the body; I was sure he would have to die." (4385–4410)

When Gui heard about the wretch who had killed his beloved lion, he at once left the room and went looking for the seneschal everywhere. He entered a stone chamber and found the seneschal there, advising one of his nephews. When he saw Gui, he was terrified. "Traitor," said Gui, "you stabbed me in the back! Why did you kill my lion? It never did you anything but good—why did you slay it? Twice you have betrayed me: by my head, you shall pay for it!" Angrily he drew his sharp sword and split the seneschal's head down to his teeth. (4411–26)

When the nephew saw his uncle struck dead, he was impatient to avenge him. In the act of taking a sharp spear, his right arm was cut off. When he begged for mercy, Gui left in great fury and came into the emperor's presence. "I have served you, my lord emperor; you have requited me in evil fashion, since in your court I have lost my dear lion, which I loved so much. The wicked seneschal killed it, but I have rewarded him for it: he lies in a room, cut down—I have rewarded his service. Who will serve you now, since you cannot protect a stranger in your land without your people mistreating him? I will go to my palace; I can't remain, I have a great longing to see my father and my friends. I don't know whether they are dead or alive. And if you need me, whether in peace or in war, to carry out a mission, indeed you may be sure I will come and serve you as far as I can.' (4427–54)

When the emperor heard Gui, who was so angry, he said: "Sir Gui, mercy, for God's sake! If anyone has wronged you, I swear to you I'll do you whatever justice you like; you yourself can decide what is just. They are now your men and will remain so; take my daughter and they will fear you. I want you to marry her, with great honour, tomorrow, at the start of the day." "My lord," Gui said, "don't talk about that: I am not minded to take a wife. If you had given me your daughter and I had married her, among themselves the Greeks—who are often proud[45]—would say that the son of a poor vavasur[46] had been made their emperor. Among themselves they would consider me base, and[47] among themselves would often say that your daughter, when she was given to me, was mismatched. I would rather have a little honourably than great wealth dishonourably, so I tell you, my lord emperor, I shall not on any account stay here. I want to go away, I ask for leave. I commend you, my lord, to the Son of Mary." (4455–82)

When the emperor could not detain him, and saw his great longing to go, he wept for unhappiness, and so did all the court. Then he had his great treasure-chests opened and freely offered Gui as much as he wished, but Gui disdained to take anything; he had acquired enough from the Saracens. The emperor behaved like a noble man in that he handed over his rich treasure-chests to Gui's companions; he gave them plenty of gold and silver, as much as each wanted to take, by imperial command. They praised the emperor exceedingly, saying he was a man of great worth. Gui had his ships prepared and plenty of food stored in them. He took his leave of the emperor, and the weeping emperor granted it; and Gui took leave of all the knights in the city. You could see the people there grieving for him, who now had to depart. The women and all the children, the high and the low, wept, because as long as he was in the land they would not fear war from anyone alive. (4483–4510)

The emperor called for Heralt and spoke to him just between the two of them: "Sir Heralt, stay with me: I tell you for certain, and you can be quite sure, that within this year I will give you the richest fief I have in my land." "My lord,

---

[45] See Rebecca Wilcox, "Romancing the East: Greeks and Saracens in Guy of Warwick," in *Pulp Fictions of Medieval England*, ed. Nicola McDonald (Manchester and New York: Manchester University Press, 2004), 217–40 (222–29).

[46] 4471 **vavasur** *vavasur*: A *vavasur* was the petty holder of a fief, a country nobleman. See Marc Bloch, *Feudal Society*, trans. L. A. Manyon (London: Routledge & K. Paul, 1962), 332.

[47] 4474 **and** *En*: Ewert's text here has a misprint, *en* instead of *e*.

thank you!" he said. "You know well that I am with Gui; I will never leave him for any wealth I may obtain." Now Gui set sail. He was much lamented in the city, for he had brought much honour to the English, who are still there to this day, much feared in the land, considered trustworthy and much loved.[48] (4511–26)

Now lord Gui travelled over the sea, and his companions with him. They sailed so far across the sea that they arrived in Germany. Gui went straight to Speyer and found the emperor, who received him most splendidly, for Gui was very welcome; the emperor was very glad of his coming. He treated him and his companions with honour. Gui was with the emperor for a while, but he longed for his own country. He took leave of the emperor, who had done him much honour. He travelled so long that he entered Lorraine, arriving there with great joy because he recognised the land and the country. (4527–44)

It was a day in May when every flower blooms. Gui entered a forest which was nearby a city. He happily asked his men to go at once to the city to secure his lodging, while he wanted to linger a little, to hear the birds sing; this would delight him. They went on their way and he remained alone in the forest. He heard the sweet songs of the birds and fell into profound thought, and so, absorbed in thought, he got lost. He left his path for another and went astray through the forest, which was very wide and big. From far off he heard a lament, and he stopped to listen. He went straight in that direction and looked underneath a hawthorn; he saw the body of a knight and marvelled at the sight. He saw he was handsome, tall, and noble; indeed he said to himself that he had never yet seen such a handsome person. He turned his mule around and went in that direction. The knight's first beard was sprouting; his face was drained of colour because of the blood he had lost, which had left his body. His eyes were bright, his face shapely, his forehead broad, and his nose well set; he had a long and very white neck, mighty arms and burly hands, wide shoulders, and a broad chest. His flanks were handsome and well made, his pelvis fine and long; Gui had never seen a man of such fine stature. He had been struck through the body. He was clothed in a short tunic and hose of rich silk; there were gold spurs on his feet, and he was girded with a steel sword. By his head lay a quartered shield. (4545–90)

Gui looked at him and was seized with pity. He asked him very gently: "Sir knight, who wounded you? What is your name and where were you born? Tell me, I beg you, on condition I promise you faithfully I will do you no harm: who wounded you in this woodland?" The knight replied: "I won't tell you, because I have such great pain in my heart from it, I can't relate it to you. For you can easily see how hurt I am; if I were now to tell you of my suffering, it would be so much the greater. Go away, don't speak of it! Indeed, you shan't know about it

---

[48] 4526 **much loved** *mult amez*: After 4526, F adds 2 lines on the love the emperor feels for the English because they serve him most honourably. On the English colony in Constantinople see K. N. Ciggaar, "Western Travellers to Constantinople 962–1204" (Leiden: Brill, 1996).

from me, unless you were to do something for me and promise me firmly to do what I tell you: I would tell you all about myself, who I am and what my name is, and who treacherously wounded me. Otherwise you shan't know of it through me and henceforth will talk of it in vain." Gui then began to consider whether he could promise him this. He saw him lie bleeding on the ground and was very eager to know who he was. "Knight," said Gui, "I promise you that I will do what you want as far as I can." Gui then pledged him his word, on condition he told him the truth. (4591–4622)

"Sir knight," said the wounded man, "I shall tell you my name and where I was born. I am from Worms, and am called Terri, son of the old Count Alberi. I was with the duke of Lorraine, whom as a youth I served. He held me very dear, for which I thank him, and I served him well, to the best of my ability. He had a daughter, who was very beautiful; there's no maiden so fair in the world. We loved each other above all else, and promised each other our love so that she would love me above all others and would not leave me for anyone else. I took up arms for her love; then I left the country. I often went seeking renown in many foreign lands: in both France and Burgundy, in Germany and Saxony, I never heard of a tournament, or of a war on this side of the sea, that I didn't go there seeking glory. I was a powerful knight: I was renowned as far as pagan lands and was much esteemed for feats of arms. Then I heard talk of a war — Saracens from overseas had come into Romanie[49] and had laid the whole land waste — and I went there seeking renown, with Remis, prince of the country. I was on very good terms with him, because I served him well in his war: I beheaded many a Saracen and through my valour brought his war to an end. (4623–58)

"Then a messenger came to me, telling me of great trouble: Duke Otun of Pavia would seize my beloved, Osille, and if I wanted to have her, I would have to come for her that day, in secret, or I would lose her for ever. I set out very speedily, with seven of my bold companions, each on his excellent horse. We didn't stop travelling, night and day, and came straight to the city where the dukes were gathered for the wedding of Osille, my beloved, for whom I lead such a wretched life. Then I sent word to my beloved, the creature I love most in the world, that she should come to me, and she quickly did so. She came to me without delay; she had herself quickly brought down from the castle. I had her mounted on an ambling mule and then we took to the road. In this I was too foolish: we delayed too long. As we left the city, the light of day appeared; at a bridge I was spotted, having come for my beloved. Outcry rose throughout the city that Osille had left with me. You could see knights mounting there, vying with each other on their steeds. They pursued me with great vigour, all threatening me on account of Osille. I fought them boldly, and my companions too; we gave them a fierce

---

[49] 4651 **Romanie** A name for the Byzantine, or Eastern Roman, empire, but also used of the Holy Roman Empire. See note to line 5710.

battle and killed plenty of their men. Then I lost my companions, because we were without armour.⁵⁰ (4659–4700)

"When I saw my companions killed, I thought I would go mad, I was so angry. I struck a man from Lorraine; I avenged myself very well on him. I did the same to a Lombard; I struck him down dead and bleeding in the field. Then I fought them; I don't think there's a knight in the world equally brave or fierce, except for the valiant Gui of Warwick, who could attack them more boldly than I did, to my knowledge. Then I saw Lorrainers and Lombards coming from all directions, all coming to seize me, and I couldn't oppose them any longer. I lifted my beloved on to my horse and most speedily set off; I went at a great rate, carrying my lovely mistress with me. Then the pursuers began to chase me, and I went off on my horse; all that day they chased me and didn't stop until night-time. I crossed the countryside and the regions, the mountains and the valleys; I came to a very big stretch of water. From all directions they came following me, and I could find neither boat nor bridge for crossing the river. The river was swift and wide, and there was no way I could avoid it; I put my trust in my good horse, entered the water, and crossed over. (4701–34)

"When I had crossed the river, I saw my pursuers stop at the watercourse. They dared not enter it, and so they turned back. I came at once into this forest, gently carrying my beloved with me. I feared neither thief nor robber, but believed I was quite safe. What with keeping watch, with fasting, and above all with hardship, I was very sleepy, so I went to sleep in this place. My beloved was sitting in front of me; my horse was tied to a branch. Then knights appeared, fifteen very fierce robbers. They wounded me mortally while I slept; I have no life left at all. I've told you my whole life-story: how I have, alas, lost my beloved, for whose loss I suffer more than for my death—I have no solace except in her. I'm very afraid she may have been dishonoured by the robbers, God curse them! You have heard my misadventure: I believe so harsh a one never befell any man. (4735–60)

"Now I entreat you, by your word which you here pledged to me, that as soon as I am dead you will have my body buried either in an abbey or a church, so that animals cannot devour it, and that you will go up that mountain, where the fifteen robbers are; you will find them all together. If you can kill them, you will regain, before evening, what you will not give away for any possessions, my mistress, the noble Osille (as far as Sicily, there's no one so lovely), and my horse, which is so swift (in the world there's none so valuable). I won him by force in pagan lands from the son of Sultan Salakis. They offered me plenty for him: fifteen castles and seven cities and fifteen packhorses with gold and silver. I certainly

---

⁵⁰ 4700 **we were without armour** *en pleines armes eriuns*: In E, F, and A, there is no word between *pleines* and *eriuns*; C, F, and M have *armes* which Ewert inserts, presumably following the pattern of 6571, *en pleines armes*. See note to line 1669.

wouldn't give him up for a hundred today. Take this shield and this sword and set your mind to rescuing the maiden. I see you are handsome, tall, and noble; you should certainly carry out your oath." (4761–86)

When Gui heard it was Terri, the brave, the valiant, the bold, he began to weep for pity. When he saw the knight lie bleeding, he knew he would never be happy if he did not avenge him. He lamented bitterly over him, took his strong shield and his sharpened, keen blade, and went straight to the mountain. He looked up to the top and saw a large hut there, in front of which he recognized the good horse. With the utmost speed he went spurring up there, dismounted from the mule, and drew his sword. As he entered the hut, he said aloud, and very fiercely, to them: "Wicked scoundrels, you're all dead; may God destroy every one of you. Why did you kill the knight? You are all dead and defeated." He made the head fly off the first one he reached, and he hacked to pieces the next and the third. He did great damage to the fourth and cut off the arm of the fifth, rent right down to the belt. Before they could seize their weapons, he made up to eight of the robbers lie prostrate and dead on the spot; thus he got rid of the wretches. Then he attacked the remaining ones and very soon defeated them. Not one there remained alive; they were all killed and slain, except for one alone, who had escaped, but not before Gui had given him a mortal wound. (4787–4822)

Gui went straight to the maiden and spoke to her in courteous words: "Beautiful lady, cease your grieving; get up and come away! I will bring you to your beloved under the hawthorn, where I left him." "My lord," she said, "if you will take me to my beloved, thank you!" She fell at his feet and fainted. Gui raised her up in his arms, then mounted the good horse, making the maiden mount the mule, and they returned to the hawthorn. They did not find the body of the knight there. (4823–36)

When Gui did not find him, he was wretched. In his heart he truly believed that wild beasts had eaten him, or his enemies had found him there and had carried him away to harm him. From now on, he would not stop looking for him. He left the maiden there; no woman ever showed such sorrow. She wept and swooned and cried aloud, longing for death more than life. Gui felt so unhappy that he did not utter a word. He saw the hoofprints of horses, which he followed at great speed, putting himself in danger for Terri's sake. The horse was good and went fast. In a large wood, he saw four knights riding on their horses, shields round their necks, and he saw they were carrying Terri's body over the neck of one of their horses. Speedily Gui caught up with them, and addressed them in the friendliest fashion: "May that Lord who created the day give you great honour, my lords. If you please, my lords, talk to me and hear what I have to say: I have promised that knight, whom I see you carrying on that horse, to bury his body. I have pledged him my word." (4837–66)

Then a knight turned around, Duke Loher's seneschal, who had crossed the river in a boat he had found. He had come upon the body in the great forest and one of his knights had carried it off. "Fellow, who are you? You're very foolish and arrogant if you've come here to contest the body of this knight. You are his friend, so we shall seize you and bring you before the duke; you will both be sentenced together and handed over to die, like traitors. It was your bad luck you ever thought about the maiden and wickedly carried her off. I defy you; now take care, and think of defending yourself!" In great anger he struck him and cut off the principal ornament from his shield, so that the seneschal's whole lance broke. Gui, who did not care for him, struck him back; he severed lung from liver and knocked him dead, far along the path. Another man went to strike Gui, and Gui had no intention of sparing him: he threw him down far from his horse and cut his heart in two. And the third went to strike Gui, and Gui struck him back like a brave fighter, so that he knocked him dead from his horse; no one would ever get solace from him. And Gui struck the fourth a great blow on his shield blazoned with a leopard; with great violence he knocked him from his horse, making him break four ribs. He took Terri's body in his arms and set off back along the road. (4867–4904)

Now I shall leave Gui and tell you about his companions, who had gone to the city. They were very frightened for their lord; they had returned to the forest and were unhappy and distressed. Some sounded their horns and went here and there, calling; they sought him everywhere and did not find him. Then they returned. Heralt went searching through the forest, great sorrow in his heart. Close to him he heard a lament, as if of a pregnant woman. It was wretched and frightened, and he thought it was coming from an enchanted being. He looked to one side of him, saw a maiden, and asked her who she was and where she came from. But she would not say, and instead said she came from the neighbourhood and was lost. Heralt saw she was beautiful and took her with him; unhappy, he returned to the city. She began to grieve and there was no one who could comfort her; in their presence she lamented in many ways. Heralt put her in a chamber, fearing lest her great sorrow would upset their followers. (4905–35)

Gui came to the hawthorn and found no trace of the girl. He put the body on the ground and often called himself weak and despicable. Up and down he went searching for her, lamenting most bitterly; he was sure she had been taken by scoundrels or devoured by wild beasts. He felt such misery at heart that he did not know what on earth to do. He did not know what to do, the night was dark, and he wanted to go to the city. He placed the knight on the neck of his horse and came to the city. He found his men miserable, but when they saw their lord coming, they rejoiced greatly. "My lords," he said, "take this body and put it very gently on the ground." They took the knight's body and put it on the ground, on a rich cloth. Gui asked for all the best doctors in the city. "My lords," he said, "now listen: if you can heal this knight you see here of his wound, I will reward you well. I don't know if he is dead or alive. Now I beg you, dear friends, to set about healing him, for which you shall have a hundred gold besants." They examined the pulse and the veins and found them quite sound. They looked at the wound in his body and could easily see he was not dead. The doctors said they would cure him, which they could do with God's help. (4935–72)

Then Gui heard the sound of grief—weeping, wailing, and lamenting. He called one of his servants and in anger quickly asked him who was making such a noise; he should at once tell them to go away. And he replied that it was "a very beautiful girl, whom Heralt found in the forest where he was looking for you. Because of her great laments, and thinking of you, he put her in a chamber, so that she would not vex you." And Gui replied: "Bring her here; I want to see her, go and fetch her!" The servant went for her and brought her into the hall in front of him. When she had entered the hall, in tears and distressed, Gui recognized and greeted her. There wasn't a single person who did not take pity on her. Then she saw the body lying on a rich Tyrian cloak. "Alas, Terri, handsome and sweet friend, how pale I see your face now, which was so rosy and fair! No one better than you was ever born. Alas that you ever saw me, since you have died for me, wretch that I am! I want to die with you; I don't want to live, my grief is so great. If I can't die, I shall kill myself; I don't want to live any longer. Since your death occurs because of me, I want to die along with you." She fell on to the body and swooned. God, how she grieved! She kissed his mouth and face and often called herself wretched and unfortunate. Again she swooned; her soul nearly left her body. (4973–5012)

Gui then took her in his arms and said to her very lovingly: "Beautiful lady, give up this grief! I will have your beloved completely healed of his gaping wounds. The doctors have told me they will cure him entirely. And if by chance he should die, you can be quite certain of this: I would not choose another person for you. I could not give you to anyone better. The doctors say they will cure him and will make him sound within a fortnight." With that, Gui comforted her for the great grief she felt. From then on, Gui saw to Terri's healing; he had him looked after with the greatest affection. He did not want to tell anyone who he was and where he came from. He found him as many good doctors as he wished, and desired his health above all. Terri stayed so long in the city that he was quite cured of his wound. (5013–34)

When Count Terri was well, Gui was delighted. They went hunting and hawking, and truly felt much affection for each other. One day they were returning from hunting, and noble Gui said: "My lord Terri, I have done you much honour by staying behind so long in this land and in this city; you ought to be very grateful to me. Now I want us to swear to each other that henceforth we shall be friends and that, in our lives from now on, neither of us will fail the other." And Count Terri replied: "My fair lord Gui, many thanks! If you, my lord, love me so much that you wish to be my friend, you have done me great honour. May God yet allow me to see the day I can reward you, because you are a most noble lord. You have saved me from death, sir; I would certainly be very much in the wrong if I didn't love you as my lord. I ought to show you very great honour." Then they kissed each other, quite certain of their friendship. Next they went to the city, glad and happy men; they returned to their lodging and gave themselves over to great rejoicing. (5035–66)

Then Gui wanted to get ready; he intended to go to England. He would take Terri with him, and his sweetheart, Osille, whom Terri loved so much. He wanted to get to know the king and stay in the land a long while, for he had in mind to give all his castles to him. He leant against a window and talked to Terri about their journey. Then they saw a wayfarer, who certainly looked like a knight and like a man who had been travelling. Gui therefore called him over: "Sir knight, where do you come from? What are you seeking? Don't hide it from me." And he replied: "I will tell you, my lord, and I won't hide it from you: I seek Terri of Worms, son of the brave Count Alberi. I have been seeking him in many kingdoms." And Gui replied: "To do what, my lord?" "My lord," he said, "indeed, you shall know; now you can hear about a great wrong. Terri served Duke Loher; the duke loved him and held him dear, giving him weapons with much honour, and he became a most valiant knight. The duke had a beautiful daughter, who had been given to the duke of Pavia. Terri loved her and carried her off, for which many men lost their lives. Knights made every effort to pursue him; I don't know if he is alive or dead. Then Duke Loher decided to take vengeance upon his father; he went there with the army of Lorraine, taking the duke of Pavia with him and his good band of knights, the best in Lombardy. They besieged the count in Worms and laid waste the countryside round about. If God grant I find Terri, he should come and help his father, or he will lose all the land and will never get it back. His father is old, he can't help himself; he can no longer bear arms." (5067–5114)

"Sir knight," said Gui, "stay here with me! I will tell you about Count Terri, my fair friend, whatever I happen to know." "My lord," he said, "thank you! Above all else, I would like to hear about Terri." Then Gui ordered his men to lodge him most splendidly. "My fair friend Gui," said Terri, "I beg you by God, my lord, to come with me now, according to what we swore to each other. We will now go and help my father. I need that very much: if my father is killed or captured, and I am dispossessed for ever, for want of your help, our friendship would not be a good one." "Sir Terri," said Gui, "what are you saying? May God hold me in contempt the day I fail you, my lord Terri. I shall at once summon knights and I'll go with you to help your father, subject to God's good Providence. I won't fail you, you can be sure, as long as I can stand on my feet." "Sir Gui, thank you," he said. "Fair friend, how lucky I was to come across you!" (5115–42)

At once Gui summoned German and Saxon knights, who were so fierce. Great numbers of them came to him; before a week had passed, he had five hundred bold knights. "Terri, fair and sweet friend," he said, "let's go and help your father; I think we ought to do so." Then they prepared themselves thoroughly and travelled so far on their journey that they were delighted to arrive at the city of Worms. They entered the city one evening without letting the besiegers know. Count Alberi was very glad of his son Terri's arrival, and especially of the arrival of Gui, the brave and valiant knight. He wept for joy; then they all went to kiss him. "My dear father," said Count Terri, "show great honour to my lord Gui. We are sworn friends; I certainly want you, dear sir, to know that. Indeed, he has saved my life." The count replied: "I thank him! From this very day on, I want my whole land to be at his disposal, to do all his bidding: in your presence, I give complete control over to him. I am a very old man: I haven't borne arms for twenty years and I've lost my knightly abilities. Take control of my land." With much happiness, they took lodging in the city, and the city-dwellers were delighted with these newly-arrived lords. (5143–80)

In the morning, the company rose and after mass gathered in front of old Count Alberi. Then they heard a great outcry from the citizens of the city. Gui very quickly asked for the cause of this great noise he had heard from the city. "My lords," said a knight, "indeed it's the constable of Duke Loher, behaving arrogantly in front of the city. If he had his way, he would certainly do some bit of knightly daring." "My lord," said Gui, "let's arm and attack the men from Lorraine." They went off to their lodgings to arm; they wanted to make the effort to strike effectively. They armed themselves splendidly and then re-assembled. "My lord, Count Terri," said Gui, "take two hundred knights here and attack the men from Lorraine. Have confidence in Heralt and me. We shall stay here in the city and will help you when you need it." (5181–5204)

Terri took the two hundred knights, armed and on their horses, and went out of the city. Before the end of the day he would shatter many a shield. He struck a knight, to whom no weapon was a pennyworth of use. He put his lance through the man's body and knocked him incontestably dead. He speedily struck another high on his shield; he did not want to miss. With great violence, with great impetuosity, he knocked him dead on the grass. Each of his companions struck more blows, as certainly appeared to be the case. You could see so many felled knights, lying prone in the fields, one with his face covered with blood, another pierced through the side. Count Terri and his companions did very well, for they fiercely attacked the men from Lorraine and cut down many, bleeding and dead. (5205–26)

Terri struck the constable and knocked him far from his horse. He would certainly soon have released him on parole when some hundred excellent knights all ferociously struck at Terri. He fought them like a lion, making many of their heads fly; whatever he reached, he completely overthrew. At that moment, his luck turned, since he lost some of his companions, owing to the great strength of the men from Lorraine, who numbered more than five hundred. Terri's companions were defeated, some of them taken, killed, and captured. But Terri went at them, fighting and striking many great blows with his sword. Disdaining to yield a single foot, he turned his horse round to face them. Like a brave fighter, he rescued his companions and knocked many a man dead from his horse. (5227–46)

Heralt said: "My dear Sir Gui, don't you see Count Terri? He's a warrior of great worth; except for you, I don't know any better in the world. Now let's boldly go and help him!" And Gui replied: "So we shall!" Then they went off at great speed and attacked the men from Lorraine fiercely. Gui went to strike Count Garner, the nephew of Duke Loher; with his lance he knocked him off his horse and released him on parole into the fray. Then he went back to strike Garner's companion and knocked him from his horse into the sand. Heralt went to strike a man from Lorraine, whose armour was not worth a herring; he put his steel blade through his body and knocked him dead from his horse. Like a good fighter he struck another man and propelled him far from his horse, into the field. From then on, both sides exchanged blows, neither sparing the other; they struck each other most forcefully and killed and cut down many. (5247–70)

What a sight was Count Terri, along with his friend Gui and the good Heralt of Arderne, whose brave deeds never failed, seizing and felling so many knights that day! There is no one who could decide who was the best of the three lords, they did so well! Wherever they went, they thinned out the ranks. Gui went to strike the constable and—no lie—knocked him off his horse; after a struggle he captured him in the fray. The other side retreated, vanquished. Gui and Terri pursued them energetically and their companions did the same. They captured and killed all of them; not one of the forty survived. Gui and Terri returned, taking their prisoners with them. (5271–88)

Then a knight came forward to announce the news to Duke Loher. "My lord duke, now think about taking revenge! This morning we appeared in front of the city of Worms, five hundred brave knights, and great hardship befell us. We were all taken and captured; forty did not come back. Count Terri has returned, and with him Gui of Warwick and Heralt of Arderne, the marquis, and some five hundred prized knights, who are very brave and fierce, and the cause of your knights' deaths." The duke replied: "Is this true? Has Count Terri then returned, and Gui of Warwick and Heralt, with their invaluable aid? Devils have brought them; from now on we shall have war indeed." Then the duke of Pavia said: "My lord, Duke Loher, with your permission I shall go outside the city tomorrow with a thousand good knights. If the traitors are found there, they will be killed or captured, you can be sure." The duke rose in the morning and went straight to Worms, with a thousand knights in his band, the most famous in Lombardy, who all threatened Gui and Terri; if they were found, they would be in trouble! (5289–5322)

As Gui returned from church, he looked at a great plain which stretched in front of the duke's army; he saw many knights coming. He called Count Terri and showed him all that he saw. "My lord count," said Gui, "what shall we do? We can see the army from Lorraine approaching. The duke of Pavia has arrived; I recognize him from his weapons. He's my enemy, I feel no affection for him. I'm very eager to fight him." The count replied: "Now let's arm; we'll take a thousand knights with us. Go boldly and attack them. Make every effort to avenge yourself!" Then they quickly armed and had their horns sounded throughout the city. When they were armed, they assembled to assail the duke fiercely. They went out of the city and attacked the Lombards with great violence. Each side struck the other great blows with lances and knocked the others far from their horses. Then they drew their steel swords and gave each other great blows, killing many on both sides. But the Lombards were unlucky to this extent: they lost many of their knights, some killed, some captured. (5323–52)

Gui struck Count Jordan, at that time count of Milan, a great blow on his golden shield, which knocked him far from his chestnut horse. Then Terri came spurring up and with great force struck Amalri, Duke Otun's constable, knocking him dead onto the sand. Heralt struck Guischard, a cruel seneschal, and knocked him far from his horse, so that Duke Otun saw him. Then the Lombards fled and the others pursued them from all sides, constantly capturing and killing them; they howled and cried throughout the plains. The defeat was considerable; the Lombards had bad luck. The duke fled from the area, holding his sharp blade in his hand. Nobody pursued him except Heralt, who followed him vigorously and in haste. As the duke was distant from them, nobody alive saw him except Heralt alone who pursued him. He did not fear the duke at all because he saw his weapons were cut to pieces; he scorned him all the more. "As God is your salvation, turn round, duke of Pavia!" said Heralt, "and deny the evil you once did to us in Lombardy." In great anger, the duke turned round and attacked Heralt with his sharp sword. There the two lords fought: the hills rang with their blows, they cut through helmets and bright hauberks, and blood streamed out from various places in their bodies. The battle between them was very hard; neither of them knew any other way. (5353–92)

Then Heralt reflected that if he were not avenged, he would never be happy. He attacked Duke Otun and cut one of the quarters off his helmet. The blow fell on to his shoulder and cut a full span into it, making him fall on his hands. Then he advanced to seize him by the nose-piece. He would gladly have cut off his head, but thirty knights arrived who all struck at Heralt, doing their best to kill him. Heralt fought them well; he gave no sign he was wounded, instead fighting a Lombard and making his head fly from his body. He defended himself like a great warrior, but then his luck turned: he wanted to go back towards the city, but his horse was mortally wounded. All around they struck him with swords, with mighty blows on his helmet, cut through his hauberk and drew blood, reddening what was formerly white. But he defended himself as best he could and bloodied many a face. (5393–5418)

Then a cruel Lombard came up called Betuer. He struck Heralt with his sword and wounded him through the shoulder. Heralt sought revenge on him and intended to give him a great blow on the helmet. This time he missed him: the sword descended to the saddle-bow. By force he pulled the blade back so that it broke at the hilt. "My God," said Heralt, "what shall I do if I can't defend myself any longer? O sword, may Christ curse whoever made you! Why have you let me down so soon? Now I shall be ruined through you. Indeed, I would rather die than be taken alive." (5419–36)

Then a Lombard came up; in the end he behaved like a scoundrel. He seized Heralt by the nose-piece and most unpleasantly said to him: "Scoundrel, you shall pay for this! This very day you'll be torn limb from limb." Heralt hit him with his fist and broke his neck. "You shan't judge me," he said, "you are far too insolent." Then a knight came up, born in France, from Montdidier; he was a mercenary of Duke Otun's who had served him for his livelihood. "Now yield to me, Heralt," he said, "and you can be quite sure you will not be harmed in any way by the duke or any living man." Heralt replied: "I agree, and I entreat you, upon your word, not to hand me over to the duke of Pavia; I would rather you killed me." The knight captured Heralt and then put him on his horse. They went off towards the army, where the Lombards were glad about Heralt. (5437–62)

Gui returned and with him Count Terri. They had defeated the Lombards and killed or captured their leaders. They asked about Heralt, where he was and where he had gone. Then a knight told them he had seen Heralt leave the scene of defeat, very vigorously pursuing a knight; he thought it was Duke Otun. "My God!" said Gui, "how I have been betrayed if now I've lost my friend Heralt, who loved me so much! I can't do without him. My lords," he said, "now leave and take your prisoners with you. From now on I shall seek Heralt. I shan't stop, night or day, until I've found him dead or alive; if I lose him, I'll never be happy again. Friend Terri, you shall come with me; don't hesitate to help Heralt!" (5463–84)

They struck spurs into their horses; the two lords went off quickly. They went spurring in the direction of the army, intending to mount a mighty pursuit for Heralt. Gui looked at the entrance to the army, recognized the duke of Pavia there and Heralt of Arderne, who had been captured. Gui was very wretched at heart. "My God!" he said, "Heralt is captured; I've seen him in my enemies' midst. Let's strike them; cursed be he who, for fear of death, fails to go and help Heralt!" They advanced with great speed. Gui struck a Lombard and knocked him to one side, dead; Terri struck another and knocked him dead from his horse. Then they drew their swords, from which many battles had sprung, and they cut down and killed with ferocity. You could see so many dying a painful death! Next they rescued Heralt and gave him a sharp sword. Then they defeated the Lombards, some of whom fled. (5485–5510)

The duke went off towards the army and Gui, who had no affection for him, pursued him. Within the army, a staff's throw away, Gui caught up with Duke Otun. He intended to give him a mighty blow with his sword, for he was very keen to take revenge on him. The warrior's blow descended between the body and the saddle-bow, cutting the golden saddle, and the horse with it, in two pieces. The duke tumbled to the ground; if, in his great anger, Gui could have given him another blow, Otun would never have enjoyed life again. Then knights came out from the army, striking Gui on all sides; he returned through the middle of the army with Lombards fiercely pursuing him. He met Terri and Heralt, and they marvelled greatly at how he had escaped from the army under those circumstances; each felt great joy because of him. They often struck at the Lombards and would not deign to flee for half a mile[51] without turning round on them and giving them great blows with their swords. (5511–36)

Gui and Terri and Heralt rode off; the Lombards, mortified, turned back. Hale and hearty, Gui and Terri returned to the city. But Heralt was badly wounded: he had many gashes to his body. The town's citizens often thanked God that Heralt had come back alive; he was a good and much feared warrior. Heralt had doctors summoned and his wounds tended in comfort. In the city people rejoiced greatly at the luck God had sent them to defeat their enemies; henceforth they would not fear them in any way. (5537–52)

Duke Otun returned, disarmed in his tent, and had his wounds treated. Then he went to the duke and showed him what great danger he was in; he wanted a decision about this. "My lord, Duke Loher," said Otun, "listen, sire, to my words. If you don't take a decision quickly, you will lose all Lorraine through these traitors who have arrived—would that they were all strung up high! They have killed our knights, our kin and our friends; the loss can't be made good. Furthermore, you can be sure they will do more. The city is strong: you won't be able to take it, however hard you try. They will get help from many lands, through which you will suffer a great deal of harm. If you will trust my advice, you will avenge yourself through a ruse: a man should take revenge on his enemies and harm them in every way. Send a friendly message to Count Alberi that you want to give your daughter Osille to his son, Count Terri, that you will gladly be reconciled with them, and that they should go back together with you, quite unafraid and confident of their safety, to your splendid city where your barons will be gathered. There you will give him your daughter and thereby be reconciled. And when they are a day's ride away from their homeland, then you shall seize all your traitors and judge them in your court. But this much I want to beg you: hand over Gui and Heralt to me; they are my deadly enemies and will never be my friends. I will take them with me to Pavia and put them in my dungeon. They will never get out and will die there in misery and rage. Have Count Terri judged and him and his father killed. Then give your daughter to me. In that way you will set your land free." (5553–5602)

Then Duke Loher replied: "My lord, Duke Otun, let that be! Indeed, I shall never do a treacherous deed. For all the world's goods, I would not betray Count Terri, who is my vassal, and whom I brought up.[52] Nor, as God is my

---

[51] 5534 **half a mile** *Demi arpent*; see note to line 3620.
[52] 5608 **whom I brought up** *jol nurri*: A young nobleman was often sent out to the household of a *magist*er or *mestr*e, usually a knight, who "nurtured" him, becoming responsible for his education.

help, will I betray Gui of Warwick or Heralt. Not for all the possessions in my land would I behave treacherously to them. If Count Terri has done me wrong, he can still put it right, and the others too, who are most noble people." Once more Otun answered "My lord, all you have said is good. If you are so fond of the traitors that you don't want to kill them, have them thrown into your dungeons. There have them well guarded until they find valuable hostages, so that they can't harm you. I shall have Gui and Heralt guarded; I shall put them in an honourable prison until they are punished and have renounced their animosity. In that way I can be reconciled and very soon obtain their affection." In his heart his thoughts were quite different: if he could get them together, in the city of Pavia, all Lombardy would not stop him from having them torn limb from limb, burnt in a fire or thrown into the sea. He entreated Duke Loher so hard, both through demand and prayer, that the duke finally allowed him to seize them in such a way. (5603–40)

Then they got a bishop, a very wise man from that land, and expounded all this to him and how they had decided on reconciliation. The bishop went straight to the strong city of Worms, where he found Count Alberi, Gui of Warwick, and Terri. "My lords," he said, "now listen: know that Duke Loher greets you and sends word that he would like to be reconciled with you. If you set his wrongs to right, he will gladly accept reparation. He will give his daughter to Count Terri and bring him to his city; he wants to hold the wedding there and will make all his barons attend, so that the bond of love will always be binding. This should be five days from today; assemble from both sides. There, in the plains before the city, you will come to an agreement; forever after you will be friends." They all replied together: "Almighty God be thanked that our lord, Duke Loher, wants to be reconciled with us!" (5641–68)

"My lord bishop," said Count Alberi, "listen to this, if you please: thank Duke Loher very much for wanting to honour my son by giving him his daughter. He will receive her most joyfully. We shall gladly come before the duke, and accept the day you have said. If we have done him wrong in any way, we shall certainly set it right as it pleases him." "My lord count," said Gui, "beware you are not deceived! I am deeply suspicious of the duke of Pavia, who is thoroughly wicked; he would readily give evil advice, by which many men would lose their lives. I know very well that Count[53] Loher would not do wrong even if he were to have his limbs cut off." The bishop relied: "Don't be afraid; put your confidence in God for everything! Let none of you fear treason; he will do only what is good." Then the bishop departed and the others were left rejoicing. (5669–92)

When it came to the fifth day, the noble lords of the city made ready with great splendour. Count Alberi, his son Terri, Gui, and Marquis Heralt went to

---

[53] 5685 **count** *li quons*: On the difference between Continental dukes and counts, see Bloch, *Feudal Society*, 399.

the parley and with them five hundred knights of great renown, on their horses. All were dressed in magnificent tunics and fine cloaks of beaten gold. They brought the maiden with them, not suspecting treason. They arrived at the parley; many and various people came to it: the very proud duke, Loher of Lorraine, with his assembly of barons, and Duke Otun of Pavia, and four counts of the Empire.[54] (5693–5710)

"My lords," said Duke Otun, "listen to my words; listen to me, all of you gathered here. You know very well that Count Terri of Worms, son of Alberi, has wronged our lord, who once did him very great honour: formerly he brought him up in his court and loved and cherished Terri so much that he equipped him splendidly with weapons. And he repaid him wickedly, by giving his daughter bad advice and abducting her from her chamber. Next he brought foreigners, who have a deadly hatred for the duke and who have killed his barons and destroyed the countryside round about. There are plenty of other things, which shall not be mentioned now. But I, along with my other friends, have certainly entreated the duke so much that he has quite pardoned him, and on top of that will pay him great honour: he wishes to give him his daughter and pardon all wrongs. He will accompany him to Lorraine and there hold a splendid wedding. I will go with Terri; I will come to the feast for love of him. We shall always be friends. Then I shall leave for my own land. The duke informs you of this through me; I have told you in good faith." (5711–44)

"Yes, my lord," said Duke Loher, "I certainly want to agree with all you have said. I renounce my ill-will to him and henceforth will hold him very dear." "One more thing!" said Duke Otun. "Before you all I entreat Gui: if I have done him wrong, I will gladly put it right, on condition that we kiss each other and henceforth be friends." "My lord duke," said Gui, "no more of that! I certainly don't care to kiss you. Once, in your country, you treated me with treachery: you had my friends killed. But now I must let matters rest. You did what you liked long enough. Go and kiss Count Alberi and be reconciled with his son Terri; establish love between them and the duke. You will accrue great honour from it!" Then they kissed each other in love and great friendship. Gui withdrew to one side; he never kissed a Lombard that day. He went and kissed all those from Lorraine, and Duke Loher first of all. (5745–70)

"My lord, Duke Loher," said Count Alberi, "I entrust my son Terri to you; I shall go back to my city. May you all be commended to God, and you, Sir Gui and Sir Heralt, may God, who sits on high, restore you! I am old, I can't travel, so I want to go home." The count turned back, and the duke took to the road, a great gathering of lords with him, who were unaware of his wicked intention. Heralt brought the young lady, who was overjoyed at the news that she was rec-

---

[54] 5710 **Empire** *Romanie*: Probably the Holy Roman Empire, but it could refer to Byzantium. See note to line 4651.

onciled with her father and would be married to her beloved. They went straight off towards Lorraine. Gui and Terri were delighted about it;[55] they were unaware of the treachery plotted by Duke Otun. Before the day had passed, they would be separated with much suffering. They journeyed quickly until they had travelled from the city of Worms to a plain, where the dukes dismounted. They at once ordered their men to dismount straight away; because of the great heat, the men wanted to rest a little. When everyone had got down on the ground, the dukes together stood up. (5771–5802)

"My lords," said the duke of Pavia, "my party, those from Lorraine and Lombardy, all those on our side and on the side of Duke Loher, listen to this. I order you: wait no longer, but seize all these traitors quickly and tie their hands behind their backs. We shall take them to Lorraine and tomorrow sentence them to death, and whoever hesitates to seize them will be sentenced alongside them." Then you could see the Lombards jump up, like young goats running from the slaughter, and with them those from Lorraine, who were unhappy with the order.[56] They rapidly went to attack Terri and held him tightly so that he could not leave. They took Heralt in exactly the same way, because their men there were more numerous. (5803–22)

"My lord, Duke Loher," said Gui, "why have you betrayed me? I always considered you a trustworthy knight; why have you betrayed us all? Then didn't we kiss each other and become reconciled in front of your barons? You have put your trust in Duke Otun, who never counselled anything except evil; he plotted this treason. God, who created everything, destroy him! You would never have decided on this if the traitor hadn't plotted it." Duke Loher felt such misery that he could not say a word to Gui. He withdrew to one side; never had he been so sorry about anything. (5823–38)

Then a knight from Lombardy came up, a real scoundrel. He seized Gui by his cloak and jerked him towards him, so that the fastenings broke; many knights watched. Gui turned round towards him and struck him with his fist, making him fall dead to the ground: he would never again seize a knight. Lombards came running and seized Gui on all sides. The tunic he wore was torn into so many pieces that each one bore in his fist a scrap which he had pulled off. Gui fiercely rushed away from them, landing many punches. He saw his good horse standing in front of him. Instantly he jumped on it and dug spurs into the horse, soon emerging from the great throng. When Duke Otun saw that Gui was spurring off, he called loudly to his knights: "My lords, mount your horses and hasten to capture Gui, if you want my love! If he gets away, I'll be in a sorry plight, for

---

[55] 5788 **were delighted about it** *grant joie en funt*: After 5788, F adds 2 lines.

[56] 5818 **who were unhappy with the order** *Qui del comandement sunt dolenz!*: Ewert puts an exclamation mark here, perhaps suggesting irony—i.e., the reverse was true—but without such a mark, it can be taken seriously: the men from Lorraine are not as villainous as the Lombards.

I'll then be greatly betrayed. If he gets away from you, may it please all-seeing God that you never have any joy in this world and all soon die a painful death! Whoever brings him to me, alive or dead, shall have a thousand gold besants before the end of the day." (5839–74)

The knights mounted their horses by their hundreds and thousands, and they pursued Gui, who went off on his own, without a single weapon in the world. He fled in one direction; if almighty God did not look after him, he would surely be maimed and killed. The men from Lorraine and Lombardy surrounded him on all sides and very soon would strike him from every angle. Then a knight came up, shield round his neck, on his horse; he held a sharp sword in his hand and came quickly towards Gui, meaning to hit him through the body. But God would not allow it: the sword's blow came down between his arm and his side, cutting his tunic and shirt. And Gui met him in the following way: he punched him so hard with his fist that he knocked him off his horse. Then Gui rode past, but met another, holding a cutting blade, who meant to hit him on the head. The blow fell on Gui's horse and sliced half a foot into its hindquarters. (5875–5902)

Then Gui ran away from them; it is no wonder he was afraid. He went at great speed and the others pursued him vigorously, until Gui saw a fellow holding a stake. He went towards him and spoke to him in a friendly way: "My friend, give me that stake! You can be quite sure I'll reward you as soon as I can." And he replied: "My fair, dear lord, I'll gladly give it you; I can certainly see how much you need it. God defend you from harm!" Gui then took the stake in his hands and quickly turned to face his pursuers. He met a knight and gave him a blow with the stake so that he knocked him dead to the ground. He seized the horse by its reins and went back to the man. "My friend," he said, "I give you this horse as a reward; God bless you!" The fellow gave him many thanks, took the horse, and led it away. (5903–30)

Then Gui turned away; no disarmed, solitary man ever defended himself better in a single day. When he could bear the fighting no longer, he fled, still defending himself, until he came to a big river. He entered and crossed it, at which each of his pursuers marvelled; no one dared cross behind him because they were too afraid of drowning. Then they turned around and went back to their lord. Duke Otun was very angry that Gui had got away from them; he blamed his men, his Lombards and his Lorrainers, very much for letting Gui go; he was absolutely intent on killing him. "My lord, Duke Loher," said Otun, "that scoundrel has gone. I want to go to Pavia and there marry your daughter; I will hold a splendid wedding. Take Terri and Heralt along and put them in my prison there. They will just suffer there until you do what you please with them, deciding whether they should live or die. Keep the other prisoners; you can do what you like with them." (5931–60)

"My lord Otun," said Duke Loher, "I could not bear it if you had Count Terri killed. Indeed, dear sir, I can't allow it. If you want to be in charge of Count

Terri and retain my friendship, have him guarded with great honour and much cherished and respected. Until he does my will, I want him to be honourably kept. I shall keep Heralt with me and have him guarded in prison. I don't want you to keep him, for I know you will never be fond of him." Then they exchanged kisses and parted on very affectionate terms. (5961–76)

Duke Loher went off to Lorraine and had Heralt guarded with much honour. The duke of Pavia departed and took the maiden with him, and also Count Terri; if God did not help him, he would be in a sorry plight. They chained him, tied his hands behind his back, and then put him on a hack, and in this way brought him into Otun's land. When his beloved saw him being led thus, she began to weep for sorrow; she fell from her horse and swooned; her heart almost broke. When the duke saw her fall, he said very angrily to her: "My dear, you behave very badly when you lament in this way for a lowly fellow. Henceforth you can be sure that if ever I see you making such a show in any way, I'll have Terri torn limb from limb, strung up or maimed in front of you. Don't be upset, my my fair love; we shall go joyfully to Pavia and there I shall marry you and keep you with great pleasure. I shall guard Terri in my prison, where he'll get nothing but good treatment, for sure. I've bitterly hated him on account of both Heralt and Gui, but I'll have him attended with great honour so that you no longer look sad." (5977–6010)

"My lord," she said, "thank you! But now I beg you one thing: give me forty days' respite, for my grief to subside. Then I want you to marry me and keep me with great honour." "Certainly, I consent," replied the duke. Then they went to Pavia. But the maiden's thoughts were very different from what she revealed: that before he married her she would kill herself with a knife. She took comfort inasmuch as she trusted strongly in Gui because he had escaped; she believed that through his great valour he would contrive to free his friend Count Terri from prison. Then they arrived in Pavia. The duke lost no time, seizing Count Terri and putting him in a dark dungeon. Terri suffered greatly there, not knowing if it was night or day. He had little to drink and less to eat. His beloved never stopped grieving, at night when she was alone, when no one saw her. (6011–38)

Now we shall tell you about Gui once more. When God had saved him from death and he had crossed the river, he looked in all directions and saw he was alone and friendless. He remembered his companions and nearly went mad with grief. "Lord God," he said, "what shall I do? Alas, wretch, what will become of me now I've lost Count Terri and Heralt, who was such a good friend to me? Since the wicked duke has captured them, I know they'll be killed. Alas, my lord, Duke Loher! How can you put up with wicked Duke Otun carrying out treachery in front of you? From now on you'll be considered a traitor; no one will defend you. My God!" he said, "what can I do? Where shall I go and to which land? This morning I was feared as I went out of the city, five hundred knights with me, all mercenaries who belonged to me. Now I haven't even a squire to hold my horse. Because of me they are all killed or imprisoned in Pavia. Alas for my good friend Terri; we are so far apart now! I shall never see you again; I would certainly give my life for you. The duke will never be able to protect himself from my cutting him to pieces, and I will have avenged you in that way. I am sure I will die there." (6039–76)

Then Gui rode off and journeyed all that day until he saw a very fine castle by a river. He wanted to lodge there: it was dark and he could go no further. When he came to the gate of the castle, he found a young man, a powerful and courteous knight, with what looked like three companions; Gui could see easily by his appearance that he was lord of the company. "My lord," said Gui, "listen to me: God, who created the whole world, bless you this day and give you very great honour. I am a knight who has lost his way; I ask for lodging out of charity." The lord answered very gently: "You shall have lodging most willingly." Then he had his horse taken and cared for beside his own. Next he took him by the hand, they sat down in the hall, and he had a silk mantle brought and thrown over Gui's shoulders. The knights who were in the hall looked at him in amazement: [*he was powerful and handsome and well-proportioned, and everyone gave him much attention.*]⁵⁷ (6077–6106)

"Sir knight," said the lord, "I entreat you in a friendly way to tell me your name and not conceal it from me." Gui replied: "You shall indeed hear it, since you want to know: I am called Gui of Warwick, and I am in great trouble." When the lord heard that this was Gui of Warwick, he said: "My lord, welcome! You are lodged as if in your own home. You are very welcome now that I have recognised you. I should hold you dear above all others; you once did me much good. When I served you, you cherished me fondly, gave me weapons with honour, and then led me to many lands, to tournaments and to wars, until my renown was great. Then I returned to my country. I am called Amis de Champaine; you certainly ought to know me." ⁵⁸ When Gui looked at him carefully, he recognized him and at once kissed him. (6107–32)

"My lord," said Amis, "since you journey so secretly, where have you come from? You certainly look like a frightened man who has escaped from danger. Where is Heralt the marquis and where are your companions staying?" "My lord," said Gui, "I will tell you; it's no wonder I grieve for them." Then he told him everything: how he found Count Terri wounded and how he had him cured of his wound, and how they went to help his father, and how they were all betrayed at a parley they had accepted, and how he alone had escaped through great fortune, and how Count Terri had been captured, as well as Heralt of Arderne,

---

⁵⁷ 6105–6 **he was powerful ... gave him much attention** *Granz ert ... esteit mult esgardez*: these lines are not in E; they are supplied from M and F.

⁵⁸ 6129 **Amis de Champaine** Amis has not appeared before; he is symbolic of friendship (see 6173). His sobriquet varies from Champaine to Muntaigne (6417); the latter is more convincing, because Champagne has no border with Germany (see 6417–18). He is said to return to Alemaigne, "straight to his land," 12566.

the good marquis, and with them five hundred knights, very valiant and bold. He did not know if they were alive or dead, but had seen them all being captured. (6133–54)

When Gui had informed him of everything and of what bad fortune had befallen him, Amis said: "My lord, now be patient, and please listen to me. I have castles and strong towers—there are many in my land. I will have them all handed over to you, and then I will summon my knights; I can summon five hundred of them, who will all be at your disposal, without counting my people, who are good, and not counting the aid which will arrive for us. We shall make war on Duke Otun; we can ruin and burn his land. Thus you can take revenge on him and certainly soon kill or harm him. From now on we shall not stop making war until we have killed him." (6155–72)

"My friend," said Gui, "thank you! Any delay would now be too great; even were I to make war on the duke, vengeance would be delayed too long. I will take revenge speedily; fear of death will not stop me." He stayed there eight days and never stopped grieving. Amis comforted him night and day and felt much sorrow for him. Gui then took leave and went towards Pavia; Amis wanted to go with him, but Gui would not take him. Amis stayed behind, very unhappy; he often prayed God to defend Gui from harm and to bring him back safely. Gui went straight to Pavia; he dressed himself like a squire, stained his whole face with an ointment, and dyed his hair, which was in fact blond, completely black. There was no one, however discerning, who could recognize him. (6173–98)

Gui arrived in Pavia and was recognized by no one. He found Duke Otun and spoke to him as you shall hear. "My lord, Duke Otun, may God save you, as a noble and worthy man! I am a man from a foreign land; I have come from afar to seek you, and I've brought you a war-horse. He certainly has no equal in this world. A Saracen raised him and then a cousin of mine gave him to me. Nothing under heaven is as fast: neither leopard, goat, nor dromedary ever went so fast that this horse would not soon pass it. You'll never fear any arm of the sea which you won't be able to cross on him. If you don't believe me, I would certainly like you to try him. But the horse has one practice, which has caused many men harm: he will devour anyone under heaven who approaches him, except me, for I have taken care of him and loved him above all else." (6199–6224)

"My friend," said he, "thank you! This is a most noble gift. I shall keep you with the horse and make you rich with gold and silver. I could do with such a horse, which I can really trust: I've had enemies I've been revenged on, and I've thrown some of them into my prison, but one of them escaped from me: God, who created everything, grant I can get him back in my power! He would have such a hard life: tomorrow, for sure, I would hang him, because I would have every right to do so." "My lord," said Gui, "who is this, who is in so much danger?" "My friend," he said, "I will tell you: it is Gui of Warwick, whom I never loved. I shall never be safe, for sure, as long as he's alive." (6225–44)

"My lord," he said, "I know Gui well. God, if only he were here now! He killed one of my kin, which still gives me sorrow. And I know Count Terri well: he is my mortal enemy, for he wickedly killed my father and then disinherited my brother. May God never let me die before I can hold him captive as I like." "My friend," said Duke Otun, "I have Terri in my prison; now I want you to guard him and humiliate him in every way." "My lord," he said, "thank you! And I tell you truly, I will entirely change his circumstances, for I myself will keep an eye on him." The duke handed the keys over to him; from now on he would be chief jailer. The duke asked what he was called. "My lord," he said, " people call me Yun."[59] The duke ordered him to take good care of the horse; he had a house handed over to him which would otherwise be unoccupied. The duke had no idea how Gui hated him. Gui was at court and nobody knew him; he did many things on his own authority and there wasn't a single person to gainsay him. (6245–74)

Gui went off to a tower and found a nasty dungeon; it was forty fathoms deep in the ground. Inside it he could hear a lament. Gui at once asked who in there was showing such sorrow. "I am surely a wretch," he said, "indeed it grieves me that I'm alive. I'm called Count Terri; now I'm feeble, but once I was a lord. I'm placed in this dungeon here; I never harmed the duke in any way. Now I'm more laden with iron than a burdened hack, on my arms, my legs, and my body—I would very much rather be dead. Because I was the friend of the best warrior I knew, whom the duke mortally hated, revenge will be exacted from me: this is the third day I have not eaten and I shall not last five days." "My friend," said Gui, "don't be afraid! I am Gui whom you love so much; I will deliver you from this prison as soon as I can." (6275–6300)

"For God's sake," said Terri, "my lord Gui, my good friend—get out of here! How did you get here? Your arrival will do me great harm: if the duke were to find out it's you, you would be killed before the end of the day. I would rather die alone than see both of us perish. So, my lord, go away; for God's sake, don't stay!" As they talked together, a Lombard, who had followed Gui into the tower in order to know for sure what he would do, heard everything. He called out in a loud voice: "Gui, your arrival will be your misfortune! Both of you will be hanged, since you have joined each other." "For God's sake, no more of that!" said Gui. "You can certainly harm us, but what will you gain if you have us killed? I will become your liege man and serve you as my lord, and Count Terri along with me; I give you my word we shall give you half our lands and whatever we can gain in the world." (6301–28)

---

[59] 6266 **Yun** At 8270, Gui calls himself "Jun." Both "Yun" and "Jun" form the second sound in the name "Guiun."

"Be quiet, you scoundrel!" said the Lombard. "May God never look after me if I don't tell this to Duke Otun; I won't for anything fail to do that."[60] He went running from the tower and Gui quickly followed him, straight to Duke Otun's feet. Gui hit him with a large stick and struck him a great blow to the head, so that he knocked him dead to the ground. "My good sir," said the duke, "what have you done? You will certainly be torn to pieces by horses. Why have you killed my man? How were you so presumptuous?" "My lord," said Gui, "now you shall hear; don't be disturbed but listen. I had gone into that tower; I wanted to see the situation there. I found this wretch there, talking to Terri in the prison; he had brought him food, great quantities of bread and wine. When I saw this, it troubled me, and he threatened to kill me. Because I told him that indeed I would tell you about it before evening, he hit me a great blow with his fist, so I followed him into your presence and struck him in anger with my stick. I beg you, fair sweet lord, to pardon me this misdeed; I did it for you, you can be sure of that. Others along with him will be punished, who feed your prisoners without your permission." (6329–62)

The duke swore a great oath: had Yun done differently, he would speedily have been killed or soon strung up high in the wind, "but now you may be forgiven." Gui thanked him very much. As soon as it was night, Gui went off into the city, bought plenty of food, and took it to Terri in the dungeon. He did this for I don't know how many days and much relieved Terri's suffering. He set him free from the irons and made him as comfortable as he could. One day he entered a room and found the maiden there, lamenting bitterly like someone in danger. "My lady," said Gui, "listen: you should know me well. My name is Gui of Warwick, a friend of your beloved. I've come in this fashion so as not to be known by anyone, in order to free your sweetheart, who is so dear to my heart." (6363–88)

When the maiden heard it was Gui himself, she swooned from the joy she felt, and Gui at once raised her up. "My lady," he said, "don't do that! Do you want to betray me? If I were discovered through this, I would be quickly killed or hanged." "Sir Gui," she said, "in God's name, thank you! Three days from today is the time I shall be married, but I have decided something: I will kill myself the day he is to take me to the church for the wedding." Gui replied: "My friend, don't do it. You should follow all his orders. Before he arrives at the church, a great calamity will befall him: I will sever his head from his body and take you away with me." (6389–6410)

Gui left, and as soon as night fell, he went off to the dungeon and at once set Terri free. "Now, my lord Terri, go—don't stop, night or day—straight to Amis de la Muntaigne. Greet him on my behalf and stay there until I come or someone in my name does." "My lord," said Terri, "I promise I will." Then they

---

[60] 6332 **I won't for anything fail to do that** *Ne larreie pur esperlun* is E's reading. I have adopted C's reading of 6332, *Ne larreie pur nul dun*.

exchanged kisses and both wept at parting, each for pity of the other, who had been in great danger. Gui lowered him from the tower and commended him to the Holy Spirit. (6411–28)

 Gui stayed behind, Terri left; he travelled unceasingly that night. He travelled so hard that he arrived at La Muntaigne and recognized it: it had a castle and a fine city, surrounded by an ancient wall. There were many beautiful halls and strong towers throughout the city. On the one side there were rivers, on the other thick forests. He entered the city and went straight to the hall. He found Amis playing chess with one of his brave companions, and with them some thirty knights, all his mercenaries, who had stayed with him because there was war in his land. "My lord," Terri said, "listen to me: please talk with me, and privately, by your leave, so that people don't hear it." Amis replied: "I'll do so most gladly, dear and fair sir." Then he rose from the chessboard and called him over to a window. (6429–54)

 "My lord Amis," said Terri to him, "Lord Gui sends you greetings. He has sent me promptly, to stay with you until he can come here; that is what he very much wants." "My lord," he said, "I thank him for sending you here. What is your name? Tell me!" "My lord," he said, "I will do so. I am called Terri of Worms, and I've escaped from a mighty prison." "Count Terri," said Amis, "welcome to this land!" He kissed him more than a hundred times. His eyes filled with tears of pity when he saw him in such a wretched state, and he rejoiced that he had escaped. He had him bathed in great comfort and his head washed after bloodletting. Terri was served as he wished, and clothed with splendid garments. He gave him horses and weapons, the most precious in the land. He would not leave there until he received news of Gui. (6455–80)

 We shall tell you about Duke Otun, and after that we shall speak of Gui. The duke sent for his barons, for all those from Lombardy to gather in the city of Pavia. When the time came, the duke was delighted; he came to the maiden like a happy and joyful man. "My beloved," he said, "now make yourself ready! This very day you will be married." "My lord," she said, "I will most gladly do what you command." She quickly went to dress herself in magnificent Tyrian cloth.[61] Then they put her on a palfrey—neither king nor prince mounted a better; the saddle-cloth was very splendid, with much gold and silver in it. They went off to the church, expecting a joyful wedding. (6481–6502)

 Gui armed himself most splendidly, for he had as many weapons as he liked. These, presented to him by the maiden, had been given to the duke. Then he mounted his good horse and caught them up without delay. "Duke," he said, "listen to this! I order you to go no further. Don't you remember the treachery you

---

 [61] 6496 **Tyrian cloth** *drap de Tyr*: A garment dyed in Tyrian purple would be rare and expensive: the dye, made from marine molluscs, was from earliest times used for cloth exported by the Phoenicians.

did to Gui, on the way back from Benevento? My heart is still sad about it. And you did me greater treachery when you seized Count Terri and Heralt and my companions and had them put in your prisons. This is Gui you see here, and by my head, you will pay for it!" He struck him through the middle of the body, so that the Lombards saw it clearly. Then he swore by almighty God that if anyone made the slightest move he would sever his head from his body. Next he turned to the maiden, took her quickly in his arms, put her on the horse in front of him, and went off at high speed. The cry was raised in the city, and the people made every effort to pursue him. Gui rode off, and they returned, back to their lord's body, but a most courageous young man, a very brave nephew of Duke Otun, named Berard, followed Gui entirely on his own, with neither friend nor companion, his shield round his neck, his sword in hand; in a time of need, he was most valiant. He chased Gui for fifteen leagues and saw him in front of him in the distance. "Gui," he said, "turn around! As God is your help, fight with me!" Gui at once turned round, like someone not at all afraid of him, set the maiden on the ground, grasped his shield by its leather thongs, and went to strike the young man, who encountered Gui bravely. (6503–50)

The young man struck Gui first so that he split his golden shield, cut his strong hauberk, which was of no more use than a button, and cut into his flesh as far as his rib. Gui was astonished by the blow. He struck the young man back, putting his sharp sword through the shield, and wounded him through the shoulder, knocking down his horse along with him. When the young man realized he was on the ground, he jumped quickly to his feet, then drew his steel sword; he would readily have killed his horse. "A curse on you, horse," he said, "when you can't hold me up! You certainly deserve to die since you can't hold me up. Turn around, Gui!" he said. "Remove your hauberk; let's fight without our weapons[62] and we'll see who's more valiant! If I don't cut off your head before I leave this place, I don't expect ever to gain honour or, indeed, live beyond this day." (6551–76)

"My friend," said Gui, "we shall not strike now; we'll have enough occasion to resume our fighting." He took the maiden, carried her off, and then crossed a river. The young man returned, very sorrowful, to the city. They buried the duke most solemnly in the cathedral church. The young man went to the emperor and told him of his uncle's death; the emperor gave him the whole domain and kept him with him with great honour. He soon bestowed weapons on him and showed him great affection; he made him seneschal of Germany, which later caused harm to many men. (6577–92)

Gui rode off with the maiden, who started to grieve once more. "My lord Gui," she said, "now what shall I do? I shall never see my beloved again! Now I am sure he will die. Would to God I were there, so I could die along with him;

---

[62] 6571 **without our weapons** *En pleines armes*: See note to line 1669.

that would certainly please me." "Terri is unharmed, be sure of that! You will see him again, safe and sound. I had such a talk with the jailers that they will gladly serve him." He travelled so long on their journey that he arrived at the city of La Muntaigne, which was beautiful, where Gui had sent Terri. He joyfully entered the city and then went to the hall. When Amis saw him, he recognized him. "My lord Gui," he said, "welcome!" (6593–6612)

When Terri saw Gui coming, and the maiden with him, he gave Gui the most joyful of welcomes. He took the maiden in his arms. "My lord Gui," he said, "welcome, and my beloved whom you bring here! God be thanked we are now together! God and St Mary forbid we should be parted for a long time!" Then they kissed each other and shed many tears of pity. When the maiden saw Terri, her sweetheart whom she loved so much, she swooned for joy amongst them; she did not expect to find him there. Terri took her in his arms and kissed her, then said to her: "My fair love, don't be afraid, for I'm quite hale and hearty." They rejoiced greatly amongst themselves, and stayed there as long as it pleased them; Amis had them splendidly served. (6613–36)

One day Gui reflected that they had stayed there a long time. He called Amis and Terri. "My lords," he said, "listen: we have stayed here enough. Now we ought to go to Worms, to Count Alberi; I am sure he grieves for us. Next I want to summon knights, avenge myself on Duke Loher, and free my companions; I can never forget them.[63] Everyone should make every effort to take revenge on his enemies." "My lord," said Amis, "I shall go with you; I shall take five hundred knights and a thousand men at arms on their horses, who will most gladly help you." "My lord," said Gui, "thank you; I put great trust in you." Amis summoned his knights and assembled them at once, and the men at arms along with them, who were bold and brave. (6637–60)

When everyone had prepared himself, they left that place and went quickly towards Worms. In Lorraine they inflicted great damage: they seized castles and burned cities, and many of them caused much harm there. Then they came to Worms; the citizens were overjoyed, especially Count Alberi when he saw Gui and Terri. He swooned for joy in front of them, for he thought he had totally lost them. Then there was great joy between father and son; each told the other how Gui had saved them from death. Gui lost no time in gathering a band of knights; he had done the duke great harm and certainly seemed to be taking his revenge. (6661–80)

When Duke Loher heard that Gui and Terri had arrived, and his daughter, the maiden Osille, he was very glad at the news. He called for Heralt of Arderne and speedily told him how Gui and Terri had come and were waging war on him with great violence, and with them the count of La Muntaigne, who had a most noble company. When Heralt heard that Gui and Terri had come, never was he

---

[63] 6648 **I can never forget them** *Nes puis unques oblier*: After 6648, FM add 2 lines.

so glad of anything; he kept praising God. "My lord Heralt," said Duke Loher, "now I shall make you a messenger. You shall go to Count Alberi, to Gui and to Terri, and tell them I want to be reconciled with them and put right all wrongs. I shall give my daughter to Terri, and I shall give him the right to inherit my land. I would very much like you to be the guarantee that the friendship is binding." (6681–6704)

"My lord," said Heralt, "I will go there and will assume responsibility for the agreement." The duke sent for his prisoners and handed over all their weapons to them; there wasn't a single one who lacked anything, not even a farthing's worth. They all accompanied Heralt and concerned themselves with the agreement. Then Heralt made ready and went straight towards Worms, and the knights along with him, who would seek a reconciliation with Terri. Gui was returning from hunting one day, with Count Amis and the brave Terri and some hundred knights, girded with swords, on their horses. They were going towards Worms and looked to one side of them; they saw so many knights coming that they feared there would be treachery. The count of La Muntaigne said: "I see a great company arriving over there. I don't know who they are. They want to come this way; I don't know if they seek war or peace. I shall go and find out all their circumstances." Then he mounted a Gascon horse and, with his shield round his neck and lance in hand, he went at great speed in that direction. He arrived at the right moment: he stopped alongside them and Heralt recognized him at once. Then he asked him where he had come from and where Gui, his lord, was. (6705–38)

"My lord," he said, "I will tell you; I will take you to him. He's coming back from hunting; I left him close by this mountain." Heralt said: "My lord, now let's go there!" They struck spurs into their horses and rode there at a great rate. When Gui and Terri looked at them, "My God!" said Gui, "I can see Heralt and my companions, as God is my saviour; they've escaped from prison, or else the duke has released them." Both of them went to kiss Terri and they rejoiced greatly. (6739–52)

"My lord, Count Terri," said Heralt, "wise counsel is most valuable. This is what Duke Loher sends to you. Certainly I ought to love him for it, since he has honoured me above all others and held me dear and loved me much. He wants to be reconciled with you and greatly to love and honour you. He will gladly give you his daughter and the right to inherit his land, and he wants to be reconciled with your father and to guarantee to you everything I have said. And he will most gladly, my lord Gui, be likewise reconciled with you. Whatever you decide he will gladly do, you can be sure, and I shall be pledge of this, that he will do everything I have said to you." Together they all begged Gui, and Terri likewise, to be reconciled with Duke Loher, for such a man was much esteemed. They prayed and begged them so hard, as did Count Amis, that the reconciliation was agreed and completely guaranteed. (6753–78)

Then they went off to the city and told Count Alberi how Heralt had arrived and had agreed to the reconciliation; the count consented to it since Heralt had agreed it. They waited no longer but went to Lorraine—Count Alberi and his son Terri, Gui and Heralt and Count Amis and a great crowd of knights who gladly went along. When they arrived in Lorraine, they were received with great joy. There they were reconciled and all wrongs were pardoned. There was great joy in the city that they were agreed in that way. The duke gave his daughter to Terri, and gave him the right to inherit his land, in front of counts and barons who were from many regions. Then they held the wedding—a more splendid one was never seen, whether of a king or an emperor, because it was carried out with great honour. (6779–6804)

At the conclusion of this feast, which was so splendid and honourable, the barons took their leave and went back to their lands. Count Amis took his leave and went to his land. Gui stayed on afterwards. One day he went into a wood, and Duke Loher along with him, for they wanted to hunt in the direction of Brabant.[64] Count Terri went, and many other knights with him. They entered a great forest and, finding a fierce boar there, they unleashed all their hounds and hunted it energetically. The boar soon fled away, doing great harm to the hounds and killing more than a hundred of them. It speedily passed through the countryside; skilled hunters followed it, crying out, shouting and making a lot of noise. The large boar made off, fearing neither huntsman nor hound. It crossed the land and the districts, the tall mountains and the valleys; horses and steeds grew weary, knights and huntsmen fell behind. All the hounds which followed it were exhausted and dead, except just three good ones; they followed it as far as Brabant. Neither huntsman nor knight, young man or even squire, knew where the boar was nor into which land it had been chased. (6805–40)

Gui pursued it on his horse; he had his steel sword in his fist and his horn round his neck, which he often sounded while vigorously chasing the boar. It gave Gui no pleasure to pursue it: the boar fled as far as Brabant, into a large forest. As fast as it could, it got inside a thicket it knew, taking a short detour around it to put the dogs off the scent. It resisted the hounds and defended itself as a fierce boar would. When Gui saw it, he dismounted from his horse, held his sword with both hands, and quickly went towards it. The swine met him like a bold creature, and Gui struck its hoof and cut its body in two with his sword, throwing it dead to the ground. He disembowelled it and then sounded his horn, thinking he had been accompanied. He was too far from his men; if almighty God did not take care of him, before the end of the day he would, rightly or wrongly, be in mortal danger. (6841–66)

---

[64] 7002 **Brabanter** *Brabaçon*: Brabant was made a duchy in 1183–84; it covered approximately the present North Brabant (in Holland) and Flemish Brabant, Walloon Brabant, Antwerp, and the Brussels region, all in Belgium.

When Gui had disembowelled the boar, he sounded his horn loudly. "My God!" said Count Florentin, "who can that be, by St Martin, whom I hear blowing his horn like that in my forest? He has taken a stag or a boar." Then he called to a knight, his son, whom he dearly loved. "My son," he said, "to horse! Whoever he is, bring him to me!"[65] "Sir," he said, "I certainly will." Then he mounted his swift horse and went straight to the forest, finding Gui at once. Florentin's son seized a big stick of apple-wood, an act that would bring him great harm. "Fellow," he said, "who are you, who have entered this forest without my lord's permission? You will regret taking his boar today; you did not deign to ask permission to do so. Quick, hand over your horse and that horn you are carrying; you are coming with me, entirely on foot—you shall certainly not ride." (6867–92)

"My friend," said Gui, "indeed I shan't do so. I'll not hand over my horse to you; it's not customary for a knight to go on foot for any length of time. I shall go with you, if you wish, and you can show me the layout of the country. You can certainly have the horn, if you ask for it in a friendly way." "Fellow," he said, "no more talk of that! You'll never escape in that way." He advanced to seize Gui's reins; he was very keen to have the fine horse. He struck him with the stick and Gui nearly went mad with anger. "Wretch," he said, "you've struck me; by my head, you shall pay for it!" With his horn he hit him on the head and made his brains fall on the ground. "Fellow," he said, "take the boar and be generous with it. Never again think of striking a knight; you were too violent a fellow." (6893–6914)

Then he left that place and travelled for so long through the forest that he emerged very tired. He did not recognize the country round about; he looked in all directions but saw neither castle, town nor city. It had been a long day and he had not eaten. Then he did not travel for much longer before seeing, beside a fence, a very well-situated castle. He went straight in that direction and met a man from the region. "My friend," he said, "this castle—to whom does it belong? It's very fine." "My lord," he said, "you shall hear at once: you'll never see a better man. He's Count Florentin; a truer man never drank wine.' Gui speedily left him, came to the gate, and entered; he then came to the door of the hall and quickly dismounted. At the high table he saw a knight whose hair was quite white, with a long beard and a proud face; he certainly looked like the lord of an important land. He speedily went before him and greeted him politely. (6915–42)

"My lord," he said, "give me a hearing; may God who created the world bless you! I'm a weary knight who begs you, for charity's sake, to give me something to eat; then I will depart." "My friend," he said, "you shall have it; please sit down!" Then the count quickly sent for water and Gui rapidly washed his hands. Then he sat down to the meal. They put bread and wine in front of him and a great quantity of meat. When he had eaten some of it, he heard bells ringing in the town, with loud lamenting, great weeping, garments being rent and hair being

---

[65] 6876 **bring him to me!** *sil m'amenez!*: After 6876, FM add 2 lines.

torn—you never heard tell of greater grief. "My God!" said the count, "heavenly King! What can this great lamentation be for?" At that, two men entered the hall carrying a body, and placed it in the middle of the floor. "My God!" said the count, "that's my son."[66] He rent his clothes and tore his hair, so much pain and anger were in his heart. "My fine son," he said, "who slew you? Would to God and St Denis I had that man in my power in this house! For the whole Roman empire I would not fail to kill him on the spot, burn his body, and scatter it to the winds." (6943–74)

"My lord," said a squire, "I see him sitting here at the meal, the man who killed your son; I give you my word, I see him with my own eyes." When the count heard this, he rushed to the table. He grasped a short sword in his hand, raised it high, and then said to Gui: "Wicked scoundrel, now you'll die! Why did you kill my son?" Raising his arm very high, the count threw the dagger violently at Gui. That time it missed him, for Gui at once jumped up and it went half a foot into the post. "My lord count, mercy, in God's name!" he said. "If I killed your son, I did it in self-defence." Then knights attacked him and assailed him on all sides. Gui seized a shield and a good axe and moved towards one part of the house, where he defended himself like a brave fighter. They attacked him from all directions and he defended himself courageously. Then the seneschal came up, a Brabanter, a very wicked fellow; he struck Gui high up on his shield with a sword. Gui's return stroke did not miss him: he struck the Brabanter a great blow with the axe, so that he split his head in two and he fell dead to the ground. That was how Gui continued to defend himself, and they attacked him very fiercely. He killed three knights, the boldest in the court. (6975–7012)

"My lord, Count Florentin," said Gui, "mercy, in the name of the True Cross! Aren't you so virtuous a man that no one as far as Rome is as true as you? If you kill me in your own house, it will be considered treachery. You will always be greatly reproached if you kill a man whom, out of charity, you willingly sheltered in your house. Whether rightly or wrongly, it would be considered a very treacherous act, and especially at a meal where I could not defend myself. In God's name, my lord, do as much to me as will not bring you censure: give me my horse and let me leave the castle in peace. Then, if I am killed or captured, the country will never blame you." (7013–32)

Thereupon the count retreated. He suffered very greatly at heart to see his son lying dead; never again would he have solace from him. "My son," he said, "what shall I do now that I've lost you? Who will rule my land and my great fiefs when my days are done? I'm an old man and quite feeble; God help me, I would like to die." He fell swooning over the body; there was no one under heaven who did not pity his great suffering. Then he said to his knights that no one henceforth should be so bold as to attack Gui in front of him: so long as Gui was in his

---

[66] 6966 **that's my son** *ja est ço mun fiz*: After 6966, F adds 2 lines.

court, no one should touch him. Then he ordered his people to give Gui his horse speedily, but once he had left his court he was to be instantly cut down. Then Gui's horse was handed over to him, and in great fear he mounted it. With him he carried the shield and he took his sharp sword; then he went out of the castle and made his way towards Lorraine. (7033–60)

Then you would have seen the count, armed, and pursuing Gui fervently, along with his knights, forty of them, on their horses. Gui turned his horse round and struck a knight, piercing him through the body; he boldly knocked another down. Then the count came spurring up on his charger, shield around his neck, sword in hand—completely armed, ready to strike Gui. Gui turned, refusing to flee, and went to strike Count Florentin; with sharp swords, each struck the other's shield. First the count struck Gui through the middle of the shield with his sharp sword. Gui struck him back,—he could not do otherwise—and knocked him far from the horse to the ground. Gui reined the horse in; he felt great pity for the count and for his son whom he had killed, for the count was so old—a full fifteen years had passed since he had last been armed. "My lord count," he said, "now take your horse and mount it! Devils made you take up arms; from now on, you should certainly give them up. I give you as a reward the horse that you gave me today. You should be lying in your chambers or serving in church in God's name. I give up all claim to your lodging: I would certainly rather die of hunger than come and eat with you again, either at dinner or supper."[67] (7061–98)

Then Gui went off at great speed, with no more wish to stay. On all sides he saw knights, burgesses, men at arms, and squires, with all those in the land who had been mustered. He did not want them to catch him, and delaying served no purpose. He struck spurs into his horse and entered a forest. He often turned his face to them and wounded and killed many of the boldest and strongest. Then Gui left them behind and went fleeing through the forest on his good and valuable horse. The count returned like a man in great distress who had not avenged his son. He had his son's body buried with great solemnity in a church. (7099–7118)

Gui journeyed all that day until evening came, and then did not stop journeying all night until bright daylight appeared and he had arrived in Lorraine: he knew the country well. He went straight to the city and found the counts together, who were deeply mourning him: they had looked for him throughout the land. Now they were overjoyed when they saw him coming, perfectly safe. Gui told them all about what danger he had escaped. They all thanked God who had delivered him from such danger. Then he had no wish to stay there any longer, but wanted to go back to his own land. (7119–36)

---

[67] 7098 **either at dinner or supper** *Ne al digner ne a soper*: At this period, dinner was the largest meal, eaten between midday and 2:00 p.m. Supper was a light meal, eaten before retiring for the night.

Gui took leave of Loher, but he granted it unwillingly. The duke offered him plenty of gold and silver, but he would not deign to take any of it. Then Gui went to Count Terri and spoke to him as you shall hear. "My lord Terri," said Gui, "now I shall go without delay to my country, to England. I cannot refrain from going there and seeing my father and my friends. I don't know if they are alive or dead; seven years and more have already passed since I was in the kingdom. If it happens that during this journey you should need me in any way, whether in peace or in war, never be in any doubt: quickly send for me, and I won't leave off, for all that belongs to Rome, to come to you speedily when I've received the summons. We have finished our battle, and you have wed your beloved, and we have destroyed our enemies—dukes, counts, and barons—and brought peace to the land. What man should you fear from now on? And you are renowned as such a man that you will never fear your enemies. I shall send you messages and often give you word of my situation, and you shall do so with yours—you shall tell me all your circumstances. And I myself shall come to you, once I am comfortably situated." (7137–72)

"My friend, thank you!" said Terri. "But what a sorry state I'm in now! You have often saved me from death and I have never rewarded you for it. If you leave me now, I don't know if you'll ever see me again. When our enemies know that we two are separated, they will make war on me from all sides—Germans, Teutons,[68] and Lombards kin to Duke Otun, for he was a lord with many relations. The king of Spain was his uncle, the duke of Moraine[69] married his sister, and noble dukes and counts will accuse me of Otun's death. I shall always be at war and in sorrow, as long as I live. If we two were together, we should never fear war. If you were to stay here, you would have plenty of gold and silver, fine cities and strong castles, and the very best land. I shall stay with Duke Loher, and I will give you all Worms and the splendid fief belonging to it. Then I shall give you an oath never to seek to contest even as much as a pennyworth of the fief." (7173–7202)

"My lord count," said Gui, "don't talk of that! It's no use asking me, because I am very eager to go; were I to die for it, I would not stay. Were it not for love of my beloved I would not leave you; we would always stay together and never part. I must go, whether I want to or not. Don't let it grieve you, my dear friend." Then they exchanged kisses and both began to weep, shedding tears from their eyes most tenderly. People felt great pity; there was not a man under heaven who did not feel great pity for them, at the parting of the friends who were such noble lords. (7203–20)

---

[68] 7182 **Germans, Teutons** *Alemans e Tyeis*: These terms presumably signify different kinds of Germans. *Tieis/Tyeis* is also used at 2838 and 4221, where I have translated it as "Germans." The word may be close to *Teutsch*.

[69] 7186 **Moraine** See note to line 884.

Gui mounted an ambling mule[70] and set out, with much sorrow. Terri stayed behind, in a similar state, greatly mourning his friend Gui. He showed such grief, night and day, that no one under heaven could show more. From then on Gui never stopped travelling, and came straight to the sea; he had a good wind, made the crossing, and arrived in England. He went straight to York[71] where King Athelstan was. When he came to York, he was received with great joy; the king went to meet him with the city burgesses. The king showed him much joy and they went arm in arm, talking together; the people from the city watched him with wonder because he was so renowned. (7221–40)

Gui stayed with the king. One day he was playing chess when four wayfarers, peasants of the land, appeared. They said to the king: "My lord, listen: you will now hear harsh news. If you don't soon give some thought to it, you will lose your whole land. An evil beast has come into your country, from the kingdom of Ireland into the region of Northumberland. Not a single man is left who hasn't been maimed or killed, except for those who have escaped by good fortune to the cities. The beast eats animals and people. We tell you truly that there was never such a fierce brute. It has a large and hideous head, its neck is thicker than a tower, and it is blacker than a Moor. It is ugly, large, and very horrible, all covered with scales above the navel. Because of the fine scales covering it, no weapon can touch it in any way. It's as thick in the chest as a pack-horse, and it could easily outrun a horse. It has paws in front like a lion and the people say it is a dragon. It has large wings for flying. I can't tell you about its whole appearance. The body gets larger towards the tail; such a beast was never seen before. The tail is very large and long. You can't know a man in the world today, however well armed, who, if he got a blow from its tail, would not soon have to die; he would never escape from there." (7241–80)

When the king heard what the man was telling him, he began to think and for a long time did not want to say a word. "Sire." said Gui, "don't worry about it! Do not ever fear it. I shall go to Northumberland; if I can find the beast, please God I will surely defeat it because I am very willing to fight it." "Gui," said the king, "you shall not do it; I don't want you to go there alone. You shall take a hundred knights and will be thus much safer." Gui at once replied: "Almighty God forbid that one should gather so many men for a single beast." Then he took leave of the king and went to his lodging. As fast as he could, he got ready and went off to Northumberland. He left all his followers behind and took no companion with him, except for Heralt and two knights, spears in hand, on their

---

[70] 7221 **ambling mule** *mul amblant*: As at 4572, Gui is mounted on a mule, rather than a horse, because he is "off-duty." Whereas a warhorse would be used on the battlefield, mules were preferred by gentlemen and clergy for their strength, endurance, and patience, so it is sensible for Gui to use one for a long journey.

[71] 7231 **York** *Everwic*: FM has Warwick at 7231 and 7233; C has Warwick at 7231 and York at 7233.

horses. When he arrived there and was informed where the beast lived, he armed himself most splendidly. Then he said to his men that none of them should be so bold as to come after him. (7281–7312)

Gui went off into a wood, where the dragon had been pointed out to him. It was exceedingly large and ugly; when Gui saw it, he was not reassured. With great force he struck it with his spear, which was very sharp, so that the spear shattered into pieces, but in no way touched the body. When the beast felt itself struck, it raised its head high, then shook itself and jumped on Gui, speedily knocking him and his horse over. Gui was quite stunned by the blow; never before had he suffered one like it. Hastily he jumped to his feet. "Almighty God," he said, "who made day and night and suffered death for us sinners, and saved holy Daniel from the lion, defend me, Lord, from this dragon." Then he drew his steel sword and attacked the beast; he struck it on the front of its head with a great blow from the sharp sword, but no sign of this appeared on it. Gui thought he was defeated, since he could not harm the beast or damage it with a swordblow. The battle between them was fierce, neither failing to attack the other. During one attack, when Gui struck, he was unlucky in that he approached the beast too quickly; it struck him with one of its paws, so that it pulled off one of the flaps of his hauberk, on which he greatly relied. (7313–48)

Now Gui was greatly perplexed. He retreated to a great tree; there he would defend himself and wait for the beast to fight him. The beast turned to come alongside him and struck him with its tail, high up on the shield, splitting it down to the ground as if it had been hit by a sword; Gui was nearly felled. Then the beast encircled him with its tail and with great violence strained him towards it, so that it broke three of his ribs. Gui struck the tail vigorously, cutting it in two halves, and set himself quite free on this occasion. He had cut eighteen feet[72] off the body and saved himself with great distress. Then Gui realized that from the navel upwards it would never, for all the world, be slain by a sharp weapon. (7349–70)

When the beast felt itself struck, it uttered a cry heard far and wide, making the countryside around resound. People could hear it throughout the region; anyone there would have feared dying. Gui retreated to a tree and there fiercely defended himself. His hauberk was all torn, as if it were a piece of Flemish[73] cloth. Gui fought hard. He finally realized it was no use attacking straight on, nor would he ever kill it that way. As the beast turned, Gui lost no time in hitting it near its wings, and he cut the body through the middle into two. The beast fell, unable to move; it cried and bellowed, showing great pain. Then Gui retreated

---

[72] 7365 **eighteen feet** *treis teises*: A *teise* is a measure of length, about 6 feet. Gui cuts off three *teises*.

[73] 7380 **Flemish** *flamengé*: M has *file*, spun, here.

backwards, because of the violent stench, and did not therefore dare to approach it; he rested at a distance. (7371–94)

Once the beast was dead, it measured thirty feet—the people of the region all measured it, in wonder. Then Gui cut off its head and carried it away with him. He returned to his companions, who were praying for him. Then he went off to York[74] and presented the head to the king, who was happy and glad when he saw Gui hale and hearty. They hung up the head in York and considered it a great wonder. (7395–7408)

Gui took leave of the king and went off to his own land. He went to Wallingford and found his men from the fief, who were delighted to see him; they had not had news of him for many a day. His father had died, and there was no other heir but him. He called Heralt of Arderne and gave all the fief to him; and the men who had served him he rewarded very well, knights and men at arms, the lesser and the greater. Then he went off to Warwick, to the count who paid him much honour, and all those in the region rejoiced for him. The count loved him and greatly honoured him; he did not want to be without him for a moment. Together they went to the woods to hunt and to the riverbank to hawk. Then Gui went to talk to his beloved and told her all that had happened: how mighty kings and emperors had offered him very great honours, and how he was beloved by maidens, by daughters of princes who were very beautiful, but he had not wanted to love anyone except her, nor would he ever do so. (7409–38)

"Sir Gui," she said, "thank you! And I tell you truly that the noblest in the kingdom have constantly sought me in marriage, but I wouldn't love any of them, nor from now on would I ever do so. I give and promise myself to you; do what you please with me." Gui kissed her for joy; he had never been so happy about anything. Then he took leave of his beloved and went to his lodging. Night and day he was joyful because he was certain of her love. (7439–52)

One day the count called for his daughter and spoke to her in front of her mother. "Daughter," he said, "take a husband; we have no other heir but you. Dukes and counts have sought you in marriage, coming from foreign lands; you wouldn't take any of them. How long, daughter, do you want to wait?" "My lord," she said, "I will think about it and will tell you three days from now." When it came to the third day, the count most lovingly sent for his daughter Felice, who was so wise: "Daughter, tell me your thoughts." "My lord," she said, "I shall certainly tell you what my heart intends. Don't take offence if I tell you, good sweet sir, I beg you. It is Gui, your knight—I believe he has no equal in the world. If I don't have him, I shall never take a husband." (7453–74)

"Daughter," he said, "you've spoken well. Now bless you that you didn't lie about wanting the man who will bring honour to all of us. I would love him even more than I loved this city, should he be pleased to take you in marriage. He

---

[74] 7403 **York** *Everwic*: FM have *werewic, warwick*.

never deigned to love a maiden; he has refused so many—the daughters of kings and emperors who are far more important than you are or ever will be. But since you, my beauty, love him so much, I will certainly speak of it to him; I'll find out all his intentions." (7475–88)

One day, when the count had returned from the riverbank where he had taken great quantities of birds, he sent for Gui in private. "Gui," he said, "listen here: tell me what you think—if you want to take a wife, you shouldn't hide it from me." "My lord," he said, "I'll tell you: there's no woman in the world I know whom I esteem, except for one; it would be useless to ask me." "Gui," he said, "now listen to me: I have a beautiful daughter, as you well know. I have no other heir besides her; I will give her to you, Sir Gui.[75] I give her to you; do take her and be lord of all my land, of castles and of cities, and do what you please with all of it." "My lord," said Gui, "thank you: this is a great honour! I would rather have your daughter, just herself alone, than the daughter of the emperor of Germany with all the land as far as Spain." The count kissed him repeatedly and thanked him with all his heart. "Gui," he said, "now I know for sure that you love me above all other, since you are willing to take my daughter and have refused so many beautiful women. In that case, a week from now, let the wedding be held with great splendour in the city of Warwick; a great assembly of lords will be gathered there." (7489–7524)

"My lord," said Gui, "as you please; I shall most gladly be there." Gui told Heralt everything the count had said to him. "Heralt," said Gui, "it gives me delight that from now on I shall have to myself the creature I love above all other. I intend never to leave her." When the time came, a great assembly of lords was gathered, of dukes, counts, and barons, who were summoned to the wedding. The maiden was splendidly prepared and was married to Gui with great honour. Then they held the wedding-feast and celebrated for four days. There were plenty of minstrels, the best in the kingdom—good harpers, players on viols and rotes,[76] fiddlers and tambourine-players. There were all kinds of jugglers, and monkeys and bears frolicked there. Poor knights and prisoners were given rich gifts; they were splendidly paid with plenty of gold and silver, robes and precious cloth, white and grey furs, and good horses. On the fifth day they left and went back to their own lands. (7525–54)

Now Gui had everything he wished, since he could fulfil his desire for his beloved. They were together for fifty days; their love-making lasted no longer

---

[75] 7504 **I will give her to you, sir Gui** *Jo la vus durrai, sire Guiun* is the original reading of E, which I preserve here. Because this statement is virtually repeated in the next line, Ewert substitutes C's line *Grant tere l'atent, ço svez mun* (a great deal of land will be hers).

[76] 7544 **players on ... rotes** *Roturs*: The rote was a triangular zither with strings on both sides of the soundbox. See note to line 3100 in *Boeve*.

than that. It happened that on the first night of their mutual enjoyment, Gui slept with his wife and she conceived a child with him. (7555–62)

It was in May, in summertime, that Gui was in the city of Warwick. One day he had come back from hunting, having taken a great quantity of game, and was very joyful and glad. On a beautiful evening, Gui climbed a tower and leant out of the high gallery. He looked at the country round about and at the sky, which was so full of stars, and at the clear, calm weather. Then Gui began to think how God had done him great honour; He had never done greater to any knight, for he was never in any place or fight that he was not considered the best. And he thought of how he was a man of influence, and renowned in foreign lands, and how he had killed so many men, captured towers and cities by force, and had exerted himself far off in strange realms, for the sake of a woman whom he loved so much and for whom he had borne so much suffering — but never for his Creator, who had done him such great honour, nor had he bothered to serve Him. But now he wanted to repent of this. He began to sigh, and resolved in his heart that he would completely change his life and put himself at God's service. (7563–94)

Then his wife appeared. When she saw her husband so pensive, she said: "My lord, what are you thinking? In God's name, I beg you not to hide it from me. I've never seen you so downcast; are you distressed about something?" "My love," he said, "I'll tell you about it; I'll tell you everything that's in my heart. From the first moment I loved you, I've borne so much suffering for you; I believe there's no man ever born who endured so much sorrow for a woman as I have for you. For you I've caused great havoc, killed men, destroyed cities, and burnt abbeys in many kingdoms. And whatever I've done in this world, whether bad or good, from the moment I first knew you, I've not wanted to hide anything from you. All that I've exerted my body for, and all that I've done and given, I've done for you, you can be certain, and much more than you've heard here. If I were lucky enough to have done only half for the sake of God who created us, who has lent me such great honour, I would truly have heavenly glory and be a saint, together with God. But I never did anything for Him, and so I am wretched and despicable. I've killed so many honourable men that the sins remain with me. From now on I shall go in God's service; I want to expiate my sins. The place where I lie one night I shall never be seen in a second time. I shall give the credit to you for half of all the good actions I henceforth do." (7595–7634)

"My lord," she said, "what have you said? Do you scorn me then? Now I know you have another woman and want to leave me for her. Now go off to her; you shall never come back. My God, alas that I was ever born!" Then she fell swooning to the ground. Gui raised her in his arms and spoke to her most lovingly. "My lady," he said, "no more of that! What is the use of such sorrow? Nothing will make me stay; I've undertaken this journey for God's sake. And you will remain here, with the friends you have. Behave wisely and take comfort for love of me, for you are with child, from which you will have great comfort." (7635–54)

"My God!" she said, "what shall I do? Wretched and unfortunate, what will become of me? If you now leave me, you could not find a better way of killing me. Be sure I won't live any longer once you've left me. If you want to do good deeds, you need never go from here: have churches and abbeys built, plenty of them here and there in your lands, which will always pray for you, nor stop praying night and day. You can surely save your soul here; why go into exile?" (7655–68)

"My lady," said Gui, "now be silent! In God's name, beloved, no more words. I have undertaken this journey for the sins I did, for the many noble men I have killed. For you I have committed many great sins. What I have done wrong with my body, I want to expiate with my body." When the lady heard he would not stay, she often called herself weak, wretched, and unfortunate. She fell to the ground, completely miserable, and swooned and wept and lamented bitterly. "My love," Gui said, "now I'm going, and I commend you to God. If it please God, I shall come back again, when I have performed my penance. But for the future I tell you this much: make no fuss at all that people may see, for you will lose my love for ever; keep your peace. Never again make an outcry about it, if you want to have my love from now on. Often greet Count Rualt, your father, from me, the good countess, your mother, and Heralt of Arderne likewise, and my other men with him. When the time comes to bear the child, I command you to look after him well, until he can walk on his own; then have him handed over to Heralt, who will know how to look after him well and instruct him in everything. He will receive him with great joy and look after him with great honour. I believe there never was a man who was as faithful to his lord as he has been to me; this is why I love him and trust him so much. Take this sword, my lady, and keep it for your son's use: in no land is there such a good one, and he can win great renown with it." (7669–7714)

Then he kissed the lady; out of sorrow he could speak no more. You could see them in such grief—both fell swooning to the ground. When Gui recovered from his swoon, he sadly turned to leave. "My lord," she said, "listen to this: take this gold ring with you and think of me when you see it, so that you don't forget me, in God's name."[77] Gui took the ring from the lady and showed great sorrow at their parting. Then he descended from the castle keep and secretly left the city, without speaking to anyone, not even to Heralt whom he loved so much, but went straight towards the sea, intending next to go to Jerusalem. From then on he resolved he would not stop travelling; he would indeed come to Jerusalem and to many foreign lands, where he could seek God's saints. (7715–36)

---

[77] 7724 **so that you don't forget me, in God's name** *Que vus pur Deu ne me ubliez*: This could also carry the meaning: "so you don't forget me for God."

The lady stayed in the tower in great distress. "My God!" she said, "what shall I do, since I shall lose my husband, the person I most loved in the world? And how can I live?" Then she fell swooning to the ground. You never saw a woman make so much sorrow—rending her clothes, tearing her hair; it was uncertain if she would live. She wrung her hands, which were white, so that she broke the rings on her fingers and blood appeared. That night she had a hard time: she never stopped swooning and weeping, and she continually lamented her good husband. Then she took a sword and drew it out of the scabbard; she said she would kill herself, since she had lost her husband. She had put the sword close to her heart when she thought she was doing something very foolish: was she not with child? She could not kill herself without the child having to die. If she killed herself like that, her father, the count, and her mother and her friends, and all the people of the land, when they knew about it, would at once think her husband had killed her in a fit of madness, and had thus fled. Otherwise she would surely have killed herself. She had no rest at all that night but lamented bitterly. (7737–72)

She rose very early and went to her father's bed. "Father," she said, "you don't know it yet, but now you will hear bad news indeed. My husband has gone; you will never see him ever again. Believe me, he has gone into exile; never again will he be seen in this realm." Then she fell down, and swooned seven times or more before stopping. "Daughter," he said, "give up this idea! I cannot imagine or believe that he has gone into exile, nor that he has put himself at such risk. He has done it to test you—and to see how much he can trust you." "My lord," she said, "it's not like that. You'll never see him again, you can be sure." Then the count rose, and speedily had Gui sought throughout the city. When he did not find him, he summoned all his barons, and then told them how Gui had left the kingdom. When the barons heard this, they sorrowed greatly for him, and everyone in the city lamented him deeply. (7773–7800)

When Heralt heard that his lord had gone away, he felt from then on such grief that it never ended, night or day. He went to the count: "My lord, what shall we do now, in God's name, when we've lost my lord? I don't think we'll ever see him again. Let's quickly send messengers to look for him throughout the land. If he's not to be found here, then he has gone to Lorraine, to talk to his friend Terri, whom he loves so truly." They collected their messengers, and they searched for him throughout the land, but when they did not find him, they came back. (7801–18)

When Heralt was informed that they had not found him, he soon decided he would go and look for him in other realms. Next he took twelve messengers, who were brave, quick-witted, and wise. He gave them plenty of gold and silver and sent them through various kingdoms, so that they should go searching for a whole year, to see if they could find his lord. Then Heralt got ready, dressed like a pilgrim. Next he went off to Count Rualt and gave him his land to look after, and said he would go and look for his lord in the lands where he had been. The count was very distressed when he saw Heralt going away like this. (7819–36)

The count stayed behind and Heralt departed, straight towards the sea without stopping. He crossed with a good wind and went to Normandy, from there into France and Burgundy, then into Germany and Saxony, then Lorraine and Spain. Then he came back through Brittany. He never could find anyone to tell him anything about his lord, whom he was seeking, which made him very unhappy. He came back to England, very perplexed about his lord, since he had not found him. Gui was much mourned in the kingdom: the king was very sad about him and also everyone in the land. They thought they would never see him again, and everyone felt much grief for him. (7837–56)

Now we shall tell you about Gui, as we have found it in the story. He exerted himself so much that year, and travelled through so many foreign lands, that he arrived in Jerusalem, having experienced great exhaustion. Then he journeyed through the land and visited the holy places. Next, he left Jerusalem and decided in his mind that he would go to Antioch. A day's journey away from this side of it, at a fountain under a pine tree, he saw a pilgrim sitting, lamenting bitterly, his head bowed. In appearance he looked like a Saracen, but he had a large, proud face; he was very like a man of great nobility. His head was white, his beard white, whiter than snow on the branch. He was exceedingly sorrowful, and when Gui saw him he felt pity: he was tearing his beard and his hair, and often fainting as well. He cursed the hour he was born because he had been so ill-treated. (7857–82)

"Pilgrim," said Gui, "who are you, who are so tormented? I can certainly see from your appearance that there's great suffering in your heart. Tell me about it, I entreat you, in the name of God, our creator." "Good man," said the pilgrim, "what you've in effect asked me to do is to tell you about my grief, so that I shouldn't hide it from you. I am sure you will consider it astonishing when you have heard the truth about this great sorrow of mine, because of which I often call myself unfortunate and wretched. I was a man of great renown; a country was subject to me. I was once count of Durazzo,[78] and they called me Count Jonas. I had fifteen very valiant sons, aggressive and brave; I don't think a man was ever born, since the founding of the world, whose fifteen sons were so good, each in his way, as mine were; but I've lost them in a great battle, and because of this I'll never be happy again. An infidel, unbelieving people had come to Jerusalem and destroyed the whole land. Then we gathered a great army and went to attack those Saracens. The battle was very fierce; many that day received their deathblow. Through me and my fifteen sons, the Saracens were defeated; we captured seven emirs and three kings on that occasion. (7883–7920)

---

[78] 7899 **Durazzo** *Duraz*: Dyrrachium, part of the Byzantine empire; now Durres, in Albania.

"I vigorously pursued a king, my fifteen sons with me. The king was called Triamor; a better pagan never wore spurs. He was fleeing towards Alexandria, whose powerful king he was. We committed the very great folly of pursuing him into his land. In a wood, in ambush, lay three hundred armed Saracens, who jumped out of their hiding-place and attacked us on all sides. We hit them back boldly; like worthy men we defended ourselves well. Then they killed our horses, which caused us great hardship. We put up strong resistance and killed many of their brave fighters, and before they captured us, we had killed so many of their men that even the most stout-hearted of them was distressed. Before we surrendered to them, they cut our hauberks and shields to pieces so that the blood streamed down from our bodies. We defended ourselves well, like valiant men, until our swords broke in our hands. Then we could not defend ourselves, and we surrendered to King Triamor's mercy on this condition, that he would let us be held to ransom. Then he took us to Alexandria and threw us into his dungeon. We drank little there and ate less, leading a very hard life. A whole year we lay there, with little to drink and less to eat. Two years and more have now passed since we have been in such distress. (7921–58)

"It happened that the sultan, their lord, held a feast with much splendour. Thirty kings were gathered there, his men, sworn to him, and forty very powerful emirs, who were all attending him. King Triamor went, and took his son, a young man called Fabur, brave and recently made a knight. On the third day of this feast, which was so splendid and honourable, after the sumptuous meal—no one could tell you of a finer—the sultan's son, called Sadoine of Persia, got up. 'Fabur,' he said, 'let's go and play chess and amuse ourselves.' 'My lord,' he said, 'and so we shall; since you want to, we'll certainly do so.' Then they went to Sadoine's lodging and at once asked for the chess-set. They then sat down to the game, which would bring distress to both. Before they had finished playing the game, each was angry with the other. Sadoine of Persia took offence at Fabur telling him 'checkmate'; then he said it again, at which Sadoine was angry. He called Fabur son of a whore, and with a castle struck him on the head so that he broke it open; blood streamed down his face. (7959–92)

"'My lord Sadoine,' said Fabur, 'you have done me much dishonour, by breaking my head and insulting me in your father's court. Were you not my lord's son, you would certainly die in great pain.' 'Wretch,' said Sadoine, 'what did you say? Did you threaten me then? By my head, it was unlucky for you that you said it; never did you do anything so stupid.' He was going to strike him with his fist, when Fabur could stand it no longer; he jumped quickly to his feet, seized the chessboard with two hands, and struck Sadoine on top of his head, so that he knocked him dead to the ground. When he saw he had killed him, he at once fled and went to his father's lodging, who had returned from court. As soon as he could, he told him how he had slain the sultan's son. Triamor was very frightened; he was sure he would lose his life. At once they mounted their horses and speedily left the city at a great rate for Alexandria. Before the news of this offence got out, that the sultan's son had been killed, they had left the country and arrived in Alexandria. They were in great fear of the sultan. (7993–8024)

"When the sultan heard that his son had been killed, he was sad and angry, as were all those in the city. He had the body buried, then gave thought to revenge. He summoned King Triamor, like someone for whom he had no love, to come to his court and defend himself from the charge of felony, and his son Fabur with him, because of Sadoine whom they had killed. If he would not do this, he would have to leave the country, or they would die a violent death, or endure the judgement of his court. So King Triamor went there, taking his son Fabur with him. When they appeared before the sultan, they were very frightened they would die. (8025–44)

"The sultan strongly accused them, blaming them for his son's death. If they could not defend themselves, they would be given over to great harm. Then he made a Saracen come forward; there was no one so strong in the kingdom of Tyre. He had come from Ethiopia and was large, ugly, and terrifying; he was blacker than a firebrand and his look was like a dragon's. He had thick shoulders and a large body; there were not twelve men in the land, however strong, whose strength, in comparison with his, was worth any more than a little piece of bark. He was four and a half feet larger than any knight who stood next to him. If King Triamor wanted to deny that his son had caused the death of the sultan's, this Saracen would prove it and would defeat him in battle. (8045–64)

"King Triamor was very frightened when he saw the Saracen's size. Nevertheless, he denied that he had destroyed the sultan's son or that his own son had killed him with his knowledge.[79] Whoever accused him of the death, he would defend himself in front of the sultan. He was given a year and forty days' respite, without opposition, because that was the custom of the kingdom, and it was decided in court that if he dared not fight, he could seek someone else on his behalf. Then he returned to Alexandria, summoned all the men in the country, and searched throughout his lands to find a knight who would take on the battle on his behalf, to whom he would give the third part of his domains. But not for anything could he find a man who dared undertake the battle against the pagan, who was so strong. His equal would not be found in the world. (8065–88)

"Then he had me leave prison and at once appear before him. He began to ask me if I knew any knight in the world who would take on this battle for him. He would make him a rich man, without fail: he would give him plenty of gold and silver and the third part of his fief. And I replied that I didn't know—I wouldn't lie to him—who would dare do the battle; there was nobody anywhere, except for the valiant Gui or the brave Heralt of Arderne. If he could have either, from that time onwards he would be sure one of them would certainly de-

---

[79] 8070 *Ne par lui ne par sun fiz*: In E this line is missing. Ewert supplies *Ne par lui ne par sun fiz* from C to complete the couplet, which begins *Ne par sun seu n'esteit oscis*.

fend him from the charge of felony, against the strong pagan. But when the king heard me mention Heralt and Gui, he put his right arm around my neck. 'Thank you, my lord, Count Jonas. If I can't get Gui through you, I shall never get him through another. If I could have Gui, or the bold Heralt of Arderne, I would be sure of winning the battle. I would like Gui above all others. Now you shall go to England and make every effort to find Gui. If you can't find Gui, bring me Heralt of Arderne. If you do what I have told you, I will restore your sons quite safely to you and give you much gold and silver; I will have twenty pack-horses loaded for you.' Then he made me swear over holy relics that I would go on this mission and return to him. If I couldn't bring back either of these, he would kill me painfully (nothing would be able to save me) and my fifteen sons with me; then I would rather be dead than alive. (8089–8132)

"Then I left the country, wretched and distressed. I went straight to Germany, Lorraine and Spain, and into Apulia and Saxony and France and Burgundy. I likewise went to England. I kept asking people, and I asked in Warwick, the noble city of which he was called lord. I found nobody, great or small, who could tell me anything about where I could look for either Gui or Heralt—neither where they were nor in what land. But the people of the land told me what they had heard tell: that Gui had gone into exile, they didn't know to what kingdom; and Heralt of Arderne had gone looking for him in the lands where he used to dwell. Then I left that place and searched many lands, but I could never find anyone who could give me any news of them. (8133–56)

"From there I came here with great suffering. It's a year to the day that I've borne this distress.[80] Now is the time I must go to the fierce king Triamor, to say what I have accomplished, for which, alas, I shall be maltreated: if I go there, I shall die. I don't want to stay behind, because I promised the king I would come to him at this time. I know very well that my sons will die as a result; they will be killed in great ignominy, and I shall die with them, for I cannot live without them. My death is nothing to me; I prefer death to life. Their death will be very sad, because they are knights of great worth: I know very well that, if they live, they will advance Christianity's cause. Now I shall go to them; I wish to suffer death with them." He fell fainting to the ground. When Gui saw him in such misery, he felt great pain in his heart, but he did not want to show any sign of it. (8157–84)

"Pilgrim" he said, "you are suffering now and you feel great grief for your children. You have sought Gui and Heralt for a long time in foreign lands. It's no wonder you grieve when you can't find them: through them you intended to save yourself and release your sons from prison. I was once a famous knight in the kingdom where I was born. For the love of mighty God—may He help me from now on—and for Gui for whom you have searched so hard, and for the

---

[80] 8160 **this distress** *cest ahan*: After 8160, F adds 2 lines.

Gui de Warewic 187

good marquis Heralt, I will undertake the battle for you and free your sons from prison." (8185–8200)
When the pilgrim heard that he wanted to undertake the battle, he looked at his face and at his feet. He saw he was very poorly dressed, but he was large and strong and indeed appeared to be a very powerful man. His beard was long and his face hidden; he certainly looked like a man who had spent time in the wilderness. "Good man," he said, "may St Mary, mother of Jesus, bless you for wanting to take the battle on. But you don't know the Saracen: if he were once to look angrily at you, and firmly roll his eyes at you, you would never again be bold enough to undertake battle against him." "Good man," said Gui, "don't be afraid! God is very strong, as you well know. Many men have rolled their eyes at me, and often given me angry looks. I never fled from them on that account, or forsook a battle from fear. If you think I am weak, I know for sure that God, who performs so many wonders for others, will give me strength, through which I shall win the battle." (8201–26)

"My lord," said the pilgrim, "thank you! May the rightful God, who has never lied, give you thanks even now!" He fell swooning for joy to the ground; then he kissed his foot. Gui raised him up at once. "My friend," said Gui, "let's go; with God's help, we shall give the Saracen a good fight." They went straight off to Alexandria and arrived before King Triamor. When the king saw the count, he hardly recognized him. "Count Jonas," said the king, "you are very poorly dressed. Tell me, where is Gui, and Heralt, since I don't see him?" "My lord," said the count, "you shall find out. You shall never see Gui or Heralt. I have since been in England and asked many men about Gui; the people of the country told me he had gone into exile, seeking saints' shrines, for ever, which has put the land in danger. Heralt is looking for him everywhere. No one knows anything about them. I have brought you this knight, most renowned for his strength, who will do the battle for you, with the help of God, who created everything. He will defend you very well against the pagan from the charge of felony, whenever it pleases you." (8227–58)

The king replied: "My lord, Count Jonas, take care this is not a joke! If I am ruined by this man, you shall die, be sure of that, and your sons with you, in great ignominy. You shall be hanged or burnt at the stake." The count replied: " I agree; if he meets with misfortune, it will grieve me." The king called Gui and spoke to him briefly. "My friend," said he, "what is your name?" "My lord," he said, "people call me Jun."[81] "Friend Jun," said the king, "now tell me, upon your word, where you were born and where you come from." "My lord," said Gui, "you should know for certain that I'm English; in England, that's where I was brought up; and since I was first knighted, I have dwelt in many lands." "Are you

---

[81] 8270 **Jun** *Jun*: "Yun" was the name adopted by Gui when deceiving Otun; See note to 6266.

English?" the king said. "I ought to hate you. So do you know Gui, and Heralt of Arderne, his friend? If they are still alive, they are very brave and valiant. I should feel great hatred for Gui—he killed King Hesman of Tyre, my brother and a powerful king, whom I now miss greatly. And he killed my uncle, the sultan, right where he sat at his meal. I saw his head when Gui cut it off and took it with him; I was in the tent that day. We chased him most vigorously, but devils protected him so that he wasn't killed. He often turned his face towards us. If you were his relation or his friend, you would now be in a very sorry plight. Would to God he were here! Then I would be saved. If he wanted to fight for me, he would be spared my anger." (8259–8302)

Gui answered the king: "My lord, I know Gui very well, and Heralt of Arderne too; I saw a lot of them in England. If you had one of them now, you could be sure of winning the battle." The king replied: "Tell me: you're in a very shabby state. You must have served a bad lord, since you left him in such a state; I believe he probably chased you away because of your wickedness." "My lord," Gui said, "that may well be; you know something of my situation. It's true, I served a lord who once did me great honour; through Him I was given great glory, and cherished in the company of kings and princes. Then through misfortune I did Him wrong. I left the country and the land and at the same time as this I travel like a penitent, constantly awaiting His mercy. When I am reconciled with Him, I will return to the kingdom." (8303–26)

"Friend Jun," said the king, "will you fight here for me? Or I shall look for another. Tell me: will you fight for me?" "My lord," said Gui, "that's why I came here. Please God, who created everything, I shall fight the battle for you. With God's help, I shall defeat the pagan, on condition that Count Jonas's sons are set free forthwith." The king replied: "And I agree. May Mahomet always be your help!" But Gui replied: "May the Son of Mary give me strength and help, for Mahomet isn't worth a straw, nor is his strength worth a shell." The king said: "Listen, Jun, and pay attention carefully to my words: if you can win the battle and deliver me from death, I shall treat your God with great honour, so that there will always be much talk of it. I shall set all imprisoned Christians free; there'll be no Christian, great or small, men, women, even children, as far as greater India, whom I won't set free with great honour. And I shall establish such peace in all the land, as long as I live, that Christians will be able to journey safe and sound and without harm. I shall never find anyone so brave who maltreats them in any way whom I won't have at once hanged, his body burnt and scattered to the winds." (8327–62)

"My lord," said Gui, "thank you; here's a very fine promise!" Then the king had baths prepared, and wanted to have Gui bathed and dressed, clothed in silk garments. But Gui did not care for that. "My friend," said the king, "do dress yourself: put on these splendid clothes." "My lord," said Gui, "I shall not do so; I'm not able to wear such garments. I was never wont to wear clothes woven with gold. Give me something to eat and drink; I don"t care to wear silk clothes." The king had him splendidly looked after, served and honoured. (8363–78)

When the time came which the sultan had set for the king, the king made magnificent preparations. He took a large group of lords with him and went off to the sultan's court, in his splendid city, Persia. They arrived before the sultan, with proud lords and great might. Gui was splendidly equipped, armed with magnificent weapons: he had an enchanted hauberk, which had been given to King Charles when he was in Jerusalem. Charles had put it in his treasury afterwards, whence a thief stole it and carried it to the land of the Saracens. The forebears of Triamor bought it and kept it as very precious; in their plight, they gave it to Gui. Thirty years on, it was not rusty, but shone brighter than silver; the hall was resplendent with its light. He had a helmet from ancient times, encircled most cunningly on all sides with great skill. Whoever had it in battle would never be defeated, for it belonged to the brave King Alexander when he killed King Porus. He had a good sword, which Hector the brave had in Troy, with which he killed many Greeks before he lost it. He had good and well-worked boots, which would not have been exchanged for their weight in gold. He had a shield edged in gold, which was never touched by a weapon; there was no weapon on earth which could damage it in any way or cut so much as a flake off it. It had once belonged to King Darius; the father of Triamor had bought it. (8379–8418)

When Gui had been made ready in this way, many Saracens looked at him. Each asked the other who he was and from which kingdom, this man who was to fight for the king—never was there anyone so finely armed. "My lord sultan," said the king, "listen to me, sire. I have come here to your court to defend myself, through this man standing here, against him who will accuse me of felony in the death of your son Sadoine, given that he was not slain by any of my people." "King," he said, "no hurry: you shall now have a battle indeed!" He had the Saracen, Amorant from Ethiopia, come forward. He was very large and well armed; everyone watched him with astonishment. For build and height, there was no one so large at that time. (8419–40)

When Gui saw the Saracen, who was so big and strong, "Heavenly God!" he said. "That's not a man, that's a devil. Who could bear his blows without at once having to die?" Then they decided that the battle should speedily take place, without fail, in a meadow on an island below the city, which was surrounded by a river. There the very fierce battle occurred. They arrived by boat on the island where they were to fight.[82] Then they mounted swift horses and boldly advanced to strike each other. They made pieces of their sharp spears fly through the fields, then drew their sharp steel swords. Amorant drew his blade, which was

---

[82] 8453 **they arrived by boat** *Par batels venuz i sunt*: Fighting by boat on an island recalls the Scandinavian custom of *holmgang*. See note to line 3583 of *Boeve*.

sharpened on one side only; there was no weapon which could resist it, no matter how excellent. It had once belonged to strong Hercules, who had killed many men.[83] A goddess gave it him; she thrust it into the river in Hell. No one who could get hold of the blade, however great a battle he was then in, could fail to win the fight, because of the power in the sword. If God did not now look after Gui, he would be hurt by the sword before the end of the day. They struck each other great blows with their good sharp swords. (8447–76)

Like a man angry at heart, Amorant advanced. He struck Gui very fiercely so that it was very visible on his painted helmet; he knocked off its gold flowers, and a foot and a half from the strong shield, which had never yet been damaged in any battle it had been in, and split the saddlebow across, in front, and pierced right through the caparisoned horse, so that the steel sword fell more than a full foot and a half into the earth. Gui fell down on the ground, his horse sliced to bits beneath him. "Almighty God," he said, "who made the four elements, defend me this day, Lord, as you can well do, so that, if it pleases you, I'm neither killed nor mutilated nor injured!" (8477–96)

He jumped at once to his feet, like a man with distress in his heart. Then he drew his steel sword and struck Amorant a blow. He cut his horse's neck in two, so that Amorant fell down to the ground. But he jumped up at once, like a man filled with courage. He struck Gui angrily, and Gui struck him back furiously. The warriors exchanged great blows and their attacks upon each other were very fierce: they cut through strong shields and the shining helmets above, and through bright hauberks, making their links of mail fly into the fields; with their swords, they cut into weapons which had never been damaged. The battle between them was very bitter; henceforth each mortally hated the other. (8497–8516)

Then Amorant thought he had endured many mighty blows; he raised his arm high and gave Gui a blow on his helmet, which was bright and shining. He made the flowers and the ornaments drop out, and violently cut into the golden browband, damaging the strong helmet with his sword. The blow descended to the shield and split it to the boss. As he withdrew the blade, he pulled it towards him so violently that it brought Gui to his knees, but he soon jumped up, like a brave fighter; at heart he was deeply angry. "Oh God, fair and sweet Lord!" he said, "it's never yet happened that I knelt for any knight's blow." Then he raised his sword and struck Amorant with great violence on his bright and shining helmet, so that he scattered its gold and jewels, and damaged and cut to pieces its nose-piece, ornamented with gold, and all the ventail,[84] without a doubt—not a

---

[83] 8465 **strong Hercules** *Hercules le fort*: This may refer to the story of Hercules's Twelfth Labour (as told in Apollodorus's *Library*, 2.4.11 and 2.5.12) where he descends to Hell and abducts the dog Cerberus; he is aided in his journey by various gods, including Athene and Hermes, but it is the latter who gives him a sword.

[84] 8541 **ventail** *la ventaille*: See note to line 3566.

mail-link availed him. He cut into his flesh and the blood flowed; he injured and wounded his face, damaged his double-meshed hauberk, and cut more than thirty links off it, and he split and shattered the shield edged with gold, bringing his steel sword down to the boss of fine gold. Then he pulled it out with such force that he made Amorant hit his knees and one of his hands against the ground. He did not resemble a peasant as he jumped up, but rather a brave knight; he held his sword in his right hand and quickly attacked Gui. Then they struck each other fiercely on their gold-painted helmets; neither failed to strike well. They made the meadows round about resound, so fiercely did they strike each other; they struck each other with such force that they made sparks fly from the helmets. The battle between them was bitter: everyone said who saw it that never did two men born of women fight each other so violently. (8517–68)

As we have found in the story, the weather was hot, as in summer, because the battle, between warriors fiercer than lions, was on the day after St John's day, at the division of the year.[85] Amorant drew back and kept his face lowered; from the blood he had lost and the heat, which greatly troubled him, he was so thirsty he could not bear it. He had to drink or die. "My friend," he said, "who are you? Never before have I found one so brave. I've won in person forty pitched battles—such battles as you've never heard of—and I never found anyone who could endure my blows without soon dying of them. Tell me, on your oath, who are you? I believe you are very valiant." Gui replied: "Indeed, you shall hear. Know that I am a Christian; I was born in the kingdom of England and there I was raised and knighted. King Triamor brought me to defend him, because he is guiltless, from the charge he is accused of, of causing the death of Sadoine the quick-witted." (8569–98)

"Are you English?" said Amorant. "Now, please Tervagant it could be Gui the valiant, whom people talk about so much! My heart would be filled with joy: I would gladly see his face and cut off his head before the end of this day. He has inflicted much destruction on our race: the loss of those he wrongfully killed will never be made good. He killed forty thousand of us in agony one day in front of Constantinople. If I killed him, and Heralt of Arderne, the marquis, with weapons, I would then have slain and conquered, killed and defeated, the very bravest in all the world." "What!" said Gui, "why? Did Gui ever misbehave towards you? Why would you cut off his head? You would be horribly wrong, and sinful." Amorant replied that he would not; rather, it would confer great honour on the race of Saracens. (8599–8622)

"Christian, listen to this," said Amorant, "the heat is great, as you well know. In the name of that God you believe in, now give me this much respite so that

---

[85] 8571 **St John's day** *demain de saint Johan*: St John's day, June 24th, was when the summer solstice was celebrated with festivities all over Northern Europe. The weather would not only have been hot but the daylight very long.

I can drink in the river, for I have such severe thirst that my heart, I think, will burst if I can't quench it. If you killed me now, and defeated me through the anguish of my thirst, you would never be praised for it, but it would be considered a base action. Now I ask you for this respite, in the name of Jesus, your powerful God, who is son of the Virgin Mary—may He now help you—and on these terms: that I return you the favour today, that if you want to drink, you should drink as much as you like." (8623–42)

"Sir," said Gui, "I agree: now I permit you, in good faith, to drink enough, quite safely. Return me the favour this very day." When Amorant had leave, he was exceedingly joyful and glad; he went speedily to the river, entirely unlaced his ventail, and drank copiously. He soon came back. "Knight," he said, "now surrender! Your end is near, you can be sure. You were badly tricked when you gave me leave to drink; now I'm fresher than I was this morning. Now your end is at hand, truly. I shall tell you about my habit: however much I have fought, from morning to evening, if I can get enough time, truly, to wet my mouth once, then I fear no danger. Now I defy you, this very day." Gui replied: "Do not feel secure." Then they struck each other on their bright helmets, which were so strong. (8643–68)

From then on, battle started again; neither refrained from attacking the other. No one knew who was accuser, who defender or who attacker; neither, on that occasion, deigned to flee from the other for fear of death. They hit each other with such great violence that their two bodies often crashed into each other. They cut into their helmets and their shields and their faces with their sharpened blades, and on both sides they often damaged their hauberks, which were so strong. They often made each other kneel, from the great blows they exchanged. Amorant was furious: he advanced angrily to strike Gui. He cut the gold knob from the helmet, so that one of the sections fell out completely, and he knocked one of the shield's quarters far away to the ground. The blow slid on to Gui's shoulder, so that it damaged a full span of his hauberk and his tunic with it; nothing was left as far as the flesh. Then, from the ferocity with which he struck, the blow came down on the knee, and it made the knee-piece and the whole boot fly far away into the battle arena, and a full foot into the earth. Many Saracens talked about the blow. When Gui looked at his bare flesh, he was quite amazed that the blow had not broken the skin in any way; he thanked God who had protected him. (8669–8702)

When Gui felt himself hit in this way, he was most mortified and angry. He had a keen desire for vengeance; in anger, he quickly struck Amorant on the top of his shoulder, so that he shattered his hauberk. With his steel blade Gui cut a full half foot into Amorant's shoulder. Then he drew back, like someone who is very hot. "Amorant, mercy, in the name of God!" he said. "Now I tell you truly, I'm so thirsty I have great difficulty standing or even talking to you. Now I beg you, for the love of God, the creator of the world, to return the favour I did you—you know it well—when you promised me earlier, and truly said that you would do me the favour, when I asked you for it, of giving me leave to drink, as agreed between us." Amorant replied: "No more talk of that: by my head, you won't get leave! I'll cut off your head first; I certainly won't give you leave." (8703–30)

"In God's name, Amorant," said Gui, "honourable and noble knight — mercy! If you were to kill me now, [and defeat me through the anguish of my thirst],[86] it would never be considered praiseworthy in other kingdoms or in this land. But wait now until I've drunk and recovered my strength; then we shall fight each other. We shall see, indeed, who will win." "Be quiet, fellow!" said Amorant. "Even for this city filled with pure gold, I won't keep my promise to you now lest I fail to destroy King Triamor. When I've cut off your head, and the king is killed or maimed, the sultan will give me his land, for he has promised it to me in front of his court. The sultan has a beautiful daughter, there's no fairer maiden in the world; I've loved her above all else. He will give her to me, which will make her happy. I've conquered two kingdoms in person; this will be the third I shall get. Now surrender quickly to me and lay down your arms. I will grant you your life; if you don't do so, I shall kill you." Gui answered him very angrily: "Indeed I shall not, fair sir! That's not the custom in my country. I would rather let horses pull me to pieces than admit defeat; I would rather die a hundred times." (8731–64)

"Tell me then, fellow," said the pagan, "I know very well you're a Christian — I've seen that in your behaviour. You've thoroughly pierced my shield, you've wounded me badly in the body, and still I see you hale and hearty. Tell me now, upon your word, what is your name? Tell it me. Then you shall have leave to drink, on condition you tell me the truth. You have people call you Jun,[87] but that's not your real name; were you called Jun, your name would be much better known." Gui replied: "Now you shall hear it, on condition you don't betray me: my name is Gui of Warwick, from the realm of England. I'm fighting now for King Triamor, not to take his silver or gold but to free his son from death, who is most wrongly accused." (8765–86)

When Amorant heard this was Gui of Warwick, of whom he had heard so much praise, he began to look at him in amazement. "Gui," he said, "welcome! You are the person I've most wanted. Now I see very well that what people say of you is true. This very day I shall fulfill my desire because I shall cut off your head; I've wanted to do that above all things. I shall present it to my beloved. From now on, you can be quite sure that, even if I were given seven kingdoms, I wouldn't give you leave to drink, for you're too likely to trick me." (8787–8802)

---

[86] 8734 **and defeat me through the anguish of my thirst** *E par destresce de sei conquis*: This line is missing in E; Ewert supplies it using C, whose *seif* he emends to *sei*.
[87] 8775, 8777 **Jun** *Yun*: in the French the name is here spelt *Yun*.

"My God!" said Gui, "now what shall I do, since I can't get leave to drink?" Then he decided he would go straight to the river; he went towards it with great speed. Now he had to drink or die. Amorant followed him with his steel sword; he wished to harm him with it. Gui entered the water; if God, the mighty King, did not look after him, he would never come out of it but die there in great pain. (8803–14)

Now Gui was in great danger; he was in the water up to his waist. He plunged his head into the river as far as the shoulders, then raised it. Amorant hit him as he got up, forcing him to his knees in the river, and all around the water enveloped him. But he quickly jumped up, like a brave man, shook his head and said: "Now thanks be to Jesus Christ. You've baptized me in cold water, but you haven't given me a name." He leapt out of the river and angrily struck Amorant. They started the battle again, both sides from now on thinking how to inflict harm; there was no more need for agreement between them. (8815–32)

"Wicked Amorant," Gui said to him, "thanks to God, who created everything, I'm now well refreshed from plunging into the river. I'll never trust you again; you are a traitor, as I know well." They struck each other fiercely, like strong warriors of great power. They fought so long that day—from morning to night, when the bright star appeared—that nobody knew who was better. They saw the stars in all parts of the sky, so long did they fight. As Amorant launched a blow, Gui fiercely countered it; he made his right hand, with the sword in it, fly far away into the meadow. (8833–50)

When Amorant felt himself hit, he felt great pain and anger. He took his sword in his left hand and made some thirty attacks on Gui, like a furious lion who has fasted for three whole days. But Gui defended himself like a brave man, and in no way deigned to flee. Amorant was very warm; from bleeding so heavily, his blows became much weaker.[88] When Gui noticed this, as Amorant moved away for a moment, he boldly followed him; he cut his arm off close to the shoulder, so that it flew far away on the ground. (8851–62)

When Amorant had lost his arm, he called himself feeble and weak. Fiercely he jumped at Gui so that he nearly knocked him to the ground, but Gui suddenly leaped aside and angrily pushed Amorant, throwing him down to the ground. And Gui seized him by the nose-piece, unlaced his ventail, and at once cut off his head. Then, since he had cut the head off the body, he was, with great fatigue, the victor. He came to the boat, crossed over, and presented the head to King Triamor. The king received it with great joy [*and then came before the sultan and*

---

[88] 8859–61 **Amorant was very warm . . . much weaker** *Amorant est mult eschalfé . . . mult afeblisant*: I have altered Ewert's punctuation (*Amorant est mult eschalfé/ Del sanc qu'il ad tant seigné, Ses colps vont mult afeblissant*.), which suggested that Amorant was very warm from heavy bleeding. It was believed that an abundance of blood led to fever, for which blood-letting was prescribed, so Ewert's punctuation makes less sense than one which gives the meaning of feeble blows caused by blood-loss.

gave it to him in front of the court]⁸⁹ so that kings and emirs saw it. And the sultan released the king and he went back very joyfully to Alexandria, his splendid city, taking Gui with him. Then he sent for Count Jonas and embraced him affectionately, kissing him more than a hundred times. He released all his sons and gave them plenty of gold and silver and many precious silk garments. (8867–94)

"My lord, Count Jonas," said the king, "listen to me, sir. You have saved my life through this knight I see here. This very day I promise, by the God I believe in, to grant you all my land and my cities, so that you can do all that you wish with them." The count at once replied: "My lord king, many thanks!" (8895–8904)

"Listen, Jun," the king said, "may it please God, who created everything, to let you stay with me! Truly, you would have very great wealth. I want to pay you great honour: I give you the third part of my land. I don't want you to abjure your faith, for you are a good man and a true believer." (8905–12)

"My lord," said Gui, "I shall not do that—I shall take no land from you." Then the count took leave of the king and took Gui with him. They went towards Jerusalem. Jonas had decided that at all costs he wanted to find out who had fought on his behalf. He was sure he dared not reveal himself, so he wanted to talk to him in private. [*Do tell me, sir knight, who call yourself Jun*]:⁹⁰ I am sure you are concealing your identity and you don't want to reveal yourself. Now I beg you, in the name of the God who let Himself suffer on the cross, through whom you will be saved, don't hide your name from me." (8913–30)

"My lord," said Gui, "you shall hear it, since you have entreated me. But don't betray me to anyone, for you would commit a very great sin. I am called Gui of Warwick; don't betray me, noble lord. For your benefit I have fought just now; I defeated the pagan with God's power." (8931–38)

When the count heard that it was the valiant Gui, he fell in a swoon at his feet, whereupon Gui raised him. "My lord," said the count, "thank you, in God's name! What business makes you go about in this fashion? Your worth is indeed so great—God never made anyone better than you. I shall give you the county of Durazzo and become your liege man, and my fifteen sons with me, who are your men and your friends. We shall all swear to you, over relics, never to contest anything, not a pennyworth, of the fief; you have won it through your great strength. If it were not for you, we would be dead; we would never in any way have escaped." (8939–56)

"My lord, Count Jonas," replied Gui, "fair sir, many thanks. Were you to give me your land, you would reward me too dearly. Now go to your own country; be in God's hands, and I shall stay in my land. I shall never see you again."

---

⁸⁹ 8882–83 **and . . . the court** *E devant . . . ad rendu*: These lines are missing in E and are supplied from C.

⁹⁰ 8923–24 **Do tell me. . . call yourself Jun** *Di mei ore. . . Yun vus faites apeler*: These lines are missing in E and are supplied from C.

Then they kissed each other. The count wept, and then returned to Durazzo, like a man who has escaped from death. (8957–68)

Now Gui departed, giving many praises to God for the great adventure which had befallen him. Then he went to the land of Greece and sought out the relics there. He stayed for some time in the land, often visiting Constantinople.[91] (8969–74)

Now I want to talk about the lady, Gui's wife, that good woman. There was no one in the world her equal for goodness nor so deserving of praise. After her husband went into exile, she truly never stopped feeding the poor, furnishing churches and restoring poor abbeys, making roads and repairing bridges; she often gave clothes to prisoners. No matter what amusement was made for her, no one ever saw her laugh. (8975–86)

This lady had a son, and at that time there was no more handsome boy. They raised him with great honour and gave him the name of Rainbrun. The boy was handed over to Heralt, as his father had ordered. Heralt looked after him most honourably, as he should have done for his lord's son; he had him looked after by two knights, who had no other occupation but to guard him. (8987–96)

At seven years old, the boy was handsome and fair, big and well-proportioned; indeed, he grew more in two years than others did in three. It happened that merchants from another land, from Russia, as I've heard tell, brought a great deal of gold and silver there, copper and brass too, white and grey furs and ermine robes, silk garments and sables, pepper and cumin and oriental fabrics, spices and Alexandrian incense. They arrived at the city of London and gave King Athelstan gifts; then, with their merchandise, they travelled throughout the land and the cities, until they came to Wallingford, which still exists, close to Oxford. It was a strong city, and enclosed by a wall; in those days it was most imposing. Later it was destroyed by a war between Heralt and the king of the land, and totally razed to the ground; it has never been so well restored since.[92] The merchants were well-bred and courteous; they brought a Spanish mule and presented it to Heralt, because he was lord of the region, and he received it in a very friendly fashion, thanking them for it more than once. (8997–9026)

When the merchants saw the boy, who was going through the hall playing, it seemed astonishing to them he was so handsome and comely. They asked the knights who this child was, who was so beautiful, and they told them that indeed he was the son of Gui the wise. They praised the child's beauty greatly and often thought privately that, if they could get him, they would sell him most

---

[91] 8974 **Constantinople** *Costentinoble*: Before the Fourth Crusade, Constantinople housed the greatest collection of relics in Christendom. See Jonathan Riley-Smith, "Peace Never Established: The Case of the Kingdom of Jerusalem," *Transactions of the Royal Historical Society* 28 (1978): 87–102, esp. 89.

[92] 9020 **never been so well restored since** *Unc ne fu puis tant ben estoré*: See Introduction, 12.

dearly. Then they talked to the porter and promised and gave him so much that he handed the boy over to them. They returned to London and at once entered their ship without the people of the city knowing. They raised the sails, had a good wind, and travelled straight towards Russia. (9027–46)

As they approached Russia, they saw land and were very joyful, for they believed they would land safely. But, on the contrary, great trouble befell them, the sky began to darken on them and the clouds to thicken greatly, violent thunder increased around them and a great storm came upon them. The four winds which were blowing overturned everything in their path. The sea began to roil, and they had no idea which way to go. The waves overwhelmed the ship; there was no one whose head wasn't wet. The ropes broke, their mast shattered; there was no one who did not think he would die. The tempest increased on all sides, and they called upon almighty God. At that moment a wind blew upon them from the north, sending their ship far out to sea. They were driven along all day and night, and then arrived in Africa. (9047–68)

When the merchants realized they had come to Africa, they agreed among themselves that they had arrived in a foreign land. They would take the boy Rainbrun and present him to the king of the country, so that they could travel through his land, sell their merchandise, and buy more. Then they selected three merchants who were courteous and well spoken, and they presented the boy to the king, and he received him most willingly. The king had a daughter, who was the same age as Rainbrun on that day—she was hardly any older. On her mother's advice, she asked fierce King Arguz, her father, if she could raise Rainbrun in her chamber, so that in future he could serve her. The king gladly consented, for she was the being he most loved. (9069–90)

When Heralt realized that the boy had been seized and was lost, he had him sought throughout the city, throughout the land and throughout the kingdom. But when he knew that the boy had indeed been stolen, his sufferings started again because he had lost his two lords. He sent to Russia to seek him, and to many other foreign lands, but when he could not find him, he lamented most bitterly. It was not long before King Athelstan gathered people from the kingdom—his counts and his barons—who were wise and sensible. Heralt of Arderne went there, whom the king honoured very much more than he did any man in his land, because he was of nobler character. The others were very envious, and that day they often said among themselves that the king was very wrong to pay Heralt, who was the son of a poor vavasur,[93] so much honour; he did great dishonour to his barons. (9091–9116)

"My lords," said the king, "listen to me. You are my men and my trusty supporters; I ask for advice, so give it me! I am sure you have heard tell that King Anelaf of Denmark, who is so fierce and has such wicked intentions, is coming

---

[93] 9115 **vavasur** *vavassur*: See note to line 4471.

upon us with a great army; if he can, he will crush the whole land and drive us out of the kingdom, or he will kill us all if he can. A long time has passed, indeed, since he has laid claim to the realm." (9117–28)

"My lord," said Heralt, "we shall succeed: with God's help, we shan't fear him. If he wants to invade the land, he must die a painful death. You have good men and strong cities; never, my lord, doubt them like that. My forbears once used to tell me that the Danes formerly had rights in this land, but that was a long time ago;[94] then their people lost their land and were then slain in battle, killed and destroyed and maltreated. In this way they lost their rights, because they were defeated in battle. But now, send word to your barons who have castles and keeps, and live beside the main shores and alongside your borders, that they should get ready with horses and weapons, so that if you need them, they can help you when necessary. If the Danes invade this land and want to conquer the kingdom by force, gather your army quickly and fight them boldly. With God's help you will defeat them, if you want to do what I have said." (9129–56)

"My lord Heralt," said the king. "now that's very good advice; I've never heard better. Thank you; I'll do that." Duke Modred got up, Cornwall's liege-lord. He was an old and wicked knight, but he was very bold and brave. "My lord," he said, "listen to me: you don't behave as you should when you believe rogues, and love and honour them more than you do your barons—we are wrong to serve you. We should know how to advise you about war, and be of more use and more help than that traitor I see over there. From now on people should point him out, because he betrayed his good lord, who once did him such great honour that from being poor he made him rich and powerful. But he is rewarding his lord badly, for he has shown him poor gratitude, since he sold his son, Rainbrun: he sold him to Russian merchants and got silver and polished gold for it. Should he be a close friend of yours for a year, he'll never be happy or really glad unless he's been able to trick you, for he's a proven traitor and evil-doer." (9157–86)

When Heralt heard himself criticised in this way, he could not utter a word for grief. Quickly he jumped to his feet and stood like someone feeling shame and great sorrow. "My lord duke," he said, "when you accuse me before our lord the king of a wicked act, you're lying. You do me very great shame. If you wish to maintain that what you have said is true, arm yourself speedily and make good your false speech that way. If I can't defend myself from this, I want the king to have me hanged. If I don't cut your head off before the end of today, I never want to enter a ship again. You've mistreated me badly now, and shamed me before

---

[94] 9136 **Danes formerly had rights** *Daneis jadis dreit aveient*: See Gaimar, *L'Estoire des Engleis*, ed. Alexander Bell (Oxford: Blackwell, ANTS, 1960), lvii–lviii, 39–816 and 2063–84. The *Estoire* starts with the story of Haveloc, a Dane who through marriage becomes king over part of England; when Danes invade later, they refer to Haveloc to support their claim of ancient rights over the land.

my lord the king, by saying that I meant to sell Gui's son, the son of my lord, the noble baron. I never did so, nor did I ever think of it, so help me the true Christ! When I knew for certain that merchants had stolen the boy by night, I never felt more bitter grief, nor will I ever at any time. I sent my men to look for him in Russia and in other lands; when they didn't find him, it grieved me and I'm still very upset. Whether lies or truth, I shall always be blamed. What will the people of the kingdom say except that what you've accused me of is true? But now I say to you in front of the king, and indeed I pledge my word to you, that from now on I shall go looking for my lord's son, whom I've lost. I'll never stop until I've found the child. And if God grant I find him, and I can return safely, I'll cut your head from your body; that I won't fail to do for all the gold in the world." (9187–9230)

"Be quiet, villain!" the duke said. "May God who created everything destroy you! You'll never be seen in court again without being thought a proven traitor." When a knight heard this—he was called Edgar, and was very valiant, the seneschal of Heralt of Arderne, and full of courage—when he heard his lord accused, and charged with treason before the king, he felt such distress he did not know what to do. He would not abstain from speech; he jumped to his feet before the duke, the picture of an angry man. "Wicked duke," he said, "when you accuse my lord here of crime and treason, you're lying; you've lied through your teeth. Now five hundred curses on you, and may you never be honoured at court, if you don't at once arm yourself and fight me. If I don't cut off your head, I never want to come to a feast again." They would have exchanged blows there, but the king forbade either of them, for fear of life and limb, to defame the other. (9231–58)

When the king had spoken to his men, he ordered them to protect his land carefully and be sure their horses and weapons were ready. Then they all departed and each one went home to his region. Heralt went back to his fine city of Wallingford, very ashamed and angry. He called his seneschal Edgar: "Seneschal," he said, "what shall I do? I shall never be glad again, since I'm accused, in the king's court, of having sold the son of Gui, our liege lord, to merchants. I would rather be burnt or hanged. But alas, now I don't know what to do. I shall go and look for my lord's son and I shall never return until I've found him, alive or dead. If I were now to leave it at this, so that I didn't go looking for my lord's son, what would the people of the kingdom say except that everything wicked Duke Modred said was true? May God, who ascended into heaven, destroy him! Edgar," he said, "you will stay and look after my land well for me, and my wife and my son and all my land round about. You are a good man, I know—I have never found one more loyal." (9259–90)

"My lord," said Edgar, "thank you, in God's name! You shall not leave here, my lord, but I shall go and look for the boy; I say to you, indeed, by almighty God, that I shall not stop, every day of my life, until I have found Rainbrun. I journeyed on the sea for a long time; I was a seaman for seven years. There's no country in all Christendom, my lord, to which I haven't been. You are white-haired and elderly; you have suffered pain and grief. Now you should rest and send another person on your behalf." (9291–9304)

"Edgar," said Heralt, "don't talk like that! Truly, for all the gold in England, you can be sure, I wouldn't stop looking for Rainbrun. But you shall stay in this city and give thought now to guarding my land. I am sure that my enemies, when they know I'm out of the country, will come and besiege you with a great army; you will defend yourself like a noble fighter." "My lord," said Edgar, "we shall certainly do so. If they attack us, we shall defend ourselves." (9305–16)

Then Heralt left his city. Taking leave of his people, of his wife and of his son, he went sorrowfully from the land. As soon as he could, he put to sea, and from then on would not stop looking for Rainbrun, his lord's son, for whom he underwent much suffering. To Denmark and to Ireland, to Norway and to Gothland, to Germany and to Russia, to Saxony and to Turkey he went, looking for his lord's son, but he did not find him. When he could not find him, he put to sea again. He was travelling towards Constantinople when a great storm met him and, willy-nilly, blew the ship along; straight away it arrived at a port in Africa. They saw a city beside the shore which was fine and splendid and very large; the walls, the battlements, and the high towers were razed in places. (9317–40)

"My God!" said a seaman. "Now we're in for great trouble. We've all come to Africa, to the land of the evil King Arguz. He's a mighty king and very valiant; there's no mightier, all the way to the East." Heralt asked: "What is this city and this land, which is so ravaged?" The seaman said: "I'll tell you who it belongs to, as far as I know. Now it belongs to the emir, Persan; there's no one so wicked as far as the river Jordan. He hates Christians more than any others; we shall be killed in great agony. King Arguz has attacked him and laid his land and his country waste." Then they saw Saracens coming, who soon seized their ship. They captured Heralt and his men and took them at once before the emir, and he had them thrown into his prison. They had little to drink and less to eat. (9341–62)

Now Heralt was in prison; if God in Paradise did not look after him, he would never be freed from prison but would die there in a most wretched state. My lords, now you have heard about Heralt, the good vassal who was so courageous, who for the son of his earthly lord underwent such suffering. (9363–70)[95]

When Duke Modred heard that Heralt of Arderne had gone away, he gathered the Cornish army and besieged Edgar, the seneschal, in the fortified city of Wallingford,[96] and ravaged the surrounding countryside. But Edgar defended

---

[95] 9363–70 **Now Heralt... such suffering** *Ore est Heralt... tel dolur*: These lines are missing in CM.

[96] 9375 **Wallingford** *Walingford*: Wallingford was strengthened and fortified in the early days of the struggle between King Stephen and Matilda, daughter of Henry I. Between 1139 and 1152 it was repeatedly, and fruitlessly, besieged by Stephen. King John also fortified it in 1193.

himself impressively, like a bold and valiant knight. He summoned mercenaries throughout the land and gave them plenty of gold and silver. That year he defended his lord's cities and castles most honourably, so that he never lost anything, so impressive was his defence. He attacked the duke frequently, killing many of his men—the duke lost more than a thousand men that year, killed in pain and distress. The duke besieged him for a year without accomplishing anything. He returned to Cornwall, leaving behind many of his men, dead. (9371–92)

Now we shall tell you about Gui again, the noble lord, the brave lord. Once he had stayed in Constantinople, and visited the relics of the kingdom, he decided he wanted to return to his country. He left Constantinople and made so much progress on his journey that he came into Germany, where once he had been held in great esteem. As he came to the division of four roads, a crossing-point for pilgrims, at a carved crucifix a day's journey from Speyer, Gui saw a pilgrim sitting, and saw him lamenting bitterly: he often cursed his destiny, which was so bad and harsh. When Gui heard him, he pitied him, and then he asked him in a friendly way: "Tell me, good man, I entreat you, as God may relieve your grief, tell me truly now who you are and where you come from." And the pilgrim replied: "Fair and dear sir, if I were now to tell you of my trouble, I am certain you would feel pity, and I would be in even greater anguish!" And Gui replied: "You wouldn't be; may it not please God that you should be! But I would gladly advise you, if I can do so; it often happens that strangers can give good advice." The worthy man said: "That's true; I should be glad to have advice." (9393–9428)

The worthy man said: "That may well be so. Now I shall tell you, my lord, of my situation. I was once a powerful count; I had castles and cities in my lands, and many good men, and I was much feared in the realm. There was no Christian land where I wasn't acclaimed for feats of arms. I was very greatly esteemed, and I had very many good friends, and I had very many noble followers, and I gave many noble rewards. Now I don't have a pennyworth with which to buy food; now I'm wretched and a beggar—it's no wonder I suffer so much." He could no longer speak, from grief, but began to weep bitterly, to sorrow and to lament his great unhappiness. "Sir pilgrim," he said, "let me be; in God's name, leave me in peace! My lord, ask no longer who I am or what I'm called, because my pain will be too great. If I were to relate my whole life to you, I would stay here too long. What is the use of asking me so much, when you can't help me? I'd be better off looking for a meal, since I'm in great need of it—I haven't eaten since nine[97] yesterday morning, nor will I, I think, for a long time." (9429–60)

Gui replied: "In the name of God, the true and mighty, now tell me this much—your name, without hiding it from me, and why you are dispossessed, so that almighty God may give you relief before the end of this day. Then we will go and look for a meal, for I still have a whole penny." "My lord," he said, "I

---

[97] 9459 **nine** *terce*: Terce is the third hour of the canonical day.

shall tell you; I don't want to lie to you. I was once called Count Terri, and I was a most noble lord. Now I am weak and wretched; indeed, I'm sorry to be alive. I was liege-lord of Worms, a knight of great power. I had a friend whose name was Gui; since the time of Christ's passion, such a good knight has not been born, nor indeed ever will be. We were sworn friends; truly we had much love for each other, and he was such a true friend to me that on two occasions he saved me from death, and restored my county to me twice. You never heard of such a loyal man. It so happened that this Gui, who was such a true friend to me, made the great mistake of killing Duke Otun of Pavia, because the duke had often treated him treacherously, and he took revenge in such a way that he killed the duke amongst his men. Then he left, most courageously, carrying my beloved in his arms, on whose account we had had a very hard life. (9461–96)

"This duke who was slain had a nephew through his sister, called Berard of Pavia—there was no one so wicked in the world. He was a young man then, and afterwards served the emperor, who greatly cherished him, for a long time. Then he gave him the fief of Pavia. This Berard I spoke of became a man of such great cruelty, and became so proud and arrogant, and above all envious, that I believe there wasn't his equal in the world, nor one so brave or so bold, because he had such great courage that he was never in a battle or a fray without being much more feared than a hundred of the most famous knights. Never was there a knight so well armed that, if Berard could strike him with his sword, he would not split him with his blade, from the top of his gleaming helmet down, with great ferocity, to the waist or lower, to the crotch. (9497–9520)

"You never heard tell of such a man, for he has such great strength in his arms that there's no bear so big in Germany or in Saxony as far as Spain, that if he gave it a blow with his fist, he would not break its neck or throw it down dead on the ground. It would never escape him. And he is so extremely wicked of heart and so extremely fierce of face that in the whole court there was no knight so proud or arrogant that, if Berard got angry with him and rolled his eyes angrily at him, he would not shake all over with fear and, if he were a coward, soon lose his reason. Because he was so renowned and so feared in the land, the emperor made Berard seneschal and took great pains to advance him. Because the emperor feared him, and his barons feared and liked him, if there were a duke or a count in the land who would not do his command, Berard would at once have him burnt or exiled: this seneschal would descend on him and soon take him, alive or dead, put him in the emperor's dungeon, and for ever disinherit him; the man would never recover possession. Berard is still so greatly feared through the land and through the kingdom that, if he loves, or loved someone, born of no matter how poor a lineage, he made him wealthy and influential, a duke or a count or more powerful still, and if he hated someone, no matter how wealthy a duke or count, that man was soon exiled, killed and destroyed and ill-treated. (9521–60)

"It so happened that the emperor held a council in the following way: dukes, counts, and barons were summoned to it. And I went there in most splendid fashion, up to a hundred knights accompanying me. As soon as I had come into court, and Berard the seneschal recognized me, he immediately got to his feet and went straight to the emperor, accusing me of his uncle's death, in front of the whole court and without desisting, saying that I had betrayed him by my advice and wickedly killed him. When I heard myself accused of a felony, I didn't deign to delay any longer: I quickly defended myself against the charge of crime, like a brave and bold knight. I held out my pledge to the emperor that I would defend myself against Berard and against any other who accused me, who dared undertake an act of such great boldness; against him I would indeed defend myself and would defeat him in the field by force. (9561–84)

"The emperor received our pledges; I didn't then know what that meant. I found not a single man at court, however true a friend he had been to me, who did not believe he would be in a sorry plight if he dared to stand surety for me against the seneschal. But the seneschal found plenty; nevertheless, not one of them loved him. But he was held in sufficiently greater regard and, by the wealthy, in greater fear. When I could find no one to dare to stand surety for me in court, I was sad and very angry that everyone whom I asked failed me. The emperor then took me and put me in his dungeon at Speyer, on the advice of the wicked seneschal—God bring him great trouble, this very day! He went at once and seized all my land, and he wanted to shame me through my wife, but she fled into a foreign land. I don't know where I could look for her. (9585–9606)

"When I was put in prison, I had a very sorrowful life. Berard thought, through me, to get hold of Gui, whom he never loved, for if he could take revenge on him and kill or maim him, he could then have me most painfully killed, and in that way would be avenged. I lay in prison for a whole year; I cannot tell you the sufferings which I bore in the dungeon. I never saw the light nor did I ever eat my fill; I spoke to neither friend nor relative. Then my friends got together, and went to make a request of Emperor Reiner: they begged and prayed him so hard, and gave him so much of what they owned, and likewise gave to Duke Berard, the wicked and cruel seneschal, that they released me from prison then, on condition that I went to find Gui, that I would never stop until I found him, alive or dead, and brought him to the emperor's court to defend ourselves against Berard—God curse him—from the charge of felony. (9607–34)

"Then I left the realm, like someone who had borne much suffering. I went looking for my friend; I thought I would find him in England. When I came there, I didn't find him, nor Heralt, the loyal and good vassal, for Heralt had at that time gone off to seek the son of his liege lord, whom foreign merchants had stolen and carried into a foreign land. And Gui had gone into exile; I never found anyone in the country who could tell me anything further about him. I left in distress and anger. I've travelled through so many lands since and never found anyone who could teach me anything of him; for this reason, I'm sure he's dead." Then he began to weep, to wring his hands and sigh. (9635–54)

When Gui heard Terri speak, who once was such a noble lord, and whom in his heart he held so dear, he began to look very hard at him. He saw Terri was wretched now and sorrowful, and he saw he was in more torment than anyone else. His body, which used to be so well clothed, was, Gui saw, nearly naked, and his legs, once so well covered, were maimed. He fell to the ground and swooned three times before stopping. When Terri saw him, he took pity, ran quickly to him and lifted his body in his arms. Then he asked him: "Good man, how long have you had this sickness, which is most evil and deadly? This is falling sickness,[98] the disease most hated in the world." And Gui replied: "Hardly for long: it's only since I've been sitting here that it has struck me down in this way." (9655–78)

"Truly," said Terri, "I believe it; you have been in a very bad way. It's a year today, to tell you the truth, that I left this kingdom. I've never since stopped travelling, either by sea or by land. Throughout the land I've heard tell that our emperor, Reiner, will hold a council at Speyer; there is no king or duke in the Empire who attends on him who won't appear there. That's when my day has been appointed. I have sworn and pledged that I will bring Gui there, if I can find him alive on earth; and if I can't find him, I should never again return to the realm. If I go there, I know for sure I will die before evening. For this reason, I don't know what to do, nor where to go, nor in what land." (9679–9700)

Gui, in floods of tears, listened to him; there was great pain in his heart. "True and powerful God!" he said, "now why have I lived so long, to see this noble knight demonstrate such affliction? I never saw so faithful a friend, nor will there ever be such, I believe. May God never give me food again if I don't speedily avenge him and, if I can find the wicked duke and get the opportunity to speak to him, if I don't strike him such a blow with a stick or a big stake that I kill the evil wretch, to avenge my dear friend. Sir Terri," said Gui, "good sir, don't grieve like this: grieving will not help you, from now on. As God is your salvation, let it be! If God has ordained any good thing for you, no man will ever take it from you so that you don't have it, be sure of that. Why give yourself over to this sorrow? Now let's go to the court; we may hear some news there, and you may hear such news as will give you great pleasure." "My lord," he said, "I agree. Let's now go there in good faith." (9701–30)

After this, they went straight to the city, Terri showing great sorrow, and Gui also, for his heart was very sore. When he saw the noble knight, he could no longer refrain from weeping. He sorrowed exceedingly and could no longer restrain himself; he covered his face with his mantle so that Count Terri would not notice. (9731–41)

---

[98] 9673 **falling sickness** *la gute*: *Gute* can mean gout or arthritis, but it is more likely Terri means *gute chaive*, "falling-sickness," which we know as epilepsy.

They had not been travelling long towards the good city of Speyer when "My God," said Terri, "what a sorry state I'm now in! Such great sleepiness has seized me: now either I must sleep here, or my soul must leave my body." "My lord," said Gui, "do so; rest in this place and I will be at your bed-head and care for you. "My lord," said Terri, "thank you; then I will rest here." (9741–52)

Thereupon Terri sat down, put his head on Gui's lap, and at once went to sleep. Gui, weeping and often fetching great sighs, was looking at him when he saw come out of his mouth a pure white ermine,[99] whiter than snow falling on the branch. It rapidly went towards a mountain, which stood at the end of a plain, and entered a hollow in a rock. It did not stay there long but immediately came back and entered Terri's mouth in the way it had formerly come out—there it was, returned! Gui saw everything and was greatly astonished. Then Terri woke up, opened his eyes, and saw him; next he gave a great sigh. "By God, the creator of everything!" he said. "This is what I dreamt, sir pilgrim—that I went onto that mountain and found a hollow rock. I was much astonished when I found a great treasure, beneath a dragon which was lying dead on top of it, and a sword inside it; of all the swords in the world, there wasn't one as good as this. And I dreamed a lot about Gui, who was such a true friend to me: that he was sitting at my bed-head and held my head in his lap." (9753–88)

Gui replied: "Fair and gentle friend, God willing, who was put on the cross, you will have great joy, you can be certain: you will see your friend Gui again and recover your lands through him. Have great confidence in God! Rise, let's go. Almighty God willing, from now on we are quite safe: we shall succeed with God's help." Both of them then rose and now made their way towards Speyer. "Sir pilgrim," said Gui, "fair and gentle friend, listen: let's go up to that rock where you dreamt about the dragon and about the treasure and the good sword. Please God, the true and mighty, if we could find that treasure, it would be very useful." Terri replied: "Do let's go there; let's hurry there without delay." They came to the rock and went inside through an opening, where they found all the treasure just as Count Terri had dreamt it.[100] Gui at once seized the sword and drew it, gleaming brightly, from the scabbard; it lit up the plain round about. "God, almighty Lord!" said Gui, "whoever saw such a sword before? I'm certain it's enchanted." Then he looked at the pommel, which was very richly carved, and the relics and precious stones set in it in various ways. He put it back into the scabbard and said to his friend: "Sir Terri, I give you all this treasure I see here; I'll have the least, you have the most." Terri replied: "It's all yours; all this treasure has no value for me, I'm so

---

[99] 9759 **ermine** *hermine*: An ermine is a member of the weasel family; its fur is white in winter.

[100] 9814 **Just as Count Terri had dreamt it** *Cum li quons Terri l'ad sungé*: The source of this episode is probably Paul the Deacon's *De Gestis Langobardorum*, Book 3, Chapter 34, where the "little animal" is "in the shape of a reptile."

overwhelmed with grief. Why don't we go to the city? We can easily return here." "So we shall!" replied Gui. Then they went off to the city. (9789–9834)

When they came to the city, Count Terri was apprehensive; he feared he might be recognized and thus he was very frightened. They took lodgings at the further end, far from the city. In the morning, Gui rose and commended himself to Jesus; he handed over his good sword to Terri and he guarded it carefully for him. Then he went to the emperor's court. As the latter was leaving church, he went to meet him and greeted him courteously. "My lord emperor, listen to this: may God, who made and fashioned everything, bless you, my lord emperor, and give you great honour. I am a pilgrim from a foreign land, and I have come to ask you for something of yours. You will see clearly that I badly need you to give me something you own." The emperor replied: "Gladly! Now, my fine, dear friend, listen to me: you shall come to the palace with me and have something of mine, with pleasure." (9837–62)

The emperor entered the palace, dukes, counts, and kings with him, then sat down on the high dais; on this occasion many of the nobility were there. "Pilgrim," said the emperor, "now tell me, by your father's soul, which lands you have been in; you look like a well-travelled man." "My lord," he said "I shall tell you: I have been in many lands, in Jerusalem and in Syria, in Constantinople and in Persia." "Then tell me, pilgrim, upon your word, what they say about me in Constantinople." "My lord," he said, "now you shall know, since you wish to know it. Many say bad things about you: that through the advice of a seneschal, you have disinherited Count Terri, and many other barons with him, which is a very great wrong. You are blamed severely in foreign lands for being in the habit of disinheriting your barons through the advice of a rogue, who is an evil-doer and a scoundrel." When the duke heard himself blamed in this way, he began to roll his eyes; he was fiercer than a lion or boar. He would surely soon have struck Gui with his fist, had the lords not held him. (9863–92)

"Pilgrim," he said, "you're lying when you slander me so much. I've never been considered a scoundrel. So God and His might help me, if it weren't for the emperor's presence, now I would shame you in the following way: I would shake your long beard so that I made your teeth fly out of your mouth. You're a wretch and a rascal; you've led this life many a day. If I can meet you outside, this day I'll have you thrown in such a place that you won't get out of it for seven years, nor will you see your feet once; thus other scoundrels will beware of slandering lords." (9893–9908)

"Is that you, my lord?" said Gui. "You're very big and strong. I never saw you before, I believe; you look like a very valiant and bold man. If you were now to mistreat me, you would never gain any honour from it: it would be considered great insolence if you, who are of such high rank, were now to do me shame and dishonour in your emperor's court. You would esteem him very little should you do me wrong in his court. But if I were before a full assembly, I would now show the emperor that Count Terri is disinherited most wrongfully and criminally, and you have wrongfully had him expelled and exiled from the realm. Nor is he guilty of the charge made against him, in which you blamed him for your uncle's death—I know that very well, I've often heard the truth about it." (9909–30)

The duke replied, filled with anger: "Now may our Lord grant you are a fellow capable of defending Count Terri!" And Gui replied boldly: "Now your anger will prove disastrous! I am ready to defend Terri of Worms, son of Alberi: that he is not guilty of the death of Duke Otun, the evil-doer, the traitor, the scoundrel, nor did he kill him. See here my pledge before the emperor! I am ready, this very day, to defend Terri from felony towards you, my lord duke of Pavia." (9931–46)

Duke Berard jumped to his feet, like someone completely furious. "Fellow," he said, "you're a complete scoundrel, mad and arrogant and stupid, since you've challenged me to battle. Now I'm absolutely sure that you are pursued by devils, since you're taking on battle against me. Now, since you are taking up arms against me, I realise you hardly know me. In a short while, I will have cut off your head; devils have brought you here." "My lord emperor," said Gui, "listen to this, if you please. I am not known in your court; I've come here from foreign lands. Here I have neither friends nor relations to lend me their equipment with which, my lord, I may defend myself. You should now see to this, so that you maintain me in your court and find me weapons, if you please. You should help the poor; that befits you, as you know very well." (9947–70)

Then they both held out their pledges, and the emperor quickly accepted them. He ordered them to be armed early next day, because he wanted to see the battle and nothing would prevent him. The duke left, like someone whose heart is swollen with anger. The emperor summoned his daughter and in a friendly manner asked her to look after this pilgrim and equip him nobly with weapons. And she did so most willingly; she took him at once to her chamber, and wanted to clothe and bathe him and dress him very splendidly. He did not care about that, but asked her for good weapons. Then throughout the city there was talk of this pilgrim, about where he came from, who dared to undertake battle with the duke. Everyone that day prayed to God to help this pilgrim to defeat the wicked seneschal. (9971–94)

In the morning, the emperor rose and returned from church, and with him kings, dukes, and barons from various lands. When the court, with a magnificent retinue, was all assembled, Duke Berard arrived, more arrogant and prouder than a leopard, and well armed on his charger. He advanced into the court. The maiden lost no time in arming the pilgrim very well, and had his good, swift horse given to him, all caparisoned. Gui acted like a brave fighter in that he did not intend to forget the good sword he had found on the treasure; by secret signals he sent Terri for it, so that everybody would not notice. He will have great need of it, as you will hear later. (9995–10016)

When the maiden had armed him and most splendidly equipped him with whatever he wanted, she made him come before the emperor. The court looked at him with amazement, so handsome was he when armed. [*Some—Teutons, Lombards, and Germans—often said to each other that this was not the pilgrim, the poor wretch, who yesterday had pledged to do battle; many swore it certainly wasn't he.*][101] (10017–28)

The emperor said: "Now listen, my lords gathered here. Know that these knights you see are indeed brave men. They have undertaken to fight a battle, of what kind you well know: this pilgrim standing here will defend Count Terri against accusations of felony, treason, and Duke Otun's death—this duke you see before you accuses Terri, as you well know, of the death of his uncle, duke of Pavia, for through Terri the duke lost his life. After that Terri went to look for his friend, in what foreign land I don't know, for if he had succeeded in finding him, he was to have brought him here or forever be disinherited. I have determined that they should defend themselves on this day from accusations of felony in the death of the duke of Pavia, uncle to Duke Berard, who is a brave, noble knight. Now this pilgrim has come here, apparently a knight of great strength, who wants to defend Count Terri here and now. [*If you now jointly consent, you shall at once see their battle.*][102] Everyone said: "We consent; let's bring them together soon!" And they did so at once; they decided on the battle. On an island, below the city, there the battle was judged to take place. [*Gui and Berard took an oath; then both went on to the island, fully armed on their horses, arrogant and proud, on the brink of battle.*][103] (10029–68)

With great violence they advance to exchange blows, each eager to harm the other. With sharp steel spears they strike great blows on the double-layered shields,[104] and break stirrups and stirrup-leathers and saddle-girths in various ways. The hauberks, which are not damaged, are good, and both men come off their horses. (10069–76)

Now the strong warriors are on the ground, their horses' saddles between their thighs.[105] The noble lords, fiercer than lions, jump to their feet and draw

---

[101] 10023–58 **Some ... certainly wasn't he** *Entr'els ... maint le jura*: These lines are missing in E. It is not clear where Ewert's supplied lines come from, but they seem to be a mixture of C and M (line 10027).

[102] 10057–58 **If you.. battle** *Si entre vus. . . verrez*: These lines are missing in E and have been supplied from F.

[103] 10065–68 **Gui and Berard took an oath ... battle** *Les sermenz unt eschargez ... fers*: These lines are missing in E and supplied from F. C has *les sermenz unt eschariz* (they declared/affirmed oaths) in 10065, which Ewert thought was probably the correct reading though he kept F's *eschargez* (impose). I have used C for my translation.

[104] 10072 **double-layered shields** *escuz dublentins*: Shields may have been lined with leather or wood. See Christopher Gravett, *Norman Knight 950–1204* (London: Osprey Publishing, 1993), 12, 20.

[105] 10078 **saddles between their thighs** *Entre lur quisses les seles des chevals*: It sounds as if the saddles, possibly not strapped down, have come off the horses at the same time as the riders.

their steel swords, strking great blows on jewelled helmets [*and splitting shields and lacquered hauberks, making large sections fly onto the meadows*].[106] They strike fire from gleaming helmets, like sparks from burning wood. Both are very well armed, but the duke has a superabundance of iron: he has two strong hauberks, well fashioned, two helmets on his head, well banded[107] — there are many precious and potent stones in them.[108] One helmet was flat-topped, the other conical.[109] Round his neck hung a double-meshed shield, whose strips of gold would be burdensome even for a pack-horse, and in his hand he held a good steel sword which had belonged to the noble Emperor Constantine. (10077–96)

The battle between the knights was bitter. They were on foot on the ground, for they had lost their horses. [*The fine shields round their necks suited them well. No clerk in the whole world could have counted the attacks.*] [110] Then all those in the city, and all the other lords gathered there, said that this pilgrim was no mortal man but an angel sent from heaven by God, to kill this treacherous devil; God didn't want Berard to rule beyond that day. If this pilgrim weren't an enchanted man, the duke would already have slaughtered him — there wasn't a man in the world now alive who could have borne his great blows. No one knew which of them was harsher; they looked at them in amazement. All the people from the city ran there together — monks, nuns, and even children, young and old, little and large, except Terri alone who, in a church, never stopped praying to God to help Gui, as he was in need. A priest found him before an altar.[111] [*"Fellow," he said, "get up; you are far too pious. Why don't you go over there to see the battle between the arrogant duke and a pilgrim, who is fighting for Count Terri?" "Who is this pilgrim?"* said

---

[106] 10083–84 **and splitting shields . . . meadows** *Trenchent escuz . . . prez*: These lines are missing in E and supplied from C.

[107] 10090 **well banded** *ben encerclez*: For bands round helmets, see note to line 2333.

[108] 10091 **there are many precious and potent stones** *mainte pere i out de grant vertu*: Magical and medicinal powers were ascribed to precious and semi-precious stones from classical Greek times. Such beliefs were often presented in lapidaries, which were particularly popular in Anglo-Norman England. See Paul Studer and Joan Evans, *Anglo-Norman Lapidaries* (Paris: Champion, 1924); some of the texts they print describe stones which protect warriors in battle.

[109] 10092 **One helmet was flat-topped, the other conical** *L'un healme ert plat, l'altre agu*: The conical helmet was in use throughout the twelfth century, but around 1180 cylindrical types with flat tops appeared; Philip of Flanders is shown wearing one in his seal. See Christopher Gravett, *Knights at Tournament* (London: Osprey Publishing, 1988), 53, and Gravett, *Norman Knight*, 17.

[110] 10099–100 **The fine shields . . . attacks** *Ben lur seent . . . assals*: 10099 is missing in EC and is supplied, with correction, from F. 10100 is missing in E and has been supplied from F.

[111] 10120 **A priest found him before an altar** *Un prestre le trove devant un alter*: In E this line is: *E li defende de encombrer*; Ewert has substituted C's line, which makes more sense.

Terri. "God help me, I don't know," he said, "but he's very brave and tough; he's pierced the duke's shield full of holes."]¹¹² Then the Count Terri got up and went straight to the battle. He was very frightened he would be recognized, and hid himself amongst the people. (10097–134)

When Terri saw the duke standing in the field, saw his armour was damaged in some places and blood was coming out in others, this gave him enormous pleasure. When he saw that the pilgrim was attacking Berard strongly, "God almighty, Lord," he said, "this isn't the pilgrim who overtook me on the road some days ago. This man is strong and extremely big, brave and bold, of great might; that man was weak and poverty-stricken, feeble of body, quite starved. This one is so fine and so good a fighter, I don't think he can be a mortal man. When I see him, I remember Gui; he's like him in body and face. If Gui weren't dead, I would say truly he must be him in all his strength." Terri began to weep for sorrow, and as fast as he could returned to the church; he never finished praying God to help him that day. (10135–56)

The battle lasted a long time, from morning to evening, because they never stopped fighting, and did each other a lot of damage. From early morning to the evening they fought each other, truly, until the stars appeared. The barons did not know what they should do, but they pointed out to the emperor that daylight was fading and what he should do with these lords, since they lacked the light of day. (10157–68)

Then the emperor called four dukes whom he trusted. "My lords," he said, "pray take Duke Berard and guard him for me, as you love your domains, so that you return him to me in the morning in this same state. I will have the pilgrim guarded until tomorrow, when daylight comes. Then we shall put them together: we shall see who wins, to be sure." "My lord," they said, "as you please!" They halted the battle. The four dukes took Berard and that night guarded him very well. The emperor took the pilgrim; he had him guarded until morning and ordered that he be well guarded indeed until morning, until he should get up. (10169–86)

Duke Berard was very angry and decided on a most wicked act. He called his four nephews and ordered them to go and kill the pilgrim. "Gladly, fair sir," they said. At once they armed themselves, with hauberks and their steel swords, and went straight to the court. They entered the room secretly, where the pilgrim was lying in a large bed of fine gold; it was decked with silken sheets and he was lying inside them. The guards were asleep. The nephews grabbed the bed, raised it onto their shoulders, and carried it straight to the sea. The pilgrim lay there and slept; if God, who never lies, did not look after him, he would now be killed, for they threw the bed down into the sea and quickly left. They

---

¹¹² 10121–30 **Fellow ... full of holes** *Vassal ... tut estroé*: These lines are missing in E and are supplied from C.

abandoned the bed in the sea, returned with all speed, and went straight to their lodgings. (10187–212)

Now they had put the bed in the sea and transferred the pilgrim to a poor lodging! The waves lashed at him, now up, now down. When the pilgrim awoke, he raised his head, looked around, and saw the stars and the sky. He saw nothing else on any side except only the sea, where he was floating. It is no wonder he was afraid. "Jesus Christ, the Almighty," he said, "who rules the wind and the water, now remember me when I need you! My God, where has this trouble come from? I never fought for reward, nor for any castle or keep, but for my good friend whom I want to deliver from danger—which he very much needs, for I saw him poor and unhappy and felt great pity for him, a once rich and powerful man, now a poor beggar. I wanted to give my life for him, and that's why I fought the duke; had I defeated him in the field, I would have defended Terri against the charge of felony. The court, I believe, would see that he got his lands back. My God! if it were true that he could, through me, recover his castles and his whole fief, on condition that my life would not be prolonged for a single day afterwards, it would give me great pleasure. But now, alas, I am bound to die, there is no help for it, through Duke Berard's treachery. May God never take his side, for he is evil and full of treachery; God curse him!" (10213–54)

At that moment, a seaman came by, who had come fishing in the sea. From far off he saw the bedstead floating and very quickly rowed in that direction; he thought it was some enchanted thing brought by the sea. As soon as he drew near it, he called upon the pilgrim, in God's name, to say what this was which he saw floating in the sea. The pilgrim raised his head and immediately spoke to the seaman. "Friend," he said, "don't be afraid! Know that I am sent from God. Were you born in the city?" He replied: "I was born there." "Don't you remember yesterday's battle, which Emperor Reiner held in his court, between the seneschal and the pilgrim, who fought each other from yesterday morning?" And he replied: "Yes, indeed, I watched the battle until the evening; the emperor had them separated and ordered them to be well guarded." (10255–78)

"I'm the pilgrim," he said, "who was fighting Berard. We were separated yesterday evening, and I was put in a room: I lay down and slept in this bedstead you see here. Because I was weary, I fell asleep at once. I have arrived here, I don't know how, in sorrow and great torment—I believe I've been betrayed. So help me, good and gentle friend; by your faith and your loyalty, take pity on me." The good man had pity on him and let him enter the boat, and then he took him to his lodging and assisted him as much as he could. (10279–96)

In the morning, the emperor rose and heard mass at St Martin's church. Afterwards he came into the marble hall and asked for the duke and the pilgrim, and the four dukes went off and brought the duke forward. The emperor then ordered the pilgrim to be brought to him, but people came before him and told him the pilgrim was lost, and with him the bed where he had been put, and the guards in charge of him did not know what had become of him. The emperor was extremely angry and swore by God and His might that they would be killed and hanged, drowned at sea or burned at the stake, if the pilgrim were not returned to him. The emperor was very angry and spoke to the duke in fury. "Duke," he said, "now listen to me: if you don't speedily return the pilgrim to me, whom you have taken from my custody, you will never again have my friendship. I want to have him from you quickly, alive or dead, without delay, or else you will be judged in my court. I know very well you have murdered him." (10297–324)

Duke Berard jumped to his feet, like someone completely furious. "My lord emperor, now I can well see that good service counts for nothing. I have served you for a long time and protected your great domains well, but now you want to judge me in your court; I wouldn't give a single penny for it. If there were anyone now so bold as to judge me in such a manner in your court, I would give him such a blow with my steel sword that I'd make his head fly from his body. And you, who have judged me here—I certainly want you to know that I'll go back to Lombardy, summon my country's army, and enter Germany. I won't leave you a single foot of land." (10325–42)

When the emperor heard this and understood the duke's threats, he became extremely angry and swore a great oath that the duke should leave his court, and the duke swore in turn that he would do so. At that, the fisherman appeared. He came quickly into the principal palace, went straight to the emperor, and prodded him with his finger in a friendly way. "My lord," he said, "listen to this; please speak to me. I shall now tell you about the pilgrim and where he is, because I know all about it." "My friend," said the emperor, "now, by your father's soul, if you know anything about the pilgrim, tell me: I shall give you a hundred marks of fine gold." "Yes, sire," he said, "most certainly! I won't lie to you about anything. Late last night I went fishing. As I was in my boat on the sea, I found a bed floating and a knight lying inside. I asked who he was, and he told me truly that he was the pilgrim who fought Berard. Then I pulled him into my boat and brought him straight to my lodging. I've guarded him well all night. Send for him and I will hand him over to you." (10343–74)

[*"My friend,"* said the emperor, *"it was lucky you saw him, by St Peter. Now I'll give you many possessions, so that you'll always stay here."*][113] Then he sent him and others for the pilgrim, who was brought at once. Battle was decided on and the pilgrim and Berard were soon brought together without fail. They fought each other vigorously and often exchanged great blows with their good sharp swords on their brightly gleaming helmets. They knocked out the ornaments[114] as well as the flowers and the stones of various colours. [*The blows were great and powerful,*

---

[113] 10375–78 **My friend ... stay here** *Amis ... ci manant*: These lines are missing in E and different in C; they are supplied from F, with correction.

[114] 10387 **ornaments** *esses*: *Esses* are S-shaped ornaments.

like thunder from above.]¹¹⁵ They fought until nine in the morning; a fiercer battle had never been seen before. (10375–92)

The duke became very angry and furiously struck the pilgrim on top of his helmet, knocking out whatever flowers there were and cutting into the gold brow-band, damaging his ventail, shaving his face and his chin, and all the hair from the left side of his moustache. The blow fell on to his shoulder, shattering many mail-links there, but did not cut into the bare flesh because God did not at that time permit it, though it cut off a large section of the shield. Pulling out his steel sword, Berard forced the pilgrim to kneel and kiss the ground with his mouth. Gui's sword jumped out of his hands, and he was most ashamed, but he jumped at once to his feet. He struck the duke very angrily on top of his bright helmet, making a portion fly off, and likewise he knocked the flat-topped helmet quite down to the ground and made his ear with the whole cheek fly far away on the battleground. [*And the hauberks, which were so strong, were both damaged by the sword-blow.*]¹¹⁶ He cut off his arm along with his shoulder; the sword struck as far as his hip. [*It cut through his entrails and ribs, so that his body was severed in two.*]¹¹⁷ Gui wrenched his sword out and the other fell, and he cut the body in two with his sword. Life left the body; the entire city was delighted. (10393–428)

Then Gui withdrew to one side. "Ah, Duke Berard," he said, "alas for your valour! Had you been honest, so good a knight was never born [*or ever begotten.*"] Then he rested beside the body. The people of the city said: "This man is truly enchanted: such a blow was never yet dealt since the creation of the world."]¹¹⁸ Gui went straight to the emperor and told him how he had justified himself in the field. He asked for his court's decision as to whether Terri should be acquitted. Everyone shouted with one voice: "This pilgrim has spoken very well: if it pleases the emperor, he has entirely acquitted Terri." Then the emperor spoke: "I shall never deny it. " (10429–50)

"My lord emperor," said Gui, "Have mercy, my lord, on Count Terri! I have defended him against the charge of felony and beaten the duke in battle; I ask for the decision of your court on whether Terri should be freed forthwith and if he should recover his lands." The emperor replied like a noble man: "Pilgrim," he said, "well said. Now, speedily and without delay, I give up my anger towards Terri, and restore all his fief to him immediately. [*Now if I knew where he was, I would not wait another day to seek and send for him, and restore to him all his land.*]

---

¹¹⁵ 10389–90 **The blows ... from above** *Granz ... de la sus*: These lines are missing in E and are supplied from C.

¹¹⁶ 10419–20 **And the hauberks ... sword-blow** *E les halbercs ... falserent*: These lines are missing in E and are supplied from C with an "E" ("And") added.

¹¹⁷ 10423–24 **It cut ... two** *La boele ... severez*: These lines are missing in E and are supplied from C.

¹¹⁸ 10434–39 **or ever... the creation of the world** *Ne james ... le mund fu estoré*: These lines are missing in E and are supplied from C.

The pilgrim replied: "You will certainly find out: if it please you, you shall see him before the end of today." "My friend," he said, "then make haste and don't hesitate to look for him."][119] (10451–70)

Then Gui was disarmed. The emperor wanted to pay him honour: he wished to hold him very dear and dress him in splendid clothes, but Gui did not care for that. He asked for his poor pilgrim's cloak and at once it was brought to him, and he took off the magnificent armour, quickly put on his cloak, and went straight into the city. He went up and down looking for Terri; then he entered a church and found the count there, beside an altar, where he was praying. "Terri," he said, "get up! The emperor asks that you come to him. Quickly, don't delay; let's go, don't be afraid." (10471–88)

Count Terri raised his head. "God, who created everything," he said, "now whom can one trust, or tell one's secrets to, when you, who looked so loyal, have denounced me to the emperor? He will have me killed or maimed. You've received a bribe in order to have me killed. [*Like a scoundrel, you've betrayed me. Alas that I ever told you my name! I considered you such a faithful pilgrim; alas that I ever came into company with you!*]][120] I will get up and go with you; I see clearly I can't stay. If I die, it will be because of you; please God, He will take care of it." (10489–504)

"Terri," said Gui, "don't be afraid! Today you shall hear good news. The wicked Duke Berard is now dead; his body lies below the town. A pilgrim has beaten him; he has indeed defended you against felony." They arrived in front of the emperor. Count Terri did not feel safe. "My lord emperor," said Gui, "here is the good Count Terri." The emperor looked at him, and Terri hung his head, because he was very frightened of him. The emperor said to him: "Are you Count Terri of Worms, son of Alberi?" "Yes, my lord," he said, "indeed I am; now I am a poor wretch but once I was a lord." "Tell me, Terri," said the emperor, "where now is your splendid appearance? [*Once you used to be so powerful; where now is your great pride? You were so arrogant and proud; there was no more noble lord in the world.*]][121] You're not Count Terri, who was once so brave and bold." (10505–30)

"My lord," he said, "yes, I am indeed, but for too long I've been painfully waiting. I've suffered greatly: for a year and a half now, I've been travelling. Without a single day's rest, I've kept going, in order to look for my friend Gui, in many a far-off, foreign land. But in the country where he was born and raised, they told me Gui had gone into exile and that he'd died in a foreign realm. Now

---

[119] 10463–70 **Now if I knew ... don't hesitate to look for him** *Se seusse ore ... De lui quere ne vous targez*: These lines are missing in E and are supplied from F and C; 10467 is from F only.

[120] 10497–500 **Like a scoundrel ... came into company with you** *Trahi m'avez ... tant mar vinc*: These lines are missing in E and are supplied from C.

[121] 10525–28 **Once you used ... in the world** *Tant soliez ... plus noble ber*: These lines are missing in E and are supplied from C.

I've heard tell that a pilgrim—may God give him a good end!—has killed the wicked Duke Berard. I am sure God has sent him here. I don't know who he is; I never saw him before. In the name of God, my lord emperor, mercy!" He immediately fell at the emperor's feet. "Mercy, my lord, in the name of God and His might!" And some thirty courteous counts and all the princes of the palace fell at the emperor's feet: there was not one of them who did not weep for pity, and they begged the emperor for mercy. The emperor looked at Terri and was seized by great pity for him, and his face was wet with tears. "Terri," he said, "fair and gentle friend, in what lands have you spent your time? [*You have suffered much affliction; you look, indeed, like a man who has dwelt a long time in the wilderness. Now I feel great pity for you.*]¹²² This very day, Terri, I am restoring to you all your lands and your fief. I shall return your fief splendidly. Today I make you seneschal of Germany, as Duke Berard was; he had authority over my realm. This I promise you, my lord Terri." And they all answered in a shout: "Noble emperor, thank you! The count has often rendered you service." The emperor kissed Terri and renounced all his anger, and all the princes of the palace kissed him on this occasion. (10531–79)

There was then great joy in the city that Terri was reconciled with the emperor. "My lord Terri," said the emperor, "now tell me, as St Peter may help you: who is this pilgrim? Is he a relation or neighbour of yours, who has fought for you? He defended you excellently against felony; I didn't think there was a knight in the world, however arrogant or proud, who dared fight Berard or in his heart considered doing so." "My lord emperor," said Terri, "so help me God, as far as I know, I never saw this pilgrim except when he overtook me on the road. I never knew before, I swear to you, that he fought for me. I never knew it, but now I do. May Jesus Christ, the true God, reward him for it; he has delivered me from misfortune." The emperor behaved like a noble man: he had Terri enter his chambers, had him bathed and dressed and splendidly supplied with garments. He gave him harness and good horses, the very finest in the city. Then Terri went to Worms, taking the pilgrim with him. The emperor wanted to retain him, offering him very great honours, but he did not care about those—he went with Count Terri. The count too offered him plenty: half his castles and his cities; and he wanted to make him lord and ruler of all his lands forever. But the pilgrim refused everything, for riches held no value for him. (10579–618)

Count Terri came to Worms and was welcomed there with very great joy. He then had the countess sought for immediately throughout the land. He found her in an abbey of nuns, where she had hidden herself out of fear, for she was very frightened of Duke Berard who wanted to take her by force. Now the count was important and proud; he was the principal governor of Germany and now accomplished much with his power. All Germany was under his control. (10619–30)

---

¹²² 10561–64 **You have suffered much affliction . . . pity for you** *Maint grant mal avez suffert . . . pité me prent*: These lines are missing in E and are supplied from F.

One day Gui reflected that he had stayed in the land rather a long time. He thus took his leave of the count and spoke to him sorrowfully. "My lord count," he said, "I am going away; I shall not stay with you any longer. Now I ask you, out of friendship, to come with me outside the city. You shall hear such a thing as will astonish you, but let no one come except you alone." The count replied: "I agree." He readily mounted a mule and went through the city quite alone, taking no one with him except the pilgrim, who accompanied him. Soon after they had left the city, they came to a cross half a league away, and there they halted. (10631–50)

"My lord count," said Gui, "now listen to me. I'm well aware that you've failed to recognise me. You ought to know me well, if you gave it much thought. Don't you remember Gui, who was once your friend, and who killed the evil Duke Otun and freed you from his prison? And how he found you wounded in the forest, where he was travelling, and how he defended your beloved from fifteen robbers, whom he killed? Then he saved you from four knights and left all four there dead. Then he carried you on his horse and healed you completely of your great wound. Then he came to your father's aid—he has helped you in many an hour of need. Just now he took revenge for you on Duke Berard, who wrongly expelled you from the realm. This is Gui you see here; why will you not recognise me?" (10651–72)

When Terri studied his face, he could not, for all Paris, utter a word. He fell swooning from the mule to the ground; you never saw a man grieve so much. "Ah, Sir Gui, my good friend! Alas, how deceived and wretched I am! If I didn't recognise you before, now I am most unfortunate; I ought to have realised, from your mighty deeds, from your strength, that you were Gui the valiant, the courageous, the bold, the brave. Who would have such courage to enter battle against the treacherous Berard, against such a strong knight, if it weren't you, good Sir Gui? In God's name, forgive my misdeed! For the love of Jesus, forgive me, my lord, for not recognising you!" Quickly he fell at Gui's feet, which were split with cracks. Weeping, he kissed them, and saw that Gui's feet and legs, which once used to be so well shod, were all battered. He wept and mourned bitterly; there is no one alive under heaven, however hard-hearted he might be, who would not have had great pity on Terri. Gui had such sorrow and anguish in his heart that he could hardly utter a single word. He raised him up in his arms and they kissed each other. Each felt such great pity for the other that both fell to the ground in a faint. (10673–708)

"My good friend Terri," said Gui, "I am going away; you will stay here, and I commend you to Him, the powerful king over this world. I have a son from my wife; I don't know if he's a knight by now, but if he ever needs you, take care to help him." "My good friend," Terri replied, "in the name of that God who made the world, stay here with me! I pledge you my word that whatever I possess in this world I will share with you, good friend. If you won't do this, grant me, without refusing, a prayer which I ask you: that I may go with you. I would certainly never leave you as long as I live. I would rather accompany you and constantly endure great suffering, bearing misery with you, than be a wealthy emperor without you. If we now go together, we shall quite easily be able to bear the great sufferings we shall endure, since we two shall be together. As long as I am together with you, there's no misfortune under heaven, however painful, that I wouldn't bear very well, so long as I am with you." (10709–40)

"My friend," he said, "indeed you shall not come with me; never speak of it again. You will return straight away and loyally serve your lord. Beware of pride; help him well in case of need. Never think to disinherit a man, for if you wrongly disinherit anyone, I want you to know you will be disinherited of God's kingdom. Remember Duke Berard, who was so powerful and arrogant; he wrongly expelled you from the realm and disinherited many others. Now he is disinherited, slain in ignominy and pain. I am going away, you will remain; I commend you to God." (10741–58)

Then the friends, who were such noble lords, separated. At their leave-taking, they lamented bitterly: they kissed each other lovingly and then left, in floods of tears. They would never in their lives see each other again. The count went back home and went into a vaulted chamber; for three days, he never ate, nor even talked to anyone. When the countess knew for sure that it was Gui who had gone away, she lamented most sorrowfully and blamed her husband very much: if he could not keep Gui through affection, he should have detained him by force. (10759–74)

Then Gui departed, very miserable; he kept remembering Terri. In his travels he journeyed so much [*and crossed distant lands, that he came straight to the sea*][123] and crossed into England. He asked the people he saw there where King Athelstan was, and they told him that he was obliged to be at Winchester with large forces. He had summoned all the army of his land—dukes, counts, and barons and everyone who could bear arms—for never had there been so great a need. His bishops, his abbots, and all the vassals from his lands were all gathered at Winchester. Throughout Christendom it had been decided they would fast three whole days and pray to God, night and day, to send them a man who would undertake the battle, because King Anelaf from Denmark and King Gunlaf from Sweden had arrived in the land, with fifteen thousand armed men. They were ravaging the land and the countryside; all the way to Winchester not a tower or castle or city was left which they had not totally laid waste. (10775–804)

King Anelaf was extremely fierce, wicked, arrogant, and conceited. He had brought a Saracen[124] with him, whom people said was born in Africa. He was

---

[123] 10778–79 **and crossed distant lands . . . straight to the sea** *E terres lointeines . . . dreit a la mer*: these lines are missing in E and are supplied from C.

[124] 10807 **Saracen** *Sedne*: *Sedne* can mean Saxon, but "Africa" suggests *Sedne*'s other meaning, Saracen. See Flutre, 294. On Danes as Saracens, see Diane Speed, "The Saracens of *King Horn*," *Speculum* 65 (1990): 564–95.

more feared in battle than a hundred armed knights. They said he was called Colebrant; a fiercer warrior was never born. Anelaf had sent word to King Athelstan that he should give up this kingdom to him, or become his man, loyal to him, and pay him tribute willingly; the truth was, his ancestors had received it.[125] And if he refused to agree to this, he should rapidly find a knight who would, at once and without delay, join battle against Anelaf's champion, in order to prove the right of the king, his lord. They had fixed a day between them, but our king could not find anyone who dared undertake battle against the Saracen, who was so hideous and large and strong and powerful. (10805–28)

"Then where is Heralt," said Gui, "who never failed in the hour of need?" Someone replied that the truth was he had left the kingdom to look for the son of Gui, his liege lord, taken away by merchants. "Then where is Count Rualt, the noble lord who was so valiant?" And he replied that he was dead; he had died long ago. Gui wept for sorrow and readily prayed for his soul. "What is his daughter, the countess, doing?" And he replied that no abbess, nor any woman born, gave so many alms, to feed poor brethren and build abbeys, to make roads and paths. She never stopped praying God that He would let her see the day when she could again find her lord Gui, alive or dead. (10829–50)

Gui then went towards Winchester. No one, except God, knew who he was. He joined those who were suffering[126] and with them went towards Winchester. It was on the feast of St John.[127] King Athelstan was at Winchester, where he had summoned all his barons, and spoke to them in a loud voice. "My lords," he said, "now listen to me. You are my men, as you know well; how can we defend ourselves and take up arms against the Danes? In God's name, now advise me, and, starting now, deliberate among yourselves, for King Anelaf is very cruel; there's no one more arrogant in the world. Through this mighty Saracen, Colebrant—the Saracen is the reason for the king's great arrogance—Anelaf wants to destroy and kill us, and with great slaughter drive us out. Noble knights, now prepare yourselves! Yours are the castles and the cities, the wide domains and the manors, and the forests full of animals. Remember your great possessions, your wives and your children; if you lose them through your weakness, you will be shamed forever. Furthermore, I want to ask you if you have found any knight who dares to fight the Saracen. If he can win the battle, I will give him the third part of my land during my lifetime, and the third part of my estate to his heirs for ever." (10851–86)

---

[125] 10817 **his ancestors had received it** *Ses ancestres l'urent*: See note to line 9136.

[126] 10853 **those who were suffering** *les mesaisez*: The afflicted, or the poor (*mesaisez* can mean either) are coming to Winchester in the hope of a cure, or a meal at the feast.

[127] 10855 **the feast of St John** *la feste saint Johan*: See note to line 8571.

Everyone was silent. They did not utter a word, as if someone had given them a tonsure.[128] "Oh God, good Lord!" he said. "I have so much pain and anger in my heart, since I can't find a single person who dares to fight the Saracen. Oh Sir Gui, noble lord, and your friend, Heralt of Arderne! If I had kept you with me, and much good had befallen me as a result, and I had given you as much as the third part, or half, of my land, now you would reward me; you would not fail me for anything. He is not a wise man, it seems to me, who neglects his good friends for possessions—whether it's his good dog or his good horse, his hawk or his good vassal. If a man's friend can't be of use to him every day, that's no reason for that man to abandon him, for it can very soon happen that one day such a friend will be as useful to him as he could wish. Whatever he has spent in seven years, he will recover through that friend in a single day. If I had given so much to Gui that he stayed in this kingdom, it would have been used now to very good purpose, because he would nobly have compensated for it. The Danes are getting arrogant: they consider us weak and feeble, since we can't find a man who dares to enter the field against one of theirs." (10887–918)

"My lord," said the duke of Kent, "I'll tell you what I think: summon your country's army and fight the Danes. Please God, you will defeat them with ease. You will get no other advice from us." (10919–24)

That night the king lay down in a bed of carved gold. All night he lay awake, often praying to God to send him a man he could trust for the battle. And God did not forget him; as the king slept, He sent him an angel from heaven, who gave him great comfort. "Are you asleep, King Athelstan?" he said. "King Jesus tells you this: very early in the morning, get up and go to the north gate. You will see a pilgrim enter; seize him instantly and take him with you. Ask him for the love of God to undertake the battle for you, and he will do so in good faith." Then the angel left. The king woke up and rejoiced greatly. He rose very early in the morning and went straight to the gate, taking with him two counts and two of the kingdom's bishops. They stood there until six, when the poor came in. Athelstan easily saw the pilgrim amongst them; he recognised him from the angel's words and grabbed him by his mantle. He drew him closer and said: "Brother pilgrim, you shall come with me; I shall lodge you, don't be afraid!" (10925–58)

"My lord," he said, "leave me alone. I don't want lodging yet. I'm poor, I'm going to look for food. I've only recently come to this land." But the king took him and immediately entered his chamber, bringing the bishops with him and summoning all the men of standing. "Pilgrim," he said, "listen to this. We entreat you, in the name of God who ascended to heaven, and out of charity; we shall show you our desperate need. We are engaged in battle with the Danes,

---

[128] 10888 **given them a tonsure** *lur raisist la corone*: A tonsure is the shaved part of a monk's or priest's head.

but we cannot find any man who dares undertake the combat. So I give you to understand that the combat will be undertaken in the following manner, as you will hear: I must claim my land through the person of a knight against a Saracen, Colebrant. There's no one in the world so powerful; King Anelaf has brought him. The king has such confidence in Colebrant's great might that he believes there's no knight in the world who dares use a shield against him. Now I beg you, in the name of the Lord who let Himself suffer on the cross, to take on this battle for us. God wishes you to do it." (10959–88)

"My lord," said Gui, "don't talk about it; don't ask me to do battle. You see here a wretch, weak and sick in body." Then the king rose, and fell at his feet, along with bishops and counts. They all begged him to have pity and undertake the battle, in the name of God and the holy Trinity. (10989–98)

When Gui saw the king at his feet, begging him to have pity, and the other lords with him, weeping anxiously, he said: "My lord, please rise! Since you all ask me in this way to take on the battle for you, I will do it, with God's grace." Then the king rose and kissed him with great affection. (10999–11008)

There was now great joy in the city because the king had found a man who would fight Colebrant; please God, he would easily beat him. They sent word to King Anelaf that they had found a knight who would be fully armed in the field on the day they had decided; he would fight their Saracen and defend their lord's right. When the day came which was fixed for the battle, Gui armed himself most splendidly with a strong, fine-linked hauberk. On his head he had a gleaming helmet, resplendent with a gold cross; the hoop was of carved gold, and it would not have been exchanged for a city. There were many precious stones in it, each with different properties. The nose-piece was of carved gold, with many good stones in it. On top of the forehead, above the nose-piece, there was set a carbuncle, so fine that at night it gave out as much radiance as if it were daylight. On top of the helmet was a flower, ornamented with many colours [*skilfully, they had set a crystal in it which was ornamented with fine enamel.*][129] He had good and well-fashioned boots, strong and fine and closely fitting; on his feet were some spurs, richly damascened[130] with fine gold. He was girded with a steel sword which King Athelstan cherished dearly. Round his neck they hung a shield; its straps were of woven gold yarn. Then they brought him a horse, the swiftest in the kingdom, and he at once mounted it. He made the sign of the true cross, took a sharp sword in his hand, and immediately went off towards the place of combat. (11009–52)

---

[129] 11037–38 **skilfully ... fine enamel** *Par art ... fin esmal*: These lines are missing in E and are supplied from F.

[130] 11042 **damascened** *neelez*: To damascene is to ornament metal with incised designs, filled in with gold or silver, or with a watered pattern, as in Damascus blades (OED).

When he had arrived at the place, he quickly dismounted from his horse and in an act of penance lay on the ground. He prayed to God: "Lord, who brought Lazarus back to life and saved Samson from the lion, and helped Susanna against the evil men who wanted treacherously to kill her, protect me from this scoundrel, so that through him I am not damned and may finish this battle and defend the land from servitude." Then he made the sign of the cross and quickly got between the saddle-bows;[131] he used neither stirrup nor saddle-bow. Many men gazed at him that day and praised him over all others in the world, because they had never seen such a handsome armed man. Then the relics were called for. First King Anelaf swore on them that if his man were defeated, killed, and overthrown in battle, he would return to Denmark and never again claim a right to England, nor would he ever come back there in anger, nor would any heir of his, after his death. Then King Athelstan swore in front of his whole assembly of barons that if his man were killed there, defeated, or maimed in battle, Athelstan would become Anelaf's liege man and hold all his land from him and pay him and his heirs after him a large tribute every year. (11053–86)

When they had sworn the oaths and supplied hostages on both sides, up came Colebrant, who was so big and strong that no horse could carry him or sustain him or his weapons. He always fought on foot and did not ask for a horse in battle; he had so many kinds of weapons that a cart could scarcely carry him. Colebrant was very strong. He had donned a strong hauberk; it was not made of mail-links but forged of another material. Great plates, all of steel, were joined together to protect his body, and there were many strong plates in front and behind. [132] The plates were very well joined and covered his body, arms, and hands. He had boots of the same fashion, in whch there were nothing but plates. His helmet was good, strong and proud; it feared no blow from a steel sword. He was girded with a strong steel sword, heavy enough for one man to carry. About his neck hung a round shield, stronger than any in the world, entirely edged with iron and steel; it was not formed with any other metal. He was truly ugly and hideous. All his armour was black: it had been boiled seven times in pitch and was thus totally blackened. In his hand he held a sharp spear; close by him were, to his right, seven sharp steel lances, seven pointed spears, finely decorated with feathers, strong lances suitable for a knight and long foot-soldiers' lances and sharp, feathered javelins and many other sharp spears and great axes for hacking and hatchets for cleaving iron, iron clubs, steel bludgeons, broadswords for

---

[131] 11066 **saddle-bows** *les arçuns*: The saddle-bow is the arched front or rear of the saddle.

[132] 11101 **Great plates** *granz esplentes*: Plate armour, consisting of articulated steel pieces attached to the body by straps and buckles, develops continuously through the 13th century. Full-body plate armour was usually custom-made and very expensive. Colebrant is obviously better equipped than Gui.

landing great blows, a hundred hunting-spears, and a hundred Turkish bows. The English looked at him in amazement. (11087–134)

Now those in the field were prepared. Gui was very frightened of Colebrant; he had never feared death so much in any battle he had been in before. He struck spurs into his horse, which moved more swiftly than a merlin,[133] and attacked Colebrant with great violence. But before he had reached him, Colebrant threw three spears at him; two missed, but the third struck him: it passed through his shield painted with fine gold and through the double-meshed hauberk, between his arm and side, and the length of half a mile[134] further on. Gui struck him on his shield in turn, with his ground and sharpened sword, so that he made the splinters fly up just when he was about to ride past. Colebrant drew his steel sword and was about to give Gui a blow on the helmet, but the villain's blow came down between Gui's body and the saddle-bow so that it cut the good horse in two. The blow sank a full foot into the ground. (11135–58)

Gui fell to the ground, but quickly got up again. Then he drew his good sword, of very sharp steel, and struck him back with great force, intending to hit him on top of the helmet. But Gui could not reach so high, and so the blow missed, for he was not, indeed, so close to him that he could reach high enough; even using the whole sword, which was long, he could not reach him above the shoulders. The blow came down on Colebrant's shoulder, split a big plate there, and cut into his flesh, drawing blood and making his side all red. Colebrant was very angry, raised his sword high, and with great violence gave Gui such a blow on top of the helmet that he knocked out the flowers and the crystals, the damascene work and the enamels. [*The blow fell on the shield and split it in two as far as the ground.*][135] (11159–82)

When Gui saw his shield lying on the ground, he did not know what to do; he saw one half in front and the other lying behind him. You never heard tell of such a blow. Gui began to fear Colebrant very much. He raised his sword high and with great violence struck Colebrant a huge blow on his shield, which was so strong. The blow was plain to see: it cut a foot and a half into the shield and cut through the iron bands. As Gui drew the blade out, he pulled it towards him with such great force that the sword broke in two. Then Gui was greatly dismayed; misfortune had now befallen him, since he had lost his strong shield and his good, ground and sharpened sword. "Oh God," he said, "Lord Jesus! Why am I now treated so badly? I'm fighting for this kingdom, to defend it from servitude; why has this harm befallen me?" Then the Danes grew arrogant and

---

[133] 11140 **merlin** *merilons*: A merlin is a small falcon.

[134] 11148 **half a mile** *Demi arpent*: see note to line 3620.

[135] 11181–82 **The blow ... ground** *En l'escu ... le fent*: These lines are missing in E and are supplied from C.

repeatedly said to one another: "Now the English are beaten." King Athelstan was much dismayed. (11183–210)

"Knight," said Colebrant, "you have lost your shield and your sword and you have no power to defend yourself. Now cry for mercy from me and I shall take pity on you in the proper way. Because you were so bold as to undertake battle with me, I shall take pity as is proper on you. I shall take you with me, reconcile you with King Anelaf, and give you castles and wealthy fiefs if you will now trust me." "Fellow," he said, "don't talk about that. Too bad for you if you place your confidence in that! If I've now lost my sword, our Lord has great power; I shall share your sword and put up a good fight with it. You have great quantities of weapons; you can lend me some, and then we can fight each other and see well enough who will win." (11211–32)

"Fellow," replied Colebrant, "so help me almighty Mahomet, I shall never lend you arms, but rather shall cut off your head. Now I would be a stupid fool if I freely gave you arms. On the contrary, because you wounded me, you will lose your head." When Gui heard Colebrant speak, he jumped up instantly, like someone who was young and very nimble. Before Colebrant could turn round, he had speedily seized an axe in his hands. Then angrily he said to Colebrant; "Fellow, some poor thanks! I've got your weapons in abundance." (11233–48)

When Colebrant saw this, he advanced hastily, without delay. He struck at Gui with great force, but Gui leaped aside and Colebrant, as God would have it, missed him. The sword descended far into the ground. As Colebrant drew it out, Gui lost no time but came at the Saracen very fast and, with the axe he held in his hand, cut off his sword-arm, which made Colebrant furious. When Colebrant felt himself struck, he quickly leapt to get his sword; he wanted to seize it with his left hand, since he had no recourse to his right. As he bent down, Gui got very close to him and raised his sharp axe high; as Colebrant bent down, he gave him such a blow in the neck that his head flew far off into the field. The scoundrel fell dead to the ground. There you could see the Danes lamenting bitterly; King Anelaf was very unhappy, and all his men with him. They speedily returned to their ships, embarked, and had a good wind; they went back to Denmark very dejected and distressed. (11249–78)

King Athelstan was delighted, and all his barons with him. They all went to Gui and with great joy brought him to the noble city of Winchester. A procession went out to meet him, singing *Te Deum Laudamus*;[136] they praised God again and again. Then Gui disarmed and asked for his pilgrim's mantle. The king called him to him and spoke to him with great affection. "Brother pilgrim, now listen: tell me your name. You shall stay with me; I shall give you castles and

---

[136] 11285 **Te Deum Laudamus** i.e., 'we praise you, O God'. The *Te Deum* is a hymn of praise, following the outline of the Apostles' Creed, and naming all those who venerate God.

rich fiefs, wide domains and fine cities. As long as you live, you shall always be held dear in the kingdom." (11279–97)

"My lord king," he said, "don't talk about that; I tell you, I don't look for even twopence-worth from you. If I have beaten the Saracen, give thanks to our Lord Jesus, for it was through His power that the Saracen was destroyed." "My lord," said the king, "in God's name, thank you! And, by that God who never lied, and who suffered death on the cross, here I now beg you, my lord, to tell me truly what is your name and where you were born." The pilgrim replied: "Since you have entreated me, you shall hear it. Now do what I tell you: come outside this city alone with me. Truly, there you shall hear the truth." The king gladly agreed to this, and then ordered his people that none should be so bold as to follow him. Then they left the city, but hardly travelled very far. "My lord," said Gui, "go no further. You entreated my name. I shall tell you it, but take care not to reveal it this year." The king replied: "My good and gentle friend, I give you my word your identity will not be revealed." (11298–328)

"My lord king," said Gui, "now listen to me. This is Gui you see here, your knight from Warwick. Once you loved me and held me dear. I know very well that you don't recognise me. I am just as you see me here." (11329–34)

When the king heard and understood at heart that this was the brave Gui, he had never been so astonished. He quickly dismounted and sank on his knees before Gui. "Ah, sir pilgrim, forgive me, in God's name! Are you Gui, then? Truly, it's now a long time since I heard tell you were dead. Thanks be to our Lord Jesus that you have come back here to us! God has sent you here. This very day I give you half of England in its entirety. I will increase your domains still further, provided you stay with us — do so, my lord Gui, in God's name!" (11335–52)

"My lord," said Gui, "I can't do it. I give up all the land to you. But if God grant that Heralt returns, and he can bring my son back, I beg you, my lord, to honour them; you can trust them completely. By your leave, my lord, I'm going; I commend you to God." The king felt great sorrow, and gave him many kisses of friendship. Weeping, he returned to the city, very dejected and distressed. His people went to meet him and at once asked him: "My lord, who is this pilgrim, now going on his way? He has fought for you, he's a good man with great power." The king replied: "Don't talk about it; for now, you'll not find out through me. Before this year is out, I shall tell you the truth." (11353–74)

Now Gui went off along the metalled road. He often gave great thanks to God for the honour He had granted him ever since he was born. He made such headway on his journey that he came to the city of Warwick, in which he had been proclaimed lord and ruler of the whole region. He came to the gate of the castle; there was no one there who recognized him. He sat down amongst the poor brethren, and people took great pity on him. Countess Felice was there;[137]

---

[137] 11387 **Countess Felice was there** *La contesse Felice i esteit*: F adds 2 lines after this one.

each day she had thirteen poor brothers fed in the hall, seated in front of her, with the same drink and the same food as she herself was wont to have, so that God might protect her husband Gui. When she ate at a solemn feast, she would send for the thirteen poor brethren, and people would at once bring them and would quickly seat them in front of her. Gui was at that moment one of the thirteen, and he was very afraid he would be recognised. The countess looked at him; because he was more poverty-stricken, she felt the greater pity. That day she sent him, from each course she ate, some of her table wine and her mulberry wine, in splendid gold carved cups. She sent him word, through a servant, to come to the court every day; he would have plenty of food, she said. And he gave her many thanks, but his thoughts were quite different: now he was very frightened, in case somebody recognised him. (11375–412)

When the countess had eaten and the big table had been removed, he left the hall as soon as he could, and very soon took himself outside the city. He went straight towards Arderne, to a holy hermit whom he had once known, dwelling deep within the forest; he hoped to get there straightaway. When he reached the hermitage, so deep within that wood, the hermit was dead; there was no living person there. Gui decided he would go no further but, as long as he lived, he would serve God there. He led a very holy life in this way. He spoke to a priest in the region, who would come to him at every festival and perform the office for him. He led a very holy life: night and day he served the Son of Mary. Night and day he was at prayer, and God did him great honour. As long as he served God there, he lived on the plants of the forest; he was always in front of an altar and never stopped praying to God. His body was never at rest because he always worshipped God. With him he had a boy who looked after him in the hermitage. He stayed there nine months, as we have found in the story. (11413–46)

It happened then that he became sick. God did not forget him: Gui had suffered much affliction for Him. One night, when he was asleep, God sent him an angel, who spoke clearly to him. "Gui," he said, "are you asleep? From on high, Jesus tells you to get ready now; you will speedily come to Him and He will relieve you of your sufferings, for eight days from now, you will ascend to Him in heaven, where you will have perpetual glory." Then Gui awoke and saw the angel's bright light. "Who are you who speaks to me? If you are God, don't hide it from me." The angel replied: "I am from heaven, I am called Michael, and God sends me to you because He loves you so much. Now make ready to come, for on that day you must die, and I shall come for your soul,[138] bringing a great company with me." The angel departed and Gui remained behind, not ceasing to pray to God. He was joyful and glad at the news that God had sent him from heaven. (11447–76)

---

[138] 11471 **And I shall come for your soul** *E jo pur l'alme de vus vendrai*: St Michael was traditionally the guide of departing souls.

When it came to the time of his death, he made his boy come to him. "My friend," he said, "you will go quickly to Warwick—don't delay—and carry to the countess my message, which will be of great advantage to you. You will take her this ring and tell her, on my behalf, that the pilgrim who ate in front of her, to whom she sent her food, her table wine and her mulberry wine, has sent her this ring. As soon as she sees the ring, I am sure she will recognise it. She will make you many gifts and will speedily ask you to tell her where the pilgrim is. And you will tell her: in this forest; he has now become a hermit; and you have seen me in this hermitage and have served me here. Many good things will certainly come to you because of this. When she has heard the news, I am sure she will come here with you, and you will find me here, dead. On my behalf you will tell her she should bury my body here, exactly in this spot. She should come quickly: she must die soon after me." The boy replied: "I shall go; I will carry this message to the lady." (11477–508)

The boy quickly left and went straight to Warwick. There he found the countess and quickly knelt before her. "My lady," he said, "hear this and listen to my words. The pilgrim who, this year, ate in your presence, sends you a message through me. I don't know if you know him, but he is very poor and sick. Now he's living in that forest, eating grass and roots. I think he's a most holy man, filled with the Holy Spirit. Through me he sends you this ring, which I have here on my finger." She took the ring in her hand, looked at it all over, and then said: "Thank you, my Lady, St Mary! Surely that's my lord Gui's ring!" She fell to the ground and swooned three times, without uttering a word. When she rose from the swoon, she spoke to the boy in a loud voice. "My young friend, now tell me where the hermit is, don't hide it from me." (11509–34)

"My lady," he said, "I will tell you. I left him far off in the forest, where he is dying in the hermitage. I bear this message to you on his behalf: you should come and bury his body in the hermitage, where he has died, and you should not remove it from that place but have it buried there. And you will die soon after him; you will barely survive him." When the lady heard this, she rejoiced greatly that she would see her lord; on the other hand, she grieved that she would see him die, and so lamented exceedingly. Then she asked for a mule and quickly mounted, and with the majority of the city went to the hermitage. They travelled so far into the wood that they came to the hermitage and dismounted at the door. The lady fell fainting to the ground. As she entered the hermitage, she saw the body of her lord. She uttered a loud cry and he opened his eyes; his soul departed and St Michael received it with great joy, and, singing sweetly, many angels there, who received the blessed soul, presented it to God in heaven. (11535–68)

Now the lady was in the chapel, where her grief was renewed. She swooned over the body of her lord, kissing his mouth and face, his fine hands and his handsome feet, and so did many others with her. All those with the lady mourned bitterly with her, and all went to kiss the body. God wished to do them this much honour: from the body there issued a fragrance, emitting a most sweet perfume. If all the spices in this world, and all the sweet things in it, were gathered in one spot, or heaped up into a pile, such a sweetness would not issue from them as came from the holy body. There was no sick man who would not be cured by that perfume. The fragrance lasted until the holy body was buried. The lady sent at once for the kingdom's bishops and abbots, and very many of them came, paying great honour to the body. They wanted to take it with them to Warwick, but they could not move it from the spot; a hundred of the strongest knights could not remove the body from that place. The lady said: "Let it be; I will never have it moved from here. He told me in his message to have him buried here." (11569–602)

Then they took a marble coffin and with solemnity put the body inside. Before evening came, there was, truly, a magnificent service with priests: many masses were sung and many alms given. Once the body was buried, everyone left the place and each went back into his own lands, except for the lady, who stayed and said she would never leave; as long as she lived, she would always serve there, for the sake of her husband whom she loved so much. And so she did, indeed, for she served there most willingly: she bestowed generous alms as long as she lived there. She did not live long after this; her life came rapidly to an end, as we have found in the story and is certainly to be believed, indeed—that she died on the fiftieth day after the death of her lord. She was lovingly placed next to him, and buried with great honour. They are together, in the company of our Lady, St Mary, and thus may God grant us so to serve Him that we may come to His glory. AMEN.[139] (11603–32)

Now, my lords, you have heard about Gui: how he finished his life with good deeds, always loved faith and loyalty, and honoured God above all else. And God rewarded him, as you here have heard. Gui possessed all the virtues, fine adventures befell him, and he never entered a battle or a fray where he was not considered the best. (11633–42)

When Count Terri heard that his friend Gui was dead, he came to the king of England and asked for his friend's body. He told the king of the true love between them for a long time, and how they were pledged to each other. The king granted him the body, and he took it to Lorraine. He paid the body great honour: for the sake of the soul of Gui, whom he loved so much, he had a splendid abbey built there; there was none more splendid in all the land. It is still there and always will be. (11643–56)

Now I shall tell[140] of Heralt, the good knight, who lay in prison in Africa. He drank little and ate less, barely sustaining his life. He mourned his lord's son,

---

[139] 11632 **that we may come to His glory. AMEN.** *Ke en sa glorie puissum venir. Amen*: After this line there is a space amounting to 2 lines. See Introduction, 19–20.

[140] 11657 **Now I shall tell** *Ore dirra*: E has *Ore dirra*, but I have adopted the reading, *Ore dirrai*, of FMC.

for whom he was suffering pain and sadness. He missed using his own prowess and his courage, for he must now die in sorrow in this way. One of the jailers was there, who often that day heard his lament and how he mourned his prowess. He went straight away to the emir. "My lord," he said, "something you don't know: you have a prisoner in your dungeon. You have never heard of anybody so proud of his prowess." The emir said: "Bring him here! If he is as you have said, he can be very useful to me, if I can really trust him." The jailer returned, and went to the dungeon as fast as he could. He at once brought Heralt out, who was thin and much enfeebled. They threw him a mantle and looked hard at him: his beard was white, his head overgrown with hair.[141] Because of the great sufferings he had had, no one under heaven would have recognised him, no matter how much he had seen him before. He was a large man, tall and sturdily built; he certainly seemed like a man of great ability. He was taken before the emir, who spoke to him soon enough: "Now then, who are you and from what land? Are you then as skilled in war as your words made you out to be, when you were in my jail? If I could be certain that you would consider me your lord and would loyally serve me, I would willingly retain you; I would give you the weapons you want in order to carry on my great war." (11657–700)

Heralt replied: "Good and gentle lord, I should answer your request. I am called Heralt and I was born in England. There I was once very powerful; there I was born and brought up. Here I am now wretched and weak; if my strength, which I've lost in your dungeon, were to return, and I had the weapons I wanted, I believe I would serve you well." The emir then replied: "My fine friend, from now on I will find weapons and anything else for you, and whatever you need. Since you were born in England, tell me truly if you ever knew the brave Gui, whom I've heard so acclaimed for his feats of arms." (11701–18)

"My God," said Heralt, "I knew him very well! I was his man and still am." The emir said: "Would to Apollo that he were in this marble palace! He would be very useful to me, in order to finish my great war." He sent for his chamberlain and had Heralt given splendid clothes; he was bathed and rested, and horses and weapons were prepared. The emir addressed him: "Listen to this, my friend. You know the true situation very well—that King Arguz has so greatly harmed me that, out of all my large kingdom, he has left me only this city. This is all because of a young man, an amazing new knight, who through his ferocity has quite destroyed and ravaged me. He has captured and killed my men and laid all this land waste. If I could avenge myself on him, capture or kill or maim him, then I think I could be at peace. I would make you a wealthy prince at once." Heralt replied:

---

[141] 11683–85 **his beard... recognised him** *La barbe... l'eust conu:* I have altered Ewert's punctuation (*La barbe out blanche, le chef encru/ Des granz mesaises qu'il ad eu; Suz ciel n'ad home qui l'eust conu.*)

"I shall do this; as far as I can, I shall make it my business. I think I shall avenge you properly, with the help of Jesus, Son of St Mary." (11719–48)

Then a messenger appeared, who told the emir of his great losses—that King Arguz's constable, who was conceited and arrogant, had besieged one of his castles and slain and killed his knights; not a single man was left. The emir was angry and distressed. He called his constable and told him to have all his men armed, and he speedily did so. Heralt at once armed, then mounted a swift Arab steed. They left the city and had soon crossed the countryside. They came straight to the castle and saw there many pointed helmets and many knights clad in armour, on good, long-maned horses. They boldly proceeded to attack them, each striking his own opponent. Heralt struck a Saracen and knocked him flat on the ground dead, and another, and then a third; he knocked them all dead from their horses. Then he drew his steel sword and made many a head fly off; whomever he reached, he threw down dead. With the good sword girded around him, he did not fail to strike well; many a Saracen grieved that day. (11749–80)

Heralt exerted himself so much that day that on both sides they watched him and said he was an evil spirit, brought there by devils. The king's followers were fierce, but there was a constable among them—no bolder Saracen ever served Mahomet or Apollo. [*When he saw his companions slain, he almost went mad with anger.*]¹⁴² He loudly exhorted his men and at once attacked Heralt; with his sharpened sword, he struck him a great blow in the middle of the shield. Had it not been for the hauberk, which was very good, he would certainly have pierced him through the body. Then they drew their swords and gave each other violent blows. The constable rode on, and avenged himself thoroughly on Heralt's men. Heralt lost many of his men there, but he acted very quickly: [*he recovered in a short time and gathered his men around him.*]¹⁴³ They defeated the constable, and he fled to the top of a mountain, but Heralt pursued him vigorously and so did his companions. The Saracens speedily rode away, vanquished; most of them were dead or captured. The constable was in flight, the blood streaming down his side. Heralt followed him on his Arab steed and the constable rushed on, quite beaten. Heralt caught up with him beside a mountain and there they exchanged blows, hitting each other hard and cutting through helmets and shields. Heralt captured him in the fray and then turned and went back to his companions, who were leading away many wealthy prisoners. With the booty they had won, they returned to their city. The emir went to meet them, his heart very joyous and glad upon seeing his men return in this way. They told him at once how bold and brave Heralt was—a man as good as him had never been seen before—and how

---

¹⁴² 11789–90 **When he saw ... with anger** *Quant vit ... d'ire*: These lines are missing in E and are supplied from C and M, with corrections.

¹⁴³ 11803–4 **he recovered ... around him** *En poi d'ure ... assembla*: These lines are missing in E; the supplied lines are from F, with correction.

he had captured the constable and made an amazing slaughter of others. Heralt came forward and dismounted before the emir; he delivered the constable to him, and the emir received him most joyfully. (11781–836)

"Heralt," the emir said, "you have defeated my enemies. Come forward, good and gentle friend; I give you control of this land. From now on, I want to make you constable over the army of all my land, and I want knights, burgesses, and men at arms to be subject to you. Make them come and go as you wish." (11837–46)

Now there was great joy in the city. Heralt was much respected and feared, and he hardly rested before gathering a large army. Then he went through the domains, conquering castles and cities that the emir had lost. He conquered them with alacrity, doing the king great harm; he killed his men in a great fury. (11847–56)

When King Arguz heard that his constable was captured, his men dead and captured, painfully defeated and overthrown, he was furious and sorrowful. He angrily asked for what reason, and how, he had lost his men. A knight answered him: "I don't intend to hide it from you, my lord: an old man, quite white-haired — in reality a big and strong knight — came to the emir. In the whole world there isn't such a good armed man. There's no Saracen in this kingdom, however well armed, who would not have been split down to the belt had he been struck." The king replied: "He's an evil spirit." And he swore to his lord, Mahomet: "I will summon my country's army and go and besiege the emir. I will never leave there until I have destroyed all his land; I shall put him in prison and hang the old man high." (11857–82)

He summoned his country's army and went to attack the emir. He destroyed his castles and his cities, which Heralt had captured earlier. The emir rapidly gathered his men from throughout his land. When he had assembled his country's army, he called affectionately to Heralt. "My lord Heralt, now listen to me. You can certainly see our great need: now take charge of these followers, however you like. Prepare the troops and take charge of the battle." Heralt replied: "As you wish it, good and gentle lord, so will it certainly be!" They equipped the troops and quickly prepared themselves to fight. With sharp swords they advanced to strike their enemies through their chests. From then on they hit each other vigorously, some cutting down bleeding enemies, and on both sides many blows were struck. Throughout the fields there howled and cried [*those knights with mortal wounds, and the long-maned horses roamed riderless.*] (11883–908)

[*Heralt sat on the Arab steed; anyone he reached was defeated.*][144] He did great harm to King Arguz and killed his men in his presence. Wherever he saw the king, he struck him a great blow with his steel sword. If Arguz had not had help

---

[144] 11907–10 **those knights ... was defeated** *Les chevalers ... est desconfit*: These lines are missing in E and are supplied from C.

immediately, he would have been killed in the midst of his army. The king was furious at it, shouting his war-cry, and he energetically formed a vanguard. It was a most bitter battle; thousands of very valiant knights died there in great pain. (11909–22)

The emir had the bad luck to be knocked to the ground, and he had lost many of his men, for which he suffered greatly at heart. He saw his men cut down, fleeing across the field, and being attacked on all sides by swords, lances, and hunting-spears. He defended himself with his sharp sword, like a brave and valiant knight, frequently calling upon Heralt. When Heralt heard him, he went where he was with large forces and struck the seneschal through the body. Then he drew his steel sword and cut off many heads. He had the emir mounted, and they began to rally their men. They assailed King Arguz and killed so many of his followers that the king was very frightened when he saw his men slain in front of him. Wherever he saw Heralt spurring, therefore, he feared him much more than a thunderbolt. Many were slain on both sides, but the king had the worst of it, for his followers were often defeated. That angered and distressed him. (11923–50)

King Arguz fled, thinking no one noticed him. When Heralt saw him from a distance, where he was fleeing along a valley, and recognised him from his armour, he followed him on his good horse. He would certainly have reached him and captured or killed him, when a young man appeared who was head of the advance guard. The king's daughter had raised him to adulthood; then the king had knighted him and given him splendid weapons. Arguz often had great need of him in order to defeat his enemies. When he saw that the king was fleeing, and saw Heralt pursuing him, he very speedily went to help the king, and spoke arrogantly to Heralt: "Sir Greybeard, go no further! Don't be so very stupid as to go pursuing the king. I insist you fight me. You have done us great harm, and you shall leave us your body as payment. I will present your head to the king; I've promised it to him for a long while. I shall keep the Arab steed for my use; never have I wanted anything so much." (11951–80)

Heralt saw him, and knew him by his armour and by the great blows he had struck, cutting off many a head. He turned his horse round and went to strike him, and the young man in turn struck very fiercely, so that they knocked each other off their horses. They pulled out their steel swords and at once gave each other great blows on their bright Saracen helmets; they cut into the ornamental gold circles and the fine-linked hauberks. The combat between them was very fierce, each striving to harm the other. But had one recognised the other, the battle between them would not have happened. (11981–96)

Heralt drew away a little. "Knight," he said, "as God may save you, now tell me in what kingdom you were born and to what family. I can easily see you're not very old, but you have great valour. Surrender to me—that would be wise. If I killed you, it would be a loss: I've never met a knight who could withstand me as much as you can." And the other replied: "No more talk of that; you'll never get peace that way. You'll never know who I am, either from me or from others. On the contrary, I intend to cut off your head as soon as possible, without delay, if you don't quickly tell me where you were born and from what family. If you name one particular land, I will let you go scot-free. You are very old and your hair is quite white; your power is weakening. You will be easy to beat; it would be a sin to kill you." (11997–12020)

Heralt replied: "My fine and gentle friend, the men in my country are like this: when they are old and a great age, then their valour increases. I am old and my hair is quite white, and you are young and of great strength. Before you leave me, you'll consider me very young." Then the knights hit each other fiercely; they struck sparks off their helmets and made the valleys resound with their blows. Blood streamed to their feet and they gave each other many wounds. [*They carved into hauberks and shields; they struck great blows with sharpened blades. A harsher battle was never yet seen on any day.*][145] Now they were mortal enemies, but before the end of the day they would be close friends. (12021–40)

"Sir knight," said Heralt, "now listen to me for a bit. You are very brave and bold; I think there's no better than you in the world. Were you to learn now how far I've been praised, you would certainly not be ashamed to reveal yourself to me, for there's no land in Christendom where I have not been acclaimed for feats of arms." The other replied: "Old fellow, now I think you're a real fool. Do you imagine my arms are weakened? The blows from my steel sword, with which I intend to cut off your head, can easily be seen on your bright helmet and on this quartered shield." (12041–58)

Heralt replied: "I'm not saying your arms are weak; on the contrary, they are strong and powerful. I haven't seen greater blows struck. But if you were now to give thought to where you come from and told me of it, truly I would then tell you where I come from and who I am. I would hear such news of you, or you would hear such news of me, that we would postpone this battle quite freely. I don't ask from boorishness, from pride, or from arrogance, but I beg you out of great affection to tell me what I ask you." (12059–74)

The young man drew back, his face bold and his gaze proud . "Knight," he said, "you are very wise, brave and bold, and have a proud heart. I shall not tell you in response to a boorish demand , for I would rather let my head be cut off. But since you have asked me out of affection, I will certainly heed your request. I was born in England, in Warwick, a fine city, son of a celebrated lord, who was called Gui of Warwick. When Gui went into exile, he had a seneschal whom he loved very much, called Heralt of Arderne. I was then entrusted to him, who brought me up. He loved me very much and greatly cherished and honoured me. Then merchants took me away, in exchange for substantial gifts they made;

---

[145] 12035–38 **They carved into hauberks . . . any day** *Les halbercs trenchant . . . plus fort estur*: These lines are missing in E and supplied from F and M.

they carried me to this land and presented me to King Arguz. His daughter then brought me up in her chambers, just as she wished. The king armed me, for the sake of his daughter who begged him to. They've often needed the blows from my sharp sword." (12075–102)

When Heralt heard that this was Rainbrun, son of Gui, the son of his rightful lord who had caused him much grievous suffering, he threw his shield and his sword far away and raised his hands towards heaven. "Lord God," he said, "who made the world, thanks be to you always that I've now lived long enough to see my lord's son!" He began to weep for joy and could no longer stand; he fell in a total faint to the ground. Rainbrun stared at him and then raised him up in his arms; he pitied him deeply. (12103–18)

Heralt stood up. Rainbrun was much amazed. "Sir knight," he said, "forgive me! Tell me who you are, I beg you." And the other replied: "My name is Heralt; I brought you up, my lord Rainbrun, in my city, Wallingford. I have endured much suffering because of you." (12119–26)

When Rainbrun heard it was his tutor Heralt, he at once fell at his feet. "Forgive me, sir,[146] in the name of almighty God! How could I have been so bold as to strike you with my sharp sword? Avenge yourself, for the offence is too great." Then Heralt raised him up, and there they kissed each other, partly out of joy, partly out of sorrow. They both wept for joy. They mounted their horses, went straight to the city, and told the emir everything about how they had been reconciled. He paid them much honour, because he was very happy that the king was defeated and his men captured and killed. (12127–46)

Heralt and Rainbrun asked leave to depart, and the emir gave it them. A ship was made ready for them and they embarked one evening, sailing far enough over the sea that they finally made land. They saw no castle, town, or city there, but travelled for a whole day until evening came. Then they saw a castle, but it was ruined and dilapidated. They went to the gate. Heralt said to a porter: "As God is your help, speak to me! Who is lord of this castle? Tell me, I ask you it in courtesy. If he is within, don't hide it from us. We are knights whom you see here. We are not from this realm and ask you for lodging out of charity. Tomorrow, early in the morning, we will resume our way." The porter replied: "Fair sir, I don't know what to say about the lord, but the lady is certainly within; she is very distressed and in great anxiety about her lord, whom she has lost. She will never be happy again. But I will go to her and give her your message." Then the porter left and went straight to his lady. "My lady," he said, "outside are two knights, large in stature, the one young, the other white-haired; they certainly look as if they are very strong. I think they are from a foreign land; they want to

---

[146] 12128, 12130 **tutor, sir** *mestre, mestre*: I have translated *mestre* first as "tutor" and then as "sir." The *mestre* was the knight responsible for nurturing and educating a young nobleman. See note to line 5608.

ask you for lodging, in God"s name. They will leave very early next morning and do not want to stay longer." (12147–86)

The lady replied: "Let them come in; in God's name I will lodge them. May God let me see the day that I can see my good lord!" The porter soon returned and at once let them enter. The knights dismounted at the door of the hall, where servants ran to meet them, received their lances and their shields, and brought them upstairs. The lady greeted them, then helped them to disarm, and had the meal quickly prepared. Then they sat down to eat; the food was plentiful. When they had eaten and drunk enough, Heralt asked the lady the name of her lord. The lady replied: "I shall tell you. I had a good and true lord, called Amis de la Muntaigne; there was no one better as far as Spain. There was a seneschal in Germany, wicked and unpleasant to deal with. He was the emperor's seneschal—now may God send him misfortune! He was wicked, treacherous and deceitful. Through him we are in this trouble [*He disinherited many noble lords; he expelled my lord from the kingdom.*][147] because of Gui of Warwick, whom my lord loved so much and whom he welcomed to his castle after the death of the seneschal's uncle, the treacherous and evil Duke Otun. We fled from the country and came here, to this strange and enchanted land, called Grand Arden. [*We brought many possessions with us and established this castle here, beside the forest, in this meadow; here we have led a very hard life.*][148] A fairy knight from the forest, who was dressed in magical armour, [*did my lord much damage; he slew his men in his presence.*][149] My lord quarrelled with him and struck him often with his sword, but no weapon can hurt him, neither sharpened spear nor steel sword. (12187–236)

"One day, while pursuing the fairy knight, my lord crossed the boundaries of the forest, which are such—so enchanted and so deadly—that if a man once crosses them, he will never return. I've never heard talk of him since, nor do I believe I'll ever see him." (12237–44)

Heralt said: "So is this Amis de la Muntaigne, the good marquis? We were friends, I knew him well; he was our entire refuge. [*We were friends in Germany and often led a noble company.*][150] Alas, my fair friend Rainbrun, he loved your father Gui so much! Your father loved him and held him dear, for he often needed

---

[147] 12215–16 **He disinherited ... kingdom** *Maint riche ... chasça*: These lines are missing in E and are supplied from F.

[148] 12225–28 **We ... hard life** *Od nus ... dure vie*: These lines are missing in E and are supplied from C and F.

[149] 12231–32 **did my lord ... presence** *A mun seignur ... veant*: These lines are missing in E and are supplied from F.

[150] 12249–50 **We were friends ... noble company** *Compaignuns fumes ... riche compaigne*: These lines are missing in E and are supplied from C.

him. [*Were he now to be in need, I would certainly do what I could to help him.*"]¹⁵¹ (12245–56)

Rainbrun replied: "If it please God, tomorrow I shall enter that forest. Never in my life shall I return, my lady, until I find your lord." The lady said to him: "Fair and gentle friend, don't be too foolhardy! [*If you cross the dangerous boundaries, you will never ever return.*"]¹⁵² Then their beds were prepared and they went to sleep in them. Very early in the morning they rose and quickly armed themselves. When Rainbrun had armed, he mounted his good horse. "Heralt," he said, "you stay behind with the lady. I will keep my promise to her; I shall go and look for Count Amis." Heralt wanted to go with him, but he would not take him; then he wanted to keep him back, but Rainbrun would not agree. Heralt feared greatly for him, commending him to almighty God. (12257–80)

Heralt stayed behind, and Rainbrun went off; he asked the direction of the forest and people carefully showed it to him. He crossed the dangerous boundaries and then journeyed all that day until past noon. When he saw a mountain before him with carved doors, he raised his hand and crossed himself. He entered the mountain, and the doors closed behind him; then he thought he was in a dangerous situation. He saw nothing, for it was dark. He had travelled a good half-mile when he saw a light in front of him and thereupon felt confident. At a stretch of water, he came alongside a glade. A pleasant and large river ran there, where he rested and took his ease. He saw a spot enclosed by the river, most beautiful and thick with grass — such a beautiful place was never seen. All the herbs in the world which had any power or sweetness were there [*and spices emitting fragrance grew thickly all around.*]¹⁵³ (12281–306)

In the middle of an open area there was a palace; no prince or king ever had anything like it. The walls were of crystal, ornamented with fine enamel; the rafters were of cypress-wood, which continuously gave out a sweet scent, and the beams were of fine coral, joined together with metal. Above, in the front, was a carbuncle, which lit up the whole island. The domes on top were ornamented all about: one was of sapphire, with half of it sardonyx, the other of fine emerald. Round about was the palace enclosure, with an old Saracen wall; it was all battlemented and carved with various flowers. There was not a stone which was not of marble. In front of the gate was a tree, on which every kind of bird with its sweet song dwelt, night and day. You could hear the sound of every instrument; each had its different sound. [*I cannot describe the splendour of the palace for you at this time, for I would delay too long if I were to describe the whole building. For there*

---

¹⁵¹ 12255–56 **Were he now . . . help him** *Si ore li peusse . . . a mun poer*: These lines are missing in E and are supplied from C.

¹⁵² 12263–64 **If you cross . . . return** *Si les mercs . . . revendriez*: These lines are missing in E and are supplied from F and M, with correction.

¹⁵³ 12305–6 **and spices . . . all around** *E les especes . . . tut entur*: These lines are missing in E and are supplied from C.

is no one alive in the world, however rich or powerful, who could construct the smallest pillar for all that he could provide.][154] (12307–38)

Rainbrun was quite astonished at the marvel he saw. He did not dare to cross the water; with his sword he sounded its course, but he could not find the bottom. The speed of the water frightened him very much. He decided that he would not leave the spot; [*he wanted to know about this marvel. He crossed himself with his right hand.*][155] he entrusted himself to God in heaven and hurled himself into the the water's swift current. It surrounded him, to the top of his helmet; he would have given a whole kingdom not to be there. Before he had righted himself, he had swallowed thirty mouthfuls[156] of it. He cried for mercy to Jesus Christ. The horse he sat on was a good one, and with an effort it got out of the current and rushed vigorously onto the land, sticking its four feet into the ground. Then Rainbrun rejoiced greatly and kept praising God he had escaped this danger. (12339–62)

He went straight to the palace; at the door he dismounted and went on foot, entering the splendid palace. He gazed at its great riches; he had no idea there was so much beauty in the world. He found no living person there, and that amazed him. Then he went from one room to the next. He entered a vaulted chamber and found a knight there, all alone. He greeted him in God's name. "Knight," he said, "tell me if this palace belongs to you. If you aren't lord of this palace, tell me if he's near or far, so that I can make his acquaintance. And now I would like to ask you, whom I see lying here like this, your name, and I wish to know your situation." (12363–82)

The other replied: "My name is Amis; I was a noble lord in Germany. I was exiled by an evil-doer. Now you see me in prison here. I'm not lord of this palace—I'll tell you that truly—but a fairy knight is, the like of whom was never born of a mother. All this palace belongs to him, and this forest too. The palace possesses this power: no one within it will ever grow old. If you were to remain here for a hundred thousand years, you would never be any older." (12383–96)

Rainbrun replied: "Is this Amis, the count of such great renown? I've looked for you throughout this forest. I've endangered myself for you, and now I've found you here, I shall take you back with me to your lady and good wife—there's none so good, this side of the sea." The other replied: "Don't speak of such a thing! I am much astonished by you and by how you came here, because since the world was founded, no one has entered this island, nor could ever do so, unless the lord brought him or he entered with his permission. How can you take me away when

---

[154] 12331–38 **I cannot describe ... provide** *La grant noblesce ... aramer*: These lines are missing in E and are supplied from F.

[155] 12347–48 **he wanted to know ... right hand** *Cele merveille ... se seigna*: These lines are missing in E and are supplied from C.

[156] 12354 **mouthfuls** *perchees*: Literally, "perch-lengths"; a perch is a measure of length, five and a half yards.

you can't protect yourself? [*For if you had now taken me away, before we had travelled the distance of a single mile*[157] *from this palace, we would have been killed in great agony.*][158] For the lord of this palace would have caught up with us at once. I believe there's no one so clever in the world, for if he were a thousand leagues from here, before we had left the palace he would have seen all our actions; he would oppose us very fiercely and cut our heads off." (12397–426)

Rainbrun replied: "Don't be afraid; don't give up because of that! Get up, come away! For, by almighty God, if there were anyone in the world so bold as to want to detain us here, I'd give him a blow with my steel sword, such that I'd make his head fly from his body." And the other replied: "Don't do that—such a blow wouldn't be worth a penny! You shouldn't damage your own weapons on any account, but take that steel sword in there, hanging on a pillar. If you want to beat him, you will do so with that sword." (12427–42)

Rainbrun seized the sword, drew it from its scabbard, and looked at it: the room was lit up in all directions by its brilliance, and he put it back. Next he went to Count Amis and pulled him up by his hand. Then they left that place, and both mounted Rainbrun's horse. Hardly had they gone any distance than they looked to one side and saw a mounted knight approaching, armed to the teeth. He came spurring up at a great rate. "Knight," he said, "go no further! How are you so bold as to cross this river, enter my palace, and take away my prisoner? No man born ever did that unless he had my permission. You will both stay here and never leave prison, or else you'll quickly lose your heads. I challenge you now to defend yourselves!" (12443–66)

Count Amis dismounted and at once moved away. Rainbrun very quickly proceeded to attack the knight with the good sword he carried. They gave each other powerful blows with their spears, knocking each other off the horses, far into the meadows. Then they drew their sharp swords and struck great blows on their pointed helmets; [*they struck each other very hard; they cut through hauberks of fine-linked mail and helmets and shields, with their good swords of sharpened steel*].[159] You never heard of a harsher battle. Rainbrun began to recall brave Gui, his father. He raised his sword very high and gave the knight a blow on top which laid him low on the ground. He seized him by the nose-piece and fiercely dragged him towards him. He would certainly have cut off his head, when the knight begged him for mercy. "My lord Rainbrun, mercy in God's name! Truly, you are Gui's son, son of the best knight who ever mounted a horse. If you don't kill me, I promise I shall free all the people I have captured in this forest; I shall restore them, fully at liberty, to you. I shall give you plenty of gold and silver and lead

---

[157] 12417 **a single mile** *un sul arpent*: see note to line 3620.

[158] 12415–18 **For if... great agony** *Car si... grant turment*: These lines are missing in E and are supplied from C.

[159] 12475–78 **they struck... sharpened steel** *Trop durement... d'ascer moluz*: These lines are missing in E and are supplied from C.

you out of this forest." Rainbrun replied: "Indeed not: I don't care about your possessions. But the prisoners should be freed." Then promises were made, and they went straight back to the palace. [*The fairy knight then freed the prisoners and entirely renounced any claim to them. Next he saw them across the river and had them escorted out of the forest.*]¹⁶⁰ Then he returned. (12467–508)

Rainbrun was very happy that he had freed Count Amis. They went straight to the castle where Rainbrun had left Heralt and were received there with great joy. When the lady saw her lord, she rejoiced greatly, often praising Jesus Christ, since she saw her husband in good health; she never expected to see him again. Heralt did likewise; he gave much praise to almighty God that Rainbrun had escaped from the great enchanted forest. (12509–22)

When Heralt saw Count Amis, the brave, valiant, and bold man, they both were delighted from the moment they caught sight of each other. Then Heralt told him how he had been in prison because of the son of his lord Gui, and how he had suffered pain and grief, and how it was the very same son of Gui, Rainbrun, who had saved him. And he told him all about his life and how Gui had gone into exile. There was much joy amongst them and everyone in the castle was glad. (12525–36)

A traveller then appeared, giving the news to Count Amis that Duke Berard had been slain, and that a pilgrim had killed him, in defence of Count Terri, but he did not know who the pilgrim was; the emperor had sent him to look for Amis, so that the count could receive his land. He had sought him for over a year in many foreign lands; they did not know if he was alive or dead. When Count Amis heard this, he had never been so glad of any news, and he often thanked God [*that he was avenged on Duke Berard, through whom he had been disinherited. Then he wept for joy and sorrow that God had acted for them in this way.*]¹⁶¹ Now their joy increased because of the news which had arrived. (12537–56)

Heralt and Rainbrun took their leave on the third day of their stay, and Count Amis made ready to go; he did not want to stay there any longer. He wanted to take Heralt and Rainbrun with him and give them half his land, but they were not interested in that, and took their leave of him. Then Count Amis went off, straight to his land in Germany. He was welcomed by the emperor, who gave him back all his land; he was received there with great joy and was happier than he had ever been. (12557–70)

Heralt and Rainbrun took their leave and went straight towards their country. They travelled so much in their journey, and crossed foreign lands, that they came to Burgundy, where Heralt had formerly been well known. They saw the

---

¹⁶⁰ 12504–7 **The fairy knight ... out of the forest** *Les prisons ... conveé*: These lines are missing in E and are supplied from F.

¹⁶¹ 12551–54 **that he was avenged ... in this way** *Ke del duc Berard ... eus ovré*: These lines are missing in E and are supplied from C.

land ravaged and laid waste. Heralt asked a man who it was who had so ravaged this land, and he at once told him that the brave and valiant Duke Milun, who was so arrogant and proud, had made war on one of his counts, because he was angry with him. Not a single foot of land was left to the count except a castle he had fortified on a high rock; inside it he was defending himself. "But a mercenary has joined him, a knight from a foreign land; you never heard tell of such a one, who is so renowned for feats of arms. He's very young, I think; he's not yet twenty. [*He's already been with him a year, and has used his time to very good purpose: three times he's defeated the duke and killed and destroyed his men. He's already reconquered all the castles which the count lost before the mercenary joined him, and he has all this land in his control.*]¹⁶² Esteem for the count has risen because of him, and the duke has been much diminished. (12571–603)

"At this outpost, on this hill, a hundred men have lost their lives. Travellers pass along there—knights, burgesses and merchants. There you'll see the mercenary, very well armed on his horse. No knight, if he has hauberk or horse, can ever pass by without having to leave one of them, or else lose his head without delay. If a merchant passes or a burgess, he will lose his best possessions. [*If he defends himself, then he's dead, ruined, and bodily maltreated. Turn back quickly and leave this land,*]¹⁶³ for if you pass this outpost, you will lose your heads or your equipment." (12605–22)

"God help us!" said Rainbrun. "Now I've found my match. If he asks for anything of ours, I can very easily show him that we have nothing of his, nor will we give him anything of ours. And if we can't defend what is ours, it is right we should lose it." (12623–30)

Then they left that place and had not travelled on the road for long when they saw, standing at the outpost, an armed knight on his horse. "My lord Heralt," said Rainbrun, "now I see the knight at the outpost; he is getting ready to strike us. I have a great desire to fight with him; if you agree, I shall go and strike him." Heralt replied: "Then go." (12631–40)

Rainbrun went there very speedily, and the other came down from the outpost. Each was arrogant and proud and neither designed to speak to the other. They hit each other's shields with great blows and were knocked down to the ground. They jumped to their feet and drew their swords, gripping their shields like brave men; they struck powerful blows at the bright helmets and at the strong quartered shields. They fought very fiercely and the blood streamed down thick and fast. Heralt watched the battle and often prayed to God that He

---

   ¹⁶² 12595–602 **He's already ... in his control** *Un an ... tut cest pais*: These lines are missing in E and are supplied from F.
   ¹⁶³ 12617–20 **If he defends ... leave this land** *S'il se defent ... vus en alez*: These lines are missing in E and are supplied from F.

might defend Rainbrun from calamity, for he was very fearful of the battle. In his heart he kept thinking he had never seen a fiercer battle. (12641–58)

"Sir knight," said Rainbrun, "now listen to what I have to say. You are very brave and bold; tell me now in what land you were born and what your name is. I never yet found an equal who could stand my blows, so I want to advise you now to surrender to me. I truly pledge you my word that we shall be companions and friends. You shall come with me to my country; I will give you castles and fiefs, boroughs and towns and fine cities." (12659–72)

"Sir knight," replied the other, "I shall not, by Him who made the world. You'll never discover by exhorting me who I am or what I'm called; rather, I intend to cut off your head, no matter how much you may talk. Where I've been, at this outpost, I've cut the head off many a man; to my mind, I've never found a knight there whom I rated so highly. I am saying this because I know for sure I will cut your head off.[164] And that old man standing over there—I don't know if he begot you; I'm sure he hasn't much love for you since he's sent you to me. When I've cut off your head, I'll seize him by his white whiskers and shake him with such violence that I'll make all his teeth chatter." When Rainbrun heard that the knight valued them so little, he fiercely gripped his shield, raised his steel sword high, and struck him such a blow on the helmet that he knocked off one of its quarters. The knight was stunned by the great blow, so that he hit the ground with his two hands. (12673–700)

"My friend," said Rainbrun, "no more of that: it's stupid to make many threats. In my country, it's not the custom; we are taught to strike well." The other considered himself greatly derided; he quickly jumped to his feet and fiercely attacked Rainbrun, intending to strike him on the top of the helmet. But Rainbrun received the blow on his shield and it was split all the way to its boss. The two warriors were strong and brave; the valleys rang with their blows. The battle between them was most deadly; you never heard of a fiercer under heaven. It could not last for long without one having to harm the other. Heralt watched the battle and saw that each attacked the other; he could not assess who was the better. He began to weep for the great loss which would ensue if it turned out badly for either of them. (12701–22)

Then he stepped in between them. "Sir knight," he said, "in God's name, withdraw a little and now talk to me. Leave off this battle and yield to this knight. He is a very noble and powerful man, rich with fine lands; he will give you them in abundance, he will not stay in them. Now if you want to believe me, you will put yourself at his mercy." And the other quickly answered him: "Then tell me, white-haired sir, as the Mother of Jesus may help you, what is your name

---

[164] 12683–4 **I am saying this ... cut your head off** *Nel di ... la teste te trencharai*: Literally: "I am not saying this because I don't know for sure I will cut your head off." I have replaced the double negative with a positive.

and who are you? For, once you talked to me, such fear and such dismay at your proud face seized me that all my flesh shuddered; I haven't been so afraid of anything from the day I was born. If you've come from the Devil, a thought which frightened me, then I adjure you in God's name to tell me the truth about who you are and where you come from, and if you wish me evil or good, about which I have been so fearful, dismayed, and terrified." (12723–52)

Heralt replied: "Don't talk about that; you'll never discover it from me. Rather, tell me about yourself—who you are and where you were born. Then you can hear about me, who I am whom you see here and who that knight is, standing over there, who gave you the great blows which broke your helmet and wounded your body in several places. I see your strong hauberk is cut to pieces, and I see your face is covered with blood. I shall tell you the truth about him if you do what I have told you." The other replied: "I shall do so, but not out of fear of him, rather because I want to know why I'm so terrified. (12753–70)

"I was born in the kingdom of England in a city, Wallingford. I was son of a renowned lord, called Heralt of Arderne. When he left the kingdom to look for his liege-lord's son, taken away by foreign merchants, I was only just over seven. He sent me to the count of Leicester who looked after me most honourably, for I was his daughter's son; I had many good things there. When I was a fully grown young man, strong and active and with great ability, if I maltreated anyone or said anything amiss, I would soon hear the same reproach, that I was such a coward—why didn't I go looking for my father, far off in a foreign land [*where he was either dead or captured or probably in prison.*]¹⁶⁵ I often heard this reproach. One day I decided that on no account would I fail to go and look for my father. I went to Wallingford, where I found my father's armour—his good hauberk and his horse, his shield and his steel sword. Then I equipped myself and never spoke of it to anyone. (12771–802)

"I then left the country and looked for my father in many lands; [*in Lombardy and in Spain, in Saxony and in Germany*]¹⁶⁶ I never heard of any war where I did not go to seek my father. Then I returned to this land and found a count here harassed by war: Duke Milun had ruined him, except for one castle where he was holding out. He had lost all his land so that the wretched man did not know what to do. [*I came to him in his hour of need and helped him conclude his war satisfactorily.*]¹⁶⁷ When I first came to him, I believe he had thirty knights; now he has more than three hundred—men at arms, archers, other people. I have won his castles for him and killed and destroyed his enemies. [*I have since been at*

---

¹⁶⁵ 12791–92 **where . . . in prison** *U . . . en prisun mis*: These lines are missing in E and are supplied from C.

¹⁶⁶ 12805–6 **in Lombardy . . . in Germany** *En Lumbardie . . . en Alemaigne*: These lines are missing in E and are supplied from C.

¹⁶⁷ 12815–16 **I came . . . satisfactorily** *A lui vinc . . . ben finer:* These lines are missing in E and are supplied from C.

this outpost, where people pass from other kingdoms.]¹⁶⁸ I never yet found a man there whom I didn't ask about Heralt, but no one could tell me in what land he was [*for which reason I often became angry and cut the head off many men.*"]¹⁶⁹ (12803–30)

Heralt listened to him and certainly paid attention; his eyes filled with fond tears. "Now tell me, noble knight, what are you called?" And the other replied: "My name is Aselac, son of the brave lord Heralt. Now you have heard, in truth, where I was born, and what my name is; as we agreed, you should now say who you are, who have so frightened me." (12831–40)

Heralt looked at him and for a long time could not utter a word. "Oh Aselac, fair and sweet friend, I am your father, you are my son. I am Heralt, whom you seek; thanks be to God, you have found me. I have endured great suffering looking for my liege lord's son; see him there, that's Rainbrun, brave Gui's son, with whom you've been fighting. You are both possessed of great might. Go quickly and fall at his feet and with a good grace ask him for forgiveness; give your sword up to him immediately and put yourself entirely at his mercy." (12841–56)

When Aselac heard that it was his father who spoke to him, and that it was Rainbrun, Gui's son, whom he had earlier fought, Lord! how he then rejoiced. He quickly fell to the ground on his knees. "Rainbrun," he said, "mercy, in God's name." Then he gave him his steel sword. "Forgive this insolence," he said. "Here, my lord, I now do you homage, as to my rightful lord, for I am son to Heralt the warrior." (12857–68)

When Rainbrun heard that this was Heralt's son, with his hand he raised him up and kissed him with great affection. Then Aselac kissed his father. Now their joy was much increased. Aselac took them to the castle of the count, his liege lord, and he told the count everything—how he had found his father, and his lord's son, who was very valiant; there was no better knight under heaven. The count was very happy and paid them much honour; he freely gave them all he possessed—gold and silver, lands and fiefs. (12869–84)

When they had stayed there as long as it suited them, they took leave of the count. They wanted to go to their land, and from now on they would not stop. They went straight to the sea, and after they had come there, they made a speedy crossing and went straight to London, where they found King Athelstan. The king went out to meet them, and with him the best people in the city. He greatly honoured them and gave them many of his possessions; he gave Rainbrun his county and greatly increased his fief. They stayed there three days and on the fourth took their leave, going to the city of Warwick. The people of the region were delighted. Rainbrun received fealty from his vassals and was much loved by

---

¹⁶⁸ 12823–24 **I have since . . . from other kingdoms** *Sur ceste engarde . . . d'altre regné*: These lines are missing in E and are supplied from C.

¹⁶⁹ 12829–30 **for which reason . . . many men** *Par quei . . . trenchai*: These lines are missing in E and are supplied from C.

them. Heralt went off to Wallingford, to his fine and strong castle. He wanted to remain there with his wife, that good woman, from then on, for, because of his loyalty, his body had undergone much hardship in many lands. (12885–912)

I want to bring this story to an end; after this I do not want to relate more. Whoever learns it well and wants to understand it can find a fine model in it — of loving prowess and maintaining loyalty, of following every good thing and forsaking every bad one, and scorning pride and wealth. What the book[170] tells us of Gui is that the essence of his worth was to forsake everything for his Creator. And may He, who is one God in holy Trinity, let us, through His compassion, serve Him on earth so that we may come to Him in glory. Amen. (12913–26)

---

[170] 12920 **book** *escrit*: Literally, "writing."

Bibliography

Boeve de Haumtone

Edition

Der Anglonormannische Boeve de Haumtone, ed. Albert Stimming. Halle: Bibliotheca Normannica, 1899.

Discussions in surveys of Anglo-Norman Romance

Crane, Susan. *Insular Romance*. Berkeley: University of California Press, 1986.
Field, Rosalind. "Romance in England, 1066–1400." In *The Cambridge History of Medieval English Literature*, ed. David Wallace, 152–76. Cambridge: Cambridge University Press, 1999.
Legge, M. Dominica. *Anglo-Norman Literature and Its Background*. Oxford: Clarendon Press, 1963.
Weiss, Judith. "Insular Beginnings: Anglo-Norman Romance." In *A Companion to Romance: From Classical to Contemporary*, ed. Corinne Saunders, 26–44. Oxford: Blackwell, 2004.

Articles or chapters on or connected with Boeve

Brantley, Jessica. "Images of the Vernacular in the Taymouth Hours." *English Manuscript Studies 1100–1700* 10 (2002): 83–113.
Djordjevic, Ivana. "Versification and Translation in *Sir Beues of Hampton*." *Medium Aevum* 74 (2005): 41–59.
Field, Rosalind. "The King over the Water: Exile-and-Return Revisited." In *Cultural Encounters in the Romance of Medieval England*, ed. Corinne Saunders, 41–53. Cambridge: D.S. Brewer, 2005.
Galent-Fasseur, Valérie. "Un médiateur de la Providence: le personnage de Sabaoth dans la version anglo-normande et la version en prose de *Beuve de Hantone*." *Littérales* 22 (1998): 25–38.

———. "La tentation sarrasine de Beuve de Hantone." In *La chrétienté au peril sarrasin*, 27–39. Sénéfiance 46. Aix-en-Provence: CUERMA, 2000.
Loomis, Laura H. "Jacques de Vitry and *Boeve de Haumtone*." *Modern Language Notes* 34 (1919): 408–11.
Martin, Jean-Pierre. "*Beuve de Hantone* entre roman et chanson de geste." *Littérales* 31 (2003): 97–112.
Watkin, Morgan. "Albert Stimming's *Welsche Fassung* in the *Anglonormannische Boeve de Haumtone*: An Examination of a Critique." In *Studies in French Language and Medieval Literature presented to Professor Mildred K. Pope*, 371–79. Manchester: Manchester University Press, 1939.
Weiss, Judith. "The Date of the Anglo-Norman *Boeve de Haumtone*." *Medium Aevum* 55 (1986): 237–41.
———. "The Wooing Woman in Anglo-Norman Romance." In *Romance in Medieval England*, ed. Maldwyn Mills, Jennifer Fellows, and Carol Meale, 149–61. Cambridge: D.S. Brewer, 1991.
———. "The Power and the Weakness of Women in Anglo-Norman Romance." In *Women and Literature in Britain 1150–1500*, ed. Carol Meale, 7–23. Cambridge: D.S. Brewer, 1993.
———. "The Anglo-Norman *Boeve de Haumtone*: A Fragment of a New Manuscript." *Modern Language Review* 95 (2000): 305–10.
———. "*Mestre* and Son: The Role of Sabaoth and Terri in *Boeve de Haumtone*," in *Sir Bevis of Hampton in Literary Tradition: The Metamorphoses of a Romance Hero*, ed. Jennifer Fellows and Ivana Djordjevic (forthcoming).
———. "The Courteous Warrior: Epic, Romance and Comedy in *Boeve de Haumtone*," in *Boundaries in Medieval Romance*, ed. Neil Cartlidge (forthcoming).
Wolf-Bonvin, Romaine. "Escopart, le géant dépérissant de *Beuve de Hantone*." In *La chrétienté au péril sarrasin*, 249–65. Sénéfiance 46. Aix-en-Provence: CUERMA, 2000.

Other Works Cited

Ashe, Laura. " 'Exile-and-return' and English Law: The Anglo-Saxon Inheritance of Insular Romance." *Literature Compass* 3 (2006) www.literature-compass.com.
Bevers Saga, ed. Christopher Sanders. Reykjavík: Stofnun Árna Magnússonar Á Íslandi, 2001.
Fierabras: chanson de geste du XIIe siècle, ed. Marc Le Person. Classiques Français du Moyen Age. Paris: Champion, 2003.
Kyng Alisaunder, ed. G.V. Smithers. EETS o.s. 227, 237. London: Oxford University Press, 1957, repr. 1969.
Maugis d'Aigremont: Chanson de Geste, ed. Philippe Vernay. Lausanne: Francke Berne, 1980.

Raynaud de Lage, G. "L'Inspiration de la prière 'Du plus Grand Péril'." *Romania* 93 (1972): 568–70.
Schulze-Busacker, Elisabeth. *Proverbes et expressions proverbiales dans la littérature narrative du Moyen Âge français*. Paris: Champion, 1985.
Short, Ian. "*Tam Angli quam Franci*: Self-definition in Anglo-Norman England." *Anglo-Norman Studies* 18 (1996): 153–75.

Gui de Warewic

While articles or chapters devoted to the Anglo-Norman *Gui* are few, there has been a large amount of discussion and analysis of the Middle English *Guy of Warwick*. I have thus been selective in listing works about *Guy*, since many often barely acknowledge, let alone know, *Gui*.

Edition

Gui de Warewic: Roman du XIIIe Siècle, ed. Alfred Ewert. 2 vols. Paris: Champion, 1933.

Discussions in surveys of Anglo-Norman Romance:

Crane, Susan. *Insular Romance*. Berkeley: University of California Press, 1986.
Field, Rosalind. "Romance in England, 1066–1400." In *The Cambridge History of Medieval English Literature*, ed. David Wallace, 152–76. Cambridge: Cambridge University Press, 1999.
Gaullier-Bougassas, Catherine. "Origines d'un lignage et écriture romanesque: les romans lignagers anglo-normands." In *Seuils de l'oeuvre dans le texte médiéval*, ed. E. Baumgartner and Laurence Harf-Lancner, 2:19–35. 2 vols. Paris: Presse Sorbonne Nouvelle, 2002.
Legge, M. Dominica. *Anglo-Norman Literature and its Background*. Oxford: Clarendon Press, 1963.
Weiss, Judith. "Insular Beginnings: Anglo-Norman Romance." In *A Companion to Romance: From Classical to Contemporary*, ed. Corinne Saunders, 26–44. Oxford: Blackwell, 2004.

Articles and chapters on or connected with Gui:

Calin, William. "*Gui de Warewic* and the Nature of Late Anglo-Norman Romance." *Fifteenth Century Studies* 17 (1990): 23–32.
Crane, Susan. "Anglo-Norman Romances of English Heroes: 'Ancestral Romance'?" *Romance Philology* 35 (1981–1982): 601–8.

Dannenbaum, Susan Crane. "*Guy of Warwick* and the Question of Exemplary Romance." *Genre* 17 (1984): 351–74.
Herbert, J.-A. "An Early Manuscript of *Gui de Warwick*." *Romania* 35 (1906): 68–81.
Legge, M. Dominica. "La Date des écrits de Frère Angier." *Romania* 79 (1958): 512–14.
Mason, Emma. "Legends of the Beauchamps' Ancestors: The Use of Baronial Propaganda in Medieval England." *Journal of Medieval History* 10 (1984): 25–40.
Rothwell, W. "New Fragments of a *Gui de Warewic* Manuscript." *French Studies* 13 (1959): 52.
Short, Ian. "*Gui de Warewic*." In *Enzyklopädie des Märchens*, ed. Rolf Willem Brednich, 6:289–92. Berlin: Walter de Gruyter, 1989.
Turville-Petre, Thorlac. *Image and Text: Medieval Manuscripts at the University of Nottingham*. Nottingham: The University of Nottingham, 1996.
Wathelet-Willem, Jeanne. *Recherches sur La Chanson de Guillaume*. 2 vols. Paris: Belles Lettres, 1975.
Weiss, Judith. "Emperors and Antichrists: Reflections of Empire in Insular Narrative." In *The Matter of Identity in Medieval Romance*, ed. Phillipa Hardman, 87–102. Cambridge: D.S. Brewer, 2002.
———, "Gui de Warewic at Home and Abroad." In *Guy of Warwick: Icon and Ancestor*, ed. Alison Wiggins and Rosalind Field, 1–11. Woodbridge: Boydell and Brewer, 2007.

Selected Books, Chapters and Articles discussing the Guy *story, predominantly the one in Middle English:*

Barron, W.R.J. *English Medieval Romance*. London: Longman, 1987.
Cartlidge, Neil. *Medieval Marriage: Literary Approaches, 1100–1300*. Cambridge: D.S. Brewer, 1997.
Cooper, Helen. *The English Romance in Time: Transforming Motifs from Geoffrey of Monmouth to the Death of Shakespeare*. Oxford: Oxford University Press, 2004.
Fewster, Carol. *Traditionality and Genre in Middle English Romance*. Cambridge: D.S. Brewer, 1987.
Hanna, Ralph. *London Literature 1300–1380*. Cambridge: Cambridge University Press, 2005.
Hibbard, Laura A. *Medieval Romance in England*. New York: 1924; rev. 1963.
Hopkins, Andrea. *The Sinful Knights: A Study of Middle English Penitential Romance*. Oxford: Clarendon Press, 1990.
Klausner, David. "Didacticism and Drama in *Guy of Warwick*." *Medievalia et Humanistica* 6 (1975): 103–19.

Mehl, Dieter. *The Middle English Romances of the Thirteenth and Fourteenth Centuries*. London: Routledge and Kegan Paul, 1969.
Mills, Maldwyn. "Structure and Meaning in *Guy of Warwick*." In *From Medieval to Medievalism*, ed. John Simons, 54–68. Basingstoke and London: Macmillan, 1992.
Price, Paul. "Confessions of a Godless Killer: *Guy of Warwick* and Comprehensive Entertainment." In *Medieval Insular Romance: Translation and Innovation*, ed. Judith Weiss, Jennifer Fellows, and Morgan Dickson, 93–110. Cambridge: D.S. Brewer, 2000.
Ramsey, Lee C. *Chivalric Romances*. Bloomington: Indiana University Press, 1983.
Richmond, Velma Bourgeois. *The Legend of Guy of Warwick*. New York and London: Garland Publishing, 1996.
Wiggins, Alison and Rosalind Field. *Guy of Warwick: Icon and Ancestor*, Woodbridge: Boydell and Brewer, 2007.
Wilcox, Rebecca. "Romancing the East: Greeks and Saracens in *Guy of Warwick*." In *Pulp Fictions of Medieval England*, ed. Nicola McDonald, 217–40. Manchester and New York: Manchester University Press, 2004.

Background

Busby, Keith. *Codex and Context: Reading Old French Verse Narrative in Manuscripts*. 2 vols. Amsterdam and New York: Rodopi, 2002.
Coss, Peter. *Lordship, Knighthood and Locality*. Cambridge: Cambridge University Press, 1991.
Gaimar, Geffrei. *L'Estoire des Engleis*, ed. Alexander Bell. Oxford: ANTS, Blackwell, 1960.
Gravett, Christopher. *Knights at Tournament*. London: Osprey Publishing. 1988.
———. *Norman Knight 950–1204*. London: Osprey Publishing, 1993.
Peirce, Ian. "The Knight, His Arms and Armour c.1150–1250." *Anglo-Norman Studies* 15 (1992): 25–74.
Le Roman de Waldef, ed. A.J. Holden. Cologny-Geneva: Fondation Martin Bodmer, 1984.
Thomas, Hugh. *The English and the Normans: Ethnic Hostility, Assimilation and Identity, 1066-c.1220*. Oxford: Oxford University Press, 2003.
Walpole, Ronald L. *The Old French Johannes Translation of the Pseudo-Turpin*, 2 vols. Berkeley, Los Angeles, London: University of California Press, 1976.

Index of Personal and Place Names in *Boeve de Haumtone*

The numbers given below refer to lines in the Anglo-Norman text.

ABILENT, *One of Baligant's castles*, 1501, 1506, 1509, 1523, 1533, 3402
ABREFORD, *Hermin's capital city*, 2782, 3066, 3129, 3182, 3191, 3265, 3314, 3421, 3447, 3511, 3540, 3556, 3652
AMUSTRAI, *Yvori's uncle*, 1875, 1876, 1880, 1883, 1889
APOLLO, *A Saracen god*, 3279, 3430, 3585
ARABIA, 3223, 3243
ARABS, 3485
ARAGON, *A region of Spain*, 3234
ARMIGER, *An enemy lord besieging Civile*, 2841
ARUNDEL, *Boeve's horse*, 629, 1451, 1688, 1692, 1741, 1798, 1812, 1867, 1868, 2144, 2309, 2312, 2480, 2491, 2507, 2522, 2549, 2601, 2829, 2921, 2924, 3135, 3137, 3193, 3234, 3244, 3424, 3459, 3464, 3471, 3477, 3482, 3486, 3500, 3598; *castle Boeve intends to build*, 2522, 2549
BABYLON, 3161, 3166
BALIGANT, *Brother of Yvori*, 1502
BARATRON, *A Saracen god*, 3280
BARBARY, *A country*, 1521
BEATRICE, *Boeve's daughter*, 3062
BEELZEBUB, *A Saracen god*, 3606
BETHLEHEM, 1244
BOEVE, *Hero of the poem:* (MS B) BOEFS from 3 passim until 1267; BOVOUN 637, 680, 688; (MS D) BOUN 916, 926, 3736; BOVES 1360, 2602, 2828, 3180; *name otherwise indicated by capital letter. See* Introduction, Note 4.

BOEVE, *Terri's son*, 3061, 3198, 3335, 3491, 3503, 3520, 3616
BONEFEY, *Josiane's squire*, 1435, 1436, 1438, 1496, 1499, 1541, 1542, 1560, 1567, 1577, 1608, 1618, 1627, 1629, 1635, 1646, 1651, 1654, 1656, 1661, 1681, 1697
BRADMUND, *King of Damascus*, (MS B), 496, 501, 503, 514, 567, 588, 598, 599, 605, 610, 619, 620, 621, 628, 631, 635, 637, 642, 647, 650, 654, 657, 682, 776, 794, 796, 800, 805, 808, 857, 871, 885, 888, 891, 894, 901, 903, 916, 928, 936, 937, 1036, 1121, 1146, 1147, 1149, 1157, 1161, 1166, 1170, 1176, 1181, 1182, 1184, 1186, 1195, 1202, 1210, 1225
BRANDON (MS D) 916, 928, 936, 937, 1037, 1195, 1202, 1210, 1225, 1304, 1306, 1351, 1411, 3613
BRALU, *Son of Brandon*, 3612
BRISE, *An English lord*, 2584
BRISTOL, 2584
CARTHAGE, *An African city*, 1377, 1520
CHRIST, 157, 253, 1252, 1471, 1722, 1861, 2439
CIVILE, *A city, possibly Seville*, 2818, 2910, 2913, 2934, 2968, 3011, 3013, 3058, 3185, 3377, 3523, 3527, 3542, 3618
CLARIS OF LEICESTER, *An English lord*, 2586
COLOGNE, 1895, 2052, 2098, 2386, 2648, 3727, 3797, 3800
CORDES, *A pagan city*, 3629

DAMASCUS, 497, 804, 866, 1134, 1307, 1352, 3566, 3613, 3655, 3658, 3669
DOCTRIX, *A Duke who attacks Civile*, 2909, 2947
DOUN, *Emperor of Germany*, 2008, 2282, 2293, 2306, 2356, 2365, 2366, 2369, 2377, 2434
DRY TREE, 1521
DYGON, *A French castle*, 2012
EDGAR, *King of England*, 2623, 3755, 3770, 3776
EGYPT, 362, 1365
ENEBORC, *Sabaoth's wife*, 2737
ENGLAND, 105, 386, 838, 978, 1402, 1466, 1484, 1557, 1574, 1712, 1904, 1981, 1996, 2458, 2532, 2667, 3719, 3724, 3739
ENGLISH, 331
ESCLAVIE, *The country of the Slavs*, 1520; perhaps the same as ESCLAVONIE
ESCLAVONIE, 3259; *Perhaps the same country as* ESCLAVIE
ESCOPART, *A Saracen giant*, 1781, 1784, 1799, 1801, 1804, 1805, 1815, 1822, 1831, 1834, 1840, 1843, 1850, 1852, 1855, 1860, 1865, 1868, 1874, 1881, 1882, 1885, 1916, 1931, 1956, 1962, 1965, 1969, 1978, 1989, 2052, 2062, 2064, 2066, 2067, 2070, 2074, 2076, 2079, 2081, 2083, 2088, 2092, 2153, 2155, 2159, 2167, 2171, 2174, 2179, 2183, 2267, 2271, 2289, 2340, 2343, 2346, 2348, 2646. *Called 'the' Escopart, showing he is a member of a race.*
FABUR, *Yvori's steward*, 3302, 3304, 3307, 3476, 3492, 3495
FAMER, *A city*, 1377
FAUSERON, *A Saracen warrior*, 3235
FAVON, *A Saracen warrior*, 3222, 3227
FRANCE, 2012
FRENCH, 3158, 3614, 3622, 3628
FUREZ, *A lord at Hermin's court*, 3089
GARCIE, *A Saracen king*, 1535, 1537, 1558, 1565, 1589, 1596, 1610, 1631
GAUTER, *See* Graunder
GEBITUS, *A sorcerer*, 3414
GERMANY, 25, 50, 51, 52, 72, 2247

GERNER, *A citizen of Civile*, 2819
GERRAUD, *Boeve's false name*, 2014, 2015, 2018, 2025, 2213
GILLES, *Saint; pilgrimage town*, 2749, 2736, 2747, 3382
GIRÉ, *An English archbishop*, 2464
GLOS OF GLOUCESTER, *An English lord*, 2585
GLOUCESTER, 2585
GOCELYN, *A lord at Hermin's court*, 3089
GRAUNDER, *Bradmund's nephew*, (MS B) 1148, 1149, 1151, 1154, 1178, 1181, 1213, 1226; GAUTER (MS D) 1213
GRECIAN, 328
GUI, *Baptismal name of the Escopart*, 1967, 2648, 2649
GUI, *Boeve's father*, 11, 13, 28, 34, 161, 190, 196, 207, 212, 387, 1905, 2215, 2423, 2454
GUI, *Eldest son of Boeve*, 2395, 2811, 3008, 3015, 3108, 3114, 3124, 3205, 3268, 3324, 3333, 3337, 3342, 3483, 3487, 3510, 3608, 3612, 3635, 3640, 3649, 3825, 3827, 3834, 3843
HAMTONE, HAUMTONE, *Southampton* (MS B) 3, 10, 80, 109, 177, 192, 208, 387, 626, 779, 839, 954, 1036, 1199, 1204, 1209; HAMPTONE, HAMPTON (MS D) 954, 1036, 1199, 1204, 1209, 1361, 1389, 1414, 1439, 1454, 1674, 1873, 1893, 1898, 2007, 2047, 2094, 2198, 2209, 2232, 2255, 2262, 2399, 2422, 2454, 2528, 2628, 2811, 2915, 3384, 3409, 3619, 3729, 3752, 3794, 3848
HERMIN, HERMINE, *King of Egypt, father of Josiane*, 367, 395, 488, 495, 499, 502, 503, 510, 537, 561, 607, 623, 643, 655, 659, 777, 812, 910, 957, 972, 995, 996, 1350, 3047, 3068, 3073, 3120, 3122, 3151, 3158, 3174, 3183, 3255, 3320, 3322, 3344, 3529, 3744
JERUSALEM, 1346
JESUS, 36, 157, 253, 273, 277, 402, 783, 1252, 1471, 1722, 1861, 2206, 2300, 2439

JEWS, 2414
JOSIANE, JOSIAN, *Boeve's beloved and wife*, 450, 516, 612, 663, 688, 721, 722, 733, 741, 743, 755, 911, 972, 997, 1009, 1012, 1016, 1364, 1371, 1375, 1384, 1388, 1395, 1396, 1403, 1419, 1423, 1436, 1450, 1460, 1480, 1495, 1538, 1568, 1590, 1598, 1603, 1635, 1638, 1685, 1696, 1701, 1821, 1835, 1842, 1859, 1873, 1955, 1983, 2051, 2060, 2082, 2096, 2100, 2104, 2105, 2111, 2177, 2183, 2385, 2506, 2629, 2636, 2643, 2689, 2709, 2721, 2741, 2752, 2784, 2883, 2962, 2994, 3026, 3029, 3064, 3092, 3094, 3096, 3099, 3125, 3159, 3176, 3203, 3256, 3395, 3480, 3547, 3652, 3696
JUDAS, *Judas the betrayer of Christ*, 2413
JUDAS, *One of Yvori's warriors*, 3561
KARFU, *Boeve's messenger*, 2196, 2211, 2223, 2230, 2236
LANCELIN, *One of the besiegers of Civile*, 2928
LARGE, *A city*, 2652
LAURENCE, *Saint*, 3405, 3842
LEICESTER, 2586
LONDON, 2404, 2524, 3736, 3741, 3750, 3763, 3774
LUCIFER, 2090
MAHOMET, *A Saracen god*, 381, 383, 395, 405, 407, 453, 466, 483, 500, 504, 510, 517, 526, 558, 571, 625, 639, 647, 689, 705, 746, 747, 767, 786, 801, 878, 881, 887, 888, 1047,1125, 1158, 1164, 1166, 1288, 1530, 1793, 1878, 1883, 1913, 2665, 3280, 3311, 3419, 3430, 3460, 3585, 3663
MARTIN, *Saint*, 2677
MARY, *Saint*, 402, 2135, 2623, 2707, 3357
MASEBRÉ, *One of Yvori's lords*, 3561
MILES, *A count in Cologne*, 2060, 2063, 2075, 2078, 2080, 2099, 2108, 2110, 2112, 2114, 2126
MILES, *Boeve's second son*, 2396, 3016, 3112, 3124, 3205, 3326, 3333, 3343, 3490, 3502, 3610, 3616, 3771, 3776, 3778, 3779, 3784

MONBRANT, *Yvori's kingdom* (MS D), 993, 1007, 1367, 1374, 1376, 1378, 1380, 1381, 1791, 2658, 2665, 3126, 3146, 3148, 3154, 3170, 3180, 3201, 3208, 3215, 3219, 3263, 3275, 3301, 3411, 3427, 3470, 3481, 3516, 3577, 3624, 3626, 3634, 3650, 3689, 3715, 3718, 3807, 3843; MUNBRAUNT, MUNBRAUNC (MS B) 993, 1007, 1010
MUNDOIE, *See* OUBE
MORANT, *Bishop; later archbishop of Monbrant*, 3666, 3681, 3727, 3804
MORGELEY, *Boeve's sword* (MS D) 1615, 1726, 2170, 2336, 2944, 3134, 3249, 3591; MURGLEIE (MS B) 541, 590, 632, 811, 815
MOSES, *Old Testament prophet*, 3514
NUBIA, *African country*, 1519
ORFANIE, *Country which supplies the Scottish king's horse*, 2295
OUBE DE MONDOIE, *Ally of Doun*, 2314, 2315
PAVIA, *A city*, 1524
PETER, *Saint*, 956, 1573, 1835
REINER, *Steward of the lady of Civile*, 2859
RETEFOR, *A German city*, 75, 77
RICHER, *Saint*, 97, 169, 2018
ROBANT, *Second son of Sabaoth*, 3386, 3702, 3709, 3719, 3730, 3760
ROME, 956, 3380, 3690, 3803
RUDEFOUN, *Bradmund's standard-bearer*, 570, 577, 597
SABER, *See* SABOT, SABAOTH
SABOT, *Boeve's tutor*, (MS B) 224, 229, 232, 237, 243, 321, 326, 333, 338, 840
SABAOTH (MS D) 1939, 1999, 2021, 2032, 2041, 2042, 2046, 2048, 2185, 2187, 2191, 2243, 2260, 2275, 2285, 2287, 2290, 2296, 2297, 2307, 2405, 2428, 2526, 2570, 2572,2599, 2614, 2631, 2645, 2651, 2676, 2681, 2730, 2735, 2743, 2753, 2761, 2764, 2770, 2773, 2776, 2777, 2783, 2788, 2960, 2962, 2970, 2974, 2983, 2987, 2991, 3056, 3124, 3140, 3149, 3240, 3258, 3273, 3363, 3365, 3376, 3379, 3388,

3391, 3393, 3398, 3404, 3409, 3437,
3444, 3448, 3452, 3457, 3460, 3465,
3468, 3475, 3478, 3482, 3485, 3492,
3617, 3699, 3700, 3703, 3704, 3707,
3708, 3726, 3791; SABER 3225
SARACEN(S) 355, 358, 361, 568, 1059,
1269, 1858, 2671, 2711, 2759, 2761,
3145, 3221, 3229, 3235, 3621
SCOTLAND, 20, 27, 2249, 2280, 2295
SENÉ, *A bishop in Civile*, 2896
SIMON, *Saint*, 692, 1882
TENEBRES, *An emir*, 2505
TERRI, *Oldest son of Sabaoth*, 2645, 2678,
2684, 2688, 2692, 2716, 2725, 2754,
2758, 2781, 2792, 2832, 2852, 2888,
2904, 2922, 2928, 2937, 2982, 2984,
2989, 2999, 3004, 3023, 3030, 3043,
3050, 3053, 3059, 3061, 3186, 3187,
3194, 3206, 3207, 3225, 3239, 3258,
3273, 3335, 3377, 3396, 3491, 3503,
3519, 3524, 3527, 3531, 3535, 3544,
3549, 3616, 3618, 3716, 3720, 3725,
3798
TERVAGANT, *A Saracen god*, 916, 1047,
1784, 3280, 3631, 3659, 3661, 3665
TRINITY, 1954
VALARIE, *See* YDRAC
VASTAL, *A duke besieging Civile*, 2908,
2939
WASTRANDE, *Birthplace of two contestants
in the horse-race*, 2497
YDRAC, *of Valarie, Supposedly an attacker of
Yvori's brother*, 1525
YSORÉ, *A besieger of Civile*, 2925
YVORI, *King of Monbrant*, 993, 1007,
1008, 1020, 1373, 1374, 1382, 1479,
1483, 1491, 1497, 1501, 1503, 1514,
1604, 1791, 1872, 2760, 3046, 3049,
3121, 3146, 3154, 3163, 3171, 3178,
3201, 3242, 3252, 3274, 3300, 3309,
3319, 3411, 3415, 3451, 3456, 3470,
3472, 3509, 3548, 3551, 3552, 3561,
3585, 3591, 3596, 3599, 3642
YVORI THE GRAY, *Ally of Doun*, 2313

Index of Personal and Place Names in *Gui de Warewic*

The numbers given below refer to lines in the Anglo-Norman text.

AFRICA, 9068, 9070, 9336, 9343, 10808, 11658

ALBERI, *Count of Worms, father of Terri*, 2228, 4626, 5086, 5157, 5183, 5577, 5647, 5669, 5697, 5716, 5761, 5771, 6643, 6669, 6697, 6780, 6787, 9938, 10520

ALEXANDER, 8405

ALEXANDRIA, 7925, 7951, 8019, 8023, 8079, 8235, 8887

AMALRI, *Otun's constable*, 5358

AMILERT, *A vassal of the sultan of Konya*, 3063, 3069, 3072

AMIS DE CHAMPAINE OR DE LA MUNTAIGNE, *Guy's friend*, 6129, 6157, 6181, 6185, 6187, 6417, 6441, 6451, 6455, 6467, 6611, 6636, 6639, 6651, 6657, 6718, 6776, 6788, 6809, 12207, 12245, 12274, 12383, 12397, 12447, 12467, 12510, 12523, 12538, 12548, 12559, 12564, 12565

AMORANT, *A Saracen giant, champion of the Persian sultan*, 8436, 8461, 8477, 8500, 8502, 8517, 8536, 8552, 8575, 8599, 8621, 8623, 8647, 8683, 8706, 8713, 8727, 8733, 8741, 8787, 8809, 8819, 8828, 8833, 8847, 8851, 8859, 8863, 8867, 8872

ANELAF, *King of Denmark*, 9121, 10797, 10805, 10865, 10981, 11013, 11072, 11220, 11273

ANTIOCH, 1552, 7867

APOLLO, *A Saracen god*, 3552, 4046, 11721, 11788

APULIA, 1511, 8137

ARASCUNE, *A city belonging to Seguin, duke of Louvain*, 1769, 1935, 1947, 1959, 2506, 2549, 2659

ARDEN THE GREAT, *An enchanted land*, 12224

ARDERNE, *Land belonging to Heralt*, 148 to 12774

ARGUZ, *King of Africa*, 9086, 9344, 9355, 11732, 11751, 11941, 11951, 11963, 12096

ARMARIE, *Dukedom of Cristor*, 3450

ASELAC, *Son of Heralt*, 12835, 12843, 12857, 12873, 12875

ATHELSTAN, *King of England*, 7232, 9010, 9104, 10782, 10813, 10856, 10935, 11044, 11079, 11210, 11279, 12894

BARZUNE, *A city, possibly Bayonne*, 1736

BELIN, *One of Seguin's barons*, 2527

BENEVENTO, 1184, 6513

BERARD, *Otun's nephew*, 6536, 9499, 9505, 9568, 9609, 9625, 9634, 9947, 10001, 10051, 10172, 10181, 10187, 10251, 10280, 10325, 10370, 10430, 10507, 10545, 10569, 10589, 10625, 10669, 10686, 10751, 12539, 12551

BERTULF, *A count, vassal of the German emperor*, 2141

BETUER, *A Lombard knight*, 5420

BLANCHEFLEUR, *Daughter of the German emperor*, 937, 956, 961

BLOIS, 3058

BRABANT, 6814, 6836, 6846

BRABANTER, *A man from Brabant*, 7002

BRITTANY, 750, 1171, 1190, 7844
BRUNSWICK, 2846
BUCKINGHAM, 47
BURGUNDY, 1530, 4641, 7841, 8138, 12575
BURIE, *A Saracen land*, 3053
CHAMPAINE, 6129. See AMIS
CHARLES, *The emperor Charlemagne*, 8390
CHERENBALT, *A vassal of the German emperor*, 2635
CHRIST, 5432, 8824, 9208, 10223, 10598, 12355, 12516
COLEBRANT, *King Anelaf's champion*, 10811, 10867, 10979, 11011, 11089, 11097, 11141, 11143, 11153, 11175, 11190, 11211, 11233, 11241, 11244, 11246, 11249, 11255, 11260, 11261, 11268
COLOGNE, 2104, 2310, 2346, 2749
CONSTANTINE, *Roman emperor*, 10096
CONSTANTINOPLE, 2897, 2905, 2910, 2931, 2948, 4193, 8610, 8974, 9333, 9395, 9399, 9874, 9876
CORNWALL, 9162, 9373, 9391
COSDROEIN, *An emir and nephew of the sultan of Konya*, 2985, 3177, 3947
CRISTOR, *Constable to Emperor Hernis and duke of Amarie*, 3449, 3451, 3776
DAMASCUS, 3412
DANES, 9136, 9151, 10862, 10915, 10922, 10971, 11207, 11272
DANIEL, *Saint*, 7331
DARIUS, *King*, 8417
DENIS, *Saint*, 2832, 6970
DENMARK, 9121, 9325, 10797, 11075, 11277
DURAZZO, *Dyrrachium, now Durres (Albania); ruled by count Jonas*, 7899, 8947, 8967
EDGAR, *Heralt's seneschal*, 9236, 9268, 9285, 9291, 9305, 9315, 9377
ENGLAND, 27, 872, 968, 973, 1007, 1024, 2984, 4279, 5068, 7145, 7230, 7849, 8117, 8139, 8245, 8276, 8306, 8593, 8782, 9307, 9638, 10780, 11076, 11348, 11645, 11703, 11715, 12083, 12771

ENGLISH, 2984, 4523, 8275, 8279, 8599, 11134, 11209
ERNEBURC, *Seguin's sister, married to Reiner, duke of Saxony* 2841
ESCLANDART, *A vassal of the sultan of Konya and son of the king of Burie*, 3051, 3071, 3109, 3111, 3117, 3121, 3131, 3141, 3159, 3171, 3187
ETHIOPIA, 8051, 8436
FABUR, *Son of Triamor*, 7967, 7975, 7985, 8004, 8035, 8042
FELICE, *Rualt's daughter, Guy's beloved and wife*, 75, 182, 199, 217, 232, 303, 333, 380, 447, 497, 530, 568, 585, 602, 611, 633, 675, 699, 1039, 1055, 1083, 1548, 4231, 4282, 4307, 7465, 11387
FLANDERS, 1619
FLORENTIN, *Count of Brabant*, 6869, 6931, 7013, 7074
FRANCE, 996, 1767, 2208, 3024, 4641, 5448, 7841, 8941, 8138
FRENCH, 3057
GALDEMER, *A duke*, 887; *perhaps the same as* WALDEMER
GARNER, *Count, Loher's nephew*, 5255
GARNER, *Gui's French companion*, 2206, 2214
GERMANY, 746, 995, 1644, 2530, 2879, 2945, 3030, 3062, 3196, 3299, 4530, 4642, 6418, 6591, 7513, 7842, 8135, 9327, 9401, 9523, 10341, 10568, 10628, 10630, 12209, 12249, 12384, 12566, 12806
GERMANS, 2129, 1827, 1835, 1853, 1857, 1866, 2121, 2145, 2184, 2191, 2224, 2232, 2259, 2276, 2291, 2295, 2372, 2397, 2438, 2481, 3062, 5144, 7182, 10024
GOTHLAND, 9326
GREECE, 3156, 3790, 8971
GREEKS, 2838, 3102, 3221, 3562, 3593, 3746, 3790, 3844, 4320, 4469, 8409
GUAER, *Son of the German emperor*, 809, 813, 819, 823, 2368, 2386, 2401, 2412, 2725

Personal and Place Names in Gui 257

GUELIN, *Seguin's cousin*, 2139, 2160, 2163, 2174
GUI OF WARWICK, from 129 *passim* until 12920
GUIMER, *A knight from Lorraine*, 3065
GUINEMAN, *A German knight*, 3061
GUISCHARD, *A Lombard knight, Otun's seneschal*, 1347, 1361, 1367, 1379, 1383, 1390, 1393, 1399
GUNLAF, *King of Sweden*, 10798
GUNRED, *Seneschal to the German emperor*, 2311
GUNTER, *of Pavia, killed by Gui*, 1321, 1331
GUNTER, *Seguin's vassal*, 2527; *perhaps the same as a German Gunter helping Gui*, 3029
HECTOR, *Trojan hero*, 8408
HELDEMER, *Seguin's baron*, 2528
HELENE, *A place ruled by Herkenbalt*, 2635
HELMIDAN, *A vassal of the sultan of Konya*, 3025
HERALT OF ARDERNE, *Tutor and friend of Gui*, 148, 715, 717, 723, 883, 1005, 1247, 1271, 1296, 1308, 1309, 1323, 1327, 1431, 1465, 1575, 1577, 1579, 1583, 1587, 1599, 1609, 1741, 1747, 1759, 1852, 1967, 1975, 1981, 1996, 2000, 2001, 2004, 2007, 2022, 2027, 2029, 2037, 2133, 2267, 2273, 2425, 2493, 2526, 2928, 2929, 2937, 3019, 3045, 3067, 3073, 3074, 3083, 3087, 3095, 3581, 3715, 3811, 3853, 3855, 3989, 4015, 4045, 4053, 4273, 4275, 4284, 4285, 4298, 4301, 4511, 4513, 4927, 4932, 4980, 5202, 5247, 5261, 5273, 5301, 5307, 5361, 5373, 5377, 5382, 5386, 5393, 5403, 5406, 5421, 5423, 5429, 5439, 5443, 5451, 5455, 5459, 5462, 5467, 5475, 5479, 5484, 5488, 5491, 5493, 5497, 5507, 5529, 5537, 5541, 5545, 5547, 5592, 5609, 5625, 5698, 5775, 5821, 5954, 5978, 6008, 6050, 6137, 6150, 6517, 6685, 6691, 6695, 6705, 6711, 6713, 6736, 6743, 6747, 6751, 6753, 6781, 6784, 6788, 7305, 7417, 7527, 7529, 7697, 7702, 7730, 7801, 7819, 7829, 7836, 7837, 8102, 8108, 8115, 8120, 8145, 8151, 8187, 8198, 8242, 8244, 8251, 8282, 8305, 8613, 8991, 8993, 9018, 9023, 9091, 9107, 9113, 9129, 9157, 9187, 9237, 9265, 9305, 9317, 9347, 9359, 9363, 9367, 9372, 9640, 9641, 10828, 10894, 11355, 11657, 11679, 11701, 11703, 11719, 11745, 11761, 11771, 11781, 11793, 11800, 11802, 11807, 11813, 11815, 11819, 11829, 11833, 11837, 11848, 11886, 11890, 11891, 11897, 11909, 11933, 11934, 11945, 11953, 11956, 11968, 11970, 11981, 11997, 12021, 12041, 12059, 12089, 12103, 12119, 12123, 12128, 12135, 12147, 12159, 12203, 12245, 12271, 12275, 12279, 12281, 12512, 12519, 12523, 12527, 12557, 12561, 12571, 12576, 12578, 12635, 12640, 12653, 12717, 12753, 12774, 12826, 12828, 12831, 12836, 12841, 12845, 12868, 12870, 12907
HERCULES, 8465
HERKENBALT, *A vassal of the emperor of Germany*, 2635
HERNIS, *Emperor of Constantinople*, 2906, 3737, 4102
HESMAN, *King of Tyre, vassal of the sultan of Konya*, 3497, 3539, 8286
HUENCUN, *Otun's nephew*, 1303, 1314, 1407
HUNGARY, 2326, 2633
INDIA, 8353
IRELAND, 7251, 9325
JERUSALEM, 7732, 7734, 7861, 7911, 8391, 8917, 9873
JESUS, 3668, 5432, 8210, 8636, 8824, 9208, 9844, 10223, 10598, 10692, 10936, 11202, 11302, 11345, 11454, 11748, 12355, 12516, 12737
JOCERANZ, *Seguin's baron*, 2529
JOHN, *Saint*, 8571, 10855
JONAS, *A count of Durazzo*, 7900, 8110, 8239, 8259, 8335, 8889, 8895, 8918, 8957
JORDAN, *A count of Milan*, 5353

Jun, *False name used by Gui*, 8270, 8271, 8327, 8343; *see also* Yun
Kent, 10919
Konya, *A city in Asia Minor*, 2901, 4063
Lambert, *A count and knight of Otun's*, 1193, 1293, 1409, 1297
Laurence, *Saint*, 2674
Laurette, *Daughter of emperor Hernis*, 3237, 3282
Lazarus, 11057
Leicester, 12779
Leons, *A forest*, 2578
Loher, *Duke of Lorraine*, 1654, 4703, 4868, 5091, 5101, 5190, 5194, 5256, 5290, 5312, 5330, 5556, 5559, 5603, 5637, 5651, 5667, 5671, 5685, 5707, 5745, 5770, 5771, 5807, 5823, 5835, 5949, 5961, 5977, 6053, 6646, 6681, 6695, 6755, 6773, 6813, 7197
Lombard(s), 1180, 1246, 1257, 1267, 1273, 1279, 1320, 1341, 1348, 1427, 2077, 2086, 4705, 4714, 5344, 5350, 5365, 5370, 5407, 5419, 5437, 5462, 5465, 5499, 5509, 5528, 5533, 5538, 5768, 5805, 5815, 5849, 5883, 5946, 6312, 6329, 6522, 7182, 10024
Lombardy, 995, 1177, 1559, 1987, 5106, 5320, 5384, 5634, 5840, 6846, 10339, 12805
London, 9009, 9042, 12893
Lorraine, 805, 1654, 3066, 4542, 2250, 4627, 5103, 5194, 5201, 5225, 5237, 5254, 5261, 5562, 5707, 5737, 5769, 5787, 5805, 5811, 5817, 5883, 5977, 6664, 6786, 6791, 7060, 7123, 7812, 7843, 8136, 11651
Louvain, 873, 1645, 1652, 1662, 1728, 1764, 2869
Mahomet, *A Saracen god*, 3124, 3551, 8338, 8341, 11234, 11788, 11876, 3200
Martin, *Saint*, 4116, 6870, 10298
Mary, *Mother of Jesus*, 3987, 4482, 8339, 8637, 11434, 11748; *saint*, 6621, 8210, 11527, 11630
Michael, *Saint*, 11466, 11564
Milan, 3026, 5354

Milun, *Duke of Burgundy*, 1531, 1610, 12581, 12811
Mirabel, *A young Saracen knight*, 3625
Modred, *Duke of Cornwall*, 9161, 9283, 9371
Montdidier, *A city in France*, 5448
Moor, 7262
Moravins, *A Saracen nation*, 2912
Morgadur, *Wicked seneschal of emperor Hernis*, 3263, 3679, 4407
Moriane, 884; *perhaps the same as* Moraine, 7186
Muntaigne, *See* Amis
Normandy, 733, 996, 1169, 7840
Northumberland, 7252, 7287, 7302
Norway, 9326
Nubia, *African country*, 3545
Osille, *Daughter of the duke of Lorraine, wife of Terri*, 4662, 4673, 4690, 4694, 4773, 5070, 5579, 6683
Otun, *Duke of Pavia, uncle of Berard, vassal to the emperor of Germany*, 837, 1187, 1199, 1261, 1304, 1359, 1362, 1495, 1563, 1983, 1985, 2039, 2634, 2799, 4661, 5359, 5364, 5395, 5449, 5472, 5514, 5553, 5559, 5604, 5617, 5709, 5749, 5790, 5829, 5861, 5944, 5949, 5961, 6055, 6167, 6201, 6203, 6255, 6331, 6335, 6481, 6535, 7183, 9490, 9939, 10038, 10657, 12219
Oxford, 45, 9014
Paris, 10674
Pavia, *Duchy of Otun*, 837, 848, 1306, 1384, 1386, 1925, 1940, 1945, 2347, 5096, 5104, 5311, 5331, 5382, 5457, 5490, 5595, 5633, 5681, 5709, 5803, 5951, 5979, 6002, 6199, 6485, 9490, 9504, 9946, 10041, 10050
Pentecost, 161
Persan, *An African king*, 9351
Persia, 3394, 7974, 7986, 8384, 9874
Persians, 2912
Peter, *Saint*, 10376, 10582
Plains, *A forest*, 1212, 2043
Porrus, *A king*, 8406
Rainbrun, *Gui's son*, 8990, 9073, 9083, 9180, 9296, 9308, 9323, 12104,

12116, 12120, 12124, 12127, 12147,
12251, 12257, 12269, 12339, 12360,
12397, 12427, 12443, 12450, 12469,
12480, 12489, 12499, 12509, 12512,
12521, 12531, 12557, 12561, 12571,
12623, 12635, 12641, 12654, 12659,
12693, 12701, 12707, 12849, 12859,
12863, 12869, 12899, 12905
RED SEA, 3662
REINER, *Duke of Saxony, nephew of Otun,*
843, 851, 909, 1521, 1653, 1931,
1943, 2093, 2103, 2127, 2147, 2159,
2205, 2210, 2309, 2319, 2731, 2839
REINER, *Emperor of Germany,* 764, 1643,
1900, 2323, 2386, 2511, 2535, 3300,
9622, 9686, 10272
REMIRANT, *A vassal of the Sultan of Konya,*
3059
REMIS, *Prince of Romania,* 4654
RHONE, *River,* 1734
RODOAN, *A vassal of the sultan of Konya,
killed by Gunter,* 3031
ROMANIE, 4651, 5710, *The eastern Roman
Empire*
ROME, 7016, 7156
ROUEN, 735, 1003
RUALT, *Count of Warwick and father of
Felice,* 49, 121, 649, 655, 969, 1030,
1097, 1101, 1113, 1439, 4281, 4295,
7695, 7831, 10835
RUSSIA, 9002, 9046, 9047, 9099, 9181,
9327
SABINE, *Guy's mother,* 466
SADOINE, *Son of the Sultan of Persia,* 7974,
7979, 7986, 7988, 7993, 7999, 8007,
8036, 8431, 8598
SADUC, *Nephew of the German emperor,
killed by Seguin,* 1661, 1675, 1685,
1697, 1704, 2776, 2804
SAINT-OMER, 1620
SALAKIS, *A sultan,* 4778
SAMSON, 11058
SARACEN(S), 2911, 3005, 3039, 3044,
3047, 3049, 3052, 3060, 3064, 3092,
3097, 3100, 3145, 3273, 3431, 3471,
3494, 3523, 3528, 3541, 3573, 3577,
3584, 3589, 3604, 3610, 3616, 3626,

3662, 3754, 3757, 3880, 3883, 3913,
3982, 4045, 4051, 4059, 4490, 4650,
4657, 6209, 7872, 7914, 7918, 7930,
8049, 8063, 8066, 8212, 8394, 8420,
8435, 8441, 8698, 9537, 11771,
11780, 11787, 11871
SAXONS, 10807, 10827, 10881, 10892,
10979, 11017, 11257, 11301, 11304
SAXONY, 844, 1520, 1529, 1653, 1931,
2103, 2309, 2718, 4642, 7842, 8137,
9328, 9524, 12806
SCOTLAND, 104
SEGUIN, *Duke of Louvain,* 1651, 1658,
1671, 1676, 1701, 1752, 1923, 2140,
2165, 2217, 2257, 2263, 2277, 2281,
2297, 2375, 2414, 2429, 2500, 2507,
2595, 2621, 2677, 2703, 2774, 2811,
2840, 2848
SEQUART, *Seneschal to Rualt and Gui's
father,* 111, 117, 177, 201, 205, 335,
704, 1133
SICILY, 4774
SPAIN, 749, 1172, 1175, 1787, 2529, 7185,
7514, 7843, 8136, 9524, 12208,
12805
SPEYER, *A German city,* 2880, 4531, 9406,
9600, 9687, 9742, 9800
SUSANNA, 11059
SWEDEN, 10798
SYRIA, 3020, 9873
TEBALT, *A French knight and Gui's follower,
killed by Esclandart,* 3023, 3055
TERRI, *of Worms, son of Alberi, friend of
Gui,* 2227, 2261, 2271, 2327, 2336,
2352, 2427, 2437, 2590, 2599, 2634,
2773, 4625, 4787, 4850, 4855, 4995,
5027, 5035, 5040, 5049, 5069, 5077,
5085, 5091, 5097, 5109, 5117, 5120,
5123, 5133, 5135, 5148, 5158, 5163,
5199, 5205, 5223, 5227, 5231, 5239,
5241, 5248, 5271, 5283, 5287, 5299,
5306, 5321, 5327, 5357, 5464, 5483,
5529, 5537, 5540, 5578, 5599, 5607,
5613, 5648, 5655, 5697, 5715, 5739,
5762, 5772, 5788, 5819, 5954, 5963,
5981, 6005, 6028, 6031, 6049, 6069,
6142, 6149, 6249, 6257, 6283, 6301,

6325, 6348, 6372, 6444, 6445, 6422,
6429, 6455, 6465, 6467, 6516, 6601,
6608, 6613, 6625, 6629, 6639, 6670,
6682, 6687, 6692, 6698, 6701, 6716,
6718, 6746, 6753, 6772, 6787, 6797,
6815, 7141, 7143, 7173, 7223, 7813,
9471, 9655, 9667, 9679, 9717, 9732,
9740, 9743, 9751, 9753, 9771, 9809,
9814, 9828, 9830, 9838, 9845, 9881,
9924, 9934, 9937, 9945, 10036,
10040, 10043, 10055, 10117, 10126,
10127, 10240, 10444, 10452, 10456,
10461, 10483, 10485, 10489, 10505,
10512, 10514, 10516, 10519, 10523,
10529, 10556, 10559, 10566, 10571,
10580, 10581, 10591, 10602, 10612,
10673, 10709, 10717, 10776, 11643,
12541
TERVAGANT, *A Saracen god*, 3551, 8600
TEUTONS, 7182, 10024
THOROUT, *A friend of Heralt and Gui, killed by Huencun*, 721, 890, 1277, 1307, 1460
TOLEDO, 66
TRIAMOR, *King of Alexandria, nephew of the sultan of Konya, brother of Hesman of Tyre*, 7923, 7948, 7965, 8015, 8031, 8041, 8061, 8065, 8162, 8236, 8395, 8418, 8595, 8744, 8783, 8880
TROY, 8408
TURKEY, 3000, 3019, 3179, 9328
TURKS, 2912, 3001, 3086, 3181, 3185, 3502
TYRE, 3497, 3529, 4994, 6496, 8050, 8286
URRI, *A friend of Heralt and Gui, killed by Lambert*, 721, 890, 1283, 1295, 1298, 1460
WALDEMER, *Constable to the German emperor and count of Cologne*, 1932, 2094, 2104, 2133, 2148, 2219, 2310, 2346, 2743; *See* GALDEMER
WALDENOT, *Vassal to the German emperor*, 2635, 2639
WALLINGFORD, 93, 7411, 9013, 9266, 9375, 12125, 12772, 12907, 12797
WARWICK, 28, 163, 974, 1029, 7423, 7523, 7564, 8141, 11380, 11480, 11510, 11595, 12084, 12903
WINCHESTER, 10783, 10791, 10802, 10851, 10854, 10856, 11283
WORMS, *German city, ruled by Alberi*, 2228, 4625, 5085, 5107, 5153, 5293, 5318, 5646, 5716, 5794, 6465, 6643, 6663, 6667, 6714, 6721, 7198, 9475, 9938, 10520, 10607, 10619
YORK, 7231, 7233, 7403, 7407
YUN, *False name used by Gui*, 6266, 8775, 8777, 8905, 8924; *See also* JUN

Appendix of Extracts from *Boeve de Haumtone* and *Gui de Warewic*

Boeve de Haumtone

1.

I
    Seingnurs barons, ore entendez a mei,
    si ws dirrai gestes, que jeo diverses sai,
    de Boefs de Haumtone, li chevaler curtays,
    ke par coup de espeie conquist tant bons reys.
    Si vus volez oyer, jeo vus en dirrai;
    unkes ne oistes meyllur, si com jeo crai.

II
    Seingnurs, si de lui oyer desirez,
    jeo vus en dirrai, kar jeo sai asez;
    A Haumtone fu li quens plein de bontez,
    il out a noun Guioun, chevaler fu prisez;
    meilour de lui ne fust en son tens trovez.

III
    Seignurs, iceo quens Guioun dount vus chaunt
    estoit bon chavaler, pruz e combataunt;
    mes de une chose lui alout home blamaunt,
    k'ainz ne vout femme prendre en tot son vivaunt,
    dunt pus se repenti par le men ascient.

IV
    Mes quant il fu veuz home e out long tens vescu,
    dunk prist il femme que de haute gent fu,
    file au roi de Escoce cele dame fu.
    Guioun la prist a femme, lui chevaler membru.
    Puis avint cel jour que mult iré en fu,
    ke il perdi le chef par desus le bu.

V	La dame si estoit bele e afeité.
	Le emperur de Alemaine la out avant amé
	e a son pere le out sovent demaundé,
	mes lui roi de Escoce li avoit deveé
	si la dona Guioun ov la chere membré.
	Pus en perdi le chef (allas, quele destiné!)
	pur la amour de la dame que il out esposé.

1-30

2.

CXLVIII	Ore vus dirrai de Miles l'adverser,
	ke fist Josian mal gre le sun esposer.
	Mal gre le sun la mena a muster,
	mal gre le sun la fist la nuit cocher,
	devant le list se sist, se prent a deschaucer,
	forement se hast de Josian vergunder.
	Josian le veist si comence a suspirer,
	ele prent sa seynture de sey de oltre mer,
	une lacete en fist solum son saver,
	outre le col Miles si la prent a giter.
CXLIX	Seygnurs, ore entendez, ke vus ai ci dist!
	Avant que Miles poit vener en son lit,
	Josian la bele sa seynture prist,
	outre le col Miles le gita tot de fist.
	Le lit fu haut ou il gist,
	e li quens Miles de une part se sist,
	e la pucele de altre part sailist,
	a sey le tret e le col li rumpist.
CL	E l'endemain, kant aparust le jur
	e de la clere aube apert la luur,
	les chevalers se levent tuz en tur,
	a la chambre venent ou estoit lur seynur,
	hautement le apelent chevaler e contur,
	pur nent le funt, car mort est sanz retur.

2099-2122

Gui de Warewic

1.
    Ço fu en mai, el tens d'esté,
Que Gui ert en Warewic la cité.
De berser est un jur repeiré,
Veneisun ad pris a grant plenté;
Mult joius e lé se feseit;
A une vespree, que bele esteit,
Gui en une tur munta,
En halt as estres se pua;
Le pais envirun ad esgardé
E le ciel, qui tant ert esteillé,
E le tens, qui ert serré e cler.
Gui comence dunc a penser
Cum Deus li out fait grant honur,
Unc a chevaler ne fist greignur:
Que unc ne fu en liu n'en estur
Qu'il ne fu tenu al meillur,
E cum il ert home de grant afaire
E preisé en estrange terre,
E que tanz homes aveit oscis,
Turs e citez par force pris,
E cum aveit sun cors pené
Loinz en estrange regné
Pur une femme qu'il tant amat,
Pur qui tant mals duré ad;
Mais unc pur sun criatur,
Qui fait li ad si grant honur,
Ne s'entremist de lui servir;
Mais ore s'en voldra repentir.
A suspirer dunc comença,
En sun corage se purpensa
Que tote sa vie changera
E en Deu servise se mettra.
                        7563-94

2.
    Quant Terri le vit enmi le vis,
Un mot ne sonast pur tut Paris;
Pasmé chet del mul a tere,
Tel duel ne veissez home mes faire.
'Ahi! bel compainz, sire Gui,
Cum ore sui, las, chaitif, trahi;
Quant ne vus ai einz coneu,
Trop m'est ore mesavenu;
Ben me deveie aparceveir

Par tes granz fez, par tun poeir,
Que eriez Gui le vaillant,
Le preuz, le hardi, le combatant;
Qui serreit dunc de tel valur,
Qui contre Berart le suduiur
Osereit en bataille entrer,
Encontre si vaillant chevaler,
Si ço ne fuissez, bel sire Gui?
Del mesfait, pur Deu, merci!
Que jo vus ai si mesconu;
Merci, sire, pur l'amur Jhesu!'
An eire li est as piez chau,
Qui de cravesces li erent fendu,
Tut en plorant les ad baisé
E veit ses pez tut decrevé
E les jambes decrevees,
Qui tant soleient estre ben chacees.
                    10673-98